Endorsements

If you read only one book on the history of LGBT rights, the culture, psychotherapy, religious reactions, and what the Bible really says about being gay, *Walking the Bridgeless Canyon* should be it. It is well-researched, compelling, and eye opening.

If this book had existed when I became an anti-gay Christian activist, I would have questioned if what I was doing was truly God's will or if it was nothing more than a man-made construct meant to maintain white heterosexual male dominance on the backs of gay people and women.

Kathy Baldock has spent years digging into the nooks and crannies to find the most accurate information available on the struggle LGBT people have endured for the most basic of human rights. This book is destined to be the go-to resource for everyone interested in the truth about LGBT people, our rights, and the rights of all people.

Yvette Cantu Schneider—former policy analyst at Family Research Council, former director of women's ministry at Exodus International, and author of the book Never Not Broken

Kathy Baldock is one of the most tireless, dedicated, and influential advocates for LGBT Christians in the evangelical church. Her work has helped to transform the lives of thousands of people, and her ministry is a model of the kind of effective, conciliatory bridge-building work the church desperately needs.

In *Walking the Bridgeless Canyon*, Baldock guides the reader on a fascinating journey of how the church has responded to the LGBT community—and how we all can and should do better. Brilliantly researched, accessibly written, and lovingly expressed, this book is essential reading for anyone wanting to understand the intersection between the conservative church and the LGBT community. I highly recommend it—and its remarkable author.

Matthew Vines—founder of The Reformation Project and author of God and the Gay Christian

There are those who speak eloquently about spiritual abuses levied against the LGBTQ communities and others who by their life model a different and holy path. Kathy Baldock is a national leader helping to facilitate honoring discussions with the goal of seeing latent prejudice, anger and ignorance dissipate with each handshake and hug.

Far from strident this missive lays out a solid foundation for under-standing and bridge building. And this manifesto will liberate many hard hearts and invite people to unclench fists. It's a must read.

Butch Maltby—domestic and global fundraising consultant, Senior Advisor Newton Media

For nearly three years Kathy Baldock has been quietly researching, writing, and exploring the tangled world of the American Evangelical and Pentecostal christian religious communities examining their treatment of the LGBTQ community.

Along the way she's charted the history, reasons, and purposes behind the Christian right's deeply held belief and ideology that LGBTQ people are an aberration, abomination, before their version of their interpretation of the christian bible and are forever doomed to the fires of that special place for sinners should they not give up their "lifestyle, and choice to be gay."

As I've walked that journey with her- mentoring and advising her, I've been thrilled to witness her growth as she matured into a capable researcher, solid writer, and blunt spokesperson for the real truths of her faith sans the politics in regard to the subject of God and the Gay Christian and God and Gays in general.

Walking the Bridgeless Canyon is the result of that work and in a direct, plainly written way, argues that the extremism that has been long associated over the battleground of gay rights has in fact been based in part on a political and religious animus that has no real basis in reality, but instead has been propelled forward by the christian right's need for control, power, and even wealth.

Kathy has written an easy to understand book that will educate and compel the reader- particularly in the American Evangelical and Pentecostal christian religious communities for which the book has been specifically geared towards, to reexamine the complex worldview held by those communities towards LGBTQ people and realize that there is not the black & white case to be had to condemn the LGBTQ people.

Kathy manages to condense it to one simple idea, "Love thy neighbor as thee would love thyself." (Okay, so I ripped that off the great bard himself and a version of a version of the King James Bible.) But that is in fact the point really. The intimate love that one human being has for another is not subject to a flawed interpretation nor is it proper to have the LGBTQ community at the tip of the spear of christianity which is being used as a weapon and has been for many years now.

She's done a marvelous job as a story teller and with her warm personality infused throughout this book, the readers will quite easily find for themselves that which I have known all along, she's a good mom, a great friend, and a true christian in every sense and definition of the word.

Brody Levesque—veteran journalist and Washington Bureau Chief for LGBTQ Nation Magazine

Walking the Bridgeless Canyon

Repairing the Breach Between the Church and the LGBT Community

Kathy Baldock

Walking the Bridgeless Canyon
Repairing the Breach Between the Church and the LGBT Community

Published by:
Canyonwalker Press
Reno, NV USA
www.CanyonWalkerPress.com

Edited by: Wendy Danbury, Elaine Bellamore Phillips, Jerry Reiter,
Tim Rymel, David Farmer.
Final Editor: Heidi Mann
Final Touch Proofreading & Editing
www.FinalTouchProofreadingAndEditing.com
Cover design by Rodger Peden

Library of Congress Control Number: 2014939649

Most Scriptures quoted are from the HOLY BIBLE, NEW
INTERNATIONAL VERSION [NIV] Copyright © 1973, 1978, 1984, 1990,
2011 International Bible Society. Zondervan Bible Publishers.

Also from:
King James Version (KJV) by Public Domain
New American Standard Bible (NASB)
Copyright © 1960, 1962, 1963, 1968, 1971, 1972, 1973, 1975, 1977, 1995
by The Lockman Foundation

The Message (MSG)
Copyright © 1993, 1994, 1995, 1996, 2000, 2001, 2002 by Eugene H. Peterson

New King James Version (NKJV)
The Holy Bible, New King James Version Copyright © 1982 by Thomas
Nelson, Inc.

ISBN: 978-1619200289

Dedication

To Netto Montoya, a loyal friend, who when I asked, "Do you mind if I turn around and walk with you for awhile?", trusted me with her story and life.

And to the readers who will choose to journey in love with someone unlike themselves, for this is the Gospel of Jesus Christ.

Contents

The Chasm of the Great Divide
Why This Book?

I didn't know any gay people

I sat in a restaurant having breakfast with my friends, the same three Christian women I'd been meeting with every Friday for over a decade. We talked in hushed tones about Luanne. *"Did you hear Luanne is now a lesbian?"* No, I hadn't, and it surprised me. How could *Luanne* be a *lesbian?* After all, she didn't just casually go to church on Sundays; she sang in the choir and went to Bible studies with us.

Well, Luanne had become gay; some lesbian had seduced her into the lifestyle. A recent double knee surgery had made it difficult for Luanne to get around her apartment and care for herself, so a kind woman at church invited her to convalesce in her home. And that's when it happened! The four of us tsk-tsked: "Poor Luanne" had been tricked into a lesbian relationship. With no local family for Luanne to turn to in the time of her greatest need, a lesbian had taken advantage of her crisis and made her gay.

Had any of *us* offered Luanne help after her surgery, perhaps by bringing her meals, or taking her into our homes to care for her? Nope, we gossiped about her new sinful lifestyle.

Though I could be supportive of fair treatment and *possibly* civil unions for same-sex couples, I believed marriage was reserved by God for a man and a woman. I'm one of those nice people; I'm not mean-spirited. I wouldn't intentionally harm another person, but my beliefs were the truth because they were based on verses directly from the Bible. I had a death-grip on the viewpoint that "you can't be a practicing gay person *and* a Christian." I thought *maybe* I *might* see some gay people in heaven but *only if* they had already been Christian when they became gay, were no longer "practicing homosexuals" when they died, and had committed to a life of celibacy.

I never considered examining these "long-established truths." That would have been akin to questioning God Himself. Besides, I had no reason to invest study time in the issue—I wasn't gay, my kids weren't gay, and none of my friends were gay. I didn't even have extended family members who were gay. I existed in a cocoon. My beliefs were reinforced by my insular social groups, which were an outgrowth of my church life and homeschooling circles. My life, my family, my friends, and my thinking were entrenched in conservative evangelicalism.

Then my pretty picture started crumbling. My husband of twenty years no longer wanted to be married. He'd been unfaithful and I'd forgiven him, but the two-year patch applied to his infidelity had finally lost its adhesive. To process my sorrow in healthy ways and to keep my mind and body productive, I took up two new activities: studying Italian at the local community college, and hiking in the nearby mountains.

The first person to directly tell me he was gay was Tom Durante. I had been paired with him as part of an assignment to interview and introduce a fellow student in Italian class. Tom and I met in the school cafeteria to have dinner and work on our project together. I started down a standard list of fact-gathering questions for Tom: place of birth, job, and, of course, I asked, "Are you married?"

Tom said, "I have a partner; I'm gay."

I took an extra-long sip of my iced tea, not daring to look up. Although I appeared unruffled on the outside, I was stunned and wondered, "How am I going to deal with *this?*"

I had only recently been able to relax my overzealous evangelical burden to tell sinners how they had strayed from God's perfect will for their life. I had a high success rate as a deal closer. If you invited an unsaved friend to a special holiday program or event at church, the best place to seat your guest was *right next to me.* A smile, a conversation, a well-placed question, and—"BAM!"—the sinner's prayer was offered and eternity was settled for another lost soul. But in the midst of the ending of a twenty-year marriage, I didn't feel like I had an eternity-altering moral message for Tom. So the way in which I "dealt with" Tom was to become friends with him. We met every Monday evening before class for dinner in the cafeteria.

Very few people knew I was at the end of my marriage. My husband and I had a successful retail business that brought in a great deal of cash during the Christmas season. He was concerned that the news of our divorce would create low morale among the employees and, hence, lower the bottom line. He pressured me into agreeing to stay silent about the impending divorce. We kept our sizable staff, and even our children, Andrew and Sami, 15 and 14 at the time, from knowing. Though my husband was relieved—indeed, almost giddy—to move on, his strategy left me isolated in my agony.

Not able to process the pain in front of my children, I took time every day to hike with my dogs high into the canyons near my home in the Sierra Nevada Mountains. The trails there became my sacred sanctuary. It was the only place I could take my secret and cry, lament, pray, and listen to God.

"Can I turn around and walk with you?"

I frequently ran into the same woman on the trails on the weekends. One day when I had finished my solo hike, I had extra time, so I asked her, "Do you mind if I turn around and walk with you for a while? I've seen you lots of times and I don't even know your name. I'm Kathy."

"Sure," she said. "I'm Netto."

I soon suspected Netto might be a lesbian. The pre–marriage-crisis version of me would have graciously and politely confirmed my suspicions, then kindly maneuvered the conversation to a point where I could inform Netto of her sin and, consequently, her need for Jesus. At any other time in my Christian walk it would have been easy for me. I'd been a confident and gifted evangelist. At that point, however, I was emotionally drained by the burden of my failing Christian marriage. With my own life in tatters, I didn't feel like I could "tell" anyone anything. Netto and Tom were spared my Christian attempt to rid them of sin and get them right with God.

Over the next year, on most weekends, I hiked with Netto. What a pleasure it was to exchange my solitary, sorrow-filled hike for lively conversation with my cheerful new companion! Of course, I told my friends about my new hiking buddy who was possibly a lesbian. Naturally, they wanted to know when I was going to talk to her about Jesus. Instead, I simply spent time hiking and chatting with Netto and got to know her as a friend. When she finally did come out to me a year later, I no longer cared that she was a lesbian. I had gotten to know her as a person rather than a stereotype, and I loved her as a friend. With the privacy wall between us pushed aside, I moved into Netto's social circles, and she moved into mine.

Over the next five years, through my relationships with Tom and Netto, I made more friends in the gay community. My expanding network of gay and lesbian friends started challenging assumptions I held. Still, in all those years, I hadn't met a gay person who said they were a Christian. That was fine with me.

With no one pressuring me to examine my restrictive evangelical beliefs, I saw no need to look inward and scrutinize them for myself. Gays couldn't be Christians; the Bible said so. It was settled. Christianity had established a defined wall between gay people and God, and without giving much thought to it, I obediently honored the boundary. My gay friends respected the wall as well. They wanted no part of Christianity, and Christianity wanted no part of them. Being gay and being Christian were settled as mutually exclusive conditions.

Surrendering to the process

Several years later, over the span of four months, I went from not knowing one gay Christian to knowing hundreds. The process started in
September 2006 on the final morning of a women's retreat. The women
there knew me well, as they had been part of my church home for over
fifteen years. Many were quite aware I was spending time in social circles far different from our church groups. There were "suspicions" about
me. I was an independent, single woman hanging out with lots of lesbians. I often found myself pressed to conclude stories with "Oh, but
I'm not gay . . ." when talking with my church friends about events I'd
attended with my gay friends, always making sure to make distinctions
between me and "them." But when I heard myself saying things like
that, I became frustrated. My disgraceful duplicity seemed to reek of
disrespect for my gay friends.

During the Sunday service at the end of the women's retreat, I took
my turn, as many did, to walk to the front of the room and share an
"aha" moment from the retreat. I made a declaration to God and the
women of my church: "God, I don't know what you're doing in my life,
but I recognize I have a lot of gay friends. I'm tired of cautiously validat-
ing my friendships." Looking to the women, I continued: "I really don't
care what any of you think of me. God's doing something with these
friendships, and I'm ready." I raised up both my hands in submission.
"So, God, whatever this thing is, let's do it! Let's get this thing going.
I'm ready." There were quite a few stunned reactions. But Annie, who
was sitting behind me and who has a gay sibling, pulled me back toward
her as I sat back down and whispered in my ear, "Kathy Baldock, you've
always been my favorite loose cannon. I love you."

Three months later, in December 2006, the response to my surrender happened in an unexpected way. It was a snowy morning, and my
newspaper delivery-person couldn't make it over the mountain passes.
Undeterred, I logged onto the newspaper's website to read it over breakfast. Immediately, I saw a feature story on a man named Justin Lee,

whom the article described as director of the Gay Christian Network (GCN). I stared at my monitor in disbelief. Did gay Christians really exist? I clicked on the link to the GCN website[1] and searched for their beliefs and mission statement. I was sure I would find a sexuality-focused site rather than a Jesus-focused one. I was wrong. In fact, the information on the site was theologically sound, and I agreed with the mission statement and supporting scriptures! After more than five years, my two distinctly separate worlds—religious belief and love for my gay friends—collided. It wasn't just a bump. It was a crash!

If a person *could* be both gay and Christian, how had I, in the midst of so many gay friends, missed it? I was troubled. If I started considering the possibility of people being gay *and* Christian, would I fall into an abyss of heresy? I'm not intending to be overly dramatic. For the most part, I agreed with strict interpretations of the Bible. To concede the point about homosexuality was to risk the crumbling of my doctrinal foundations. Stunned, I continued to explore the GCN website and noticed an upcoming conference in Seattle.

A few days later, I called Justin Lee and asked, "Can I come to your conference? I don't want to change you or challenge you. *I just want to see you.* I don't know anyone who says they're gay *and* Christian."

Justin said, "Sure, come join us."

On the first night of the conference, I stood alone in the back of the darkened room. I was bewildered. Undeniably, the Holy Spirit, who had been moving in my life for decades, was in the room and in the lives of the gay worshippers. Would it be possible to line up my Christian beliefs with what I was seeing in the witness of these gay Christians? That question kept running through my mind.

As confused as I was, it felt as if we were in a holy place. The sacredness of the moment was completely overwhelming; I was deeply moved. I took off my shoes, slumped to the floor, and cried.

---

[1] The Gay Christian Network, http://www.gaychristian.net.

Walking the Bridgeless Canyon

If you have lesbian, gay, bisexual, or transgender (LGBT) friends or family members, perhaps you've already faced a similar dilemma, trying to align your negative assumptions about gay people with the good you've seen in their lives. Even more challenging, once you've seen the witness of Christ and the fruits of the Holy Spirit in the lives of gay and transgender Christians, the thought of examining strongly held religious beliefs can be daunting and even painful. When I started thinking all this through, there were very few public role models, so God met me right where I was—asking questions and hiking trails.

Every day, I hike between two canyons near my home. Over the years, the area has become a sacred place for me. I first started using the name "Canyonwalker" in the late 1990s when my daughter, Sami, then eleven years old, encouraged me to get an email account. I wanted to retain anonymity and, with "Hikerkathy" taken, "Canyonwalker" was born. For the next several years, the solitude of the trails was a sanctuary for my personal healing.

In recent years, however, hiking in canyons has taken on the spiritual dimension of daily communion with God against a backdrop of dirt, snow, trees, creeks, and sky. Psalm 46:10 says it well: "Step out of the traffic! Take a long, loving look at Me, your High God" (The Message).

But now I have stepped out of the traffic and wandered onto the muddy, rocky, and often arid canyon trails of a different plane. I walk in the expanse between distant groups: the straight community and the LGBT community, as well as conservative Christians and gay and transgender Christians. From the vantage point of seeing good in each of these communities, for a long time I wondered, "How did we arrive at this point of extreme division? Good and kind people dwell on opposite sides of these canyons, convinced that their side has the truth. Christians can read the *same* Bible verses related to same-sex behavior and understand them *completely differently.* How can this be?"

We each evaluate events, people, and even Bible verses through personal filters fashioned through our life experiences, interactions, education, and even the way we process knowledge. Add to this the societal events that came before us, over which we have no control but which have been layered, one atop another, as the foundation of what we understand today. Then add to all *that* a spiritual layer, unique to each of us, shaped by our theology, the biblical teachings we've been exposed to, and our personal relationship with and views of God. It's no surprise, then, that we can arrive at diverse assumptions and conclusions in the intersection of faith and sexual orientation and gender identity.

Walking the Bridgeless Canyon examines the lenses through which we—in particular, Christians—have come to view the LGBT community. One by one, each chapter explores the historical, cultural, psychological, medical, political, and religious filters that have collectively led to our personal, social, and religious views of a minority group in America. We'll look at each layer, how it was formed, its overall impact, and its interconnectedness with other layers. Ultimately, the goal of this holistic approach is to give readers a better understanding of, and a means of untangling, the passages of Scripture referring to same-sex behavior.

As you read, you may want to ask yourself if you have erected barriers in relation to those who are LGBT based on faulty information, lack of information, or manipulation of information. You might find opportunities in every chapter, or in particular chapters, to pause and reconsider the various lenses through which you have viewed LGBT people. If you have ever wondered how the gay and transgender community came to be the target of cultural and religious derision, you'll likely have a broad and informed answer by the end of the book.

Beyond just wanting to know "how" the lenses developed, my personal faith drove me deeper. I wanted to find a way to help repair the damage and even rescue the Bible out of the midst of the rubble heap of discord. The mission of Canyonwalker Connections, a nonprofit organization I founded in 2011, is guided by Isaiah 58:6-12, paraphrased: "Loosen the chains of injustice, untie the cords of the yoke, set the oppressed free and break every yoke. Then you will be called Repairers of the Breach."

At the beginning of Isaiah 58, the Jews complained that God wasn't listening to them or blessing them. They were *sure* they were doing what God required, but they had missed the point. Isaiah said that God wanted them to end injustice and oppression. For His part of the deal, God would supply all their needs and call them "Repairers of the Breach."

A breach is a break or a gap in something that was once whole. The literal wall Isaiah 58 refers to surrounded Jerusalem and had fallen into a seventy-year decay while the people were held captive in Babylon.[2] But there was a figurative breach as well, and Isaiah told the Jews how to fix *that* broken "wall" so that God's blessings would return: They had to end injustice and oppression. The Jews needed to repair the breach in the wall, not take a shortcut and build a bridge across the top of the divide. In fact, the word "bridge" never appears in the Bible. God was clear: "If you do away with oppression, with the pointing finger and malicious talk, and if you spend yourselves on behalf of the hungry and satisfy the needs of the oppressed,"[3] the blessings will come.

Repairing the breach

The people of God are held to high standards. When we reflect on and understand how the gay and transgender community has long been treated, and our part—whether personal or corporate—in that treatment, we don't get to say "Oh, well" and move on. Nor do we get to build bridges of compromise paved with conditions. Rather, we are called to end oppression and repair the breach.

Isaiah 40:3-4 (NIV) says:

---

[2] Jerusalem was in ruins for seventy years. See Daniel 9:2, 2 Chronicles 36:20-21.
[3] Isaiah 58:9-10, NIV.

A voice of one calling: "In the wilderness prepare the way for the LORD; make straight in the desert a highway for our God. Every valley shall be raised up, every mountain and hill made low; the rough ground shall become level, the rugged places a plain."

May God bless your journey in the wilderness, raise your level of understanding, make low the mountains of discrimination, and smooth the ground for an accurate witness of God in the world.

This is the book I wish had been available to me a decade ago.

Part I: History and Culture

Chapter 1

Yearnings and "Urnings"

How Homosexuality Was Invented

Strict sexual roles

If a person who lived before the turn of the 20th century were asked about their sexual orientation, they would have been bewildered by the question. Though a wealth of literature depicts same-sex behavior as far back as the ancient Greeks, people then would not have understood terms or concepts like "heterosexual" or "homosexual." The majority of incidents of same-sex behavior were men who engaged in sex with boys, yet were erotically attracted to both females and males; the sex to which one was attracted was seen as a preference or a matter of taste.[1]

The obvious question is "How could men having sex with males not be considered homosexuals, with or without the terminology?" As early as the Roman Empire, the division between types of sexual behavior was simply based on the role one played in sex. Men took the dominant role by penetrating. The passive role of being penetrated was socially

---

[1] "Homosexuality," *The Stanford Encyclopedia of Philosophy,* http://plato.stanford.edu.

acceptable only for women, slaves, or young males who were not yet Roman citizens. Sexual relationships with younger males were temporary, typically ending when the younger male became undesirable to the older partner or entered into adulthood, usually at about twenty years of age. As the empire went into economic and social decline, and as the influence of Christianity grew, attitudes toward same-sex interaction slowly took on a negative bent.

By the fourth and fifth centuries, under the influence of St. Augustine, the mainstream Christian view of sex in general became more restrictive. Any sexual activity, even in marriage, other than with the intent to procreate was considered sinful. From the 12th century until the 14th century, theologians in the Catholic Church strictly condemned all non-procreative sex acts as sins against nature.

It's important to note that one was called a sodomite whenever one—he *or* she—engaged in a non-procreative sex act. Even people we would today call heterosexuals were labeled sodomites, immoral, sinful, or acting against nature when they engaged in non-procreative sex. Sex acts between men and boys, which had once been seen as normal or as merely a matter of an excess of sexual lust, came to be seen as perversion.

In the Age of Enlightenment during the 17th and 18th centuries, advancements in medicine and science challenged both religion and tradition; old ways of thinking were questioned. Finally, in the late 19th century, a few people started to notice that some individuals seemed to be attracted to age-appropriate people of the same sex and not attracted to those of the opposite sex.

It is here we begin to see a subtle shift in the societal perception of sexuality. A quick overview of how and when we, as a culture, came to divide men and women into heterosexual and homosexual is essential to having informed conversations about sexual identity, attraction, and orientation.[2]

---

[2] The term "sexual orientation" is very new. Prior to 1980, "sexual preference" was commonly used to indicate the sex of the person to whom one was attracted. The word "preference" suggests a voluntary choice. Sexual orientation, as reported by gays and lesbians and as supported by psychological research, is not a choice.

Sodomy: Any non-procreative sex

Before we explore how the words "heterosexual" and "homosexual" came to be, a note about terminology. My intention throughout this book is to use words historically available and appropriate to the time period being discussed. In some narratives, this historical point of view will require the use of terms such as "sexual invert" or "homosexual" rather than "gay" or "lesbian." This isn't to belabor the point, or to offend readers by using terms considered unacceptable today, but to keep us mindful of how homosexuality and heterosexuality were understood at the time of each particular narrative. Using accurate terminology is a powerful tool to help place us along historical timelines.

At the dawn of the 20th century, the idea that a person might have a consistent, lifelong, exclusive attraction to a member of the same sex was unheard of in the general population. Neither the concepts of heterosexuality and homosexuality, nor the words "heterosexual" and "homosexual," existed. This is not to say there weren't people living in an exclusive relationship with another individual of the same sex, or that romantic attractions between two men or two women did not occur. For the most part, they simply went unnoticed.

Though men who love men and women who love women have always existed, the cultural perception and interpretation associated with same-sex relationships prior to 1900 were completely different from the meanings we attach to the words "heterosexual" and "homosexual" today. We'll consider ancient words translated as "homosexual" in modern versions of the Bible in Chapter 9: "Same-Sex Behavior in the Bible." For now, let's focus on how our modern understanding of same-sex behavior developed. We'll start with the word "sodomy."

"Sodomy" is an emotionally charged word frequently swapped with the word "homosexuality." The interchange of the two words is almost always intentional and designed to cast a negative light on those who are attracted to the same sex. But where did the word "sodomy" come from? (We'll look at the biblical account of Sodom and Gomorrah in Chapter 9.)

In the 11th century, an Italian monk named Peter Damian coined the term *sodomia* in a letter he wrote to the pope. Damian was concerned about priests and monks engaging in sex with young boys (pederasty). Damian listed several specific acts he had noticed the clergy engaging in: solitary masturbation, mutual masturbation, stimulation of the penis on another person's thighs, and penetrative sex, both oral and anal. It may seem strange that solitary masturbation was on Damian's sodomy list, but remember that the Catholic Church has always viewed any non-procreative sexual act as sinful. Even today, the Roman Catholic Church's official stance on masturbation labels it "intrinsically and gravely disordered."[3]

Throughout much of history, people believed a man's semen contained all that was necessary to create a human life and that women were simply fertile ground in which to implant the seed. Because semen was thought to carry all the ingredients needed for a baby, wasting semen in sexual acts with no potential for procreation was a serious offense. The 13th-century Christian theologian Thomas Aquinas even likened masturbation to murder.

Largely due to the non-procreative aspect of sodomy, people who participated in it were viewed with religious and cultural disgust. For a time, the words "sodomy" and "buggery" were interchangeable. Until King Henry VIII of England established the Buggery Act of 1533, there were no criminal penalties associated with sodomy. Under this new law, however, all non-procreative sex was subject to criminal penalties. It didn't matter if the sexual activity was consensual, or even if it was between a husband and a wife. If the outcome of the sex act did not have the potential to plant a man's seed in a woman's womb, it was buggery and, therefore, punishable by law. When the European settlers of

---

[3] "Catechism of the Catholic Church," *Vatican Archives*, Item 2351, http://www.vatican.va/archive/ccc_css/archive/catechism/p3s2c2a6.htm.

America adopted English common law, they incorporated sodomy laws. In the new colonies, sodomy laws criminalized non-procreative sex of any kind.

Discovering heterosexuality and homosexuality

Though sexual repression was prevalent in 19th-century America, an early interest in the study of human sexuality began to emerge in Germany[4], Austria, and England. Karl Heinrich Ulrichs (1825–1895) had earned degrees in theology, law, and history in Germany. He worked for a district court until it was discovered he'd been having sexual relations with men, at which point he was dismissed. Under a pseudonym, Ulrichs wrote several essays about his own attraction to men. He theorized that there was a female psyche trapped in his body. (In today's terminology, he might have identified as either a gay man or a transwoman.[5])

Ulrichs felt he had "proof positive that nature developed the male germ within us physically, but the female spiritually."[6]

He coined the word *Urnings* in German—"Uranians" in English[7] —to describe men who were attracted to other men. Because Ulrichs thought the psyche inside him was female, he theorized that his attraction to males was a natural condition. Ulrichs imagined that his male psyche was flipped over—inverted, as it were, to a female psyche. He described and labeled the condition as "sexual inversion."

In 1867, Ulrichs spoke out at a public hearing for the repeal of sodomy laws. He argued that same-sex attractions were likely inborn in *Urnings.* Consequently, he insisted that same-sex sexual acts should not be subject to criminalization because the attractions were natural and,

---

[4] In the Province of Hanover in Prussia, which is part of modern-day Germany.

[5] Male-to-female transgender person.

[6] Hubert Kennedy, "Karl Heinrich Ulrichs: First Theorist of Homosexuality," in Science and Homosexualities, ed. Vernon Rosario (New York: Routledge, 1997), 26-45, http://hubertkennedy.angelfire.com/FirstTheorist.pdf.

[7] From the character *Uranos* in Plato's *Symposium.*

therefore, not unlawful. Ulrichs documented his work in the late 1800s[8] to foster understanding of *Urnings*. In hindsight, he is often recognized as an early pioneer for the not-yet-born gay rights movement. Though he was not successful in his attempt to decriminalize sexual actions on the part of those with sexual inversions, Ulrichs worked tirelessly to promote his belief that being an *Urning* was simply an inborn condition.

Ulrichs' discovery in the late 1860s marks a pivotal moment along the timeline running through this book. Ulrichs introduced the first attempt to distinguish between men exclusively attracted to men and men who were attracted to women. Prior to Ulrichs' observation, it was believed that men who had sex with men did so out of lust, sexual excess, or a moral deficiency rather than natural attractions.

Karl Maria Kertbeny (1824–1882), a Hungarian writer and journalist, was a contemporary of Ulrichs. As a young apprentice bookseller, he witnessed the suicide of a friend who had been blackmailed by someone who discovered his sexual attraction to men. His friend's suicide caused Kertbeny to recognize the unjustness of Germany's sodomy laws. Kertbeny, aware of Ulrichs' work on just treatment of *Urnings,* wrote a private letter to Ulrichs in 1868 outlining five groupings of common sexual behaviors he had observed.

Following are the words Kertbeny coined for each group, along with his descriptions. Though the words are recognizable, several of the meanings have changed over time. Notice the focus he placed on sexual excesses and the sexual partners in each division.

- *Monosexual* – a person who has sex with himself or herself; one who masturbates
- *Heterogenit* – one who performs erotic sexual acts with animals
- *Normalsexualitat* – one who engages exclusively in sex with the opposite sex—a label Kertbeny used for himself

---

[8] Karl Heinrich Ulrichs. *Research on the Riddle of Man-Manly Love,* 12 vols, published between 1864 and 1880.

- *Homosexual* – a person, male or female, who performs erotic sexual acts with a person of the same sex
- *Heterosexual* – a person, male or female, who participates "in so-called natural [procreative] as well as unnatural [non-procreative] coitus. They are also capable of giving themselves over to same-sex excesses. Additionally, normally-sexed individuals are no less likely to engage in self-defilement [masturbation] if there is sufficient opportunity to satisfy one's sex drive. And they are equally likely to assault male but especially female minors; to indulge in incest; to engage in bestiality."[9]

The written exchange between Ulrichs and Kertbeny in 1868 is the first documented observation which specifically categorized people by identifying the sex of their partner rather than the role one played (active or passive) in sexual intercourse. This major shift in defining a person's sexuality cannot be overemphasized. The following year, Kertbeny's terms were used in limited circles in German medical journals. From this point on, the recognition of sexual attraction as either heterosexual or homosexual began a *slow* progression into the culture.

Notice that Kertbeny observed and categorized heterosexual men as attracted to women, yet still having sex with men, and eventually going on to marry women. Self-satisfying, lustful sexual behavior of this type has been recorded since biblical and other ancient times. Further, Kertbeny noted that both heterosexual and homosexual behaviors were associated with an "unfettered capacity for degeneracy."[10]

The general population had no conscious understanding that divisions had been observed and created along a new heterosexual or homosexual axis. It would take another forty years for the word "heterosexual" to appear in an American medical textbook with its more

---

[9] Jonathan Katz, *The Invention of Heterosexuality* (Chicago: University of Chicago Press, 2007), 53.
[10] Ibid., 53.

restrictive definition: one who has sex with a person of the opposite sex. Let's follow the progression from medical text to culture.

Human sexuality studies begin

German contemporaries of Kertbeny and Ulrichs were doing early research in sex, sexual roles, and sexual relationships. In 1897, Dr. Magnus Hirschfeld (1868–1935) founded the Scientific Humanitarian Committee and, in 1919, the Institute for Sexual Science. Just as Kertbeny and Ulrichs had done, Hirschfeld used his skills to defend the rights of sexual inverts (later called homosexuals), who were often blackmailed in the 1920s under Paragraph 175 of the German penal code criminalizing sodomy.

Hirschfeld documented thousands of cases of people with sexual inversions. With a solid background in research, members of the Scientific Humanitarian Committee argued in the German Parliament against criminalizing sodomy, hoping to attain "justice through science."

Hirschfeld spent years recording the stories of people who had stepped outside the expected male and female sex roles. It is believed he interviewed over 30,000 people in an effort to create a scientific basis confirming sexual inverts as representative of a natural variation of human sexuality. For Hirschfeld, the attraction of sexual inverts for a person of the same sex was natural, to be expected, and, therefore, should not be punishable.

The Institute (and all of its over 10,000 books, articles, and research records) was destroyed by an angry crowd spurred on by Nazi storm troopers in 1933. Though much of Hirschfeld's early research and documentation was lost, he escaped to France, where he died. His tombstone is engraved *Per Scientiam ad Justitiam*—"Through science to justice."

At the age of twenty-five, Henry Gerber (1892–1972), a German immigrant to America, was briefly admitted to a mental institution due to his homosexuality. Because he was a German immigrant living in

America when World War I broke out, he had two options: serve in the Army or go to one of the internment camps. He went to war. While stationed in Germany, he became inspired by Hirschfeld's work at the Scientific Humanitarian Committee. Upon his return to the United States in 1924, Gerber established the Society for Human Rights—the first sexual invert (gay) rights organization in the country.

No examination of early modern thought on sexual inversion/homosexuality would be complete without a cursory look at the theories of Sigmund Freud (1856–1939), the "Father of Psychoanalysis." His theories outlined the healthy stages of emotional growth from infancy to adulthood. Freud put forth the idea that events from infancy and early childhood impacted adult social and psychological growth.

In 1910, Freud began postulating that sexual inverts exemplified a broken person in need of repair. If, during psychoanalysis or talk therapy, Freud could uncover evidence of childhood damage, the sexual invert could presumably become "normal." Over the next two decades, Freud's theories in the field of psychoanalysis influenced the emergence of heterosexuality as the "normal" human sexuality.

"Homosexuality" and "heterosexuality" come to America

In 1901, the word "heterosexual" was included in discourse on sexual interaction published in *Dorland's Medical Dictionary*. Defined as erotic, excessive, and "an abnormal or perverted appetite toward the opposite sex," the word still had a strong sense of perversion attached to it.

Dr. A. A. Brill, one of Freud's early German-to-English translators, was the first to practice psychoanalysis in America. Brill helped establish the American Psychoanalytic Association (APsaA) in 1911. At an American medical convention in 1913, Brill reported the distinct evidence that male sexual inverts, as they were still called, only found sexual satisfaction with men. Now, for the first time in America, it was suggested that the object of one's attraction, rather than the sexual role played, should become the distinguishing factor of a person's sexuality. Still, this new concept in America of dividing people along lines of same-sex or opposite-sex attraction only existed in obscure medical circles.

Homosexuality was first defined in the 1909 volume of *Dorland's Medical Dictionary* as "a morbid [unhealthy] sexual passion for the same sex." Fourteen years later, the 1923 *Webster's Dictionary* defined heterosexuality as "a morbid [unhealthy] sexual passion for the opposite sex." Both words were associated with sexual excesses outside of procreative sex. As we will see, this idea that sexual excess and non-procreative sex is immoral is repeated in many cultures throughout history. The terms "heterosexuality" and "homosexuality" made a slow migration out of the medical arena and into more common usage. The first time the word "heterosexual" appeared in American print other than dictionaries was in 1924 in the *New York Times* in a review of a Sigmund Freud book. Eventually, both words were defined in the 1934 edition of *Webster's Dictionary:* heterosexuality as "a manifestation of sexual passion for one of the opposite sex; normal sexuality," and homosexuality as "eroticism for one of the same sex."

To bring all of this together, using the words "heterosexual" or "homosexual" before the end of the 1920s to identify an individual's sexual attraction is meaningless. The concept of being defined by the sex of the person to whom you were attracted would have been completely foreign within the general population.

Prior to the turn of the 20th century, and throughout all of history, good sex and bad sex were distinguished in two simple ways: First, was the sex procreative or non-procreative? If the sex made babies, it was good sex. If the sex did not make babies (even sex between husband and wife), it was bad sex and presumably motivated by sexual excesses and lust.

Secondly, what role did the man perform in the sex act? Was he the penetrator—in the dominant position? That kind of sex was manly and good. Or was he the penetrated partner—in the submissive position? If the one being penetrated was male, that kind of sex was bad. Further, outside the bedroom and within the social strata, the passive male abdicated his manly position, placed himself lower than the value of a woman, and relinquished his masculinity. That kind of sex was very bad.

We can use these two simple distinctions of procreative intention and role played by the man to categorize sex as either good or bad as far back as ancient and biblical times. This is why the notion of a dividing line of the sex of one's partner in the 1930s was so significant; sexuality had never before been viewed in that manner.

The next obvious question might be: In the newly created designations and division of sexual attraction, how did one kind of sex (heterosexual sex) become the good sex and the other kind of sex (homosexual sex) become the bad sex? The answer is quite complex and can be found at the intersection of cultural and social urbanization, early feminism, and Prohibition.

Heterosexuality becomes the good sex

You may be thinking, "Cultural and social urbanization, early feminism, and Prohibition—that's quite an interesting list!" And it's a story you've probably never heard, yet need to. Eventually, the chapters of this book will navigate through psychoanalytic theories, psychological research, the American culture of the 1940s through the 1960s, the merger of politics and religion from the late 1970s to the 1990s, the six key verses in the Bible, biblical marriage, the imposition of reparative therapy on the gay community, and the status of gay and transgender Christians today. It will be quite a journey along unexpected paths and side roads, collecting insights along the way.

At the end of this trek, you should have a more clearly defined picture of how and why the gay, lesbian, bisexual, and transgender communities came to be the focus of cultural and religious discrimination that still exists today. But it all begins when heterosexuality was established in 1934 as "normal" sexuality.

With the concepts of heterosexuality and homosexuality traced through early medicine, psychoanalysis, and sex studies, let's step back a bit further to understand how sexual attitudes and roles have changed over time. The focus, for the most part, will be on male same-sex relationships because relationships between women were not, and still are not, studied to the same extent as relationships between men.

In ancient and medieval times, friendships between men were seen as nobler and more elevated in status than men's relationships with women, even their own wives. Throughout much of history, including biblical times, women were considered weak in character and inferior in moral, emotional, and intellectual abilities. Friendships between men, therefore, were often considered more fulfilling and richer than friendships with their wives. Deep, and even passionate, relationships between men were common in the 19th century. You've likely seen old photographs from the 1800s showing men in embraces that appear quite intimate to our sensibilities. Using such photos of men as "proof" that they routinely engaged in sexual relationships is to interpret the situation with our 21st-century minds and likely to overstate what was actually going on. Though often intimate, these friendships were, for the most part, nonsexual.

Men routinely used affectionate language with one another and did not shy away from loving actions, such as handholding or even putting their arms around one another. They weren't concerned that their close platonic friendships would be considered deviant or wrong. Even if male-male sexual intimacy *did* occur, it was completely normal for a man to go ahead and marry a woman.

Flagrant sexual relationships between men in the upper classes, however, were stigmatized because men of wealth and status "should" be able to control their sexual excesses and lusts. Preservation of family wealth and holdings was of great concern, hence creating heirs was essential. If a man of status did have a male lover, he also took a wife in hopes of producing heirs.

Growing cities usher in greater sexual awareness

Within the span of a few decades in the late 19th century, the United States was transformed from a predominantly agrarian society to an industrial economy. In the late 1880s, a severe ten-year drought caused many farms to fail, accelerating the migration of men to the cities seeking work. New factories and assembly lines opened in major cities, and port cities saw an influx of sailors, particularly following World War I.

Millions of immigrants flowed into American cities from abroad. Many of them were young men who worked in factories and sent their earnings home to families in other countries. A bachelor subculture formed as hundreds of thousands of men, many for the first time in their lives, were living in a mostly male environment. Of the men in New York City at the turn of the century, 40% were single.[11]

Other social changes were in the air, helping to usher in an evolution in various types of relationships. As men gathered in male-dominated urban environments, they experienced new freedom to express and explore affections and attractions they may or may not have been aware of at home on the farm or back in their small hometowns. Urban housing situations became quite conducive to male-only living environments. With the honorable intention of providing unmarried working-class and immigrant men safe and moral living quarters, the Young Men's Christian Association (YMCA) began to build single-sex housing for men. Seven YMCA residential hotels were built over a twenty-year period at the turn of the century in New York City alone. The convenience of centralized, male-only environments banning all women from visitation to the residents' private rooms led to unintended consequences.

---

[11] George Chauncery, *Gay New York: Gender, Urban Culture, and the Making of the Gay Male World*, 1890–1940 (New York: Basic Books, 1994), 76.

YMCAs became meccas for the social lives of homosexual men up to and through the 1950s.[12]

Ironically, the good intentions of Christian social justice organizations led to unexpected outcomes in other venues as well. The unwashed masses of poor, mostly immigrant laborers had no place to bathe in their overcrowded tenements; in the late 1890s in New York City, only one in forty families lived in a tenement with a bathroom. To give them sanitary relief, religiously motivated social reformers of The New York Association for the Improvement of the Conditions of the Poor began campaigns to construct public bathhouses.[13] In 1915, there were fifteen bathhouses in Manhattan alone. By the 1920s, that number had increased to fifty-seven. Over the next half century, as gay men were increasingly pushed out to the edges of society and into the corners, certain bathhouses became refuges of privacy for sexual encounters.

Before this time, women had been fenced out of many jobs, in part under the advisement of doctors who, before the turn of the century, warned them that working outside the home might damage their ability to bear children. Obviously, the threat was not based on scientific or medical research but on the presuppositions of men.[14] By the second decade of the 20th century, single women joined men in migrating to cities to secure jobs in industry and other sectors. Women began entering the workplace in record numbers.

An American imperative to be a manly man

The predominantly male-teacher culture shifted to a female-teacher culture at the end of the 19th century. The majority of the nation's teachers had been male in the middle of the century, but by the end of it, four out of five teachers were female. Many men, feeling challenged by the increased public presence and influence of women, including women

---

[12] Ibid., 155.
[13] Ibid., 208.
[14] Ibid., 112.

taking their jobs, worried that their children were being "feminized" in school.[15]

With women in the workforce and in education, cultural and social lines between men and women blurred and threatened traditional male power, control, and status. In order for men to distance themselves from women and anything perceived as feminine, becoming a "manly man" became an imperative and a common pursuit. Close male friendships, once freely affectionate and intimate, were viewed more negatively.

President Theodore Roosevelt sounded an alarm for a "manly imperative" to counter the rising women's movement and the "feminization" of American men. In his famous speech on the virtues of "The Strenuous Life" (1900), Roosevelt stated, "Let us therefore boldly face the life of strife, resolute to do our duty well and manfully."

Roosevelt led the nation by example with his strong and visible depiction of what a manly man should be. He'd been a cattle rancher, an explorer, and a police commissioner. Rather than stay in the Navy during the Spanish-American War, Roosevelt resigned, rounded up his cowboy buddies from his old ranching days, formed the Rough Riders, and led the group in a victory against Spain in Cuba. On horseback, with his rifle at his side, he challenged men to follow him. He also hunted, fished, and boxed, and altered the cultural image of what American men should strive to be.

To rescue their sons from being "sissified," men organized groups to instill masculine and rugged qualities in boys. To that end, in 1912, the Boy Scouts of America (BSA) was founded by Lord Robert Baden-Powell to forge boys into strong men. It is rather ironic, considering the skirmishes within the BSA in recent years, that the man who inspired the Boy Scouts, Baden-Powell, is speculated to have been a closeted gay man.[16] A Victorian-Age military hero and one of the British Empire's most adulated soldiers, he had a strong emotional bond with Kenneth

---

[15] Ibid., 113.
[16] Brooke Allen, "Rainbow Merit Badge," *New York Times*, July 19, 2012, http://nyti.ms/1y3HPYx.

McLaren, a fellow army officer. When McLaren married, Baden-Powell was quite jealous until he, at the age of fifty-five, married a 23-year-old woman. Without hard evidence, historians have speculated that Baden-Powell was gay.

The not-so-manly men

With the pressure to be "manly" that men felt as a result of the increasingly visible presence and cultural impact of women, an interesting and opposite dynamic arose as a backdrop in American cities in the early 1900s. Younger men, in the peak years of their sexual inquisitiveness, found themselves in same-sex environments where it was convenient to entertain their curiosities. Tolerance for men engaging in sex with men existed within the poorer, immigrant, and working classes. As long as a man took the active role and carried himself in a masculine manner, he was respected as "normal." But as we have already seen, within isolated medical circles, men who submitted sexually in the passive role were starting to be classified as sexual inverts, though that terminology had not yet migrated to the wider culture.

In the street language of the day, a man who took the passive sexual role was referred to by a variety of names. Most commonly, he was called a "fairy." It was not just having a sexual desire for men that classified him as a fairy. Fairies usually exhibited effeminate mannerisms but did not always adopt feminine styles of clothing. To make themselves recognizable, they often employed noticeable physical clues—longer hair, eye makeup, a red tie, or a feather adornment. Within the lower classes, fairies, who were thought to embody a female spirit, were seen as more of an eccentricity than an object of disgust.

Fairies were more desirable to some men simply because they were willing to engage in erotic sexual activities that the "good girls" were not socially permitted to perform. Even "loose women" were restricted by strong sexual taboos from participating in particular methods of sex quite common today. Recall, procreative sex was moral; non-procreative sex was taboo. Therefore, a man who was looking for more erotic sex sought out the companionship of the fairies, who were willing to participate.[17]

Early terminology describing gay men

Interestingly, most of the unkind terms used today to belittle gay men have their origin in words historically used to belittle women. As previously noted, throughout history women have been held in rather low esteem. Views of women as less than men—less important, less noble, less powerful, etc.—were perpetuated in the language used to describe women and, eventually, gay men.

General disrespect for women can still be observed today in derogatory language. In English, there are disproportionately more such words for women than there are for men. Misogyny spills over to labels used for men perceived as effeminate. Most of the words adopted by, or used against, the male gay community were at one time used as slurs against women.

"Fairy" was originally British slang for an ugly and, often, a drunken woman. She may have been sexually promiscuous or perhaps even a prostitute. "Fairy" was then adopted by men who, likening themselves to the less honorable status of such women, played the passive sexual role. At the dawn of the 20th century, a secret society of effeminate men who took on the role of women, dressed in women's clothing, and met for coffee and knitting called themselves "The Fairies of New York." Not all relationships with fairies were temporary or only sexual; some fairies even held respected positions in long-term marriage-like arrangements with men.

"Faggot" is a frequently used, hate-filled word in today's culture. Many words go in and out of acceptability and unacceptability within the mainstream culture. This is one such word. Though it is highly offensive in general, there is a larger reason for investigating the roots of this word.

---

[17] *Gay New York*, 85.

The word "faggot" has its origin in *fagot,* French for "bundle of sticks." Legend has it that men convicted of sodomy in the Middle Ages were burned on piles of sticks. However, that's not true. By the time civil sodomy laws were passed in England in 1533, the punishment for sodomy was hanging, not burning.[18] So, where is the inevitable connection to women? The word "faggot" was 1800s British slang describing a worthless, usually older, and rather shrewish woman. This meaning was adapted into American slang in 1914 to describe fairies, as well as men who dressed in drag. They were seen as "less thans"—less than men and less than women—by the men who had sex with them.

There are many other derogatory feminine-based terms used to describe men who took the passive role in sex. "Fruit" was originally used by hobos and tramps to describe a woman who was weak, an easy mark, or "easy pickings"—a woman who was quick to sexually oblige a man or who was easy to victimize.

Even self-identifiers used by fairies and sexual inverts were feminine in tone: queens, nances (from "Nancy"), pansies, daisies, buttercups, and sissies (from "sister"). Male-male same-sex behavior has historically evoked more reaction, outrage, and disgust in society than has female-female behavior. Hence, there were more demeaning terms for gay men than for lesbians.

Rugged, working-class, manly men who had sexual interactions with fairies and women were called "trade." Trade men were somewhat consistent with Kertbeny's definition of heterosexuals from the late 19th century. Their sexual behavior was viewed mostly as sexual excess, lust, or a lapse in moral integrity. Trade men usually went on to marry women, or were already married to women.

Sailors who might not have experienced sexual interactions with men before they left the farms and small towns came flooding into the port cities during and after World War I. They were just as likely to have a

---

[18] "'Burned for Sodomy' – The Changing Legal Framework of the Great Persecution," *Queering the Church,* July 15, 2009, http://bit.ly/1scSbU5.

sexual rendezvous with a fairy as with a female prostitute.[19] Military educational materials badly missed opportunities to limit venereal disease by depicting rather suspect-looking, loose, seductive, and evil women as carriers of venereal disease. Military propaganda about sex and the healthy use of condoms never suggested potential hazards in male-male sex. Such poorly communicated messages and warnings led the sailors to believe they couldn't catch diseases by having sex with a man. Consequently, fairies in port cities were seen as a safer, disease-free alternative to convenient sex with loose women. Even though the sailor was having sex with a man, as long as he maintained a masculine demeanor and took the active role of penetrator, he was "normal" and all was well in man-land.

Equal-status male sexual relationships

By the 1910s and 1920s, masculine men who were attracted to similarly masculine men self-identified as "queer." Queer was not initially seen as a negative term. It was used as a descriptor of how such men saw themselves in the culture. Queers were not as flamboyant as fairies and could easily pass as "normal." Regarding the use of the word "queer," an evolution has occurred. As equal-status sexual relationships emerged between men, with neither identifying in the female role, the word "queer" evolved into a cultural slur. More recently, it has been redeemed as an acceptable word used by younger gay people and others outside the heterosexual sphere, but using "queer" to describe or address an older man may be hurtful because of its recent use as a slur with harmful intentions.[20]

Use of the word "queer" marked a point of recognition that two men, neither adopting a feminine role, could experience a persistent,

---

[19] *Gay New York*, 66-67.

[20] "Queer" was unacceptable during the years of gay liberation from the 1960s to the 1990s. Older people who have lived through the years when "queer" was used as a slur strongly resist using the word as an identifier. It has been adopted, however, by younger and often urban gay youth and by the younger gay community in general. Universities have adopted it to create Queer Studies curricula. Source: Robin Brontsema, "A Queer Revolution: Reconceptualizing the Debate Over Linguistic Reclamation," *Colorado Research in Linguistics* (University of Colorado Boulder) 17, no. 1 (June 2004).

long-term attraction to each other. Beginning in the 1920s, medical knowledge about equal-status, persistent same-sex attractions began to migrate into the wider culture.

Homosexuals become gays

The word "gay," meaning "happy," came into the English language at the end of the first millennium. It is derived from the French word *gai*, meaning "merry." In the 17th century, *gai* took on a second meaning, one associated with the self-indulgent, loose, and immoral life. By the 19th century, the word was used to describe prostitutes, primarily females, and the activities in which they engaged. To "gay it" meant to fornicate. Again, we see the consistent and pervasive use of words first demeaning women coming to be used to demean gay men.

In the late 1890s, a Scottish variation of the word "gay" was used in "gey cat," which referred to a younger man or boy whom a hobo took under his wing to protect and show the ropes. A gey cat was often the hobo's catamite—a boy prostitute or sexual servant. By the 1920s, sexual inverts started using the term "gay," associated with "gey cat," in their own private social circles to refer to one another. It was a convenient form of secret code, as "gay" still had the more common meaning of "happy." By the 1950s, "gay," meaning "homosexual," moved into usage in the wider society. At first, it only indicated gay men and only later, starting in about the 1970s, included lesbians.

Gay people did not commandeer the word "gay." Repeatedly I've heard the complaint: "They changed the meaning of the word 'gay' from happy to homosexual, and now we can't even use the word 'gay' to mean happy anymore." No, no, no. The word "gay" had two completely different meanings. No one "stole" the word. As with many words, the meaning of "gay" has evolved over time. It is more likely that straight people, responding to cultural and sexual shame, didn't want to risk personal association with homosexuals by even using the word "gay." Fortunately, there are plenty of other words to indicate happy, cheerful, and merry.

What about lesbians?

Sexual relationships between women at the dawn of the 20th century were less conspicuous than male same-sex relationships. While relatively little was understood about male same-sex attractions, far less was known about female same-sex attractions. As was true of men attracted to men, women attracted to women were referred to as sexual inverts or *Urnings,* and then, increasingly, as lesbians.

Even though the word "lesbian" is derived from the ancient name of a Greek island, Lesbos, the term, as associated with women, is a modern one. Sappho, a lyric poet, philosopher, and teacher, was born on Lesbos around 600 BC. Her poetry praised beauty in nature and in men and women, but especially in women. Although Sappho was known to love women, the word "lesbian" wasn't associated with her or even used to describe women until centuries after her death. The word "lesbian," as it is now associated with same-sex attracted women, was first printed in a medical dictionary in 1890. Women with same-sex attraction had been called both sapphos and lesbians. The term "sapphos" died out, it is thought, simply because it is more difficult to pronounce.

When researching any topic involving women in history, there is inherently less documentation available because women's history has been considered less important than men's history. Consequently, information about women's sexual history is sketchy. The word "dyke," a sometimes derogatory term for a lesbian,[21] is one example of poorly documented history. There are two favored theories as to the origin of the term "dyke": One holds that "dyke" was originally a slang word for the vulva. The other possibility is that "dyke" is a shortened form of "bulldyker," a term used in the 1920s for lesbians in Harlem, New York City. Whatever the origin, "dyke" was originally used as a dismissive term but has been redeemed as acceptable by some lesbians themselves.

---

[21] This is a nuanced word. Some people use the word "dyke" in a demeaning manner. Some women self-identify with the term "dyke." The rule of thumb is: If the intention is to cause harm, do not use the term.

Until the early 1900s, women who were attracted to women were mostly invisible in society. As traditional caretakers of the home and hearth, women did not have the social freedom or independence necessary to explore their potential for romantic relationships with other women—that is, until they began entering educational institutions, the workforce, and the military.

Women who love women in the 19th century

In 1848, the participants of the Seneca Falls Convention, the first women's rights gathering, put forth women's education and the right to vote as primary social objectives. Both were novel concepts. Prior to the outbreak of the Civil War, only five U.S. colleges had allowed for the admission of women, preferring to dedicate their facilities to educating men. With men off to war in the 1860s, space opened up for the education of women in formerly all-male institutions. By 1870, almost one-third of American colleges allowed women to enroll, thereby exposing women to same-sex environments on a comparatively large scale for the first time. In all-female surroundings, some women experienced romantic and passionate attractions for one another, but, for the most part, these attractions were seen as harmless.

Such relationships, called "smashes" or "spoons," were written about openly in mainstream magazines. Though undying love was declared, gifts exchanged, and kisses shared, there was no allusion in mainstream literature to any sort of sexual interaction between women. After all, why pay attention to what women might be doing sexually? Women were thought not to have sexual needs or orgasms similar to those of men. Their intimate relationships were inconsequential. If relationships between women had a sexual element, it went unnoticed and the relationships were seen from the outside as relatively virtuous and pure.

It is not surprising that women's sexuality flew under the radar historically. Because it was impossible to "prove" the existence of female orgasm the way it could be proven for a man due to semen production, female orgasms were the stuff of anecdotal evidence with no "need" to be scientifically proven. Finally, however, in the late 1950s, human sexuality researchers William Masters and Virginia Johnson would use scientific methods to prove the existence of female orgasms. The delay of this discovery is indicative of the lack of awareness on the subject of female sexuality.

Women who refused to hide their attraction to other women were frequently diagnosed as mentally ill. In the early 1900s, many such women were admitted to insane asylums, where, under the "care" of doctors, they were abused and raped in the mistaken belief that these "treatments" would stop them from being attracted to women. Some were forced to marry despite their lack of desire for men. It is not surprising that lesbians felt pressured to keep their affections hidden.

Whether due to attraction to other women, the desire for a career, or resistance to losing freedom and becoming the property of a man in a conventional marriage, many women entered into "Boston marriages." This phenomenon was named for the relationship of two wealthy women intimately involved in Henry James' 1895 *The Bostonians*. The term "Boston marriage" was used in the late 1800s and early 1900s to refer to two unmarried women who cohabited. The number of Boston marriages markedly increased at the turn of the 20th century with the growing ranks of educated and professional women who no longer required financial assistance from men to survive. For example, 57% of the 1884 graduating class at Smith, an all-women's college, never married, compared to the 10% average of unmarried women in the general population.[22]

Some women chose to live together because they felt more drawn to women than to men. It was assumed, as per the belief about *Urnings,* that one of the women in a Boston marriage had a male psyche trapped inside. Little is documented about Boston marriages; we would in all likelihood label them lesbian relationships today. However, because

---

[22] *Gay New York*, 118.

women were typically sexually repressed until the middle of the 20th century and restrained by intense cultural taboos, many early woman-woman relationships had no sexual component.

By the late 1920s, the terms "homosexual" and "heterosexual" were making their initial appearances in the common language in limited social circles outside the medical field. An entire half century after the concept was first described in medical circles, homosexuality and heterosexuality finally arrived in the cultural consciousness of the 1930s.

The end of Prohibition sends the gays into ghettos

Prohibition made it illegal to manufacture, transport, or sell alcohol (18th Amendment, 1919, repealed by the 21st Amendment, 1933), but it never stopped people from drinking and congregating socially. Organized crime simply went underground; bars and clubs were taken over by criminals who continued selling alcohol. These establishments tended to be located in lower-class neighborhoods and catered to a free social mixing of middle-class male-female couples, queer couples, trade men and fairies, and singles. It was a carefree time; the gay-male world was visible and comfortably integrated into the party and speakeasy scene.

The Roaring '20s was a time when sexual constraints weakened and new freedoms emerged in dating and sexual behavior. Social reformers grew more concerned about the general degradation of morals and the increase in perversion among urban populations. If they could control the fairies and the queers, the reformers believed, they could control the seemingly rampant and widespread excessive sexual behaviors going on in both the homosexual and heterosexual communities. When Prohibition ended, state officials were pressured to focus selectively on sexual vices between men to clean up the effects of the social depravity of the Roaring '20s.[23]

---

[23] Ibid., 334-335.

Same-sex behavior between queers in the middle and upper classes became highly scrutinized and was seen as sexual excess, lust, and perversion. The Society for Suppression of Vice in New York City had already started arresting fairies in 1915 for "degenerate, disorderly conduct." By 1923, the dragnet was expanded to include fairies and queers who gathered in public places for the purposes of "committing a crime against nature or other lewdness." It was the first time a state law specified and singled out same-sex male behavior as a criminal offense. Though sodomy laws had been on the books previously, laws were now passed to specifically criminalize sexual activity between men.[24]

At the end of Prohibition, the New York State Liquor Authority reissued business licenses to bars with the requirement that business be conducted in an "orderly" manner. Although the laws did not forbid bars from serving gays, officials made it clear that the presence of gays, prostitutes, gamblers, and other "undesirables" would not be tolerated in licensed bars. If gay customers were served, the bar either would not be issued a license or would have its license revoked. In years prior, fairies and queers had been at the center of the speakeasy and entertainment scene in urban lower- and middle-class neighborhoods. Suddenly, they were banned from social participation.

Immediately after the repeal of Prohibition, in 1934, Fiorello La Guardia took office as mayor of New York City. Determined to fulfill his promises to clean up the city, to keep alcohol out of the hands of criminals, and to prepare for the 1939 World's Fair, LaGuardia launched an aggressive police crackdown on gay bars and meeting places. Queers, fairies, drag queens, and transvestites were arrested in rising numbers.

For the next twenty-five years, bars catering to the gay and transsexual populations were constantly on the move. Gays and transsexuals were pushed into hiding "in the closet," in the darkness and shadows, and out of the way.[25]

---

[24] Ibid., 185.
[25] Ibid., 339.

Chapter 2

Evolution of the Understanding of Sexual Orientation

Psychoanalysis and Homosexuality from 1880 to the 1970s

The beginnings of modern psychology

The foundations of modern psychoanalysis go back to the 1870s, concurrent with Karl Kertbeny's and Karl Ulrich's discoveries of human sexuality categories. In 1879, the first psychologist, psychology lab, and psychology textbook appeared. While people have always talked about their problems and stresses, no one had studied them until this time. Psychology became a new method by which behavior and mental processes were investigated and reported.

Before this period, when a person exhibited strange conduct or a neurosis, the behavior was written off as bad or weak blood from degenerate family lines, which had passed down through generations. People had a fatalistic attitude about mental stresses. Since there wasn't much they could do about "those" problems, "crazy people" were shipped off to asylums, out of public sight, to protect the reputation and image of the family.

World War I directly challenged traditional beliefs about "madness" passing through family lines and blood. The huge number of formerly sane and healthy young soldiers returning home from battle with a wide array of mental illnesses was difficult to write off according to such theories. Building upon a little over three decades of preliminary work in psychology, doctors treating the traumatized soldiers began to formulate ways to deal with the mental stresses of war. Suddenly, the study of psychology became a valuable asset. Doctors thought maybe they could fix people rather than ship them off and out of the way.

Freud and psychoanalysis

In 1896, Sigmund Freud (1856–1939) founded a new strain of psychology and called it psychoanalysis. He was a creative and brilliant theorist but spent very little time actually working with patients or studying cases. He introduced a groundbreaking ideology suggesting that only a small part of a person's motivations and actions could be witnessed. The observed part he called the conscious—just the tip of the iceberg, covering what he called the subconscious—the primary motivations beneath the surface. Freud created many outlandish and non–evidence-based theories about mental illnesses. Most of his theories, resolutions, and treatments linked to assumptions he had formulated about various stages of sexual subconsciousness, from infancy through its progression during childhood and into adulthood.

Incredibly, Freud related a variety of mental illnesses to his theories of missed or distorted childhood psychosexual stages. Most mental illnesses, he speculated, began with sexual abuse, fear of sex, or guilt about sex. Though his theories were baseless, they caught on, partly due to the scandalous intrigue they held for a culture emerging from the sexually repressed Victorian Era.

Psychoanalysis, in its infancy, was only for the very wealthy. The turn of the 20th century was still an era when people would not admit to their problems and weaknesses. The expectation was to "man up." Then, when the perception of mental illness shifted after World War I, psychoanalysis came to be seen as a respectable way to deal with trauma, and the treatment became more widely available. Freud had set the benchmark, albeit with no scientific support, little client interaction, and creative theorizing, and many psychologists followed in his footsteps.

In addition, onto the 1920s scene came the recognition of people who were exclusively same-sex attracted. Freud was bound to associate the observed same-sex behavior with disrupted childhood psychosexual stages, and he did.

While living and practicing in Austria, Freud had begun working on his theories of why some people were gay. Once again, this time in the sphere of psychoanalysis, perspectives on women as inferior beings were closely tied to views about gay men. Predictably, Freud thought the "mental illness" of both lesbians and gay men was due to disrupted childhood psychosexual stages. He didn't think women in general had sexual needs, so when they did, he thought something had gone wrong for them during childhood. The same was true for male sexual inverts. They "should" only prefer sex with women, so something had gone wrong for them in childhood.

Fortunately for heterosexual women (male and female sexual inverts were not as lucky), the female population soon escaped Freud's baseless speculations. Freud was forced to modify and modernize his theories about women as several female psychoanalysts, including Karen Horney, Helene Deutsch, and Freud's own daughter, Anna, challenged his ideas about female sexuality, sexual repression, and penis envy. Freud's theories were confronted, tested, and discarded by highly regarded female peers in psychoanalysis.

Sexual inverts, however, remained without representation far longer. In the history of the discourse on homosexuality within the American Psychoanalytic Association (APsaA) community, no analytical or influential voice arose for more than a half century to confront the formulation of theories about homosexuality. For one thing, no gays were allowed to become members of the APsaA.

(Indeed, gay people were not allowed in the APsaA until 2001—almost forty years after homosexuality was struck from the *Diagnostic and Statistical Manual of Mental Disorders* [DSM]. It was then that the APsaA finally issued a "membership non-discrimination" policy allowing gay psychoanalysts to join the organization. Before that, when gay psychoanalysts applied to APsaA, they had to lie about their orientation or they would not be accepted. Those who told the truth were asked to come back and reapply for membership when they were "cured." For ninety years there were no openly gay psychoanalysts in the primary policy-making organization in the United States dealing with the subject of homosexuality. Those who were closeted had to be careful not to rock the boat or challenge existing belief systems within the organization or they might lose their membership. This silence meant that inaccurate and poorly done research, based on cultural stereotypes and misunderstandings, was never challenged or revised by APsaA. The most abiding culturally and professionally respected discourse concerning gays was formulated by non-gays, causing the "direction of observation, judgment, and control [to extend] in one direction only."[1])

Sigmund Freud, who had believed homosexuality was an incomplete form of "normal" childhood heterosexual development but neither a vice nor an illness, softened his views further by the end of his life. In 1935, a mother wrote to Freud for advice about dealing with her homosexual son. Freud wrote back that homosexuality "cannot be classified as an illness; we consider it to be a variation of the human function,"

---

[1] Kenneth Lewes, *Psychoanalysis and Male Homosexuality* (Northvale, NJ: Jason Aronson, Inc., 1995), 225.

and added that "In a certain number of cases we succeed in developing the blighted [disrupted] germs of heterosexual tendencies which are present in every homosexual, [but] in the majority of cases it is no more possible."[2]

How then did American psychoanalysts, whose practices were founded in Freud's revolutionary thought, move from a posture of questioning and theorizing about the root causes of homosexuality to a stance of declaring "truths" about causes and treatment methods? To answer this, it is important to note that the virulent strain of homophobic psychoanalysis that developed in America from the 1930s forward was, for the most part, a purely American phenomenon.

The atmosphere within the therapy community in England was quite different than in the United States. England had absorbed a far greater number of progressive Austrian, German, and Jewish psychoanalysts from Germany and its annexed countries than had the United States during and after World War II. Freud was one such immigrant; when Hitler annexed Austria, Freud became an exile in London. He only visited America once, and his progressive psychoanalytic influence was limited to Europe.

Even Freud's conclusion near the time of his death that homosexuality was not a mental illness did not impact the American psychoanalytic community. In Europe, psychoanalysts relied on the extensive research accumulated since the late 1800s about human sexuality and tended toward more progressive attitudes. One might think that the psychoanalysts who did immigrate to America, rather than going to England, would have brought that same richness and understanding about human sexuality into the far more conservative American culture. But that didn't happen.

In large part, the psychoanalysts who came to America were tired of the social chaos and Nazi purges, including the burning of their

---

[2] Sigmund Freud, "Letter to an American Mother," *American Journal of Psychiatry* 107 (1951): 787.

research institutions, in Germany. The general unrest in Europe had enticed them to settle into the more peaceful environment available in America. At the same time, however, an overt atmosphere of anti-Semitism and anti-German sentiments prevailed in the United States, so the many immigrant psychoanalysts who were both Jewish and/or German did in puritanical America what newly arriving immigrants have done throughout the centuries: They worked hard to fit into their new communities and to not stand out.

American psychoanalysts and homosexuality

Even if once-progressive psychoanalysts wanted to speak out in favor of greater understanding for gay people, they couldn't dare to risk the consequences of the growing public anti-German and anti-Jewish wrath in America. In order for the immigrant psychoanalysts to fit in, many of them became the most conformist and conservative practitioners in their profession. It's important to emphasize: The homophobic strain of psychoanalysis during the middle of the 20th century, for the most part, was an American phenomenon.

In addition to the conservative ranks of American psychoanalysts, one cannot overlook the hierarchical structure that existed among the mental health[3] professions from the 1930s through the 1980s. It's important to recognize the differences between psychoanalysis, psychology, psychiatry, and psychotherapy in order to understand how the growing body of evidence from other mental health professionals and sex researchers was largely ignored by psychoanalysts.

The demand for psychoanalytic services increased even more after World War II (as it had first done after World War I), with returning service members needing help to deal with the aftermath of facing brutal combat. The existing psychoanalytic community in the United States was ill-equipped to deal with the tidal wave of extreme need. As the sheer number of returning service members began to overload

---

[3] The common terminology of the day would have been "mental hygiene."

and overwhelm the existing system of psychoanalytic therapy, the U.S. Government looked to other resources to meet the demand. For the first time, three other types of therapists were approved to help returning veterans:

- *Psychologists* – doctors with a PsyD or Ph.D. in psychology, licensed to treat disorders through therapy. Administering and interpreting psychological tests and using talk therapy are typical approaches used by psychologists.
- *Psychiatrists* – doctors with an M.D. who have worked in a psychiatric residency for four years. A psychiatrist treats disorders through a combination of prescription medication and therapy.
- *Psychotherapists* – psychologists who are also clinical social workers or therapists licensed to provide psychotherapy.

While the number and influence of psychologists, psychiatrists, and psychotherapists grew over the next thirty years, they carried considerably less academic weight and had little social impact compared to the psychoanalysts, who were already established as the intellectual authorities in unapproachable ivory towers.

Edmund Bergler (1899–1962) was an Austrian Jew who fled Nazi Germany and settled in New York City. He was intellectually brilliant, but abrasive. Despite his aggressive ways, he was highly articulate, a trait that allowed him to become one of the most important theorists on homosexuality in the 1950s. Bergler actually only studied the case histories of eleven gay patients, seven of whom were schizophrenic. Based on such a limited pool of therapy clients, he published on the topic of homosexuality throughout his thirty-year career. Eventually, without adding any gay patients to his small pool, he claimed "over one hundred" examples to support his theory that homosexuals could be made into heterosexuals.[4] Given his aggressive, abrasive personality, nobody among his colleagues wanted to challenge his assertions.

Bergler was not only one of the most influential psychoanalysts but one of the cruelest in terms of his assessment of gay people. In 1950, he stated, "There are a great percentage of the homosexuals among swindlers, pseudologues [pathological liars], forgers, law-breakers of all sorts, drug purveyors, gamblers, pimps, spies, and brothel owners."[5] He also declared that "homosexuals are filled with aggression, destruction, and self-deceit" and that they have an "incapacity to love. It is a masquerade of a life involving only destruction and self-deceit, exploitation of the partner and of the self."[6]

Again, let's be clear: Using his knowledge of only eleven gay clients in his practice, Bergler did not hesitate to make blanket statements about *all* gays. He explained that the penetrated, passive partner will "dress, walk, talk, and adorn themselves like a woman."[7] Worst of all, Bergler instituted the notion of a "conspiracy of homosexuals to recruit innocent children."[8] It is no wonder Bergler had so few gay clients throughout his career, given his approach to and utter disdain for gay people.

Bergler's theories dominated the conversation on homosexuality in the world of psychoanalysis for fifteen years. He claimed that 99.9% of all gays could be "cured" using the principles he had created in his limited work with gay clients. He believed same-sex behavior represented an attempt to "take revenge on the breast for having gotten too little from it" and/or an intentional withholding of milk by the mother.[9] With assistance from his therapist, the homosexual would be able to work through the aggression and attain heterosexual potential, claimed Bergler.

---

[4] *Psychoanalysis and Male Homosexuality*, 123.
[5] Ibid., 55.
[6] Ibid., 191.
[7] Ibid., 124.
[8] Ibid., 142.
[9] Ibid., 100.

By the end of his career, Bergler was known as an embarrassment to his profession for his cruel and disdainful public remarks, such as the ones quoted above. Further, the damage resulting from Bergler's unsound assumptions continues to echo to this very day among those who degrade homosexual people with the fabricated theories he fashioned from his own personal biases and unwillingness to be challenged.

Sandor Rado (1890–1972) was another immigrant who entered the psychoanalytic field. He met Freud in 1915 and decided to become a psychoanalyst. When Rado arrived in New York City in the 1930s, he set up a practice and focused on homosexuality.

Freud believed sexuality operated in the unconscious of all people and moved along a spectrum from fixed heterosexuality to fixed homosexuality; at the time, this process he called bisexuality. Moveable sexuality, Freud believed, was a potential in all people. Steady homosexuality he called constitutional homosexuality. Rado, however, asserted that the only healthy outcome of human sexual development was heterosexuality. He taught that homosexuality was pathological—a sickness caused by phobic avoidance by a child of the opposite-sex parent. Like his contemporaries, Rado had theories, formulated without the benefit of science and based on his limited work with extremely small client bases.

Whereas Freud, for the bulk of his career, had viewed homosexuality as the result of missed developmental stages and an unfixed or changeable sexuality, Rado introduced the concept of the possibility of change or reparative adjustment.[10] Rado was highly influential and taught many prominent psychoanalysts who would follow his example and perpetuate his flawed theories of homosexuality.

On the other hand, Rado seemed more open to the possibility of biological causes of homosexuality than most of today's reparative therapists who still invoke and quote his research. Rado wrote in a 1940 paper, "A Critical Examination of the Concept of Bisexuality":

---

[10] Sandor Rado, "A Critical Examination of the Concept of Bisexuality," *Psychosomatic Medicine 2*, no. 4 (October 1940): 459-467. http://www.well.com/~aquarius/sandorrado.htm.

In considering the factors so involved we must not overlook the possibility of general, i.e., nonsexual factors, as well
as innate defects of the sexual action system of as yet unknown character. It is well to recall, lest we underestimate
this eventuality, that we are still in the dark even as regards
the physiological mechanism of such an elementary phenomenon as sexual attraction. Still another possibility is of
course the presence of elements of the action system of the
opposite sex such as reflexes, or rather chains of reflexes,
susceptible to resuscitation by hormones or other agents.[11]

Such open speculation of biological influence and fetal hormonal involvement was still extremely rare. As a community, the psychoanalysts
mostly created unsubstantiated theories while other kinds of doctors
and researchers beyond the ivory towers of psychoanalysis produced
actual scientific studies. But, as would remain consistent until the
1980s, the APsaA resisted the work of any researcher not a part of its
own organization.

Meanwhile, outside the APsaA's ivory tower

There were other therapists doing research outside the field of psychoanalysis. American psychiatrist Dr. George Henry was concerned about
the growing cultural isolation and persecution of gay individuals. With
honorable intentions to help counter societal prejudices, he sought out-
patients for a study. Between 1936 and 1941, Henry and the Committee
for the Study of Sex Variants, composed of medical doctors and Ph.D.s,
compiled over three hundred personal case histories of gay men and
lesbians. Henry wanted to help decriminalize homosexuality and to
treat it as a medical condition because he believed it could be cured. He
considered homosexuality a "problem," but not because the gay people

---

[11] Ibid.

themselves were a problem; the problem and conflict, he thought, lay in the interaction between gay people and their families and society.

In 1941, Dr. Henry published *Study of Sex Variants,* a textbook depicting detailed accounts of the persecution of gay men and lesbians by friends, family members, and co-workers. His book contained highly intimate accounts about the sexual lives of gay men and lesbians. The willing participants in the study hoped to bring relief to the demeaning and aggressive acts levied by the police; to foster understanding of the pain of loss of family, jobs, and homes; and to expose the general oppressive and hostile atmosphere in which they lived. Violence against gay people had been on the rise since the end of Prohibition, and the participants in the study hoped their stories would invoke compassion that would help stem the violence. The participants were assured that the book would not be made available to the general public, but would be offered by limited distribution only to doctors so the health professionals might be better "mental hygiene leaders in their communities."[12] It was under this condition that the hopeful participants were willing to be transparent.

Unfortunately, seven years later (1948), *Study of Sex Variants* was republished with a broader distribution to public libraries, colleges, and universities. Intimate information about the private lives of gays and lesbians spurred fascination, along with even greater negativity, toward the gay community. Later (1955), the book was published to an even wider readership in pulp-fiction format.[13] With its graphic accounts of same-sex relationships, Henry's study became the subject of great interest among the curious. The book ended up doing far more harm than any of the good originally intended. Further, the psychoanalytic community ignored the information in Henry's study as it had all studies the APsaA itself did not generate.

---

[12] Jennifer Terry, *An American Obsession: Science, Medicine, and Homosexuality in Modern Society* (Chicago: University of Chicago Press, 1999), 458.
[13] Ibid., 458.

Alfred Kinsey (1894–1956) was a biologist and professor of zoology. While teaching at Indiana University, he began lecturing on topics confronting sexual myths. He eventually left his teaching position to conduct full-time research on male and female sexuality. He interviewed thousands of people about sex, adultery, masturbation, homosexuality, kinks, and various sexual habits. His two books, *Sexual Behavior in the Human Male* (1948) and *Sexual Behavior in the Human Female* (1953), documented what Americans were doing in their bedrooms but not talking about. Although the numbers were inflated as a result of the particular test populations Kinsey used, homosexuality was found to be far more prevalent among Americans than previously thought.

There are ongoing modern attempts to discredit Kinsey and his work. The two major points of contention are that he and his wife were in an open marriage with work colleagues, and that Kinsey used a dispro-portionate number of incarcerated people as participants in his survey. Both of these are true statements, but neither takes away from the groundbreaking work he completed. While Americans in general were not willing to participate in a "sex survey," by including a large number of prison inmates who *were* willing to take part in his study, Kinsey helped dismantle the shroud of secrecy surrounding sex. He brought the topic out into the public arena, and his reports heightened people's fascination about how, with whom, and how frequently Americans were having sex. (See more about Kinsey in Chapter 3.)

And still, the APsaA and its membership ignored this valuable in-formation—never mind that it had been directly gathered from a cross-section of the American population and revealed a higher rate of homosexuality than ever imagined.

Back inside the APsaA's ivory tower

Irving Bieber (1909–1991) was a psychoanalyst who wrote *A Psychoanalytical Study of Male Homosexuality* (1962), encompassing information gathered from 106 homosexual patients from his own and seven colleagues' practices, some of whom had fewer than ten patients. Over the span of ten years, these psychoanalysts collected what Bieber called "voluminous data"[14] by having their patients complete 450-item questionnaires. The majority of these patients were in treatment for major psychological issues: twenty-eight schizophrenics, thirty-one neurotics, and forty-two people with addiction problems. Furthermore, Bieber did not use a control group; that is, he did not study any homosexual men who were *not* in therapy, but only observed people who were.

Bieber claimed that all of the data collection and assessment was accomplished on a budget of $5,000. Though it is highly unlikely that a study of this scope could be effectively and scientifically implemented at such a low cost, Bieber's book became the standard definitive reference volume on male homosexuality used by the psychoanalytic community for the next twenty years.

Bieber stated that he had seen a 27% conversion rate from homosexuality to heterosexuality. His 1962 study became the basis for modern reparative therapy as a supposedly successful model offering a "cure."

Following in the tradition of Rado, prominent psychoanalysts, including Bieber, believed homosexuality was a mental illness caused primarily by imperfect parents, especially mothers, along with childhood trauma. The diagnosis most often given for the cause of homosexuality was a disruption in the pattern of "normal" growth to heterosexuality caused by a weak father and/or a smothering mother producing a son afraid of women and unable to bond with them.

Although this fifty-year-old theory has been disproven and is no longer accepted by any professional mental health organization, it is still being used in reparative therapy treatment by conservative Christian and "family values" groups. Bieber's flawed statistics from 1962 are regularly cited to this day as "proof" that a person can change from homosexual to heterosexual.

---

[14] Psychoanalysis and Male Homosexuality, 195.

Psychoanalyst Lionel Ovesey (1915–1995), another student of Rado's, also agreed with his mentor's theories concerning the ability to "fix" homosexuals and help them become heterosexuals. Ovesey's areas of "expertise" included homosexuality and transsexualism. He theorized that a transsexual male (in today's terminology, a transwoman) had developed separation anxiety in the maternal relationship during childhood. As an adult, the separation was resolved by surgically becoming like the mother and thereby creating an imaginary fusion with her.

Ovesey, who did the bulk of his work in the 1950s and 1960s, made the same errors as the rest of his colleagues: He never looked beyond the patients in his office for comparisons to the general gay or transsexual populations. His theories were constructed solely on his interactions with patients already in his practice and under treatment for psychological disorders.

Psychoanalyst and psychiatrist Charles Socarides (1922–2005) is perhaps the best-known of the influential group who focused on the pathology of "the homosexual" and the subsequent need for and possibility of repair from homosexuality to heterosexuality. Much like the others, Socarides theorized that unhealthy childhood development before the age of four resulted in homosexuality. Mothers who were "too close" or smothering, in combination with weak fathers who did not protect their sons from the grips of a controlling mother, created a homosexual son. According to this theory, because the fathers abdicated authority to the mothers, homosexual men came to distrust men and turned their affections toward feminine male partners.

Socarides warned of the dangers of the father submitting to the mother and becoming a passive male role model, thus turning sons into passive men. If the male child did not display "maleness," fathers were advised not to "shirk" their fatherly roles, but rather to take their sons fishing, or perhaps play tennis with them, to ensure that the boys would not become gay. Teaching a girl to bake, do laundry, and clean house would likewise "lesbian-proof" a daughter.[15] (During this era, the concept of gender roles was blurred with the concept of sexual orientation.)

Interestingly, theories about particular family dynamics causing male homosexuality did not cross the gender line and were, for the most part, not considered applicable to what "caused" lesbianism. There were no explanations of parental involvement or non-involvement producing lesbians. The root cause of lesbianism was rarely spoken of; the focus was mostly on male homosexuals. Shame and blame for creating homosexual children was placed squarely on the parents, who generally felt guilty and compelled to seek therapy to "fix" their children.

Dr. Charles Socarides, the go-to man who impacts the wider culture

Socarides was prominently featured along with Bieber in a 1967 *CBS Reports* documentary titled "The Homosexuals,"[16] anchored by Mike Wallace and now a classic widely available on YouTube. The show featured interviews with gay men, psychiatrists, and police officers. The "experts" were unified in their opinions—homosexuality was a mental disorder and pathological. The hour-long special, viewed by about 20% of the American public the night it aired, was the first widely seen report on the subject of homosexuality. Wallace told millions of viewers:

> Most Americans are repelled by the mere notion of homosexuality. The CBS News survey shows that two out of three Americans look upon homosexuals with disgust, discomfort, or fear. One out of ten says "hatred." A vast majority believes that homosexuality is an illness; only 10% say it is a crime. And yet, and here's the paradox, the majority of

---

[15] "Homosexuality-Prevention by Using Psychological Approaches," episode of *The Open Mind*, September 29, 1956, https://www.youtube.com/watch?v=1hFESZK5l1g.
[16] "'The Homosexuals': Mike Wallace's controversial 1967 CBS Report," http://vimeo.com/61123970.

Americans favor legal punishment, even for homosexual acts performed in private, between consenting adults.

The average homosexual, if there be such a thing, is promiscuous. He is not interested in and is incapable of a lasting relationship like that of a heterosexual marriage. His sex life, his love life, consists of a series of one-night chance encounters at clubs or bars he inhabits. And even on the streets of the city, the pick-up, the one-night stand—these are characteristics of a homosexual relationship.

In addition to his appearance on the CBS documentary, Socarides became the go-to man for the media; he, after all, was the expert on homosexuality. Thus, it is interesting to note a few facts about Socarides' own family situation: To set up a strange juxtaposition, Dr. Socarides, one of America's leading experts on the "sickness" of homosexuality, worked downstairs in his office all day, telling parents their children's homosexuality was a neurosis and a sickness; meanwhile, in the family apartment upstairs, his son Richard came to realize that he was gay.

Understandably, when Richard first chose to speak to a therapist, it was not his own father. He found someone more objective. In time, Richard's sister and the therapist encouraged him to come out to his father. Richard was in his twenties when he did so. It was the late 1970s—several years after the American Psychiatric Association (APA) had removed homosexuality from its list of mental illnesses in the DSM.

Socarides, who had been placing the fault for homosexuality on the parents, blamed himself and his role as an absent father for his son being gay. Socarides, whose typical reactions "tended to the dramatic," according to Richard, did not call or write his son for six months. When he did write, he said he was sorry that "I behaved so badly."[17] Sadly,

---

[17] "Richard Socarides Recalls Coming Out to His Dad, One of the Founders of Conversion Therapy," episode of I'm from Driftwood: The LGBTQ Story Archive, August 2013, http://imfromdriftwood.com/richard-socarides/.

the personal experience of having a gay son did not change what Dr. Socarides professed publicly. Instead, he continued counseling gay children and their parents, as well as gay adults, using the same unproven theories. He advocated for reparative therapy throughout his life, despite the fact that it didn't work for anyone, not even his own son. Meanwhile, Richard Socarides completed law school and went on to serve as a special assistant and advisor on gay and lesbian issues to President Bill Clinton.

Flawed theories continue

During those same years, Dr. Socarides founded a new "gay curing" organization, the National Association for Repair and Therapy of Homosexuals (NARTH). Socarides was the key man who brought together a small group of psychoanalysts and psychologists still disappointed about the APA's declassification of homosexuality as a mental illness in 1973.

Throughout the psychoanalytic community, the approach remained the same for over fifty years. Theories based on as few as two homosexual people from the personal practices of therapists formed the basis for understanding. These "experts" reported their data as if they were based on large numbers of clients and findings. They never observed, studied, or gave weight to gay men and lesbians who might be living in a healthy, "everyday" way within the general population. Nobody within the APsaA questioned their findings or treatment decisions; no checks or balances were provided by peer reviews. The psychoanalysts ignored or dismissed the work of psychologists, psychiatrists, psychotherapists, scientists, and researchers outside their intellectual bubble.

Psychoanalysts' theories and treatment of gays were based on imaginings and postulations that had started with Freud. Instead of conducting thorough, ethical, and scientific studies to answer the questions Freud had raised, psychoanalysts expanded on assertions created from flawed theories, gross assumptions, and insufficient research on the lives of a limited number of patients in therapy.

The next chapter investigates developments outside the psychoanalysis bubble in other branches of mental health and within the culture as a whole.

Chapter 3

Into the Closets

The Growing Persecution of Gays from the 1940s to the 1960s

World War II changes the American sexual culture

Of the many ways in which World War II affected the United States, one of its biggest contributions came in how it disrupted gender roles and sex patterns in the American culture. Sixteen million men enlisted or were drafted into the military, most of them young and leaving their homes during their prime years of sexual experimentation. Another fifteen million people relocated to urban centers for jobs in the defense industry, including women, who now entered the workforce in great numbers. In fact, at one point during the war, half of all women in America had a paying job. Women also joined military sectors in droves and, along with the young men entering the military, were exposed to same-sex environments for the first time in their lives.

The Army and Navy had established screening procedures during World War I to weed out effeminate men from serving in the military. These measures were relaxed during the World War II effort due to the sheer number of soldiers needed; fewer than five thousand potential recruits were dismissed. Often, the screening involved asking a single question—"Do you like girls?"—or simply noticing a "look" of effeminacy. Soldiers found to be gay while serving in the military were discharged, and rather than return home to probable shame and secrecy, many decided to remain in the port cities where they had been dismissed. Gays discharged from the military and those completing tours of duty congregated primarily in San Francisco and New York City.

The shortage of soldiers available to serve in stateside positions prompted Congress to pass a law in 1942 permitting women to join the Women's Army Corps (WAC). Not all people welcomed women in uniform. Within the broader culture, there was resistance to the "mannish women," often code for lesbians, who challenged the perception of what clothing was "assigned" to each gender. Women who wore masculine attire were "cross-dressers" and possibly even "lesbian threats," guilty of sexual inversion.[1] Others feared that simply wearing masculine clothing could lead to sexual inversion. Many brothers and fathers warned women not to join the WAC for fear that others might think them lesbians in their mannish clothing.

The Army unwittingly heightened the fear and misperceptions through careless planning in something as simple as the design of the WAC uniforms. The Quartermaster's Depot designing the WAC uniforms used male models to create the patterns and sizes, yielding a thoroughly ill-fitting, masculine uniform for women.[2] Certainly many heterosexual women did enlist, but the cultural stereotypes produced anxiety and additional public fear that female soldiers might *become* lesbians in all-female environments. The WAC was even called "the ideal breeding ground for homosexuality."[3] Despite all their fear of the "lesbian threat" and attempts to screen out female "sexual perverts" by asking if they were joining to "be with other

[1] Leisa D. Meyer, *Women and War in the Twentieth Century: Enlisted with or without Consent*, ed. Nicole Dombrowski (Oxon, UK: Routledge, 1999), 190.
[2] Ibid., 190.
[3] Ibid., 187.

girls,"[4] the military created an environment that *attracted* the enlistment of lesbians.

World War II also had a profound effect on American women who did not enlist, because women, during these years, made up one-third of the civilian workforce. Many of those jobs required women to trade in their flouncy feminine dresses for clothing more suitable and safer around machinery. Until the 1940s, pants and trousers were menswear exclusively. If women did wear pants, they had to buy them in men's stores and alter them, and they were immediately suspected of being lesbians. But now, for the first time, pants on women became commonplace. A seemingly tiny shift in women's apparel rippled with a liberating impact on the lesbian culture. Lesbians, many of whom naturally felt more comfortable wearing pants rather than dresses, until this time had only been able to do so at home, or in private gatherings. With a newfound freedom allowing all women to wear pants in public, lesbians blended in more easily with other "everyday" women. Working women in general became more visible in public settings, and right along with them, the pants-wearing lesbians migrated out of private settings into public spaces. Lesbian bars and gathering places increased in number, as did the social connections lesbians made.

The creation of the "traditional American family"

When the war ended, in order to make room for the returning soldiers, two million working women were either fired or demoted to more menial jobs. The overwhelming majority of women wanted to remain in the workforce, but they were told to go home, put on dresses, and start having babies. The American family structure changed dramatically in a period often called "the invention of the traditional family."[5] The Serviceman's Readjustment Act, also known as the G.I. Bill, provided

---

[4] Ibid., 194.
[5] Stephanie Coontz, *The Way We Never Were: American Families and the Nostalgia Trap* (New York: Basic Books, 1992), 25.

opportunities for veterans to get career and skills training or to go to college. Eight million World War II veterans took advantage of the offer.

In 1949, three times the number of people received college degrees as in 1940. Before the Second World War, banks required a 50% down payment on houses and extended mortgages for only five to ten years. In the postwar era, financing for home purchases came from loans insured by the Veterans Administration or the Federal Housing Administration. Only a 5–10% down payment was necessary on a thirty-year mortgage, and veterans frequently only had to put a dollar down.[6] Couples got married in greater numbers than both earlier and later generations. The average marriage age dropped, and women bore more children in fewer years starting at younger ages.[7]

With the post–World War II environment favorable for wedding bells and baby showers, one of the most significant social phenomena in America took place—the baby boom. Between 1946 and 1964, over 79 million babies were born, and the population increased by 50%. America was busy putting all the chaos of war behind it. It was time to settle into an isolationist sanctuary and to reorder the gender roles that had gotten muddled during the war. The newly created traditional American family, composed of father as breadwinner, stay-at-home mother, three children, and a cookie-cutter home in suburbia, became the standard.

Gays and lesbians have limited options

With massive numbers of people getting married and having babies, same-sex–attracted people were given three choices so as not to stand out: They could marry someone of the opposite sex—a person to whom they were not naturally attracted. (These types of marriages are called mixed-orientation marriages and are covered in Chapter 12.) They could remain single and likely invite attention and suspicion. Or the

---

[6] Ibid., 77
[7] Ibid., 24.

third option available was to continue in the military, honorably serving their country.

Many lesbians chose to stay in the military. Although Army regulations mandated dishonorable discharge for gay men, a similar action was rarely used against women. There is a famous story of a 1947 exchange between General Eisenhower and one of his most trusted staff members, WAC Sgt. Johnnie (Nell) Phelps, as told in her oral history. Eisenhower called Phelps into his office to complain about the suspected large number of lesbians in the WAC. He told her, "It has come to my attention that there are lesbians in the WAC. We need to ferret them out." To which Phelps replied, "If the General pleases, sir, I'll be happy to do that, but the first name on the list will be mine." Eisenhower's personal secretary, present in the room at the time, added, "If the General pleases, sir, my name will be the first and hers will be second." Phelps then said, "Sir, you're right, there are lesbians in the WAC, and if you want to replace all the file clerks, section commanders, drivers, and every woman in the WAC detachment, I'll be happy to make that list. But you must know, sir, that they are the most decorated group, there have been no illegal pregnancies, no AWOLs, and no charges of misconduct."[8]

Eisenhower decided to drop the issue.

What other Americans are doing in their bedrooms

At the beginning of the 20th century, most Americans held Victorian views about sex, which is to say, strict sexual restraint. In England, where many Germans and Austrians had migrated before and during World War II, sex was discussed more openly. But even after World War II, this was not happening in America.

Americans didn't talk about sex. People did what they did but they didn't discuss it. That is, until Alfred Kinsey (1894–1956) published his book *Sexual Behaviors in the Human Male* in 1948.

---

[8] Donna Knaff, *The "Ferret Out the Lesbians" Legend: Johnnie Phelps, General Eisenhower, and the Power and Politics of Myth* (Oxon, UK: Routledge, 2009), 415.

Kinsey had been raised in a devout Methodist family and was one of America's first Eagle Scouts (1912) in the Boy Scouts of America. He loved science and was a meticulous researcher. His specialty early in his career was wasps—the flying, nest-making kind. Of the 18 million insects presently in the American Museum of Natural History in New York City, 5 million were collected by Kinsey.

He was a patient scientist with excellent information-gathering skills. Based on his doctoral work on wasps, he was invited to teach biology at Indiana University.

Dr. Kinsey's biology students had questions about sex. In the mid-1930s, there was nowhere to get their questions answered, so they began to visit Dr. Kinsey's office for much-needed information. The overwhelming amount of student curiosity led Kinsey to teach a "marriage course" for students just married or intending to get married. In order to take Dr. Kinsey's class, many students got "engaged." Students—and faculty members—desperate for information about sex quickly filled the classes. Kinsey, knowing there was little information to sufficiently answer the questions, began to collect sex histories from his students and fellow staff members. Though popular with students in his classes, Kinsey became controversial as a result of the questions he was asking and the honest answers he was giving about sex. Parents of Indiana University students and alumni pressured the administration to get rid of him.

Subsequently, Kinsey obtained grant funding from the Rockefeller Foundation, enabling him to devote himself full-time to the study of human sexual behavior. For the next six years, Kinsey, along with a team of researchers who emulated his nonjudgmental mode of asking questions and recording answers, collected, coded, and tabulated the sex habits of Americans.

Kinsey reported that one-third to one-half of all married men were having affairs, 92% of men were masturbating, 70% of men were participating in oral sex, and 10% of men had had homosexual experiences.

Although Kinsey's test cases drawn from 12,000 histories were not a statistically accurate representation of the population, his report was important and groundbreaking. Overnight, Kinsey got people in America talking about sex. Americans *obsessed* about the findings in Kinsey's report. They were both fascinated and scared. The detailed descriptions of fellow Americans' sexual practices were scandalous to their Victorian sensibilities. The first printing of Kinsey's book immediately sold 250,000 copies. Americans had assumed that everyone else was conforming to traditional sexual morals. Those who didn't, they imagined, were a tiny deviant minority. The Kinsey Report (the combination of the male study and the later [1953] female study) provided facts on fetishes, fantasies, sexual behaviors, and attitudes toward sex.

In his book, Kinsey presented a scale from 0 (completely heterosexual) to 6 (completely homosexual). The Kinsey Scale became yet another tool to classify the sexuality of people outside the mainstream. The reported 10% frequency of homosexual behavior, while not accurate (it is now believed to be about 4–5% of the population), made people realize that gay men were "everywhere." The statistics also heightened parents' concerns that their own children might be homosexual. In greater numbers, parents, distressed about their possibly homosexual children, began to seek help from mental health professionals.

Rooting out Reds and sex perverts

The Kinsey Report challenged the post–World War II American isolationist culture. There arose an overwhelming fear, not only about moral decline within the heterosexual population, but also from the shock of "widespread" same-sex behavior of which people had previously been unaware. The range and variety of sexual behaviors were far greater than Americans had ever imagined themselves, or their neighbors, participating in. Judgments and delineations were made between "perverted" and "regular" sexual behavior.

Moral decline wasn't the only thing on the minds of Americans. The country was wrapped in the paranoia of the "Red Scare" in the 1940s and 1950s. Many Americans had become disillusioned with capitalism during the 1930s Depression; to some, communism looked more appealing. For still others, the Communist Party offered various attractive proposals: workers' rights, civil rights for black Americans, and the strong stance taken against fascism by the Soviet Union. Even though only 0.03% of Americans were members of the Communist Party in the late 1940s, widespread fear of internal communist subversion hit a hysterical fever pitch.

Senator Joe McCarthy was responsible for escalating the crisis and feeding the paranoia. Communists, it was believed, were the originators of a devious plan designed to attack the morality of the American family. Many Americans started believing that both their families and their moral way of life were at risk of communists and sexual perverts. Narratives about sexual psychopaths, sex deviants, and communists became commonly intertwined in the public arena. The lines between the threats of sexual perverts and communists were blurred in warnings issued in the media and by officials. Since gays were the most sexually deviant group people could imagine, they were fused in people's minds with sexual deviants and even communists.

It was assumed that communists and sexual perverts abandoned all moral restraints and seduced children. Communists were behind every parked car, and in bushes in parks trading secrets. Perverts were prowling and constantly on the lookout for innocent children. Code for both communists and sexual perverts was "twisted people," meaning they had insatiable, compulsive sexual appetites. Communists and gays were constantly paired: The communists were after children; the sexual deviants were after children. Communists were trying to indoctrinate children to their way of life; sexual deviants were trying to indoctrinate children to their way of life. Communists were an ever-present danger;

sexual deviants were an ever-present danger. Evidence of the presence of one confirmed the presence of the other.

Cryptic terms were sometimes used to conflate the words "homosexual" and "communist": security risks, moral weaklings, sexual misfits, moral risks, undesirables, and people with unusual morals.

Within the public discourse, alcoholism and homosexuality were also intermeshed. Alcoholics were thought to be a subset of repressed gays who only acted on their same-sex temptations when intoxicated. Drunks have loose lips; gays have loose lips. Gays are drunks; drunks are gays. In the early 1950s, as the fear of communists started to wane, gays and lesbians were left to carry the full burden of America's paranoia.

America became a scary place to live for everyone—not because it was *actually* scary, but because Americans were *told* it was scary. The definition of what constituted a sex crime in the late 1940s was revised in the 1950s to include sex offenses such as pornography, homosexuality, sodomy, indecent exposure, and voyeurism. All were newly listed under the heading of "rape and sexual homicide." The broadened inclusion of these related crimes inflated sex crime statistics to make it look like America was in crisis. To further elevate the statistics, additional pressures were placed on police officers to conduct more arrests. It appeared as though America were under the siege of sexual perverts, but the fact is, there was *no actual increase* in sex crimes during this period.

In 1947, J. Edgar Hoover, head of the Federal Bureau of Investigation (FBI), wrote an article for the national magazine *American Life* called "How Safe Is Your Daughter?" In it, Hoover stated, "The most rapidly increasing type of crime is that perpetrated by degenerate sex offenders. It is taking its toll at the rate of a criminal assault every 43 minutes, day and night, in the United States." Hoover informed the American public that "the sex pervert, whether he be a homosexual or an exhibitionist or even a dangerous sadist, is often regarded as merely a queer person who would never hurt anyone but himself," but, he added, "all serious sex crimes were committed by degenerates, sex fiends, or sexual psychopaths."[9]

Every action perceived as a security risk to the already fear-filled, isolationist Americans was piled onto the backs of gays and lesbians. Accusations and assumptions became truths. "Sexual psychopath" came to mean "homosexual." Supported by the "expertise" of psychoanalysts, homosexuals were understood as people who were mentally ill and couldn't control themselves.

Homosexuality wasn't believed to be inborn; it was seen as a sickness, a pathology, and a behavior that would explode in a moment of weakness. Gay men and women were thought not only to recruit adults to homosexuality, but to go in particular after susceptible and easily swayed children.

Hell on earth

Any manner in which gays naturally expressed their affectionate, romantic, or sexual attractions was against the law. Consensual same-sex sex was banned under sodomy laws. In some states, it was even a *felony* subject to a prison term or incarceration in a mental institution. Affectionate interaction between gay men in public violated some federal, state, or municipal law. Holding hands, kissing, dancing, and cross-dressing violated public and private indecency and lewdness laws and/or were seen as disorderly conduct. Acts done in private were fair game for arrest as well. Undercover police watching or raiding private parties or business establishments could, and did, arrest gays and cross-dressers. The number of proposed laws nationwide increased, and they were easily passed amid the atmosphere of fear and hysteria.

---

[9] Edwin H. Sutherland, "The Sexual Psychopath Laws," *Journal of Criminal Law and Criminology* 40, no. 5 (January-February 1950), 547.

In small towns and large cities alike, the presence, or even the possibility of the presence, of gay men prompted paranoia.[10]

Beginning in the late 1940s it was an especially dark time in America for both gay men and lesbians. They were incarcerated in prisons and mental institutions throughout the United States for being gay or suspected of being gay, and even for consensual same-sex sex. They were subjected to various medically advised treatments designed to "cure" their homosexuality.

Aversion electroshock treatments entailed attaching electrodes to the genitals—penis, testicles, or vulva—as well as fingers, chest, or arm of the patient. The patient was shown homosexual and heterosexual pornography. With each homosexual picture, the patient was shocked. No negative treatment was administered when heterosexual pornography was shown. In other treatments, the patient was injected with vomit-inducing drugs and shown homosexual and heterosexual pornography. With each homosexual picture, the voltage on an electroshock machine was increased to up to 8,200 volts for five seconds so that the patient vomited at the sight of homosexual pornography. Aversion therapy did not stop homosexuality, but it caused a high rate of suicide and long-term mental health issues for those who underwent the "treatment."

At one maximum-security facility in California where gay men were sent from the 1940s through the 1960s, the patients were regularly castrated and subjected to frontal lobotomies, a surgical procedure in which a medical ice pick was pushed over the top of the eye into the brain, then moved back and forth to sever the connectors between the frontal lobes and the rest of the brain. This procedure generally rendered the patient passive and docile, easier for the staff to control. Dr. Walter Freeman, who worked at the Atascadero State Mental Hospital,

---

[10] Two well-documented resources describing the level of paranoia in two well-known cases are worth noting. The "Boys of Boise sex panic crime" is detailed in Claudia Weathermon's documentary *The Fall of '55* (Frameline, 2005). The "Sioux City sex panic crimes" are detailed in Neil Miller's *Sex-Crime Panics: A Journey to the Paranoid Heart of the 1950s* (New York: Alyson Books, 2009).

an all-male, maximum-security prison, did over 4,000 lobotomies at the facility between 1945 and 1949. About 40% of those procedures were done on men who had been arrested for consensual same-sex acts. Because so many states had passed "sexual psychopath laws" giving state officials complete control, forced involuntary incarceration in mental health treatment facilities was allowed by law.[11]

While the fear of communism was waning by the mid-1950s, the sense that "sexual deviants" posed a grave threat was just hitting its stride. Variations of toughened sexual psychopath laws were quickly adopted in cities and twenty-nine states between 1948 and 1956.[12] Where the sodomy laws kept gays somewhat below the radar and closeted, the sexual psychopath laws flushed them out of private settings and placed their future into the hands of judges. Many states passed laws subjecting gays to imprisonment or mandatory incarceration in mental health care facilities or asylums. The "protection of society" trumped the civil rights of gays.

This time frame was hell on earth for many gay men, lesbians, and cross-dressing Americans. And, it got worse.

The Lavender Scare: Getting rid of gay federal employees

The National Security Act of 1947 had restructured the American military and intelligence agencies, establishing the Department of Defense, the National Security Council, and the Central Intelligence Agency (CIA). The director of the CIA was given authority to dismiss gay employees, calling them national security risks. In effect, the National Security Act enabled a government-approved witch hunt, setting off a period that became known as the "Lavender Scare." The term was coined by author David K. Johnson because the hysteria over

---

[11] All information in this section from: Richard Schmiechen, dir., "Changing Our Minds: The Story of Dr. Evelyn Hooker," documentary (Frameline, 1991).
[12] Most of the sexual psychopath laws were based on the Miller Sexual Psychopath Law; see "The Sexual Psychopath Laws," *Journal of Criminal Law and Criminology*.

homosexuality, with which the color lavender was associated, paralleled the hysteria over communism, the "Red Scare." The gay men in the State Department came to be called the "lavender lads."[13]

Official justifications for firing gays were based upon two completely unsupported beliefs: that a foreign power could blackmail a gay person employed in a secure or sensitive government post into becoming a spy, and that gays in political office or government agencies demoralized other employees because of the existence of perverted behavior in their personal lives. Lesbians didn't escape suspicion. A communist-lesbian narrative postulated a scenario in which female government workers were lured into lesbianism and then shamed. The communist would then easily blackmail the newly created lesbian and force her to become a spy.

The Truman White House (1945–1953) found itself in a difficult situation in 1950. If they identified gays and communists in the State Department and the Department of Defense, the Administration would be seen as lax in not having flushed them out beforehand. If they didn't locate gays in the government and identify them as security risks, they would be seen as unable to protect America from subversive dangers.

In an attempt to solve his dilemma, Truman appointed Clyde Hoey (D-NC) to create and lead a committee investigating the validity of security risks in the State Department. Wanting the findings to be accurate and not politically motivated, the committee sought out medical experts for comment on the assumed weaker moral integrity of gays. They hoped to prove the higher risk posed by blackmail of gays and its inherent danger to America. However, the medical experts testified that such accusations had no substantiation. Additional expert statements from Air Force, Army, and Navy security officers could not validate any claims about enemy agents attempting blackmail against gay people. The military representatives from all branches testified to the complete

[13] David K. Johnson, *The Lavender Scare: The Cold War Persecution of Gays and Lesbians in the Federal Government* (Chicago: University of Chicago Press, 2004), 216.

absence of records indicating a link between homosexuality and black-mail. Even the District of Columbia police concurred with military reports. They, too, lacked records linking gay government employees with *any* form of foreign blackmail.

The sole substantiation offered during all the Hoey Committee hear-ings came from the director of the newly formed CIA, Admiral Roscoe Hillenkoetter. Hillenkoetter recounted the espionage story of Colonel Alfred Redl (1864–1913), an Austrian intelligence officer. The Russians, knowing of Redl's expensive tastes for the finer things in life, began to pay him for secrets. As the exchanges escalated, they set Redl up with a male prostitute, then broke into his hotel room and took pictures. When it was discovered by Austrian officials that Redl had given the Russians documents revealing Austrian military plans, Redl commit-ted suicide. *This was the sole evidence offered to the Hoey Committee supporting the idea that gays could be blackmailed.* The only example to substantiate blackmail threats involved a thirty-year-old case from another country, involving neither a United States citizen nor a United States government employee. The Hoey Committee was not able to find even *one* instance in which an American gay federal employee had been blackmailed in exchange for government secrets. Additionally, not one gay person was called to testify as a witness during the hearing.

When the final Hoey Report was issued a year later (December 1950), it had completely ignored all the military, police, and medical expert testimony and evidence. Shockingly, the Hoey Report asserted that all of the intelligence and security agencies of the U.S. government were in complete agreement that "sexual perverts" constituted a security risk. Without any supporting evidence, the report stated that "homosexuals are at risk for blackmail, a threat to national security, and, therefore, not suitable for employment in government," adding that they were "found to be mentally unstable, morally weak, criminals, and destructive to work environments." Especially at risk, they reported, were younger workers because they could be recruited into homosexuality.[14]

The public didn't need the final report. Along with politicians and the media, they had already decided that gays were threats to the security of the nation. But based on the wholly fabricated Hoey Report, subsequent widespread purging began to rid the federal government of gays. Starting at the State Department, the "Lavender Scare" soon spread to all federal offices, as well as to private companies doing government contract work. Almost 20% of all American jobs at the time were in these sectors. Those suspected of being gay or lesbian had their lives and activities put under a microscope. Gay men and lesbians were wary of making eye contact in public places for fear that even such a slight action would be seen as suspicious. Heterosexual male workers avoided congregating together and speaking to one another in places considered private or out of the way. Even how men took part in recreation was impacted. Police crashed parties and dinners in private homes. People were arrested and asked to surrender the names of friends whom they knew to be gay.

Government workers suspected of being gay were interrogated and pressured to leave their jobs. No accurate count exists of the number of people who left or lost their jobs under suspicion of being gay, but thousands were fired, and hundreds voluntarily resigned after being questioned. In the private sector, thousands of gays and lesbians who could not get security clearance to work for government contractors were fired or pressured to leave their jobs.

Another milestone in 1950 was that Congress passed the Internal Security Act, also known as the Subversive Activities Control Act, allowing for the preventative detention of suspected subversives during times of national emergency. The law required all communists and communist organizations to register with the United States Attorney General, but it also became a tool to harass gays. Sex offenders and gays

---

[14] Ibid., 108-118.

had already become melded together under existing laws and in the minds of the public and the media. Now the same requirement placed on communist subversives to register with the Attorney General was placed on "sex offenders." (Various words were used interchangeably to describe sex offenders: "psychopath," "sex criminal," "pervert," and "homosexual"; culturally, all these words took on the same meaning.)

In the same year, the declining career of Senator Joe McCarthy (R-MN) was given new life when he famously produced his list of "205 known communists and 91 homosexuals" in the U.S. State Department. McCarthy cited a myth still used today—that even the great Roman Empire ended when its leaders became degenerate and perverted.[15]

The American public went into a panic. Gays were now known "security risks" as "proven" by the Hoey Report. Hysteria soared over the existence of a list of communists and gays in the State Department (though the existence of such a list was never verified). Amid the increasing paranoia, gays were thought to be clannish when in charge of hiring, bringing in other gays to fill all the jobs around them. (Of course, gays knew *all* other gays because they all belonged to a single secret organization!) Such fear-filled beliefs continued to push gays into hiding and out to the margins of society.

Purging the federal government of gays continued long after concerns about the infiltration by communists had faded. Unmarried men in the State Department were targeted for investigation. Every male applicant was subject to a cross-check of his name against the master files of those thought to be gay. Once past the initial screening, he was subject to a stringent interview process designed to uncover any gay tendencies. If there was any suspicion of homosexuality, the applicant was given a

---

[15] The Roman Empire, which lasted approximately 520 years, is often falsely said to have fallen because it was destroyed by homosexuality. The historically agreed-upon reasons for the fall of the Roman Empire are decline in morals and values, decline in public health, political corruption, unemployment, inflation, decay of the cities, inferior technical advancements, military spending, and even Christianity, which made citizens into pacifists. (Free Republic, December 23, 2008, http://www.freerepublic.com/focus/news/2153351/posts.)

lie detector test. The State Department also focused on weeding out existing employees who were gay. Between 1950 and 1970, more than one thousand State Department employees lost their jobs due to allegations or confessions of homosexuality. Hundreds more resigned from their positions to escape the humiliation of being fired for being gay. Because of a politically motivated, manufactured threat, careers were shortened, lives were destroyed, and some people committed suicide.

The impact on the complexion of American foreign relations in the decades immediately following the Lavender Scare may never be fully known. The need to be a "real man" became essential in avoiding suspicion of being gay. Exaggerated masculine swagger and aggressive actions were adopted to show that a man was not a "sissy" like the gays. Not only did men who remained at the U.S. State Department have to assert their masculinity, but the Department lost the positive influence of gay men, who tend toward higher communication and diplomacy skills (see Chapter 8).

When the United States committed to the Vietnam War in 1964, the State Department had, for the most part, cleared out the gays. Left behind were men who had proven their "manliness." It is only speculative, but a faster solution to the Vietnam War might have been achieved by people exhibiting less swagger and a greater openness to détente.

EO 10450 bans federal hiring of gays and lesbians

The communist-*cum*-sexual pervert-*cum*-homosexual madness impacted the presidential election of 1952. Truman and his fellow Democrats were accused of being responsible for the presumed infiltration of the federal government, particularly the State Department, by communists and gays. Eisenhower, in his run for the presidency, contended that the Truman Administration had too easily tolerated communist and other security risks in the government and defense industry. In his first State of the Union address, Eisenhower promised, now that he was president, that he would ensure the design of a new system for "keeping out the disloyal and the dangerous."[16]

Whereas President Truman had enacted a "loyalty test" for employees of the State Department and the military, newly elected President Eisenhower strung up barbed wire around government jobs by signing Executive Order (EO) 10450, "The Security Requirements for Government Employment" (1953), ensuring that only those with integrity "clearly consistent with the interest of national security" could be government employees. EO 10450 went one step farther than Truman's loyalty test, barring people from government jobs if it was even *speculated* that they might pose a risk to government security.

Some background is in order:

Arthur Vandenberg Jr., President Eisenhower's family friend and political advisor, had helped organize a national grassroots movement to promote Eisenhower as a Republican presidential candidate. Vandenberg's father, Arthur Vandenberg Sr., enjoyed enormous political clout and had valuable political capital as a bipartisan Congressional negotiator and Chair of the Committee on Foreign Relations. Vandenberg Jr. mobilized his father's extensive support structure behind Eisenhower, and once Eisenhower became the Republican presidential nominee, Vandenberg Jr. served as his Executive Assistant, coordinating the presidential staff.

After the election, Eisenhower was prepared to appoint Vandenberg Jr. as the Secretary to the President. Mysteriously, just before the move to the White House, Vandenberg Jr. was placed on leave. It was reported that he needed to take a vacation because of "ill health" associated with an undisclosed blood condition. Four months later, it was additionally reported that Vandenberg Jr. had ulcers and would be unable to return to the Eisenhower White House.

The true story was hidden until recently, but is one that must be told.[17]

16 Dwight D. Eisenhower, State of the Union address, February 23, 1953.
17 Dudley Cleninen, "J. Edgar Hoover, 'Sex Deviates' and My Grandfather," *New York Times*, November 25, 2011.

FBI Director J. Edgar Hoover, in his well-known compulsive and controlling manner, kept files on people of influence—Vandenberg Jr. and Eisenhower included. Just after Eisenhower took office, Hoover had visited him and told him he had amassed a file on Vandenberg Jr. and knew him to be gay. Because Eisenhower was intent on keeping his campaign promise to protect the American people from "the disloyal and dangerous," Hoover was able to pressure the president to fire Vandenberg Jr.

Going one step farther to eliminate any question about his serious public attention to the matter, Eisenhower, after only four months in office, enacted Executive Order 10450.

EO 10450 affected all government jobs and the military. Risk was evaluated on the basis of someone's character, reliability, and "clean living." A person with "any criminal, infamous, dishonest, immoral, or notoriously disgraceful conduct, habitual use of intoxicants to excess, drug addiction, or sexual perversion" would not be hired by the federal government.[18]

Though the wording of EO 10450 does not *explicitly* refer to gays, it does use trigger words that were commonly associated with homosexuality at the time: "criminal," "immoral," "habitual use of intoxicants," "sexual perversion." People got the unspoken message quite clearly.

Eisenhower and his wife, Mamie, felt badly about caving in to Hoover's pressure. Remarkably, Vandenberg Jr. remained friends with them, and they exchanged several personal letters even after he was fired.

Vandenberg Jr. moved to Florida and became a professor of American policy at the University of Miami. *Confidential Magazine,* a bimonthly periodical which specialized in Hollywood and D.C. gossip and the outing of gays, did an exposé on Vandenberg Jr. entitled "Why Ike Bounced Arthur Vandenberg Jr." Vandenberg Jr., publicly shamed, quit his university job, started drinking heavily, and committed suicide eleven years later.

---

[18] "Executive Order 10450—Security Requirements for Government Employment," *National Archives*, http://www.archives.gov/federal-register/codification/executive-order/10450.html.

One cannot help but see the great irony of Hoover destroying Vandenberg Jr.'s career. Hoover never married, never had a girlfriend, and lived with his mother until she died when he was forty-one. Hoover almost exclusively kept company with men. Hoover was inseparable from Clyde Tolson, whom he promoted to second in charge at the FBI. They had lunch and dinner together daily. They attended parties and events together, and on vacations, they shared a room. When Hoover died, Tolson accepted the U.S. flag draped on Hoover's coffin, inherited his $551,000 estate, and moved into his house. Tolson's grave is a few yards from Hoover's grave in the Congressional Cemetery. Hoover's life and relationship with Tolson exhibit classic indications that he was a repressed gay man. Often those most afraid of variations in human sexuality struggle with their own internal conflicts.[19]

In summation, Hoover brought down a heavy hand on Eisenhower, pressuring him to fire Vandenberg Jr. Eisenhower went a step beyond in enacting Executive Order 10450, which became a presidential-level weapon used to further destroy gays during the Lavender Scare. The heartache and devastation engendered a sense of outrage not seen before in the gay community. The most visible victim of EO 10450 was Frank Kameny, who became an early gay civil rights leader.

Early gay rights activist Frank Kameny

Born in 1925 in New York City, Frank Kameny had wanted to become an astronomer since the age of six. He entered college at sixteen to study physics but left in 1942 at age seventeen to join the Army. After the war, Kameny completed his undergraduate work and was awarded a full scholarship to attend Harvard University, where he earned his master's (1949) and Ph.D. in astronomy (1956).

While Kameny was vacationing in San Francisco, plainclothes officers witnessed another man touching him sexually. They arrested Kameny.

---

[19] H.E. Adams, L.W. Wright, and B.A. Lohr, "Is Homophobia Associated with Homosexual Arousal?" *Journal of Abnormal Psychology* 105 (1996), no. 3: 440445.

He was assured, however, that the arrest would be expunged from his record. Kameny was grateful. After all, it was 1956, and "known homosexuals" were banned from government employment and government contract jobs under Executive Order 10450.

The U.S. Army Map Service had hired Kameny to accurately map distances around the world for use in the development of intercontinental missiles. While stationed in Hawaii, Kameny received a letter from the U.S. Civil Service Commission ordering him to return to Washington, D.C. immediately to address some "administrative issues." Thinking his work was more important than a vague request from bureaucrats, feisty Kameny finished his work in Hawaii. Disappointingly, rather than getting expunged as had been promised, the arrest records from San Francisco were forwarded to the FBI, and then sent on to the Civil Service Commission, which tried to interrogate Kameny. He refused to answer questions about his sexuality, but was fired anyway for describing his arrest in San Francisco as for "disorderly conduct" rather than for "lewd and indecent acts," the actual charge.

The American-Soviet Space Race (1955–1972) was in full swing, and Kameny easily should have been employed in an excellent job. He was supremely capable and intelligent, but he couldn't get a job even as a low-level scientist. Scientists on federal projects were closely screened, and Kameny was a "known homosexual."

He launched a case against the U.S. Government in 1958, claiming that as a U.S. citizen, he was being denied rights based on his sexuality. The case was finally dismissed at the Supreme Court level in 1961. In the same year, Kameny started the Washington, D.C., chapter of the Mattachine Society, which had been founded by Harry Hay in 1948. Hay was the first activist to unite gays and lesbians—or homophiles, as they were often called—against oppression.

Kameny became a lifelong gay activist. He is recognized for organizing a group of gay men and lesbian women, outfitted in suits and dresses, carrying "Gay Is Good" signs outside the White House in

1965. Additionally, from 1965 until 1969, Kameny led a group of gay men and lesbians at Independence Hall in Philadelphia for the "Annual Reminder," a yearly protest of federal discrimination policies.

Executive Order 10450 remained in effect for a total of forty-two years. Incredibly, in 1993, the U.S. Supreme Court upheld the CIA's decision to fire a gay employee on the basis that his sexuality posed a security threat. Tragically, falsehoods propagated in the 1950s were still legally barring gay men and lesbians from serving in U.S. federal positions as late as the early 1990s. President Bill Clinton finally rescinded Executive Order 10450 in 1995.

In 2011, I spoke at the Parents and Friends of Lesbians and Gays (PFLAG) National Conference in Washington, D.C. Another speaker, openly gay Congressman Barney Frank (D-MA), described having given a group of students attending the PFLAG conference a personal tour of the Senate building and his office. He showed the students a copy of EO 10450, hanging on his office wall. Stunned, they listened to the story of the order, unable to imagine a time in the history of the United States when lesbian, gay, bisexual, and transgender people were banned from holding government jobs. Yet even as of this writing in 2014, it is still legal in twenty-nine states to fire an employee for being gay, and in thirty-four states, a person can be fired from a job because they are transgender.

In 1956, Frank Kameny was fired from a government job because he was suspected of being gay. Not only did Kameny live to see EO 10450 rescinded; he was also present and received the pen used by President Barack Obama when he signed an executive order granting benefits to same-sex partners of federal employees. For over fifty years, Kameny had been one of the most significant participants in the struggle for equality in the gay community.

In October 2011, Frank Kameny died at the age of eighty-six. At the invitation of my friend Brody Lévesque, a longtime fixture in the Washington political press core, I attended Kameny's funeral in the Old Post Office

Building. Commemorating Kameny's service in the U.S. Army, an honor guard composed of the D.C. Metropolitan Police Department's Gay and Lesbian Liaison Unit carried his casket. Several of Kameny's original protest signs were displayed in the atrium around his casket.

As he lay in state, the casket was flanked by two veterans who are also gay rights activists, Lieutenant Dan Choi and Captain James Pietrangelo II, both former U.S. Army officers who were forced out of the military under the "Don't Ask, Don't Tell" (DADT) policy. Choi, after serving in Iraq, publicly challenged DADT by coming out on the *Rachel Maddow Show* on MSNBC in 2009. In 2010, West Point graduates Choi and Pietrangelo handcuffed themselves to the White House fence in protest of DADT. The following summer, in July 2011, President Obama sent certification to Congress to repeal DADT. On September 30, 2011, the Department of Defense removed "homosexual conduct" from its list of grounds for administrative separation from the military. Kameny died just two weeks later.

It was a moving experience to participate in the public honoring of this great civil rights pioneer. An elderly man sat quietly on the back row handing out small "Gay Is Good" stickers he'd made in honor of Kameny. Noticing an empty chair beside him, I asked, "Can I join you?" I was curious about his connection to Kameny, so I inquired. He said:

> We both grew up in New York City and our mothers knew each other. When I told my mother I was gay, she was distraught and didn't know what to do with it all. Frank's mother invited my mother over for coffee, and they sat at the kitchen table until Frank's mother had answered all my mother's questions. And then it was all fine, it was just fine. My mother did not feel guilty and never made me feel ashamed. And then, Frank and I became friends for life.

Frank Kameny, the man who became one of the most significant figures in the gay rights movement, had a mom who assured him, and other kids' moms, that gay children were fine just the way they were.

Chapter 4

Out of the Closet and into the Open

Moving toward Freedom

Evelyn Hooker's groundbreaking work

Outside the bubble of the male-dominated American Psychoanalytic Association (APsaA), a female psychologist got to know a gay couple. Their relationship would eventually be a major catalyst that completely changed the status of the gay community in America.

Relationships really do matter.

Evelyn (née Gentry) Hooker (1907–1996) was born in rural Nebraska and moved with her family to Colorado. While in college, she worked as a nanny for the wealthy family of a psychiatrist. Seeing that Hooker was bright and gifted, he encouraged her to get a degree in psychology. After receiving her master's, Hooker wanted to apply to Yale University, but the head of her department in Colorado, a Yale alumnus himself, would not write a referral for her or for any woman. He disapproved of women becoming doctoral candidates.

With Yale out of reach, Hooker was accepted into the Ph.D. program at Johns Hopkins University in Baltimore. She was awarded her Ph.D. in 1932, but soon contracted tuberculosis and spent the next two years resting, thinking, and reflecting at a sanatorium in Arizona. In 1937, she received a fellowship to study at the prestigious Berlin Institute of Psychotherapy. While living in Berlin, Hooker experienced firsthand the rise of Hitler. She was standing on the streets in the midst of the frenzy and jubilation when Hitler returned from annexing Austria. She also experienced Kristallnacht, all from the perspective of the Jewish family with whom she was living—a family that later died in the concentration camps.

These events deeply impacted Hooker's sensitivity to the ability of the dominant and ruling powers to oppress, and to the injustice suffered by those who are weaker. At the end of her fellowship, she moved to Los Angeles, where she married playwright Don Caldwell and became a professor of psychology at the University of California, Los Angeles (UCLA); she was on staff there for the next thirty-one years.

Hooker taught night classes at UCLA's Extension division. She immediately noticed one of her students, Sammy From. Later, Hooker shared:

> Sammy was in one of my small introductory night classes. It became clear almost immediately that he was the most outstanding student in the class. He talked with me at intermission. He asked questions. There was just no doubt that he was the bright and shining star.[1]

After the semester was over, Hooker invited Sammy to her home for the evening. When he had left, Hooker's husband, Don, said, "You told me everything about him, but you didn't tell me he was queer."

---

[1] Eric Marcus, *Making History: The Struggle for Gay and Lesbian Equal Rights, 1945–1990; An Oral History* (New York: HarperCollins, 1992), 16.

She wondered how her husband could possibly know such a thing in so short a visit. He explained, "Well, he did everything but fly out the window."[2]

Working as a freelance writer in Hollywood, Don was amenable to friendships with gays. Sammy and his "cousin" George invited Hooker and her husband to dinner. As their friendship deepened, eventually George was reintroduced as Sammy's partner, not his cousin.

Through her relationship with Sammy and George and an expanded social circle of their friends, Hooker was able to break through many restrictive cultural and professional stigmas she had held about gays. "I think the understanding, together with the rather extraordinary cross-section of society into which I was introduced by Sammy, made the difference," she said.[3] A year into the expanding of her network of friends, Sammy suggested to Hooker, "We have let you see us as we are, and now it is your scientific duty to make a study of people like us. We're homosexuals, but we don't need psychiatrists. We don't need psychologists. We're not insane. We're not any of those things they say we are." At first Hooker declined, saying she would be unable to mix friendship with professional research. Sammy then offered to help find Hooker a different group of gay men to participate in a study. She was conflicted.

As a professor, Hooker had been teaching that homosexuality was psychopathological, a criminal offense, and even a sin. Her relationship with Sammy made her question her beliefs. She discussed the possibility with a colleague, who encouraged her, "You must do it. We don't know anything about people like [Sammy]. The only ones we know about are the people who come to us as patients. And, of course, many of those who come to us are very disturbed, pathological. You must do it."[4]

As simple and logical a suggestion as this might seem, until that time no psychoanalysts, psychologists, or psychiatrists had studied gay men outside of therapeutic settings. All of the theories developed about gays

2 Ibid., 18.
3 Ibid., 18.
4 Ibid., 19.

had been formulated from observations and interactions with clients in counseling or prison settings. No one had examined homosexual and heterosexual men in comparative environments to see if there actually were differences in their mental health.

But soon after Hooker began the work, her personal life was uprooted. Her husband, an alcoholic, realized he was destroying his own life, and he told her he didn't want to destroy hers as well. When they divorced, she abandoned the research and moved to Pennsylvania, where she began to teach again.

Hooker didn't feel the freedom or openness to conduct her research there, so when a job opened again at UCLA, she took it and moved back to California. She rented a guest cottage near the campus and resumed teaching. When she and her landlord, Edward, fell in love and got married, he fully supported her desire to study gay men. At his insistence, she quit her teaching job, ready to resume her research full-time.

Hooker noticed that the newly formed National Institute of Mental Health (NIMH) was giving out grants for research in psychology and applied for funding to help with her study of gay men in the general population. Stunned that someone would propose such research, the head of the grants division flew to California to meet with her. After all, it was 1953, the height of the McCarthy era (see Chapter 3); studying "normal homosexuals"—those living everyday lives and not in therapy—was just not done. Hooker was given the grant; later, insiders at NIMH called her research "The Fairy Project."

Hooker spent a year interviewing and studying thirty homosexual men and thirty heterosexual men with equivalent backgrounds, educations, and economic statuses. All sixty men were given three psychological personality tests. The prevailing belief in the early 1950s held that any clinical psychologist could accurately determine whether the test subject was gay or not, based on the results of such tests. Hooker selected leading experts to analyze the tests and determine which men were homosexual and which were heterosexual. The experts could not determine one from the other. There was no difference in pathology between the two groups.

In 1956, Hooker's friend, Sammy From, died in an automobile accident just months before her one-hour presentation of the research findings, entitled "The Adjustment of the Male Overt Homosexual." Hooker read her report to over one thousand members of the American Psychological Association (APA) at the organization's annual conference in Chicago. Of the experience, she later said:

> In my paper I presented the evidence that gay men can be as well adjusted as straight men and that some are even better adjusted than some straight men. In other words, so far as the evidence was concerned, there was no difference between the two groups of men in the study. There was as much pathology in one group as in the other.[5]

The room was completely hushed as she delivered her findings. Hooker had taken on the assumptions of the day concerning pathological differences between heterosexuals and homosexuals. As she chatted with her colleagues afterward, several of her peers were encouraged by the new light shed on the whole situation. Others said, "That can't be right." Later, Hooker recalled, "At the time, the hard-liners among the psychoanalysts, like Irving Bieber, would as soon shoot me as look at me."[6]

In 1991, Hooker was given the APA's Distinguished Contribution Award. For the remainder of her life, whenever she went to a gay gathering, someone wanted to meet her and tell her their story. One young woman's story really hit home for Hooker:

---

[5] Ibid., 24.
[6] Ibid., 24.

I wanted to meet you because I wanted to tell you what you saved me from, Dr. Hooker. When my parents discovered I was a lesbian, they put me in a psychiatric hospital. The standard procedure for treating homosexuals in the hospital was electroshock therapy. My psychiatrist was familiar with your work, though, so he was able to keep them from giving me electroshock therapy.

Hooker recalled:

The young woman had tears streaming down her face as she told me this. I know that wherever I go, there are men and women for whom my little bit of work, my caring enough to do it, has made an enormous amount of difference in their lives.[7]

Over the next decade, Hooker's groundbreaking results had very limited circulation outside the psychotherapeutic community. The psychoanalytic community, which dictated the overall conversation about the treatment of gays, completely ignored and dismissed Hooker's findings because, not only was she a woman, but she was not one of them. The decades of pain endured by gay men and lesbians because this study was ignored are worse than criminal. But, as we will see, from out of the shadows, Evelyn Hooker's report would resurface in 1970, helping to fuel the gay liberation movement.

1960s media messages about gays

Most gay men and lesbians who came into puberty in the mid-1960s do not recall specific or direct messages from their parents or society about homosexuality. People just did not talk about it, yet a fascination with the topic smoldered just below the surface.

---

[7] Ibid., 25.

Recall the nationwide views on homosexuality as reported by Mike Wallace on *CBS Reports* in 1967. They were quite negative: One in ten Americans viewed homosexuality with hatred; the majority thought it was a mental illness; 10% of the U.S. population thought homosexuality was a crime, and the majority was in favor of criminalizing adult consensual homosexual sex. Distrust and fear of gays ran high in the government, in the judicial system, in law enforcement, and throughout the culture in general.

Young lesbians and gay boys might have heard the word "homosexual" and wondered if it applied to them. By puberty, most knew they were different because they were not responding to the opposite sex in the way their friends did. In many towns and cities, books in the library on the topic of homosexuality were kept in locked cabinets requiring the help of a librarian to access and read them. Shaming eyes and moral judgments kept many curious gay teenagers from even the possibility of obtaining helpful resources. Unfortunately, one bestselling and highly inaccurate book did make it into many American homes.

An estimated 30 million copies of *Everything You Always Wanted to Know about Sex but Were Afraid to Ask,* by Dr. David Reuben, a psychiatrist and supposed sex expert, were sold in America. Published in 1969, it was one of the first sex manuals popularized in the mainstream. By today's standards, many of the "facts" about sex, and about homosexuality in particular, are laughable. And misogyny flows from the book like a river.

Yet, in the mainstream culture, *Everything You Always Wanted to Know about Sex but Were Afraid to Ask* was *the* authority. Everyone was reading it—including young heterosexuals and homosexuals alike. It was *the truth*. It *had* to be the truth; a doctor and sex expert had written it.

According to my gay and lesbian friends who were in their teens or early twenties at the time, *Everything You Always Wanted to Know about Sex but Were Afraid to Ask* is the single most frequently mentioned book that kept them in the closet. After reading the presumed authoritative and informed view in the chapter entitled "Male Homosexuality," young gay men were fearful about what it meant to be same-sex attracted. They were aware that they had same-sex attractions and craved information. *Everything You Always Wanted to Know about Sex but Were Afraid to Ask* was easy to find—it was hidden under the mattress in parents' bedrooms all across America.

I've read through an original copy of the book that I bought at a garage sale. I can only begin to imagine the devastating effect the words had on a young boy reading it and knowing he was attracted to other boys. *Everything You Always Wanted to Know about Sex* presents a wildly distorted image of what it meant to be gay. Today, we can read these excerpts and wholly dismiss them—even laugh at them—for their lack of credibility. But imagine a teenage boy in the late 1960s, conflicted about what he is feeling, reading passages such as these:

> Because of the anatomical and physiological limitations involved, there are formidable obstacles to overcome [in relationships]. Most homosexuals look upon this as a challenge and approach it with ingenuity and boundless energy. In the process they often transform themselves into part-time women. They don women's clothing, wear makeup, adopt feminine mannerisms, and occasionally even try to rearrange their bodies along feminine lines. Most at one time or another in their lives act out some aspect of the female role.[8]

> If a homosexual who wants to renounce homosexuality finds a psychiatrist who knows how to cure homosexuality, he has every chance of becoming a happy, well-adjusted,

---

[8] David Reuben, *Everything You Always Wanted to Know about Sex but Were Afraid to Ask* (New York: Van Rees Press, 1969), 129.

heterosexual. . . . In the "gay world" the partners are divided into "male" and "female" with the effeminate male homosexual known as a queen. Blonde hair, usually a full complement of makeup, removal of all body hair, and lots of perfume are the first steps. Then come the clothes. Most queens are in drag, that is women's clothes. Among homosexuals, expense is no object and there is never a husband in the background complaining about the cost of a new dress. No self-respecting queen would ever be caught dead in last year's outfit.[9]

When answering a question about homosexuals fearing arrest, Dr. Reuben's response was:

[Homosexuals] have a compulsion to flaunt their sex in public. The public washroom is frequently their stage. Bus stations, parks, bowling alleys are haunted by gay guys. Random and reckless selection of partners is the trademark.[10]

Another question was posed: "All homosexuals aren't like that, are they?" Dr. Reuben's answer:

Unfortunately, they are like that. One of the main features of homosexuality is promiscuity. It stands to reason. Homosexual sex is impossible; solving the problem with only half the pieces. They say they want sexual gratification and love that they eliminate, right from the start, the most obvious source of love and gratification is—women. Tragically, there is no possibility of satisfaction because the

[9] Ibid., 137-138.
[10] Ibid., 142.

formula is wrong. One penis plus one penis equals nothing. There is no substitute for hetero sex—penis and vagina. Disappointed, stubborn, discouraged, defiant, the homosexual keeps trying. He is a sexual Diogenes, always looking for the penis that pleases.[11]

Yet another question was posed: "What about all the homosexuals who live together happily for years?" Answer:

What about them? They are a mighty rare bird among the homosexual flock. The bitterest argument between husband-and-wife is a passionate love sonnet by comparison with the dialogue between the homosexual and his queen. But together? Yes. Happily? Hardly. Mercifully for both of them, the life expectancy of the relationship together is brief.[12]

Lesbians did not escape Dr. Reuben's "expert" insights. When asked about female prostitutes, Reuben wrote:

Since the majority of prostitutes are female homosexuals in their private lives anyway, making it with another girl is like a Busman's holiday. Just as one penis, plus one penis equals nothing; one vagina plus one vagina still equals zero. No matter how ingenious they are, their sexual practices must always be some sort of imitation of heterosexual intercourse. But basically all homosexuals are looking for love where there can be no love and looking for sexual satisfaction where there can be no lasting satisfaction.[13]

---

[11] Ibid., 142-143.
[12] Ibid., 143.
[13] Ibid., 218-219.

As absurd as *Everything You Always Wanted to Know about Sex but Were Afraid to Ask* seems, it can't be dismissed. The book remains an iconic piece because the information reflects the culture of the late 1960s and the 1970s. To the curious population who didn't interact with gay people, it stereotyped them as broken, sick, and perverted. In the absence of reliable resources, messages like those above settled into the souls and lives of young gay people in the 1970s and even into the 1980s, creating overwhelming trauma. Often, they were wracked with fear, thinking, "I don't want to be anything like that." *Everything You Always Wanted to Know about Sex but Were Afraid to Ask* kept many gays closeted for decades.

Activism erupts in America

Society was getting close to the breaking point. Protests for women's rights and civil rights, as well as against the Vietnam War, stirred America's youthful population. About 70 million children of the post–World War II baby boom were young adults now and moving away from the conservative traditionalism of their parents. Young people were speaking out.

Martin Luther King Jr. peacefully rallied black Americans and their supporters for change. Malcolm X preached Black Nationalism. Betty Friedan and Gloria Steinem formed the National Organization for Women (NOW) in 1966 to address the unequal treatment of women.

The decade was torn by assassinations: John F. Kennedy (1963), Malcolm X (1965), Martin Luther King Jr. (1968), and Robert Kennedy (1968). There were also happier events: In 1969, Americans sent astronauts to the moon, and hippies gathered at Woodstock to celebrate peace, love, and music. It was a decade of change—more than anything, in terms of social rights awareness.

It seemed as though everyone was marching and demanding something. But where were the gays? Gay men and lesbians (the terminology began to permanently shift away from "homosexual" by the 1970s), oppressed by mental health professionals, the government, law enforcement, and their own families, were silently off to the sides, mostly hiding. Then three incidents of civil disobedience took place in the late 1960s—two on the West Coast and one on the East Coast—and together began to energize, organize, and empower the gay and transgender communities.

The "Last Dance Raid"

A group of heterosexual ministers from mainline Protestant churches agreed to sponsor a Mardi Gras Costume Ball for gay men and lesbians set for January 1, 1965, at the California Dance Hall in San Francisco. This was still a time when a bar could be raided if gays happened to be present. A big private event where gay couples could socialize was a novel idea. The group wanted to do it right. They went to City Hall and to the San Francisco Police Department to get a permit for the dance, which they estimated would draw five hundred people. Though it was legally permitted, the night of the dance, hundreds of police officers showed up and lined the entrance to the dance hall. Despite a string of provocations by the police, none of the dance attendees took the bait. Enraged at the sight of men wearing dresses entering the dance, the police officers raided the event.

Using batons to beat bloody anyone they got close to, the police dragged hundreds of attendees off to jail simply for the crime of dancing together. One police officer, who was known for his brutality toward gays, kicked the genitals of two men. When the men were taken to the hospital, the doctors refused to treat their injuries because they heard that the men were "dirty, filthy queers."

Until now, gays had just had to take the beatings and brutality, but this time was different because the heterosexual ministers, men of God, the hosts of the dance, called a press conference the next day and told the media what had happened. Suddenly, the entire city knew of the events that had unfolded at the dance. A lawsuit was filed against the city, and when the gay side won, things began to change. This true story is covered very well in the award-winning 2013 documentary film *Lewd & Lascivious: 1965: Drag Queens, Ministers and the SFPD.*

The first-ever instance of gays fighting back set a new tone in San Francisco, which was not yet known for being friendly to gay people. The Castro District, which later became known as "the gay district," was still mainly Irish-Catholic, blue-collar, and very homophobic.

T-girls are tough

The Tenderloin District in San Francisco was one of the few places where transsexual women (called transgender today) felt comfortable living, socializing, and working. In the 1960s, if transwomen did not pass well enough as "real" women, traditional employment was out of their reach. Prostitution was often the only way for them to survive financially. Late at night, after working the streets, transwomen prostitutes would congregate at the Compton Cafeteria.

One night in August 1966, a few of the transwomen got rowdy, and management called the police. Historically, the women had been quite compliant with management and the police. They were accustomed to being handled roughly and inappropriately by law enforcement. It happened all the time.

On this hot August night, however, they decided to fight back. After being verbally abused by a police officer, one of the women threw her coffee in his face, and bedlam broke loose. Glasses, dishes, and windows were broken. The women were arrested.

This event marked a radical turning point for the treatment of the transgender community in the Tenderloin. For the first time, they didn't comply but, rather, fought back. Community leaders and police began to listen to the needs of the transgender community. This little-known story is well covered in an inspiring documentary called *Screaming Queens: The Riot at Compton's Cafeteria* (2005).

Stonewall: The famous event

Three years later, on June 28, 1969, in New York City, the gay and transgender community again fought back against abuse.

The Stonewall Inn had been located in lower Manhattan since the repeal of Prohibition, when the gay community was ghettoized in that part of the city, mostly in Greenwich Village. Typical of the bars that did welcome gay and transgender people, the Stonewall was, by the late 1960s, owned and operated by the Mafia without a license. The sanitary conditions were disturbing. There was no running water in the bar, and the bathrooms were insufficient. The alcohol was watered down and the drinks, overpriced. Still, it was a relatively safe place for gay men and transgender people to gather.

Though subject to raids and arrests, customers still flocked to the Stonewall because it was the only gay bar in New York City where same-sex dancing was allowed. Regular payoffs to the police ensured that the Stonewall evaded frequent raids. Occasionally, if one did happen, all the lights were turned on as a signal for the patrons to stop dancing and stop touching one another. Everyone knew and complied with the established procedures. Typically, all the patrons lined up and the police demanded their ID cards. Drag queens and transvestites/transgender people were aggressively targeted by police and humiliated; policewomen checked their genitals. If drag queens were not found to be wearing at least three pieces of men's clothing (not counting socks), they were subject to arrest and, often, to beatings.

The police planned the June 28 raid on Stonewall. It started quietly with undercover officers in plain clothes slipping in one at a time to collect information and take notes. Then, at just the right moment, several police officers walked through the door in the early morning hours.

The lights were turned on, and the police announced their presence and ordered all the patrons to line up. It was expected to go as it usually did. Those arrested would be loaded directly into the Public Morals

Squad paddy wagons waiting outside. But things didn't go as usual this time.

Some of the patrons left the bar but congregated outside. Some refused to leave, and others resisted arrest. Within a short time, there were several hundred people gathered around the Stonewall entrance. Bystanders began to mock the police; paddy wagons were overturned and their tires slashed. When the crowd discovered the raid had occurred in part because the Stonewall's Mafia owners had not paid off the police, people in the crowd began to throw pennies (coppers) at the cops. Drag queens and transvestites started hitting the police with their purses. The crowds continued to gather.

Skirmishes between the police and the gays stopped and started repeatedly for the next three nights. Some older gays, including those who had worked with the Mattachine Society since the 1950s, felt it was important for gay men and lesbians to behave like every other respectable member of society. They were shocked at the violence and the feminine behavior displayed. But this riot, or series of riots, would be a turning point in the thinking of the gay, lesbian, bisexual, and transgender communities.

A massive resistance hadn't been organized, but after years of police mistreatment and targeted abuse, the gay and transgender communities had had enough. In the midst of American social upheaval and protests, no one expected the gay and transgender communities to rise up. They had spent years in stealth mode, hiding in the shadows. But something within the Greenwich Village gay community had shifted. In response to the Stonewall Riots, the Gay Liberation Front (GLF), the first organization to use the word "gay" in its name, was formed.

Coming out in the society

The shadows and margins of society had been relatively safe places to hide. People in the mainstream had not known gay people; they were stereotypes—not their sons, daughters, friends, and co-workers. But

Stonewall was the beginning of the gay liberation movement. Gay men and lesbians were now encouraged to come out to their friends, family, and colleagues. Coming out in the late 1960s was frightening. Laws banning gay, lesbian, and transgender people from housing, employment, and even public gatherings were deeply seated in the culture. But consistently it has been shown that attitudes change when people realize that someone they know is gay, and indeed, for those to whom people came out, "gay" went from being a behavior to being a *person*.

The Gay Liberation Front was soon joined by the Gay Activists' Alliance, both formed in 1969 as immediate responses to the Stonewall raids. The GLF was created as a split from Frank Kameny's New York City chapter of the Mattachine Society. Within weeks of the riots, gays, lesbians, bisexuals, transvestites, and transgender people gathered to organize a march in New York City. They suggested that the proposed march replace the Annual Reminder, led yearly by Kameny, along with Barbara Gittings, since 1965 to protest federal hiring discrimination policies. While planning for the march, several events were added to expand awareness of the issue. Bisexual Brenda Howard suggested that the word "pride" be attached to the entire observance, and it was scheduled for the third Sunday of June.

The first Gay Pride March took place in June of 1970. It began with just a few hundred people.[14] The bravery of those first marchers cannot be overstated. Homosexuality was still viewed as a mental illness. Participants in the first Gay Pride March risked losing their reputations, jobs, professional licenses, and even apartment leases. But by the time they crossed over Christopher Street and moved out of the Village, the group had swelled to several thousand participants. And before long, the line of marchers stretched from Greenwich Village to Central Park, fifty-one blocks away.

---

[14] For excellent historical background, watch the documentaries *Before Stonewall* (1984) and *After Stonewall* (1999).

The number of cities where marches were held grew quickly. Most such events were called Gay Liberation Marches, Gay Liberation Day, or Gay Freedom Day. In the 1980s, the term "Gay Pride" would become standard, marking it as less of a radical activist event and more as one with a celebratory atmosphere. After so many centuries of being shamed, pride seemed a natural antidote and a statement of healthy self-esteem for a community once rejected and imprisoned by the stigmas forced upon them.

Perhaps thinking of Gay Pride events as a kind of Independence Day for the gay, lesbian, bisexual, and transgender community puts it in perspective. The gay and transgender communities and those who support them participate in Gay Pride events to commemorate the June 1969 Stonewall action signaling the end of oppression and the beginning of liberation, and to celebrate diversity in how human relationships are expressed.

In the spirit of expanding national gay activism, various groups sprang up in the early 1970s. The new breed of empowered gay activists began splintering into special-interest groups, such as Radicalesbians and the Street Transvestites Action Revolutionaries. The GLF spread throughout the United States, mobilizing the gay and transgender communities against oppression. Within months of Stonewall, all over the country, local GLF chapters began staging direct actions.

Barney's Beanery, in what would later be West Hollywood, was the site of one of the first actions by the gay community. The owner, John Anthony, had long been an aggressively antagonistic opponent of the gay community. A sign posted over his bar proudly declared "FAGOTS [sic] STAY OUT." Even after Anthony died, the offensive sign remained. In February 1970, a group of GLF-ers decided to remove it. The protest soon led to compliance by the restaurant's management. The success of the direct-action method inspired other GLF groups to confront injustices in their own local areas.

Another mainstay of the gay rights movement, the organization called Parents and Friends of Lesbians and Gays (PFLAG), was born in 1972. Its founder, Jeanne Manford, was a schoolteacher and the mother of Morty Manford, a gay rights activist and member of the Gay Activists' Alliance. Morty had come out to his parents in 1969 at age fifteen. Jeanne remembers her reaction: "I wanted him to be happy, and whatever made him happy was fine with me. Morty was no different from the way he'd been the day before."

Morty was arrested for the first time in 1971 for sitting with a friend in a doorway on Christopher Street, Greenwich Village, the heart of the New York City gay community. A police officer urged the two to move along, and they refused. Simple actions like walking along holding hands could get a gay couple arrested even in a predominantly gay neighborhood.

The next time Morty got into a confrontation with police he was handing out flyers at a dinner for politicians and the press in April 1972. He was there to raise awareness about the oppressive and demeaning language used by the media about the gay community. Along with several other activists, Morty was severely beaten and arrested by police, and then taken to the hospital. Early the next morning, a police officer called Morty's mother, Jeanne, and her husband at home: "Your son has been arrested. And you know, he's a homosexual."

Jeanne replied, "Yes, I know. Why are you bothering him? Why don't you go after real criminals and stop harassing the gays?"

That same week, she wrote a letter to the *New York Post* which began, "I have a homosexual son and I love him." She told the story of Morty being beaten while other police officers stood by. Her name was later on the front page of the *New York Times*. The principal of the school where Jeanne taught requested that she be more discreet. "Look," she said, "my professional life is one thing. And my private life is another, and I'll do as I please."[15]

---

[15] *Making History*, 240.

Two months later, while homosexuality was still considered a mental illness and sodomy a crime, Jeanne joined her son Morty in the Gay Liberation Day march, carrying a handwritten sign that read: "Parents of Gays: Unite in Support of Our Children." Both mother and son were wildly cheered along the parade route. Later, Morty said:

> We are the only minority whose parents do not share our minority status. In other words, a black child who is fighting for civil rights is going to have his parents share that issue with him. Because of the importance of family to all of us, being estranged from your parents is a very traumatic thing. Being forced to closet your life from them is very devastating. The symbolic presence that my mother provided was a sign of great hope that parents could be supportive, that the people we are closest to, whom we love the most, need not be our enemies. I think the desire on the part of the gays to share the totality as people, as gays and lesbians, was very much the reason why the parents have always gotten such an overwhelming response.[16]

In the days following the march, many gay people called Jeanne, asking her to talk with their parents. Clearly, there was a need to organize and assist parents who supported their gay children and wanted to help in the efforts to bridge the gay and the heterosexual communities. Soon, Jeanne Manford and her husband were holding meetings for other parents with gay children at a Methodist Church in Greenwich Village. Twenty people attended the first parents' meeting. Originally, called Parents of Gays, the organization eventually became PFLAG, now with 350 chapters and over 200,000 members in the United States.

---

[16] Ibid., 243.

The American Psychiatric Association challenges the APsaA's theories

Psychoanalysts continued to counsel gay youth and their parents that homosexuality was a mental illness that could and should be fixed. Charles Socarides and his peers held firmly to their limited observation-based theories of same-sex attracted people in therapeutic settings. Meanwhile, the Hooker Study was finally gaining followers beyond the American Psychiatric Association.

In 1961, Hooker had been invited to present her findings as a lecturer in Europe. Then, in 1967, the National Institute for Mental Health (NIMH) had asked her to chair its Task Force on Homosexuality and requested that she compile a position paper for the Institute on the treatment of homosexual men. The paper was ready for publication in 1969, but members of the Nixon Administration wanted Hooker's task force report withheld because they considered it "too liberal and tolerant."[17]

During these same years, psychiatrists were talking among themselves about gay men and women they were treating in their practices. One such doctor, Judd Marmor (1910–2003), had been treating gay patients since after World War II. Many desired to change their sexual orientation. While Marmor was pleased to try to help them do so, he admitted that people were buoyed by the false expectation that psychoanalysis could cure everything "from frostbite to homosexuality."[18] Most of Marmor's clients were in literary or show business fields; although he was able to help them better cope with social and professional stresses, they always remained gay.

Sex, scandal, and sexual perversion were hot topics in America in the mid-1960s. A publisher approached Marmor and asked him if he would write a book about sexual inversion, as same-sex attraction was still often called. Marmor was conflicted: When he was with his peers, he heard conversations about gay men as vindictive, aggressive,

---

[17] *Homophile Studies Quarterly* (ONE Institute of Homophile Studies, 1970).
[18] *Making History*, 250.

untrustworthy, and unable to have healthy relationships, but none of this was true based on Marmor's experience with his own clients. He consented to writing *Sexual Inversions* (1965) and began collaborating with Evelyn Hooker, with whom he had worked on NIMH's homosexuality task force.

In 1970, a magazine got hold of the as-yet-unpublished 1969 NIHM Task Force report and printed an unauthorized copy of it. (The official report was published in 1972.) Thanks to the Task Force report and Marmor's book, gay activists became aware of Hooker's 1956 study.[19] Seeing the value and truth of her work, they became more vocal about their rights. A small group began disrupting professional medical conferences whenever homosexuality was discussed. They wanted the only scientifically completed study included in the discussion of their lives.

At the APA conference held in San Francisco that year, several gay and lesbian activists were able to obtain press passes from sympathetic connections within the APA. They rushed into the convention hall targeting a behavioral therapy meeting led by Dr. Irving Bieber. The activist group disrupted Bieber's meeting, yelling, "Stop talking *about* us and start talking *with* us. We are the people whose behaviors you're trying to change. Start talking *with* us!"[20]

Some psychiatrists ran out of the room, but others, wanting to hear what "actual homosexuals" had to say, stayed and talked with them.

Behind the scenes, a shift had already begun to take place inside the APA. Overwhelmingly, the very conservative membership still believed homosexuality was a mental illness. But while gay therapists were strictly banned from APsaA, some were members in the APA. Deeply closeted regarding their sexual orientation, a tiny number were actually among the membership of APsaA, too.

Over the previous decade, several gay therapists had been meeting secretly at conferences to discuss mobilizing for change. These gay APA

---

[19] Richard Schmiechen, dir., "Changing Our Minds: The Story of Dr. Evelyn Hooker," documentary (Frameline, 1991).
[20] *Making History*, 222.

members were called the GayPA and were informally headed by Dr. John Fryer. While they had quietly begun to challenge the APA from the inside, unexpectedly, pressure from the outside, brought on by gay activists, added more intensity to the process.

Concerned about activists disrupting the following year's conference (1971), meeting organizers invited them to host an information booth and to sit on a session panel. Since most studies about same-sex attraction only observed gay people in treatment or in jail, it was considered a revolutionary and progressive step to invite them to speak on the panel entitled "Lifestyles of Non-Patient Homosexuals." (The activists, when referring to their participation, called the panel "Lifestyles of Im-Patient Homosexuals."[21])

Frank Kameny, present among the small group, had written "Psychiatric Option," a paper directed to the APA. Kameny, never at a loss for words or opinions (or literary alliteration), called the APA's work on homosexuality "shabby, shoddy, slipshod, slovenly, sleazy, and just plain bad science based on insufficient definitions of terms like pathology and neurosis."[22]

Along with leading lesbian activist Barbara Gittings (1932–2007), Kameny hosted an exhibit at the conference called "Gay, Proud, and Healthy: The Homosexual Community Speaks." Taking advantage of a rare opportunity to engage the professional mental health community directly, they answered questions, distributed literature, and met members of the APA and the secret group, the GayPA. An alliance between outside efforts and inside efforts was forged.

Gittings and Kameny accepted an invitation to the conference again the next year (1972), where they were asked to appear as guests on a panel called "Psychiatry: Friend or Foe to Homosexuals? – A Dialogue" alongside Dr. Judd Marmor and another heterosexual APA member. Gittings' partner, Kay Lahusen, noticed that the proposed panel lacked someone

---

[21] *Making History*, 222.
[22] Holly S. Heatley, *Commies and Queers: Narratives that Supported the Lavender Scare* (Ann Arbor, MI: ProQuest: 2007), 134.

who was both gay and a psychiatrist. The panel moderator agreed to the suggestion to add such a person, but only if one could be found who was willing to publicly take the position, as no APA members were openly gay.

Based on rumors of his homosexuality, Dr. John Fryer, the informal head of the GayPA, had recently lost his job at the University of Pennsylvania. Kameny and Gittings asked him to make a bold move and give a speech about the damaging effects of the DSM's diagnosis of homosexuality as pathological. Already out of a job, Fryer was concerned he might never be hired if he stood up and openly admitted he was a gay, so the group devised a plan: Fryer could appear as "Dr. Anonymous" while wearing a large tuxedo, a Nixon mask, and a wild wig. He agreed. Speaking into a voice-distorting device inside the microphone, Dr. Anonymous described to his fellow psychiatrists how harmful the wording in the DSM was to him and other gays. Gittings followed Fryer and read several statements anonymously submitted by members of the GayPA. When Dr. Anonymous was done, the panel received a standing ovation.

Later in the same year, Dr. Robert Spitzer, a member of the APA's Committee on Nomenclature and Designation, attended a behavioral therapy conference in New York City. During a meeting, Ron Gold, an early gay lobbyist and one of the five original founders of the National Gay and Lesbian Task Force, stood up to object to the APA's lack of understanding of homosexuality.

Intending to tell Gold how inappropriate his actions were, Spitzer sought him out after the meeting. The conversation took an unexpected turn as both men agreed that Gold, along with some other gay men and lesbians, should participate as invited guests in a panel discussion at the next convention.

Goodbye, stigma

At the 1973 American Psychiatric Association convention in Honolulu, in a filled-to-capacity room, the opposing sides spoke about the designation of homosexuality as a mental illness. On one side were Charles

Socarides and Irving Bieber, while on the other side were Ron Gold and Judd Marmor. The group engaged in a panel debate.

Now comes my favorite part of the story, the relationship part. Many of the following details are omitted when conservative "family values" groups or religious groups recount the events leading to the removal of homosexuality from the DSM. These biased storytellers depict the gay activists as charging and disruptive. The fact is, after 1970, when they first crashed the conference, as mentioned, they attended the subsequent conferences as invited guests, hosting booths and serving on session panels. Conservative groups also always leave this next part of the account out of their narratives:

As had been traditional for years, the secret GayPA group gathered at a local gay bar at the end of the conference day. They invited activist Ron Gold along, calling him the hero of the day following his successful engagement on the panel discussion. Gold, now friends with heterosexual Spitzer, invited him along to the bar, too. Spitzer went incognito as Ron Gold's closeted gay psychiatrist friend. As he was sitting off to the side observing, Spitzer was stunned to discover that some very well-known colleagues were part of the secret GayPA.

Spitzer's identity was uncovered when he started asking the members of the GayPA questions. Understandably, they became very uncomfortable and asked Gold to leave and take Spitzer with him. As the two groups were arguing, a man in a full Army uniform walked into the bar.

He saw Gold, walked over to him, and, overcome by emotion, began weeping in Gold's arms. The soldier, a closeted Army psychiatrist stationed in Hawaii, had attended the conference. Moved by Gold's speech, the soldier had felt brave enough to visit a gay bar for the first time in his life. Spitzer, after witnessing the entire event, grabbed Ron Gold and said, "Let's go write the resolution." The two went back to Spitzer's hotel room and wrote the proposed language to declassify homosexuality as pathological in the DSM.

Their suggested language stated that homosexuality was a normal variant of human sexuality. It also allowed for another option—that if a person was concerned with their own same-sex attractions, they would still be covered by the DSM for purposes of treatment. Members of the APA Task Force on Nomenclature and Statistics researched the mounting scientific evidence accumulating on the question of homosexuality as pathological. The proposal was reviewed and approved by the APA Reference Committee and the Assembly of District Branches prior to going to the APA Board of Trustees for a vote in December 1973.[23]

As expected, the most vocal APA opponents were the handful of therapists with joint memberships in APsaA and APA; they were furious. They fought the reclassification. Sure that the majority would not vote for the change, they insisted that the vote go before the entire APA membership. They were wrong. In April 1974, the resolution passed: 58% voted for the change to declassify homosexuality as a mental illness.

Dr. Marmor became president of the APA the following year. About the removal of homosexuality from the DSM he said:

> We didn't merely remove homosexuals from the category of illness; we stated that there was no reason why, a priori, a gay man or woman could not be just as healthy, just as effective, just as law-abiding, and just as capable of functioning as any heterosexual. Furthermore, we asserted that the laws discriminating against them in housing or employment were unjustified. Therefore, it was a total statement, and I think it was a very significant move. Shortly after that, the American Psychological Association and the American Bar Association came out in support of homosexuals. It was an important step that we took.[24]

---

[23] Ira Glass, "81 Words," episode of *This American Life,* NPR, January 18, 2002.
[24] *Making History,* 254.

Homosexuality was next listed as a "sexual orientation disturbance" (SOD) so those who were uncomfortable with their orientation, or found it to be a distraction to their lives, could still get help if they wanted help. There was controversy from the psychoanalysts at APsaA regarding this step too. The DMS-III, published in 1980, replaced SOD with "ego-dystonic homosexuality" (EDH), which essentially acknowledges culturally induced pressures. In 1987, EDH was removed from the DSM, effectively removing homosexuality entirely as any type of psychiatric condition.

Even after his son Richard came out to him, Dr. Charles Socarides never stopped fighting against the removal of homosexuality from the DSM. Throughout the prolonged battle, he invoked the dismissal of scientific evidence at each stage of every decision.

Science had never been used to classify homosexuality as pathological. Homosexuality had been misdiagnosed through biased, careless, morally based observations and false assumptions by a select few on the basis of a very small group of gays in therapy.

Backtracking just a bit: In 1973, things were looking hopeful for the gay and transgender communities. The mental illness designation had been lifted from homosexuality, the government had eased back from its wholesale witch hunts, and gays and lesbians were coming out of the shadows and organizing for civil rights. However, storm clouds were gathering on the horizon: Conservative politicians and religious leaders would soon merge to try to block the gay community from fully attaining their newfound freedom from oppression.

Part II: Religion and Politics

Chapter 5

Getting the Faithful into the Voting Booths

Turning Politically Unengaged Christians into Republicans

First theology book on homosexuality paves the way in England

In the early 1970s, the future was beginning to look quite hopeful for the gay, lesbian, bisexual, and transgender (LGBT) community. They were coming out of the closet and walking toward newfound freedoms. Though a few Bible translations included the word "homosexual" when copyrighted in 1946, 1958, and 1966,[1] the only religious groups in America that seemed to be making any noise about homosexuality were some travelling fundamentalist Methodist preachers in West Texas in the early 1970s. They had discovered that talking about gays was a good way to fill their revival tents.

---

[1] Revised Standard Version, Amplified Bible, and Revised Standard Version-Catholic Edition, respectively.

So, does this mean there were no fiery sermons about homosexuality coming from American pulpits in the early 1970s? Yes, apparently it does. None are recorded until W. A. Criswell (1909–2002), senior pastor of First Baptist Church in Dallas, Texas, two-time president of the Southern Baptist Convention, and the man widely considered the "father of modern fundamentalism," preached a sermon on homosexuality on September 21, 1980.[2]

In his message, Criswell completely ignored the seven-year-old American Psychiatric Association (APA) decision that had declassified homosexuality as a mental illness. Criswell did, however, quote from the book *Everything You Always Wanted to Know about Sex but Were Afraid to Ask* (1969) to drive home his point that homosexuality was a sickness, a perversion, and a sin.

Twenty-five years before Criswell launched this attack on the gay community from his pulpit, an English Anglican priest, Rev. Dr. Derrick Sherwin Bailey (1910–1984),[3] had noticed the growing tendency, starting at the end of World War II and continuing through the 1950s, to make sexual inverts the scapegoat of pervasive social, moral, and family problems in England. When several high-profile men were arrested under sodomy laws, public attention brought more weight to the issue.

Alan Turing (1912–1954) is known as the "father of computer science," the "father of artificial intelligence," and the cryptographer who broke the German Enigma code, helping the Allies win World War II. In 1952, his home was burglarized, and Turing reported the incident to the police. While taking the report, the police were surprised at how frankly Turing reported that the theft might have had something to do with his young male lover. Rather than address the robbery, the police

---

[2] Mel White, *Holy Terror: Lies the Christian Right Tells Us to Deny Gay Equality* (New York: Magnus Books, 2006), 36.

[3] Jonathan Sinclair Carey, "D.S. Bailey and 'the Name Forbidden among Christians,'" *William A. Percy Christian Studies of Homosexuality* 12: 94-113. http://webcache.google-usercontent.com/search?q=cache:v9Sx_Wk5dJAJ:www.williamapercy.com/wiki/images/DS_bailey_and_the_name_forbidden_among_christians_studies_of_homosexuality_volume_12.pdf+&cd=16&hl=en&ct=clnk&gl=us&client=safari.

arrested Turing. He was convicted for "gross indecency" under British sodomy laws dating back to 1885.[4]

Though he had previously earned the honor of Officer of the British Empire for his wartime work, Turing came under suspicion. English government officials feared Turing knew too many national security secrets; being gay, they believed, opened him to blackmail by foreign agents.

Turing was stripped of his security clearances and followed by government agents wherever he went. He was given a year's probation for his crime and forced to undergo chemical castration. Two years later, in 1954, Turing committed suicide by eating a cyanide-laced apple.

In the same period, 1953–1954, Sir John Gielgud[5] and three other high-profile men were arrested and convicted under similar English indecency charges. Sensing that the timing was right to challenge the prosecution of modern-day sexual inverts/homosexuals under English sodomy laws that were decades and, in some cases even centuries, old, D. S. Bailey helped establish a call for reform of the laws. Bailey, operating within the Church of England's Moral Welfare Council, established in the 1920s to aid prostitutes and the homeless,[6] formed a group to investigate a simple question: Why were fornicators and adulterers not prosecuted as harshly under morality codes as were gay men?

---

[4] David Leavitt, *The Man Who Knew Too Much: Alan Turing and the Invention of the Computer* (New York: Atlas Books, 2006), 18.

[5] Sir John Gielgud (1904–2000) was an English theatre director and recognized as the most accomplished English stage actor of the 20th century, as well as for his roles in movies (*The Elephant Man, Chariots of Fire,* and *Gandhi* are a few titles) and on television. Sir Gielgud was honored and knighted in 1953. Four months later, he was caught in a sex scandal in a public restroom in Chelsea. He was charged with "persistently importuning men for immoral purposes." There was a call to strip him of his knighthood and horse-whip him, yet most prominent politicians refused to sign the letter to the Prime Minister. Gielgud remained publicly closeted and saved his career. In 1988, he publicly acknowledged his relationship with his longtime lover, Martin Hensler, who died in 1999. Sir Gielgud died just a year later at the age of 96. Sir Gielgud's popularity brought light to the issue of criminalizing homosexuality.

[6] "D.S. Bailey," 95.

Bailey and the Moral Welfare Council set out to help reform the harsh and unequal penalties. Gay men had been the clear target; only they were punished—never lesbians. Men caught in same-sex acts, even when private and consensual, were subject to a range of penalties, from fines to life in prison. Bailey was concerned about the abuse and mistreatment of gay prisoners and the disparate age of consent for heterosexual couples (16) and homosexual couples (21).

To study the issue from a wider base, Bailey assembled a group of leaders and experts across several disciplines. Together, theologians, medical doctors, historians, anthropologists, lawyers, and legislative leaders studied homosexuality and the sodomy laws, interviewed sexual inverts who were both in and out of therapeutic situations, and concluded that, other than the negative pressures imposed by society, many sexual inverts lived "normal" lives.

The gays informed the panel that they had never known a time when they were not attracted to the same sex. They didn't suffer guilt about their same-sex behavior; to them, their attractions and sexual behavior were quite natural. Still others, Bailey observed, were aware that their actions violated not only established traditions but their internal "law of nature" as well. Bailey differentiated between the "sin" of those who transgressed their internal nature, and the actions of those who had a clear conscience about their attractions.

Consistent with psychoanalysts' theories and the terminology of the 1950s, Bailey referred to homosexuality as a sexual inversion. However, he made an interesting distinction between sexual *inversion* and sexual *perversion*. Psychoanalysts in both the United States and England had used the two terms interchangeably and, by doing so, made sweeping assumptions about the mental state of same-sex attracted people. Bailey concluded that, although homosexuality was sin, it should not be a punishable crime.

Hoping to persuade Parliament to treat male sexual inverts more justly, in 1954, Bailey and his group of experts published and submitted to the governing body "The Problem of Homosexuality," a pamphlet summarizing their findings. The combination of Bailey's pamphlet and the sensationalism surrounding the recent rash of high-profile arrests prompted Parliament to form the Wolfenden Committee, charged with studying homosexuality and prostitution and the civil penalties associated with each crime for a period of three years.

Once "The Problem of Homosexuality" was completed, Bailey returned to a book he had been working on, *Homosexuality and the Western Tradition,* which would be published in 1955. Until then, psychoanalysts, sex experts, psychologists, and legislators had looked at homosexuality, but no modern-day theologian had done so. Not only was Bailey's approach scholarly; it was far more compassionate than Criswell's sermon.

Bailey went beyond simply reading translated words on the pages of the Bible. He searched ancient scriptural texts and studied church and English history to uncover and expose long-held traditions and biases and their influence on sodomy laws. He concluded that the church had an obligation to correct the part it had played in the creation and perpetuation of destructive attitudes and laws used to punish sexual inverts. Church doctrine, he said, had blurred the concepts of immoral perversion and consensual inversion. The actions condemned in the Bible, Bailey concluded, were sexual excesses in which sexual perverts engaged, as opposed to the behavior of sexual inverts, who acted according to their nature.

Upon completion, *Homosexuality and the Western Tradition* was submitted to the Wolfenden Committee as an additional resource. Largely due to Bailey's contributions, at the end of the three-year study period, the Wolfenden Committee recommended doing away with criminal punishment for consensual same-sex acts and lowering the age of consent for gays and lesbians to sixteen, the same as for heterosexual couples.

The Wolfenden Report moved through to the British Parliament for debate. Parliament Home Secretary Sir David Maxwell-Fyfe was notoriously anti-gay. Even though the Wolfenden Report detailed excessive injustices against gays, Maxwell-Fyfe delayed the vote and petitioned for even harsher penalties, as well as additional studies. In response to Maxwell-Fyfe's aggressive stalling, the English gay community organized itself into the Homosexual Law Reform Society and advocated for changes to the sodomy laws.

It took another decade for the Wolfenden recommendations to come to a vote, but finally, the Sexual Offences Act of 1967, decriminalizing sodomy, passed by a narrow margin. Though Bailey did not approve of same-sex acts personally or theologically, his Christian faith and sense of fairness had motivated him to protect those he felt were being treated unjustly. His work and book had paved the way to decriminalize homosexuality in England and Wales. His comprehensive, impartial, and compassionate view was groundbreaking and indeed remarkable for the time.

It took thirty-seven more years for the United States to join England in erasing the sodomy laws criminalizing consensual sex between adult men. Bailey's work and research remained unsurpassed for decades.

Roots of American fundamentalism

Before the mid-1970s, conservative Christians, for the most part, avoided public involvement in cultural issues. They were nose-down, do-the-work-of-the-Lord people. It was unthinkable for many fundamentalists, evangelicals, or conservative Christians to involve themselves in politics. So how did conservative Christians become a significant voting bloc, eventually turning their focus on the LGBT community in the late 1970s? To answer the question we need to step back to the 1920s.[7]

The evangelical movement of the 19th century's Second Great Awakening eventually drifted into two divergent groups at the turn of the

---

[7] Robert B. Horowitz, *America's Right: Anti-establishment Conservatism from Goldwater to the Tea Party* (Malden, MA: Polity Press, 2013), 64-72.

20th century: the Modernists and the Fundamentalists. Interestingly, it was the publication of the Scofield Bible (1909) that, in part, caused the division.

The Scofield Bible had several innovations: The side margins contained dates of past events and cross-references to related verses. Most uniquely, the Scofield Bible promoted dispensationalism—a belief that the timeline of the Bible can be broken into seven eras, the final one being Judgment. When post–World War I events fit conveniently into the "pre-tribulation dispensationalism" model, the Scofield Bible became the voice alerting Christians of the quickly approaching end times. Armed with warning signs, Fundamentalists—those who read the Bible literally—became more passionate about repentance, soul saving, and the impending vengeance of an angry God. Seeing the moral looseness and self-indulgence of the culture during the Roaring '20s, along with the excesses brought on by the repeal of Prohibition, the Fundamentalists preached about a national imperative to turn back to God before it was too late.

In contrast, the Modernists took a more expansive view of the Bible and focused on the social issues set before them: poverty, injustice, hunger, disease, equality, and slavery. They, too, believed the Bible to be divinely inspired, but focused their attentions on understanding Scripture passages in context rather than taking isolated verses literally, like the Fundamentalists. A key example of the difference between the two groups lies in their respective understandings of the creation narrative. While Modernists viewed the Genesis 1–2 stories as figurative, the Fundamentalists believed creation had happened precisely as written in the Bible and, thanks to the Scofield Bible[8], they even had a date for the beginning of the world: 4004 BC.

---

[8] The Scofield Reference Bible was edited by Cyrus Ingerson Scofield in 1909. *The Incredible Scofield and His Book*, by Joseph M. Canfield (Vallecito, CA: Ross House Books, 1988), gives a historical account of the man behind this famous version of the Bible. He is depicted as a liar and an exaggerator who abandoned his first wife and children, divorcing her four years after his "born again" experience. He called himself "Dr. Scofield," yet he never earned a doctorate. His own account of his life was filled with dubious

The final break between the two groups came as a direct result of the events surrounding the Scopes Monkey Trial in 1925. It was a highly publicized court case pitting the literal creation story beliefs of Fundamentalists against the beliefs of Modernist Christians, who found evolution consistent with, and not a threat to, their faith. Legislators in Tennessee had recently passed the Butler Act, which forbade the teaching of evolution in public schools. John Scopes, a substitute science teacher, was accused of teaching evolution in direct violation of the law. The case captured the country's attention due to its content, characters, and novelty as the first court case ever aired on radio. The prosecutor was high-profile William Jennings Bryant, a three-time presidential candidate and Fundamentalist Presbyterian. The defense attorney was the famous Clarence Darrow.

In the end, Darrow lost the case, and Scopes was found guilty of teaching evolution during his one-day substitute-teaching job and fined $100. The real loser, though, was the Fundamentalist belief system. In the public contest between God and science, science won. Bryant and Fundamentalism were ridiculed in the press.

Nationwide, Fundamentalists took a beating in the power struggle for leadership in seminaries, colleges, universities, and denominations. For the most part, they retreated into the south and established their own institutions. Following the Fundamentalists' public humiliation at the Scopes Trial, many of them, and even many conservative Christians of the day, didn't want to be associated with Fundamentalism. The feeling was mutual.

Indeed, Fundamentalists didn't want to be associated with anyone outside their circle. "Good" Fundamentalists refused to fellowship, or even pray with, Modernists, liberal evangelicals, or those in mainstream Christian denominations. Over the next four decades, the chasm deepened between the Fundamentalists and all other Christians. Going

statements, outright lies, and questionable morality. He was known by many as a con man and egotist. His Bible became the crux of the division between the Modernists and the Fundamentalists.

forward, the movements became known as fundamentalism[9] and, returning to the broader term used before the Fundamentalist-Modernist split, evangelicalism. The fundamentalists became extremely apolitical isolationists. Most of them never even registered to vote.

Republicans seek a new strategy

Until the early 1960s, the Republican Party and the Democratic Party were more ideologically similar and far less polarized than they are today. The division between the parties began with the 1964 presidential election between Republican senator Barry Goldwater (AZ) and incumbent president Democrat Lyndon B. Johnson.

Goldwater ran on a conservative platform rejecting federal interference in favor of states' rights. Even though he had supported all civil rights legislation before his candidacy, he stood in opposition to the federal Civil Rights Act of 1964 signed into law by President Johnson. Goldwater's opposition to civil rights forced many black voters to leave "the party of Lincoln," but won him large numbers of southern white voters. Conservative Democrats, also not in favor of sweeping civil rights legislation, migrated to the Republican Party. Thus, the two parties became firmly at odds.

Johnson's landslide victory over Goldwater signaled the Republican Party's need for reinvigoration and a long-term strategy. New issues were needed to bring in a large voter base. In the 1968 presidential election, Republican Richard Nixon ran against Democrat Hubert Humphrey. Nixon mimicked Goldwater's appeal to the southern white vote in a racist approach euphemistically called the "Southern Strategy." Not surprisingly, almost 90% of black voters migrated to the Democratic Party. Still, the Southern Strategy was deemed a successful GOP election tool

---

[9] After the Scopes Trial, Fundamentalists distanced themselves from the more formal term and were called fundamentalists, with a lowercase "f." Darren Dochuk tells the history of migration from the Bible Belt to conservative Orange County, California, from the 1930s to the 1980s in his book *From Bible Belt to Sunbelt: Plain-Folk Religion, Grassroots Politics, and the Rise of Evangelical Conservatism* (New York: W.W. Norton, 2012).

because both Goldwater and Nixon had won the South in consecutive elections. The distinction between the two parties became even more strongly established and has remained so to this day.

As early as the 1960s, a young Goldwater strategist, Paul Weyrich (1942–2008) began to conceptualize ways to link the anti–big government Goldwater followers, called the "New Right," to the largest untapped voting bloc in America—unregistered conservative and fundamentalist Christians. The strategists were faced with an obvious problem: Conservative Christians were not involved in politics. They had retreated into relative isolation way back in the mid-1920s following the Scopes Monkey Trial. They had eschewed politics for decades and weren't even registered to vote.

Though Weyrich saw the benefit very early on of seducing conservative Christians into politics, Goldwater felt it was a bad idea. He was extremely outspoken in his opposition to the unholy marriage of politics and religion. A decade later, in a September 16, 1981, speech to the U.S. Senate, Goldwater said:

> On religious issues there can be little or no compromise. There is no position on which people are so immovable as their religious beliefs. There is no more powerful ally one can claim in debate than Jesus Christ, or God, or Allah, or whatever one calls this Supreme Being. But, like any powerful weapon, the use of God's name on one's behalf should be used sparingly. The religious factions that are growing throughout our land are not using their religious clout with wisdom. They are trying to force government leaders into following their position 100 percent.
>
> If you disagree with these religious groups on a particular moral issue, they complain, they threaten you with a loss of money or votes or both. I'm frankly sick and tired of the

political preachers across this country telling me as a citizen that if I want to be a moral person, I must believe in "A," "B," "C," and "D." Just who do they think they are? And from where do they presume to claim the right to dictate their moral beliefs to me? And I am even more angry as a legislator who must endure the threats of every religious group who thinks it has some God-granted right to control my vote on every roll call in the Senate. I am warning them today: I will fight them every step of the way if they try to dictate their moral convictions to all Americans in the name of "conservatism."[10]

Though it seems Goldwater foresaw the disaster that would overtake both the GOP and conservative religious groups for the next three decades, he couldn't possibly have imagined how accurate his warning and insights would prove to be.

Conservative Christians eyed as a potential voting bloc

Goldwater's top political strategist, Paul Weyrich, didn't heed Goldwater's warning about the potential damage of an unholy alliance between religion and politics. Though Weyrich is not well known outside the conservative political core, his name seems to pop up everywhere in the landscape between conservative politics and religion. Over a 35-year period, Weyrich created or co-founded many of the most prominent conservative organizations in the political and religious arenas: The Heritage Foundation; Christian Voice, a conservative political organization widely known by its newsletter of the same name; and Free Congress Foundation, just to name a few. With the help of direct political marketing and fundraising pioneer extraordinaire Richard Viguerie (1933–), Weyrich's Christian Voice was

---

[10] Bill Moyers, "Religion in Politics," *Public Broadcasting Service*, December 7, 2007, http://www.pbs.org/moyers/journal/blog/atheism/.

the first organization to successfully use direct-mail campaigns to build a voter base and to raise money and awareness for socially conservative causes among its targeted group—unregistered Christians. Though Weyrich could reach out to conservative Christians, he still needed an issue to inspire them to register to vote. He found a rallying point during the Carter presidency.

Jimmy Carter was the first self-identified "born-again" evangelical Christian to win the White House. For people of faith, it was empowering to have an "out and proud" Southern Baptist leader and role model as president. It was problematic, however, to the Republican New Right because Carter was a Democrat. Some evangelical Christians, still a relatively untapped voting bloc at the time, had supported Carter during the 1976 election. Now, the New Right hoped to win the Carter Democrat Christian voters to the GOP and regain the White House in 1980. But they had a challenge: How to get that group to shift their allegiance to the Republican Party?

Shifting conservative Christian voters to the GOP

Because of the Civil Rights Act of 1964, the Internal Revenue Service (IRS) ruled that "private schools with racially discriminatory admissions policies" would lose tax-exempt charitable status. In 1927, Bob Jones (1893–1968), a product of the isolationism of southern Fundamentalists after the Scopes Monkey Trial, founded Bob Jones University (BJU), Greenville, South Carolina. BJU's policy included belief in the "God-ordained" separation of the races based on a long-popular fundamentalist way of interpreting the Bible's "curse of Ham" (Genesis 9:18-27) so as to justify slavery, segregation, and bans on interracial marriage. No black students were allowed admission to BJU. By upholding segregation, BJU was clearly breaking the 1964 Civil Rights Act.[11]

---

[11] The Easter Sunday 1958 sermon delivered by Bob Jones, President of Bob Jones University, was the university's position paper on segregation that remained intact until 1986. The paper was sold in the campus bookstore and mail-delivered to ministry supporters. The language and theology in the position paper are shocking to our

In late 1970, the IRS notified BJU that it was planning to revoke the university's tax-exempt status due to its admissions policies. Under pressure, the BJU administration began admitting black students, but only if they were married so they would not participate in interracial dating. In January 1976, the IRS did revoke BJU's tax-exempt status, retroactive to December 1970.

To onlookers, BJU was involved in an obvious attempt to justify segregation and discrimination. But remember, Paul Weyrich had been looking for an issue that could be used to wake up and inspire the conservative and fundamentalist Christian voting bloc. While it would have been a public relations disaster to ask Christians to support segregation and discrimination, Weyrich cleverly repositioned the issue as an attack on religious liberties and a threat to the tax-exempt status of Christian institutions.

Weyrich led the charge and accused Democrat Jimmy Carter, in his role as President, of revoking the tax exemption of Christian schools and, "if we are not careful," warned Weyrich, possibly other Christian organizations, too.[12] It was a slick political maneuver. Though the IRS had made its decision about BJU a full year before Carter was sworn in as President, the false accusations succeeded in getting formerly unregistered Christians to register and vote, and in getting Democratic Christians to shift to the GOP.

But the numbers were still not high enough. As early as 1975, Weyrich was looking for a longer-term strategy. His ultimate goal was to join faith leaders to the GOP's New Right. They needed a broader issue than just tax-exempt status for religious institutions. On a 1975 Weyrich-hosted conference call with conservative religious and political leaders, someone suggested that abortion be considered as the much-needed sweeping issue. But this suggestion presented problems with both timing and logistics.

---

sensibilities. Reading it will afford excellent insight into the extreme level of racism prevalent in the fundamentalist religious community: Bob Jones, "Is Segregation Scriptural?" (Greenville, SC: Bob Jones University, 1960), https://docs.google.com/file/d/0B6A7PtfmRgT7Q1kzZEVXUThMLWc/edit.

[12] *America's Right*, 91-95.

For one thing, the Supreme Court had handed down the *Roe v. Wade* decision, making abortion legal, two years before this conference-call conversation. And if you imagine that there was quite an outcry from the ranks and pulpits of the conservative church as a result, . . . well, you're wrong.

In fact, W. A. Criswell, head of the Southern Baptist Convention (SBC) in 1971, had put forth at the SBC conference that year a resolution supporting "legislation that will allow the possibility of abortion under such conditions as rape, incest, clear evidence of severe fetal deformity, and carefully ascertained evidence of the likelihood of damage to the emotional, mental, and physical health of the mother."[13] After the *Roe v. Wade* decision, Criswell again affirmed his belief that life begins at birth. There was no official SBC stance on abortion in 1973.

Roman Catholics, with their longer tradition of focus on reproductive issues, had been more deeply engaged in the abortion issue[14] than had evangelicals and fundamentalists at the time of *Roe v. Wade*. Now in 1975, the Religious Right[15] and New Right leaders saw the political advantage of joining forces with the Catholics on the matter.

Christian Reconstructionism: Small number, wide impact

Not all Christians avoided politics until the mid-1970s. In 1965, R. John Rushdoony (1916–2001), a strong Calvinist Christian from an Armenian immigrant family, started the Christian Reconstructionist

---

[13] Randall Balmer, *Thy Kingdom Come: How the Religious Right Distorts the Faith and Threatens America* (New York: Basic Books, 2006), 11-12.
[14] The Right to Life Committee is a Catholic organization instituted in 1968.
[15] Jerry Falwell used this term to refer to himself and like-minded Christians who associated with conservative Republican politics. The Religious Right was known by other names: the New Christian Right and the Christian Right. The basic tenets of this politically conservative, religious voting bloc are small government, undefined strict separation of church and state, support of Israel as a sovereign nation, conservative politics, no or limited sex education in public schools, school prayer in public schools, school voucher systems to support private Christian schools, anti-abortion, anti-homosexuality, and belief in Creationism as opposed to evolution.

movement in Southern California. The movement is known by several names, including dominionism and Kingdom theology.

In its most basic form, Christian Reconstructionism is a spin-off of Calvinism that started with a detour at the turn of the 20th century.[16] It was then that Danish theologian Abraham Kuyper declared, "There is not a square inch in the whole domain of our human existence over which Christ, who is sovereign over all, does not cry: Mine!"[17] Next, Cornelius Van Til (1895–1987), another Danish theologian, refined and narrowed the ideology, drawing stricter lines between Christians and non-Christians. Next, Rushdoony created the most extreme form of dominionism—Christian Reconstructionism, which holds that civil government should decrease, and even wither away, while church government moves into its place. All institutions, whether educational or social-welfare institutions, should be administered by Christians so they may bring the kingdom of God to earth more quickly. Ideally, the federal government would be stripped down to matters of defense, justice, and a State Department.

Reconstructionism held sway in the Southern California evangelical movement from the 1960s to the 1990s. It impacted many of the televangelists and high-profile religious leaders of the 1970s and 1980s, who believed they had been given a call to rescue America from destruction and immorality by ushering in an age of biblical law. Though many evangelicals may not call themselves Reconstructionists, the policies have infiltrated much of the conservative church. The goal of a theonomy, in which God's Law supersedes human law, hovers just at their horizon.

Today, we see three movements, all rooted in Rushdoony's Christian Reconstructionist theology, blurring lines and sharing values as they intersect: dominionism, the Tea Party, and the citizen militia movement.

---

[16] James C. Sanford, *Blueprint for Theocracy: Examining a Radical "Worldview" and Its Roots* (Providence, RI: Metacomet Books, 2014), 57-119.

[17] Ibid., 70.

Looking ahead to the 1980 elections

Looking toward the coming years, the New Right and the Religious Right still needed to expand their voter base further. They needed something powerful enough to reach deep into the fundamentalist and Reconstructionist base which, since the turn of the century, had been motivated by fear and belief in a mandate from a holy and vengeful God to save America from moral decay and destruction.

Enter the gays.

Chapter 6

The Start of a Bad Marriage
The Religious Right and the New Right Merge

Anita Bryant, the catalyst for anti-gay and pro-gay activism

Anita Bryant (1940–) began a one-woman crusade to halt proposed non-discrimination policies that would have protected gays in her local municipality, Dade County, Florida. Bryant's story warrants attention because she was the catalyst not only for the anti-gay conservative Christian movement but for the nationwide gay liberation movement as well.

Bryant was America's darling. A former Miss Oklahoma (1958) and second runner-up for 1959 Miss America, she met and married Bob Green, a Miami disc jockey, at the age of twenty. With Green as her manager, she recorded several moderate hits over the next fifteen years. Bryant travelled with the Billy Graham Crusade and the Bob Hope Tour to Vietnam, sang at the Super Bowl, and performed at both the Republican and Democratic Conventions, the White House, and Lyndon Johnson's funeral.

In 1969, she became the spokesperson for the Florida Citrus Commission and was nationally known for the ditty "Come to the Florida Sunshine Tree," with the famous tagline "Breakfast without orange juice is like a day without sunshine." She was a well-paid and recognizable celebrity, and in March of the same year, Bryant spoke at the Rally for Decency, held in Miami.

Three weeks earlier, a warrant had been issued for the arrest of The Doors' Jim Morrison for indecency. Morrison, just twenty-four years old and addicted to both drugs and alcohol, had incited the crowd at one of his concerts. Stunningly handsome, he took off his shirt and offered to do the same with his pants. In reaction, it's estimated that perhaps half of the concert-goers completely stripped down. All reliable testimonies indicate, however, that Morrison himself never did anything lewd; he was too intoxicated to strip.

In reaction to the mayhem and arrest warrant, a grassroots effort on the part of a Catholic teen and his youth group spearheaded the Rally for Decency, which drew 30,000 people, half of them youth and half adults, to the Orange Bowl. The rally featured several notable conservative voices calling for a higher level of decency in the entertainment industry. In attendance were Kate Smith, The Lettermen, Jackie Gleason, and Anita Bryant. Bryant, after all, had an image of wholesomeness about her that attracted public attention.

By the mid-1970s, Bryant and her husband/manager were raising their four children in the Miami area, home to a sizable gay community during those years. Under the organizational skills of a wealthy gay Miamian, Jack Campbell, enough support was raised to lobby for anti-discrimination laws in Dade County. Ruth Shack, a newly elected Dade County Metro Commissioner, had a record of experience and success in civil rights and feminist causes, so gay equality was a natural extension of her work.

Shack's husband and Bryant's husband had established a friendship over business dealings. Ironically, considering the actions Shack would soon take, as a favor to Shack, Bryant had recorded a radio campaign ad promoting her election. One wonders what Bryant thought when, one month into Shack's term as commissioner, she sponsored an amendment to the county's non-discrimination policy to include those with variant "affection or sexual preferences." The amendment got past the first hurdle; by a vote of 9–0, the County Commissioners approved it.

Since the Stonewall Riots, there had been little objection anywhere in the nation to the gay community speaking out for and obtaining equal civil rights. In fact, gays had already succeeded in winning non-discrimination ordinances in several cities. The vote might have proceeded unnoticed, but instead of passing into obscurity and going the way of such efforts in other cities and counties, the Dade County non-discrimination proposal became the genesis of a major clash between two movements: the political New Right and the Religious Right, versus the gay liberation movement.

Robert Brake, a Roman Catholic lawyer who had spent two years serving on the Dade County Metro Commission, was a friend of Bryant's. He happened to read in the newspaper the public notice of intent to add gays to the county's non-discrimination policy. Brake knew the county charter and understood that the non-discrimination bill could be forced to go to a popular vote if an opposing petition could gather enough signatures. Brake, whose children attended a local Catholic school, lamented to Bryant that he feared the hiring of gay men and lesbians as teachers for his children.

Bryant attended a Baptist church where her four children were enrolled in parochial school. Her pastor approached her about his concern that gay teachers might be legally protected in church jobs. Bryant, with an established connection to Shack, visited her office and asked her to rescind the policy. Shack would not consent.

Bryant responded by organizing a group to collect signatures to fight the ordinance. At the first press conference, Bryant spoke in front of a giant banner that read: "Save Our Children from Homosexuals." She announced to the media, "Homosexuals are trying to recruit our children to homosexuality."[1]

We need to take a pause here to deal with Bryant's statement about gays recruiting children. It is an oft-repeated one. Recall the rhetoric of the period from the late 1940s to the 1960s about gays "recruiting" younger and/or susceptible people to homosexuality. Absolutely none of those claims were ever substantiated. The stereotypes, manufactured as part of the Lavender Scare, resulted from the frenzy of sexual psychopath laws targeting gays in the 1950s and 1960s. The claims that gays and lesbians recruited children have never been validated. So where did Bryant dig up this most powerful tool, which she used frequently and repeatedly to motivate people to fear what gays could supposedly do to children?

The answer goes back to the 1972 Democratic National Convention in Chicago, where a very small group of gay people, calling themselves the National Coalition of Gay Organizations, prepared the 1972 Gay Rights Platform. The platform they proposed listed nine civil rights at the federal level and eight at the state level, of which item number seven called for "Repeal of all laws governing the age of sexual consent."[2] The intent of this poorly worded platform item was to equalize the age of consent because many states' laws led to unequal treatment of gay couples compared to straight couples.[3] In my home state of Nevada, for example, prior to the 2013 legislative session, the legal age of consent for heterosexual relations was 16 whereas is was 18 for homosexual relations. This shows how long it's taken to achieve equality on this particular point of the 1972 platform.

Despite its official name, the National Coalition of Gay Organizations was not a well-unified coalition of activist groups; in fact, there were

[1] Anita Bryant, *The Anita Bryant Story: The Survival of Our Nations' Families and the Threat of Militant Homosexuality* (Old Tappan, N.J.: Fleming H. Revell, 1977), 61.
[2] "The Gay Rights Platform," *All Things Queer: Gay and Lesbian Issues*, http://www.rslevinson.com/gaylesissues/features/collect/onetime/bl_platform1972.htm.
[3] *Anita Bryant Story*, 90.

only two openly gay delegates at the conference.[4] The Coalition was simply a gathering of two men and two women who wanted to gain the support of other convention-goers and bring attention to the issue of gay rights. The hopeful group booked a convention room large enough for three hundred people; however, their meeting was not placed on the official list of events, and because convention organizers considered it low-priority, it was scheduled late at night in a hard-to-find room in the convention center. Only two dozen reporters attended, and the meeting was not generally considered a success. However, the 1972 Gay Rights Platform was published and became available to anyone who might want to read it.

This platform—specifically the wording of item seven—provided Anita Bryant and others with "proof" that gay people wanted to "recruit" children. Social and religious conservatives have repeated and perpetuated this myth for the past forty-plus years!

On January 18, 1977, Bryant led the newly organized Save Our Children (SOC) campaign into the Dade County chambers. Angry, gay-fearing protesters joined her. Still, the commissioners, led by Shack, were determined to extend equal civil rights, and passed the non-discrimination ordinance. Unlike in any other city or at any previous time, Christian conservatives had mobilized and circulated a petition at twenty local churches, gathering over 12,000 signatures in hopes of stopping the non-discrimination law. When it passed, they demanded a referendum to rescind it. The commission agreed to a June 7 special election.

Bryant's husband, Bob Green, tried to dissuade his wife from leading the movement.[5] Her involvement and celebrity was making the Dade County ordinance into a national story and battle, and he feared that

---

[4] Steve Kastenbaum, "The DNC and Gay Rights 40 Years Later," CNN Radio, September 4, 2012, http://cnnradio.cnn.com/2012/09/04/the-dnc-and-gay-rights-40-years-later/.

[5] Kate Sosin, "Talking with the Son of Bob Green and Anita Bryant," Windy City Media Group, March 7, 2012, http://www.windycitymediagroup.com/lgbt/Talking-with-the-son-of-Bob-Green-and-Anita-Bryant/36564.html.

such negative attention would snowball and that their family would suffer as a result. As her business manager, perhaps he was also concerned about the impact it might have on the family's income. But again, Bryant's pastor encouraged her to move forward, even telling her she was "God's mother for America,"[6] chosen and sent by God for this service. Bryant amassed local support from church leaders; preacher after preacher denounced the amendment whose simple goal was to extend hiring and firing protection to gay people in Dade County.

Very little response came from the local gay community. Nationwide, gays were in the infancy stage of organization and completely unprepared to step up politically.

Though Ruth Shack appealed to the recently formed (1973) National Gay and Lesbian Task Force (NGLTF) for help, they were not yet able to react to the growing impact of Save Our Children. Afterwards, a spokesperson for NGLTF correctly stated, "[This incident] wildly demonstrated just why gay rights laws are needed—in order to protect our people against this sort of ignorant, irrational, unjustifiable prejudice typified by Anita Bryant."[7]

Jesse Helms, a conservative Republican senator from North Carolina, called Bryant "a fine Christian woman fighting for decency and morality."[8] Pastor Jerry Falwell joined Bryant at a Save Our Children rally and declared, "Gays would just as soon kill you as look at you."[9]

Meanwhile, Green kept warning his wife to pull back. He was receiving complaints from pockets of Christians saying she was becoming too much of an extremist. Throughout America, the lines thickened between conservative churches and politicians on one side, and the rapidly organizing gay community on the other. But Bryant remained obsessed

---

[6] Steve Rothaus, "Gay Rights Debate Rages On 30 Years after Miami-Dade Challenge," *Gay South Florida*, June 10, 2007, http://miamiherald.typepad.com/gaysouthflorida/2007/06/gay_rights_deba.html.

[7] Dudley Clendinen, *Out for the Good: The Struggle to Build a Gay Rights Movement in America* (New York: Simon & Schuster, 2013), 300.

[8] Ibid., 300.

[9] Ibid., 306.

about the "gays-as-molesters" rhetoric and continued her tirades. "As a mother, I know the homosexuals cannot biologically reproduce children; therefore, they must recruit our children."[10]

The well-funded Save Our Children organization took out a full-page ad in the *Miami Herald* depicting a collage of newspaper articles about child molestation crimes from across the country. Any man who molested a boy was assumed to be homosexual. Save Our Children also undertook a massive television and radio campaign. The emotion-laden ads stirred up fear and hatred by pushing the myth that gays were child recruiters and molesters—an accusation that discounts all evidence that, overwhelmingly, it is *heterosexual* men who molest boys and girls.[11]

In June 1977, the anti-discrimination ordinance was repealed in a 69%–31% vote. Bryant declared, "Today, the laws of God and the cultural values of man have been vindicated."[12]

Skip ahead: Bryant's work ripples to affect gay adoption rights

In the aftermath of the Save Our Children landslide victory, the Florida legislature adopted a statute forbidding child adoption by gays. At the time the law was finally overturned thirty years later, Florida was the only state still banning gay adoption. The interesting story behind the overturning of the anti-gay adoption law shows a continued pattern of dishonesty, hypocrisy, and stereotyping of gays.

In the case of *Howard v. Child Welfare Agency Review Board,* the state of Arkansas, defending its ban on LGBT people adopting or fostering children, hired George Rekers (1948–) as an expert witness. Rekers is a psychologist, Southern Baptist minister, founding member of the Family Research Council, and former scientific advisor for the National

---

[10] *Anita Bryant Story*, 62.

[11] Gregory Herek, "Facts about Homosexuality and Child Molestation," University of California, Davis, 2013.

[12] Darren Dochuk, *From Bible Belt to Sun Belt: Plain Folk Religion, Grassroots Politics, and the Rise of Evangelical Conservatism* (New York: W.W. Norton and Company, 2011), 381.

Association for Research and Therapy of Homosexuality (NARTH), which was co-founded in 1992 by Dr. Charles Socarides and Dr. Joseph Nicolosi.

Rekers' performance as a witness was vilified by Circuit Court Judge Timothy Fox, who ruled against the state of Arkansas in December 2004, thus allowing gay adoption. Fox was strongly critical of Rekers' testimony, describing it as "extremely suspect" and saying that Rekers "was there primarily to promote his own personal ideology."[13] Despite this judge's assessment, and against strong recommendations by the Arkansas Attorney General, who called Rekers a "right-wing, religious-based expert,"[14] the Florida Attorney General hired Rekers as an expert witness in 2008 as Florida defended its thirty-year ban of gay adoption.

In his expert testimony, Rekers stated that gay people have higher incidences of substance abuse, depression, and infidelity than do heterosexual people. He claimed that gay people were, therefore, incapable of "providing a safe and secure and emotionally stable environment for the child." Rekers was paid $60,900 by the State of Florida for his testimony.[15] He promoted his personal ideology, not facts, and his testimony was again found "not credible nor worthy of forming the basis of public policy."[16]

In April 2010, Rekers went on a ten-day European vacation without his wife. He visited the website Rentboy.com, a site for gay men, to hire 20-year-old "Lucien" for the trip. When a photo of Rekers and the "rent boy" appeared in the *Miami New Times* on May 4, Rekers acknowledged hiring "Lucien" for the vacation as a "travel assistant" and denied any impropriety. He said "Lucien" was there to help carry his luggage since

---

[13] John Schwartz, "Scandal Stirs Legal Questions in Anti-Gay Cases," *New York Times*, May 18, 2010.

[14] Attorney General's Office, "Records Show Attorney General Hired George Rekers Despite Warnings." *The Miami Herald Florida*, June 5, 2010, http://www.miamiherald.com/2010/06/05/1664521/records-show-attorney-general.html.

[15] Rachel Sladja, "Rekers Was Key Witness for McCollum in Defense of FL Gay Adoption Ban," *Talking Points Memo*, May 8, 2010, http://talkingpointsmemo.com/muckraker/rekers-was-key-witness-for-mccollum-in-defense-of-fl-gay-adoption-ban.

[16] Ibid.

he had had recent surgery and was unable to carry it himself, although the photograph clearly showed Rekers lifting his own luggage.

Rekers defended himself by saying that he had "spent much time as a mental health professional and as a Christian minister helping and lovingly caring for people identifying themselves as gay." In his denial of any inappropriate behavior, Rekers said, "I deliberately spend time with sinners with the loving goal to try to help them. If you talk with my travel assistant in that story called 'Lucien,' you will find I spent a great deal of time sharing scientific information on the desirability of abandoning homosexual intercourse, and I shared the Gospel of Jesus Christ with him in great detail."[17]

In May 2010, NARTH announced that Rekers had resigned from its board, closing the chapter on this "expert's" influence. We'll revisit NARTH in Chapter 14 during the discussion of reparative therapy for gay youth, a treatment option they endorse to this day.

Back to the past: Bryant across America

Fresh from her victory in Dade County in 1977, Bryant began to tour America, pushing her gay-as-molester-and-recruiter message and leading the fight against any non-discrimination policies emerging to protect gay people. Conservative Christian leaders began to notice that Bryant had tapped into an issue capable of stirring more passionate responses than had abortion or tax exemption for Christian institutions. As more and more Christian individuals and organizations joined the cause, the gay community responded with larger and more organized national activism efforts. Motivated by the fervor surrounding Bryant's extremism, many gays and lesbians became involved in the struggle for civil rights for the first time. Gay Pride events saw record attendance in 1978 and 1979.

---

[17] Brian Montopoli, "George Rekers, Christian Right Leader, Denies Gay Prostitution Allegation," CBS News, May 6, 2010, http://www.cbsnews.com/news/george-rekers-christian-right-leader-denies-gay-prostitution-allegation/.

Bryant travelled to Minneapolis-St. Paul and helped lead a duplicate of the Dade County campaign. Once again, she focused on the core message: "Homosexuals" should not be extended "special rights" or be allowed in schools where they would surely recruit children.[18] Priests, pastors, and civic leaders testified against the gay community in public hearings. The non-discrimination bill died in Minneapolis-St. Paul. As Bryant went from city to city on her "crusade against homosexuality," she gained still greater support from conservatives. She helped block non-discrimination legislation in Wichita, Kansas; Eugene, Oregon; Champaign-Urbana, Illinois; and Iowa City and Ames, Iowa.

Along the way, she ran into a pie.

During a televised press conference in Des Moines, Iowa, in October 1977, a gay activist approached the table where Bryant and her husband were sitting and hit her in the face with a fruit pie. In iconic video footage, Bryant, with tears rolling down her cheeks, began to pray with her husband for the pie tosser, and the couple publicly forgave him. But Green, who left his forgiveness behind when the cameras stopped rolling, went out into the parking lot, found the pie tosser, and threw his one remaining pie in the activist's face.

Bryant continued her march across the country, one success following another. She finally met her match in California, where there was a growing gay grassroots resistance to her cause. The day the non-discrimination ordinance failed in Dade County, the California gay community had been watching, and five thousand protesters merged on the Castro District. Just two days after the Dade County decision, conservative Republican Assemblyman John Briggs introduced California Proposition 6, commonly known as The Briggs Amendment. Bryant went to California to help support this amendment intended to ban gays and lesbians, and anyone supporting civil rights for them, from working in California public schools.

---

[18] *The Anita Bryant Story*, 96.

Briggs was sure he could rally a majority of Californians behind him and eventually help pave his way to a State Senate seat, or possibly even the governor's mansion. Four months before the vote, the majority of Californians were behind Briggs two to one, but the gay community had begun to awaken and respond. The various legislations across the nation, intended to drive the gay community into the closet and silence them, had an unintended opposite effect in California.

Under the encouragement and leadership of San Francisco Board of Supervisors member Harvey Milk, the first openly gay politician in the United States, gay people came out of the closet by the thousands. Milk had noticed that taking a low profile while attempting to elevate the conversation to one of civil liberties and infringement on privacy had not stopped the anti-gay vote in any cities where the policies had previously been set forth. Milk also knew that people were twice as likely to support civil rights for gay people if they knew a gay person, so he encouraged LGBT people to tell their families and neighbors about their sexuality: "Gay people, we will not win our rights by staying quietly in our closets. . . . We are coming out to fight the lies, the myths, the distortions. We are coming out to tell the truths about gays, for I am tired of the conspiracy of silence, so I'm going to talk about it. And I want you to talk about it. You must come out."[19]

Within weeks of the announcement of the Briggs Initiative, emotions in California escalated. A gay sheriff committed suicide when someone outed him. Robert Hillsborough, a gay gardener, was stabbed to death by four attackers outside his apartment in the Mission District. As they stabbed him, they screamed, "Faggot! Faggot! Faggot! Here's one for Anita!"[20]

In the wake of the violence and crushing threat of active discrimination against gays, Gay Freedom Day in June 1977 in San Francisco drew over 250,000 people. Voters viewed the restrictions on gay and lesbian

---

[19] "Harvey Milk – Biography," The Harvey Milk Foundation, http://milkfoundation.org/about/harvey-milk-biography/.
[20] Randy Shilts, The Mayor of Castro Street (New York: St. Martin's Press, 2008), 163.

people as the most severe in the country. Harvey Milk had proven him-self able to gain significant respect and authority in San Francisco city government among the gays, the unions, minority groups, and blue-col-lar workers. And in the end, on November 7, 1978, the Briggs Initiative failed 58%–42%.

Dan White, one of the most conservative members of the San Francisco Board of Supervisors, grew ever angrier at the influence of Milk, the expanding tolerance of homosexuality in his hometown, and his perception of corruption in city politics. Three weeks after the Briggs Initiative defeat, on November 27, 1978, White climbed through a window at City Hall and shot San Francisco Mayor George Moscone in the head, killing him. White then went to Milk's office and shot him five times, killing him as well.

Harvey Milk's death became a rallying point not only for the San Francisco gay community, but nationwide as well. Across the country, the gay community came together. Though the conservative Christian community had organized under Anita Bryant, she soon became a victim of her own political activism. When her contract with the Florida Citrus Commission ended, they did not renew it.

After losing this major source of endorsement income, Bryant and Green needed a new strategy to win back the hearts and minds of the American public. They decided on a kinder image, one showing Bryant's loving face while still insisting that homosexuality was evil and wrong. The couple wanted to create and host a place where people could stay and work on not being gay. In 1979, Green called the offices of a fledg-ling organization named Exodus International, a Christian ministry to gays and lesbians that had been formed in 1973 in California. He spoke to Michael Bussee, one of the Exodus founders.

Green tried to make it clear that Bryant was not a hater of gays; rather, she loved kids, and protecting them was her key motivation. Green sug-gested that Exodus provide some no-longer-gay men to go on the road with Green and Bryant as a "symbol of hope," and to portray Bryant as more loving toward gays. They needed some ex-gays as public props to "prove" that change was possible. Bussee made it clear to Green that Exodus did not want to engage in activism. Exodus opted to stay away from Bryant's work; Green was angry and disappointed.

In 1980, Bryant and Green's marriage failed and they were divorced. Bryant cited emotional abuse. She remarried a year later. The conservative Christian community was still in the process of deciding what to do about Christian divorce. Many in Bryant's support base didn't forgive her when she filed for divorce. In an interview the same year with *Ladies Home Journal*, Bryant admitted several things she had hidden from the public during her nationwide crusade against the "sins" of homosexuality: She had become addicted to sleeping pills and tranquilizers; she and her husband had suffered problems from their honeymoon forward; and she strongly alluded to her own unfaithfulness in the marriage.[21] Rejected by the conservative Christian community, the woman who had made homosexuality the focal point of sin later said, "Fundamentalists have become so legalistic and letter-bound to the Bible."[22] In short, she fell on her own sword.

First American Christian books about gays

On the coattails of Anita Bryant, conservative Christians accelerated the pace and began to pump out books and create organizations for their part in the "war on homosexuals." Tim LaHaye (1928–), best known as the co-author of the *Left Behind* series, entered the "crusade against homosexuality" early on. Tyndale House Publishing approached LaHaye and urged him to write a book, pleading, "The Christian community needs a penetrating book on homosexuality. Why don't you write it?" LaHaye consented, convinced that America was experiencing

---

[21] Barbara Stewart, "Anita Bryant: From Star to Pariah, Now She's in Between," *Chicago Tribune*, May 1, 1988, http://articles.chicagotribune.com/1988-05-01/features/8803130720_1_anita-bryant-phil-varone-orange-juice/3.
[22] "Anita Bryant Says She's Altered Style of Opposing Homosexuals," *Lawrence Journal–World*, November 15, 1980, http://news.google.com/newspapers?nid=2199&dat=19801115&id=srpfAAAAIBAJ&sjid=YecFAAAAIBAJ&pg=4466,2595018.

a "homosexual epidemic."[23] Rev. Dr. Derrick Sherwin Bailey had already, twenty-three years before, set the tone for a scripturally and historically accurate, well-researched, medically supported, and thoughtful investigation into homosexuality with movement toward a biblical stance that was both just and compassionate. Though Bailey's book, *Homosexuality and Western Traditions*, was available in the United States, the American Christian public was never really given the chance to consider his findings and recommendations.

Instead of Bailey's work, American conservative Christians were presented with LaHaye's book. As a staunch fundamentalist and part of the evangelical, Christian Reconstructionist, and dominionism movements, LaHaye approached the project from his belief that God would destroy America if we did not stop "the tidal wave of homosexuality."[24] With *no expertise* on the subject of homosexuality, LaHaye authored *The Unhappy Gays: What Everyone Should Know about Homosexuality*.

LaHaye had earned degrees from Bob Jones University and Western Seminary and had pastored a church for twenty-five years. You might hope his book would be based upon biblical exegesis of the verses in the Bible often associated with same-sex behavior. One would also imagine that he might have referred to or used Bailey's book as part of his research. Unfortunately, one would be wrong on both counts.

LaHaye's "research" materials consisted of three books: Anita Bryant's autobiography, Irving Bieber's 1962 *Homosexuality: A Psychoanalytic Study of Male Homosexuals*, and *Eros Defiled* by John White. Recall that Bieber's book was based on theories about gay men in therapy and had been fully discounted by the APA. In addition to these weak book references, LaHaye cited two pamphlets, one magazine article, and a *National Enquirer* piece[25] as his resources.

---

[23] Tim LaHaye, *The Unhappy Gays: What Everyone Should Know about Homosexuality* (Wheaton, IL: Tyndale House Publishers, 1978), 8.
[24] Ibid., 204.
[25] Ibid., 207.

LaHaye's disgust with and fear of gays are apparent on every page of his book. Although he briefly mentions the Bible verses associated with same-sex behavior, his writings place greater emphasis on how disgusting, unfaithful, rebellious, sick, and sexually depraved gay people are. *The Unhappy Gays: What Everyone Should Know about Homosexuality* was the first American conservative Christian book on the subject of homosexuality, and was presumed by the church to contain expert information.

Many gay Christians who were young adults or teenagers in the late 1970s and the 1980s remember this book *vividly,* as they read it seeking answers about their sexual orientation.

Following are a few quotes from LaHaye's book:

- "Moral fidelity among homosexuals is almost unknown." (p. 31)
- "Current research indicates that the family most likely to produce a homosexual is comprised [sic] of a very intimate, possessive and dominating mother and a detached, hostile father. Many mothers of lesbians tend to be hostile and competitive with their daughters." (p. 71) [Note that this opinion was only given credence in the psychoanalytic community from the 1940s to the 1960s. By 1978, this family-origin theory of homosexuality had been thoroughly debunked.]
- "Homosexuals who want to change can marry and set in motion a chain reaction in which heterosexual experience gradually increases their ability to experience heterosexual pleasures." (p. 89)
- "All true Christians should oppose homosexuality, for it is wrong and exceedingly dangerous to society." (p. 149)
- "One major objective [of Christian parents] is to raise children to glorify God. Many such parents would prefer the death of their child to him adopting the unhappy wretchedness of homosexuality." (p. 157)

- "They are out to force the acceptance of the deviant behavior as normal in the creation of a climate conducive to recruitment. The homosexual community, by militants and secret political maneuvering, is designing a program to increase the tidal wave of homosexuality that will drown our children in the polluted sea of sexual perversion." (p. 179)
- "Many homosexuals and police officials indicate that their number is increasing at an alarming rate because they make it their business to recruit. As I have said before, if some homosexuals didn't recruit, they would become extinct because they do not propagate." (p. 193)

This information became a dagger driven into the souls of gay people, many of them young and trying to come to grips with their own sexuality. Many of my older gay friends have told me that *The Unhappy Gays: What Everyone Should Know about Homosexuality* succeeded in keeping them deeply closeted and fearful, especially if they read it during adolescence, or even their early twenties. Along with *Everything You Always Wanted to Know about Sex but Were Afraid to Ask,* it is the resource older gay adults now mention most frequently as the secret reading material they found and investigated as young people hoping to find answers about their sexual orientation. LaHaye's book in particular helped set the tone for the interaction between the conservative church and the gay community by escalating fear and paranoia.

Get 'em saved, get 'em baptized, get 'em registered

Once Bryant had stirred the slumbering conservative Christians, dozens of Christian political and activist groups formed. In 1978, Paul Weyrich (see Chapter 5) co-created Christian Voice, the first Christian political activist group, with Baptist minister Robert Grant (1936–). Its mission was to combat "legalized abortion, pornography, limitations on school prayer, [and] rampant homosexuality."[26] Using the mass-mailing marketing innovations of Richard Viguerie, Christian Voice compiled a contact list of 107,000 people, including 37,000 pastors from forty-five denominations.

Ever intent on finding new and innovative ways to rally the religious right, Weyrich and Viguerie looked to Robert Billings to help establish and organize a nationwide network of Christian schools, which had started popping up everywhere after the 1958 ban on organized school prayer.

Robert Billings had bought into Weyrich's clever revisionist view which repositioned Bob Jones University's right to segregate as a matter of Christian religious liberty. He formed the National Christian Action Coalition (NCAC) and travelled around the country meeting with pastors and televangelists and speaking about the "dangers" of the IRS "attack" on private schools. Eventually, Weyrich convinced Billings to relocate to Washington, D.C., to spearhead the Christian schools' fight against the IRS. In 1979, as President Jimmy Carter was preparing for his second term in the White House, Weyrich was trying to identify a rising evangelical leader who might serve as a figurehead for a grassroots movement to mobilize religious conservatives. It was Billings who helped Weyrich identify Rev. Jerry Falwell (1933–2007) as the best candidate for front man of a planned political/religious organization. As the host of the nationally syndicated *Old-Time Gospel Hour* TV show and founder of Liberty Baptist College (founded in 1971 and later named Liberty University), Falwell already had a substantial following.

Billings invited Weyrich and Viguerie to a meeting he had organized with Jerry Falwell. Falwell, with his fundamentalist roots, had once been *adamantly* opposed to Christian involvement in politics, but the events of the recent Anita Bryant years had changed his mind. During the group conversation, Weyrich commented, "Out there, there is a

---

[26] Robert B. Horowitz, *America's Right: Anti-establishment Conservatism from Goldwater to the Tea Party* (Malden, ME: Polity, 2013), 95.

moral majority, but it has been separated by denominational and historical differences."[27] Falwell replied, "Stop, what did you say was out there? You said that out there, there is something?" Weyrich repeated what he had said. Falwell liked the term "moral majority" and proposed it become the name of the religiously based, politically motivated group. Thus, in 1979, the Moral Majority was born.

The Moral Majority was disappointed with sitting President Carter. At the time of his election, the Southern Baptist had been given a list of hundreds of names of evangelical Christians as suggested appointments in exchange for the successful delivery of conservative votes. Because Carter did not call or appoint anyone from the list to a high-level position, the Moral Majority vowed to replace him in the next election.

The Moral Majority was driven to bring the Christian vote to the GOP. Falwell famously repeated his mantra over and over: "Get 'em saved, get 'em baptized, get 'em registered."[28] The mission of the organization was to identify, register, educate, and rally conservative religious voters, including fundamentalists, evangelicals, Roman Catholics, Mormons, and conservative mainline Christians. Falwell became the public voice of the Moral Majority, and Billings was named its executive director. Part of the organization's goal was to push back the "degradation" of the liberal culture rooted in such evils as feminism, abortion, homosexuality, pornography, and sex education in schools. (The inclusion of abortion as an issue was a Moral Majority tactic to shift Catholic voters of the John F. Kennedy years away from the Democratic Party.)

The Moral Majority was primarily a direct-mail organization claiming a membership of up to 50 million people at its peak. Falwell learned to influence the influencers. His personal interaction with pastors netted excellent results. Pastors who had previously protected their church membership mailing lists now willingly handed them over to the Moral Majority. In the midst of the Bryant war on

---

[27] "Q & A with Paul Weyrich," C-SPAN Cable, March 22, 2005, hosted by Brian Lamb, http://www.c span.org/video/?185929-1/qa-paul-weyrich.
[28] Slogan used at evangelical voter workshops and events.

gays, Falwell quickly learned that fear of gays was a good incentive for people to donate money. Thus, letters from the Moral Majority often spoke of things like losing "the war against homosexuals." A half-million targeted fundraising letters were sent out weekly, netting the organization up to $500 million per year.

Falwell also recruited Dr. James Dobson to help spread the anti-Carter message through Dobson's popular radio and media ministry, Focus on the Family.

Meanwhile, in Texas, national televangelist James Robison (1943–) emoted in a television-broadcast sermon (1979) that he was "sick and tired of hearing about all the radicals and perverts and the liberals and the leftists and the communists coming out of the closet" and was "ready for God's people to come out of the closet and take back the nation."[29] Robison, following on the heels of Bryant, and now countless others, accused gays of luring children into sex.

The owners of the television station that carried Robison's program were not pleased, and he was kicked off the Dallas airwaves. Robison's Director of Communications, a young Mike Huckabee, had dropped out of seminary after one year to take a job with Robison. Huckabee and Robison joined with local church leaders to stage a "Freedom Rally" in the Reunion Arena in April 1979 to protest Robison's dismissal from television. More than ten thousand people showed up. The majority of attendees were evangelicals, along with some Catholics who had recently joined forces with evangelicals over abortion. Weyrich was invited to speak and appeal to his fellow Catholics. The rally was successful, and the television station was pressured to put Robison's show back on the air. But something more significant and far-reaching happened at the Freedom Rally, which brought together many powerful religious leaders, including televangelist Robison, Pastor W. A. Criswell (President of the Southern Baptist Convention), Rev. Jerry Falwell, and Pastor Adrian

---

[29] "Reverend James Robison – God's People Speech," uploaded to YouTube by "Rezzonics," March 27, 2007, https://www.youtube.com/watch?v=so44kJNv9HE.

Rogers (1931–2005), three-time president of the SBC who had moved the denomination to a more conservative stance than did Criswell.

The pastors were interested in parlaying the momentum of the Freedom Rally into a culture-wide conservative political movement, so they invited the politically savvy Weyrich to offer insight on how they might achieve their goal. Weyrich told the group, "As I talk to you all, the big thing you keep telling me is that you'd like to be involved in public policy and politics, but your first mission is to Jesus Christ, and you don't think your congregations will tolerate your involvement in public policy."[30] They all agreed.

Weyrich suggested that a step in going forward would be to poll religious Americans with two simple questions: "Would you consent to your pastors becoming politically active?" and if so, "Would you be willing to give money to a religiously based political organization dedicated to furthering your religious political interests?"

Lance Tarrance, founder and president of a Houston-based national survey research company, was at the briefing. He estimated that such a poll might cost about $30,000.[31] Bob Perry (1932–2013), a Houston-based builder and owner of Perry Homes, pledged most of the money for the survey on the spot.[32]

The group in attendance became the core of the Religious Roundtable, organized to involve evangelical Christians in mainstream politics. One year later, at the 1980 Religious Roundtable meeting, Weyrich reported the results of the two-question survey: "Not only did they want their

---

[30] Dan Gilgoff, *The Jesus Machine: How James Dobson, Focus on the Family, and Evangelical America Are Winning the Culture War* (New York City: St. Martin's Press, 2010), 102.

[31] Ibid., 81.

[32] Perry was a major Republican contributor until his death in 2013. Some of his contributions include (starting with the more recent): Friends of Scott Walker ($500K), Freedom Fund North America PAC ($1 million), Texas Republican Party ($905K), American Crossroads Super PAC ($6.5 million in the 2012 elections), Mitt Romney ($10 million), Rick Perry ($2.5 million), and Swift Vets and POWs for Truth, a smear campaign against John Kerry for President in 2004 ($4.5 million). The man had money. Source: "Donor Profile: Bob Perry," The Center for Public Integrity, April 26, 2012, http://www.publicintegrity.org/2012/04/26/8466/donor-profile-bob-perry.

leaders involved in public policy, they were *clamoring* to have their leaders involved in public policy. Moreover, they said, 'Yes, we will financially support both organizations. We will not stop giving to [our home] church.'"[33]

In the 1980 election against incumbent Carter, the Moral Majority flexed its new political muscle. The candidate of choice was Gov. Ronald Reagan, a product of the evangelical base in Orange County, Southern California. A few complications did need to be addressed. Not only had Reagan divorced his first wife, which, to some voters, was somewhat forgivable, but he had also remarried, which was less acceptable to many conservatives. Divorce had been a major concern for conservative voters as recently as 1964, when they rejected divorced New York governor Nelson Rockefeller as the Republican presidential candidate. The spotlight had to be moved away from Reagan's divorce.

Complicating matters still further, Reagan had signed into law the Therapeutic Abortion Act of 1967 six months after taking office as governor of California. Whereas before the Act, fewer than five hundred abortions had taken place in California each year, after the Act, abortions averaged 100,000 per year during Reagan's two gubernatorial terms. Although his track record on abortion was less than stellar, he did alter his position once he was named a presidential candidate. (Interestingly, however, during his subsequent eight years in office, he did *nothing* about his campaign promise to reverse *Roe v. Wade*.)

While hopeful about electing Reagan to the presidency in 1980, the New Right and the Religious Right needed *another* social issue to rally the religious voters. Two years prior, Anita Bryant had handed them "the gays." When the conservative Christians gathered at the 1980 Religious Roundtable in Dallas, Falwell kept the group's focus on the gays and their threat to the morality, and indeed the very fabric, of America. He warned, "We are losing the war against homosexuality."[34]

---

[33] *The Jesus Machine*, 102.
[34] Ibid., 83.

Though the religious group was unable to officially endorse a candidate for president, savvy Reagan certainly did his part to make religious conservatives overlook his divorce and remarriage by actively courting their vote. For instance, he was the only Republican presidential candidate to show up at the Religious Roundtable conference. He told the crowd of 17,000, "I know you can't endorse me, but I want you to know that I endorse you and what you are doing."[35] He won them over.

Falwell continued to focus on gays. Gay soldiers had recently been given permission to lay a wreath at the Tomb of the Unknown Soldier to honor fallen gay and lesbian service personnel. In a subsequent Moral Majority fundraising letter, Falwell hammered home his anti-gay message, labeling the action as "[honoring] any sexual deviants who served in the military. That's right . . . The Tomb of the Unknown Sodomite!"[36] Falwell's frequent use of this type of rhetoric stirred up increased hatred and fear of the gay community.

After Reagan won the 1980 presidential race, Jerry Falwell and the Moral Majority claimed credit for securing and delivering the religious vote. In return, President Reagan appointed Moral Majority executive director Robert Billings, who had served as Reagan's religious advisor during the campaign, to be director over ten regional Department of Education offices.

In a typical show of political fickleness, religious leaders and the Moral Majority were not very pleased with President Reagan. For one thing, beyond Billings, Reagan appointed no other evangelicals to top posts in his administration. For another, as mentioned previously, in his two terms in the White House, he failed to heed the Moral Majority's expectations that he make abortion illegal again. Few Religious Right groups gained noticeable traction during the Reagan years. With a Religious Right–supported, Republican president securely in office, both the money going to and the public interest in the Moral Majority waned.

---

[35] *America's Right*, 17.
[36] Moral Majority Fundraising Letter, August 14, 1980.

In fact, neither abortion nor homosexuality was a focal point at the beginning of the Reagan White House. They had both served their purpose as vote-getting election tools.

The gay community mobilizes nationally

In March 1977, at the height of the Bryant-led uprising of conservative Christians in Florida, the Carter Administration opened the doors of the White House for the first time in history to receive a gay rights delegation. Although Jimmy Carter was not in attendance, his Public Liaison, Midge Costanza (1932–2010), a feminist and an early advocate for gay rights, invited fourteen gay and lesbian leaders for a formal meeting. In attendance were Frank Kameny and Rev. Troy Perry (founder of the Metropolitan Community Church [MCC]), both representing the National Gay and Lesbian Task Force (NGLTF). The group met in the room adjacent to the Oval Office, a symbolically powerful space. Rev. Perry was quite persuasive, telling many stories of violent and deadly attacks on the gay community, as well as recounting the burning down of the newly formed MCC home facility and other MCC churches. Although the NGLTF had gained official entrée into the White House, the gay community nationwide was in the fledgling stages of organizing and connecting.

Nationwide, gays and lesbians had become politicized in the wake of Anita Bryant's anti-gay crusades and the 1978 assassination of Harvey Milk. For the first time, the LGBT community's focus fell on the advancement of policy at the national, rather than the local or state, level. The 1979 National March on Washington for Lesbian and Gay Rights marked the beginning of the national gay liberation movement. The event included three days of workshops and a day of lobbying senators and representatives in Congress, and drew about 105,000 LGBT people and their supporters.

Delegates to the event's organizing committee, divided equally between men and women and with one-quarter minorities, had drawn up and agreed upon five demands as the focus of the March on Washington:

- Passage of a gay/lesbian rights bill in Congress
- A Presidential executive order banning discrimination based on sexual orientation in the federal government, military, and federally contracted projects
- Repeal of all anti-gay/lesbian laws
- End to the discrimination of gay-parent custody cases
- Protection of gay/lesbian youth in homes, schools, jobs, and social environments[37]

The document they produced may have been the closest thing to an authentic "gay agenda." On the day of the National March on Washington, it probably appeared as though the LGBT community, despite opposition from the Religious Right and the New Right, would continue to forge ahead toward civil equality.

Then, AIDS happened.

---

[37] "Gay & Lesbian March on Washington 1979," *Tucson Gay Museum*, http://tucsongay-museum.org/marchonwashington.htm.

Chapter 7

The Origin of HIV/AIDS and the Political-Christian Response

AIDS Is Not a "Gay Disease"

How did you respond to the AIDS crisis in America?

When AIDS was first identified in America in 1981, it was associated with a group of gay men in the Los Angeles area diagnosed with what appeared to be a skin cancer and/or pneumonia. In initial media reports, AIDS was referred to as a gay disease, the gay plague, gay cancer, and gay-related immune deficiency, or GRID. Given the existing negative attitudes toward gays in the late 1970s and early 1980s, it is not surprising that the political, cultural, and religious response to people with AIDS became another way of expressing prejudice against gay men.[1]

My own attitude was one of indifference. I didn't know anyone with AIDS, and along with one-fifth of Americans, I believed that people who

[1] G.M. Herek and J.P. Capitanio, "AIDS Stigma and Contact with Persons with AIDS: The Effects of Personal and Vicarious Contact," *Journal of Applied Social Psychology* 27 (1997): 1-36.

contracted AIDS through sexual behavior got what they deserved.[2] No one in my church or among my extended group of friends performed any form of service on behalf of those suffering from AIDS-related illnesses.

My friends Jan and Bob Bare were the rare exception. When their deeply ingrained religious righteousness was confronted with a personal experience, they allowed that experience to transform them. Through the AIDS crisis, Christians were given an opportunity to serve the sick and hurting and their families in desperate need and, in the process, be transformed into something more closely resembling Jesus. Where I failed, Bob and Jan succeeded. Jan tells their story:

> In the 1980s and early 1990s, no one in our evangelical circles believed you could be both gay and Christian. The common thread of teaching in most of the churches we grew up in was that all gay people were pedophiles. We were taught they'd committed so many horrible evils that they were turned over to the worst sin of all, homosexuality, and were demon-possessed. We believed all those things, even though we didn't know any gay people.
>
> We moved to Dallas, Texas, in 1989 with our three small children. My husband, Bob, got to know a gas station attendant named Roland, who was always upbeat with a great attitude about work. When he disappeared, Bob asked his boss where he'd gone and discovered he was in jail. Bob wrote to him, got on his visitors list, and eventually was instrumental in Roland becoming a Christian. We had no idea that he was gay.
>
> When Roland thought his dad was near death, the jailers would only release him if he had bail money, a place to live,

---

[2] Ibid.

and a job. We had just started a new business, so we offered Roland all three. He came to live with us and became a loved member of our family. Roland loved the Lord and always looked forward to going to church with us.

Roland didn't fit the stereotype of a gay man we had in our minds, and it took us six months to hear what he had tried to tell us in many ways.

Roland became a key employee of our new business, and Bob offered him life insurance. After his medical exam, a representative from the Texas Department of Health showed up at our door needing to see Roland. He had tested positive for HIV years before, and they hadn't been able to find him to let him know.

Fear, panic, and dread crashed down on us. Roland lived with us. Had our whole family been infected with AIDS? We needed help and answers, and because the church had so isolated itself from learning about HIV/AIDS, there was no one for us to turn to for good advice. One church member had a brother with AIDS and had tried to cast demons out of him. One church leader told us to "witness to homosexuals" but "not fellowship with them." There was so much we didn't know. We had been filled with years of misinformation and complete lies. AIDS Interfaith[3] became our lifeboat, and later, we joined as volunteers.

A year later, Roland woke up with a horrible headache and was admitted to the hospital. Three days later, the hospital called to tell us that he had passed away during the night.

---

[3] AIDS Interfaith Network, Dallas, TX, http://www.aidsinterfaithnetwork.org/.

Getting to know and love Roland had reshaped our thinking. At one time, we had read all the information we could find on ex-gay ministries, thinking that perhaps we were called to that. After Roland passed, we discovered a new mission.

Each day, when Bob brought home the newspaper, I would check the obituaries. At first, it started with one beautiful face, and soon I began clipping the obituaries of all the many gifted and educated young men that had died of AIDS. I began to be aware of their value and their many contributions to their friends, family, and community. So many were dying, and the church didn't seem to care.

One day, I felt compelled to go to a memorial service of a complete stranger that had caught my eye in the obituaries. The service was held at Grace Fellowship in Christ Jesus (GFIC Jesus), Dallas. I sat in the back of the church, hoping to go unnoticed. The memorial started with an extended time of worship. I didn't think gay people even knew a worship song! Wait, didn't they hate everything godly? I was sensing a presence that was unmistakably the Holy Spirit. I started to cry and could not stop. I thought God had tricked me!

That day was a turning point for Bob and me. It wasn't easy to grapple with what we had been taught compared to the visible evidence of God living in this group of people. We were invited to attend a church retreat with them in 1994, fell in love with the people, and ultimately joined the church. That was twenty years ago and we've never regretted it. We have been going to GFIC Jesus in Dallas, Texas, and love being a part of a church for ALL people.

Over thirty years have passed since the onset of the AIDS epidemic in the United States, yet when I read articles today from conservative sources regarding gay issues, inevitably the matter of HIV/AIDS is raised as a tool of condemnation.

Whatever the issue raised—same-sex marriage, the Boy Scouts, same-sex parenting, adoption, or fostering—HIV/AIDS becomes part of the discussion. For some people, "HIV is a 'gay disease'" is just a thought away. People have believed, and some still do believe, that AIDS is God's punishment unleashed on the gay community for participating in what they deem to be sexual immorality.

For some, Romans 1:27 is sufficient proof of God's displeasure: "Men committed shameful acts with other men, and received in themselves the due penalty for their perversion" (NIV). Therefore, some claim, it follows that AIDS is surely the due penalty for anal sex. A surprising segment of the Christian population believes many falsehoods about HIV/AIDS, its origins, and its connection to the Bible.

Tennessee State Senator Stacey Campfield, when commenting as recently as 2012 on how he believed AIDS started, replied, "It was one guy screwing a monkey, if I recall correctly, and then having sex with men. It was an airline pilot, if I recall."[4] Well, not quite. In fact, not at all. Yet variations on that and similar myths are common understandings of the origin of AIDS.

People with HIV or AIDS-related illnesses are hence reduced to a morality issue or a sex act: "It's God's punishment. It's God's judgment on the way gays have sex. It's deserved." Mistaken beliefs about AIDS and its origin create lenses through which some individuals, and even some whole religious denominations, view and assess the gay community.

The intended focus of this chapter is not to reconstruct the history of the HIV/AIDS crisis in America; that is well-documented in countless

---

[4] Jonathan Meador, "Stacey Campfield on the Origin of AIDS: 'It Was One Guy Screwing a Monkey,'" *Nashville Scene*, January 26, 2012.

sources.[5] This chapter takes an approach consistent with the overall structure of this book, inviting the reader to consider how something may have impacted the way in which they engage the gay, lesbian, bisexual, and transgender (LGBT) community. Here are some questions to consider as you read this chapter:

- If you were an adult between 1981 and the late 1990s, what were your reactions to the AIDS crisis? What is the truth about how AIDS came to be and how it spread?
- How does your understanding line up with the truth? What might you do with new understanding when the topic next comes up in conversation with someone?

In this chapter we'll examine the origin of HIV/AIDS, the stigma associated with the disease in relation to the gay community, and the response to the crisis by officials, the public, and people of faith, including what a Christ-like response to those suffering from HIV/AIDS in the United States in the 1980s and 1990s might have looked like. I invite you to strip away the lies and myths you might have believed about HIV/AIDS as we remove another layer of judgment used against the gay, lesbian, bisexual, and transgender community.

What is HIV/AIDS?

The human immune system is able to eliminate most viruses. That doesn't happen with HIV (Human Immunodeficiency Virus) because it attacks the immune system. Scientists don't know why HIV doesn't operate like most viruses.[6]

---

[5] *And the Band Played On* by Randy Shilts is a popular account in book form; countless documentaries are also available online.
[6] AIDS is a different diagnosis: When T-cells fall below 200 cells/mcL and there is an opportunistic infection or disease present, then a diagnosis of AIDS is made. People who have not fallen below that medical line are referred to as HIV-positive.

The HIV virus can hide in the body for long periods—even decades. As it manifests, HIV attacks T-cells, or CD4 cells, which are necessary for the body to fight infection and disease. Once inside the cells, HIV replicates itself and destroys the protective T-cells and CD4 cells. After exposure to HIV, most newly infected people experience flulike symptoms. Others, however, are asymptomatic and have no physical indication of infection.

Even throughout the latency period, the HIV virus can infect other people. The virus is transmitted person-to-person via several body fluids: blood, saliva, anal mucous, semen, pre-seminal fluid, vaginal fluids, and breast milk. HIV can be transmitted during unprotected anal, vaginal, and oral sex. It's also transmitted from mother to child during pregnancy, or in childbirth. Intravenous drug users sharing needles contaminated with HIV-infected blood can spread the disease from one user to another. Health care workers are at risk unless proper precautions are used while doing blood work. Finally, although extremely rare in the United States, blood transfusions and organ transplants from HIV-infected donors can transmit the virus.

AIDS (Acquired Immune Deficiency Syndrome[7]) is a breakdown of the immune system caused by the final stages of HIV infection. People with badly damaged immune systems develop AIDS, thus putting the body at risk for developing opportunistic diseases. AIDS is not a disease per se; rather, it is a syndrome, or a collection of signs and symptoms of diseases. In late stages of HIV infection, AIDS can manifest in an immune system so damaged that it can't fight cancer and other diseases.

In 1981, the initial cases of AIDS in the United States were identified as a rare pneumonia among gay men and intravenous drug users. People with severely compromised immune systems developed a rare opportunistic pneumonia, called Pneumocystis carinii pneumonia. Affected drug users died quickly. For reasons unknown at the time,

---

[7] Also written as "acquired immunodeficiency syndrome."

the process was slower for others. Many gay men developed a rare skin cancer called Kaposi's sarcoma.

Where did HIV/AIDS come from?

The academically peer-reviewed, widely accepted, and historically documented beginnings of HIV/AIDS are best traced in an excellent book, *The Origins of AIDS*, written by infectious disease specialist Dr. Jacques Pepin.[8] Dr. Pepin combined his education in epidemiology, his medical work in the African bush, and his research on colonial law and African history to recreate and document the most probable path of HIV/AIDS from its beginnings until now.

The HIV/AIDS story starts around 1921 in Gabon, in an area between the Sanaga River in Cameroon and the Congo River in the former Belgian Congo (later called Zaire, and now the Democratic Republic of the Congo). In this semi-isolated place, one subspecies of non-swimming chimpanzees known as the *Pan troglodytes troglodytes* (Pan t. t.), have been bound in their native habitat between the two rivers for many thousands of years. The chimps developed simian immunodeficiency virus (SIV). *Pan t. t.* SIV probably originated from the recombination of distinct types of SIV infecting smaller monkeys: the red-capped mangabeys and spot-nosed guenons, which were hunted and eaten by the *Pan t. t.*s.[9] Using scientific methods, researchers have concluded that about 6%[10] of *Pan t. t.*s may have been infected with SIV, which they then passed around their population through sexual transmission and blood from injuries sustained while fighting. SIV may well have been present in the *Pan t. t.* population for hundreds of years. Although human populations (Bantus and pygmies) had lived in close proximity to the infected *Pan t. t.* chimps for around two thousand years,[11] they never came into physical contact with the animals. Even if they could

---

[8] Jacques Pepin, *The Origins of AIDS* (Cambridge: Cambridge University Press, 2011).
[9] Ibid., 31.
[10] Ibid., 29
[11] Ibid., 221.

have captured the chimps, cultural taboos in several ethnic groups and tribes kept the native populations from considering the chimps a food source as they looked too much like humans.[12] The millennia-old natural balance and separation between humans and chimps was not upset until the early 1900s.

Industrialization in Europe demanded a constant flow of natural resources. Military forces from several European nations competitively and aggressively pushed their way throughout Africa, gaining political and economic control over the continent. By the early 20th century, all but Ethiopia and Liberia had been colonized by European powers. With the presence of the Europeans came their appetites. Whereas the native populations had avoided the chimps, white colonialists had the guns necessary to hunt the large and fast *Pan t. t.*s. So they hunted, killed, ate, and sold the chimps' meat to satisfy their colonialist desire for bush meat. SIV-infected blood in the *Pan t. t.*s entered the hunters' blood system through wounds they got while butchering the animals. Because *Pan t. t.*s share about 99% similarity in genomes with humans,[13] the SIV virus took hold in the humans and adapted, becoming HIV. Using census records, chimp population estimations, and application of molecular clock dating on HIV virus cells in archived blood samples, scientists have traced the HIV virus back to as few as two or three infected white hunters in the Congo in the early 1920s.[14] Though the HIV virus went unnoticed at the time, AIDS-related symptoms, such as brain atrophy, have been found in archival records of numerous autopsies. The numbers were simply too low then for anyone to notice the pattern.

Two cultural shifts permanently impacting the African population occurred as a direct result of European colonization: urbanization and urban prostitution.[15]

---

[12] Ibid., 45.
[13] Ibid., 18.
[14] Ibid., 222-223.
[15] Ibid., 223.

France and Belgium had staked their claims in the Congo and were engaging in the exportation of raw products (copper, cobalt, gold, manganese, rubber, coffee, cocoa, cotton, palm oil, and diamonds).[16] From 1921 through 1934, French and Belgian colonizers built two massive and competing railroad lines to carry their countries' exports to the Atlantic Ocean. The rail lines ran closely parallel from their respective capital cities, Brazzaville (French Congo) and Leopoldville (Belgian Congo), to the coast. The construction projects prompted the populations to explode to a previously unheard-of count of over 23,000 workers in the new twin cities.[17]

Where there are men, "supply women" will follow. Prostitution was at first fueled by the sexual needs of the European support population. The number of prostitutes increased over time as conscripted native African workers, often away from their villages for as long as two years, added to the demands for female companionship. Urban prostitution had never before been part of the African culture, but suddenly, it became more lucrative for a family to earn money prostituting their daughter than marrying her off.[18]

At some point in the early 1920s, the HIV-infected white hunters from Cameroon migrated to Brazzaville and Leopoldville and apparently participated in sexual activities with prostitutes. However, sexual contact between a few HIV-infected hunters and their partners would not have occurred at levels necessary to spread HIV widely.[19] Sex between partners where only one partner is HIV-infected can continue for months without passing the virus. During the first few years of the rail construction, each prostitute only serviced an average of three or four regular clients. Even when her client base extended to native African railroad workers, the sexual transmission rate of the HIV virus would still not have been high enough to cause an epidemic. HIV might have

---

[16] Ibid., 67.
[17] Ibid., 70.
[18] Ibid., 97.
[19] Ibid., 223.

gone unnoticed far longer if it had only been passed via sex.[20] So what did escalate the virus's transmission?

Epidemiologists found their answers in archived blood from the mid-1930s. Evidence of the HIV virus was discovered in blood samples from both older and younger people typically not members of the sexually active population. Further, the recorded cause of death for most of these individuals was brain atrophy, a condition consistent with AIDS-related diseases. So the scientists knew that something besides sex had started passing the HIV virus throughout the population.

Colonization leads to widespread inoculations

Several unfortunate events came together in a perfect storm at the beginning of the 20th century in Africa, causing "the mother of all tropical diseases"[21]: sleeping sickness. The tsetse fly transmitted a parasite in its bite, causing this disease that killed its victims in just a few months. Though sleeping sickness had existed in Africa for thousands of years, it had remained in isolated population pockets—that is, until colonization.

In their insatiable hunger for more resources to supply to the European economies, the colonists, along with the native workers they used to accomplish their work, pushed deeper into previously uninhabited areas of Africa, thereby removing the natural geographic barrier that had existed between humans and the tsetse fly. The natural food source of the tsetse fly had been cattle and wildlife, but an African cattle plague in the late 19th century practically wiped out the entire cattle population. With their natural food supply gone, the tsetse flies turned to close-by humans as a food source. At first, sleeping sickness spread quietly. Then workers and students attending missionary schools began contracting it in larger numbers. Severe outbreaks soon followed in the heavily populated areas that had been created under colonization.

---

[20] Ibid., 89.
[21] Ibid., 121.

Concerned about the disease spreading to other territories, officials started ordering widespread inoculations against it in the 1920s. It is estimated that three-quarters of the population in the Congo region—about 4 million people—received almost 600,000 injections total at the peak of the sleeping sickness epidemic. Because medical supplies were scarce and sterilization even scarcer, blood from one patient was transmitted to another in needles that were used up to a thousand times before they were sterilized or tossed away. In some instances, large amounts of blood were intentionally left in the needles in order to transfer antibody-rich blood from a recovering sleeping sickness patient to one who had just been diagnosed. It is estimated that the average person living in the Congo received over three hundred inoculations in their lifetime.[22]

By the 1950s, the entire population of Leopoldville had undergone a cumulative 100,000 to 150,000 injections as precautionary measures to check the spread of sleeping sickness, leprosy, yaws, and sexually transmitted diseases.[23] Once again, archived blood samples prove that the HIV virus had a growing presence in the population in and around the Congo in the late 1950s. Still, the virus wouldn't be identified for *another twenty-five years.*

In June 1960, a civil war caused the Belgians to pull out of the Congo, and a flood of hundreds of thousands of refugees began pouring into Leopoldville from outlying areas. When the Belgians left, all the medical doctors who had served the population of 14 million people were among them. The Belgian Congo had had seven hundred medical doctors, yet not one of them was native Congolese; post-secondary education of the natives had been restricted under the Belgian regime.[24]

The civil war also marked the end of government health regulations that had controlled the spread of sexually transmitted diseases and, with it, the spread of the HIV virus. Prostitution increased. Sex workers who

---

[22] Ibid., 128.
[23] Ibid., 123.
[24] Ibid., 181.

had serviced a core group of only three to four customers per year were forced to service more than a thousand customers yearly to maintain the same income in the midst of the economic crisis.[25] Now, prostitution and sex were at levels high enough to cause *another* amplification in the passage of HIV from person to person. The general population of Leopoldville and Brazzaville became infected with HIV, and thus began the inevitable spread of the virus through the rest of Africa as the population moved and interacted with others across the continent.

The HIV virus gets to Haiti

When the Belgians withdrew 87,000 nationals from the Belgian Congo, it left 80% of the government posts unoccupied.[26] All areas of the government suffered, including education. Colonization had elevated the role of European teachers and created a dearth of native Congolese teachers. The United Nations stepped into the education crisis and began to hire teachers who spoke French, the language of the Congo. Many teachers came from Belgium, but the bulk of them were French-speaking, black Haitians who were more similar in ethnicity to the Congolese than were the Belgians. Forty-five hundred Haitian teachers moved to Zaire (the country's new name).

The HIV virus migrated from the sex worker population to the general population and increased by twelve times in the next ten years. As will happen, the Haitian teachers were having sex with Zairians, many of whom were infected with HIV.[27] The virus's silent passage throughout Africa, and its manifestation as AIDS-related illnesses, still hadn't been noticed. One would expect that before long, as the Haitian teachers in Zaire moved back home, HIV/AIDS would migrate to the population of Haiti.

---

[25] Ibid., 102.
[26] Ibid., 185.
[27] Ibid., 227.

Indeed, that is exactly what happened, and once there, it again spread silently through sexual intercourse. That is, until another economically motivated disaster happened.

In the 1970s, nearly 20% of the blood plasma used in the United States was imported from third-world nations, Haiti being the largest single supplier.[28] Luckner Cambronne, also known as "the Vampire of the Caribbean," opened Hemo-Caribbean, a massive plasma center in Port-au-Prince. Due to his connections with the very corrupt President Francois Duvalier (Papa Doc), Cambronne was able to freely operate Hemo-Caribbean under extremely poor hygiene conditions from 1971 to 1972.

Hemo-Caribbean collected blood from up to 850 people each day and exported 1,600 gallons of plasma each month to the United States. Blood from donors of the same blood type was pooled at the time of collection, the plasma was removed, and platelets were injected back into the donors, along with any infectious blood from other donors in a given session. Unsterilized needles and tubes were in constant use and re-use.[29]

Following a New York Times exposé on the lack of hygiene in the blood trafficking facility, Hemo-Caribbean was shut down in 1972.[30] But it was already too late.

Ten years later, as would be scientifically expected, there was an escalation in the death rate among Haitians and hemophiliacs (the prime consumers of blood plasma) due to AIDS-related illnesses contracted from the HIV-infected blood from Haiti.

Evidence supports this: From 1979 to 1981, there were eighteen cases of AIDS diagnosed in Haitians living in the United States; all eighteen individuals were dead within six months. In interviews with the HIV/AIDS-infected Haitians before they died, all stated that they had only engaged in heterosexual sex. At the same time, several Haitians in Haiti

---

[28] Ibid., 206.
[29] Ibid., 200.
[30] Ibid., 201-203.

were diagnosed with Kaposi's sarcoma, a disease never previously seen among the native Haitian population.

How did HIV/AIDS get to the United States?

Sex tourism between the United States, Canada, and Haiti increased in the 1970s and 1980s. Straight and gay men and women travelled Haiti to participate in sex tourism. In 1979, Port-au-Prince hosted an international gay men's conference. The French-Canadian airline steward, Gaetan Dugas, famously dubbed "patient zero" by journalists, was known to have participated in sex tourism in Haiti. Dugas was later sexually linked to forty of the first 248 HIV/AIDS diagnoses in the United States. He died in 1984 of AIDS-related complications.

Early in 1980, reports emerged in California and New York of a small number of men diagnosed with a rare form of cancer, Kaposi's sarcoma, and/or a form of pneumonia, Pneumocystis carinii pneumonia (PCP). Both diseases are normally found in people with severely compromised immune systems. But in this case, all the men were young, generally in good health, and gay.

The disease cluster was first identified in the Morbidity and Mortality Weekly Report, a Centers for Disease Control (CDC) publication, in June 1981. A month later, forty-one gay men had been diagnosed with Kaposi's sarcoma. By the end of 1981, there were six new cases being reported each week.

Soon heterosexual men and women, half of them intravenous drug users, were also diagnosed with the disease. Later that same year, the acronym "AIDS" came into use, meaning acquired immunodeficiency syndrome. In December 1982, three heterosexual hemophiliacs died from PCP and other opportunistic diseases. Suddenly, a handful of Haitians living in New York City were also diagnosed with PCP and died quickly. The disease came to be associated with "the four H's": homosexuals, hemophiliacs, heroin users, and Haitians.

By 1983, although scientists were not yet fully sure about how HIV was transmitted, most strongly suspected that it was related to sexual interaction and transmission of blood; at any rate, they had ruled out casual contact, food, water, air, and environmental surfaces as possible transmission methods.

The Religious Right was not silent on AIDS

At the onset of the AIDS epidemic between 1981 and 1983, there is no recorded official statement about the disease from any major religious denomination. However, this does not mean religious commentary was absent.

Unfortunately, while the more compassionate denominational groups remained silent in the early years of the epidemic, the loudest voices came from conservative religious groups and televangelists.

In the decade before the AIDS crisis, there had been an explosion of televangelists brought on by the loosening of Federal Communication Commission regulations. Dozens of televangelists popped up across the country. They brought the "health and financial prosperity doctrine" to the evangelical, Pentecostal, and Southern Baptist communities. Prosperity teachers and preachers drew direct connections between life circumstances and obedience to God. When AIDS first appeared in the gay and intravenous drug user populations in the United States, it helped reinforce televangelists' theological position that sickness and disease demonstrated the judgment of God for perverted sexual and immoral behaviors.

The early booming voices preached the lie across America's airwaves, in stadiums, and at revivals. Just as the poisonous head of a tick gets implanted in the skin and remains there even when the tick is pulled out, so do the lies told by those voices remain among us to this day. The early messages of televangelists carried such weight that they still influence the thinking of many conservative Christians.

In the early stages of AIDS, no one was sure of its source or how it was transmitted, so conservative religious groups and televangelists took full advantage of ignorance and fear and served up their myth-filled messages. They lulled the American public into a false belief that it was only the gays who could get AIDS, thereby causing non-gays to forgo sexual precautions.

Why was the Reagan Administration silent on AIDS?

President Ronald Reagan served two terms coinciding with the meteoric rise of HIV/AIDS to epidemic levels. His lack of national leadership in the fight against it was appalling. Revisionists often imagine that the reason he remained silent as tens of thousands of Americans died during the AIDS epidemic was that he was a deeply religious man with strongly held biblical convictions about gays. This is not accurate. Though some conservatives would like to imagine Reagan as the more godly replacement for his predecessor, Jimmy Carter, evidence shows that Reagan was an infrequent churchgoer and that, once president, he rarely even invited input from a chaplain or pastor.[31]

Christian conservatives, believing they were the reason Reagan had won the 1980 election over Carter, thought the new president owed them something for their widespread support. Jerry Falwell and the Moral Majority had made clear to Reagan their expectation that federal appointments of conservative Christians would mirror the proportion of the American population they represented.[32] Falwell even gave Reagan a list of suggested conservative candidates for various positions; Reagan ignored his suggestions. Neither did Reagan, once in office, address the issues most important to the Religious Right: the reintroduction of school prayer, the repeal of abortion rights, and a strong stance against the Equal Rights Amendment.

---

[31] "How Ronald Reagan Reinvented Religion," *History News Network*, June 4, 2007, http://hnn.us/article/38958.
[32] Neil J. Young, "There They Go Again," *New York Times*, January 19, 2012, http://campaignstops.blogs.nytimes.com/2012/01/19/there-they-go-again/.

Conservative Christians again supported Reagan in his reelection bid in 1984, believing that he would focus his attentions on "their" issues in his second term; he didn't. When he left office in 1988, evangelical leaders accused Reagan of giving them nothing more than lip service to gain their votes in two elections.[33]

So why did Reagan, not a particularly religious man, fail in his political response to the AIDS crisis? The reasons likely lie in his indifference to and ignorance about the issue, as well as in his need to continue capitulating to the Christian Right to retain their ongoing support.[34] Reagan knew that a great deal of his backing came from the conservative Christian community who embraced a staunchly anti-gay social agenda.[35] Beyond that, three core advisors surrounded Reagan, helping to shape the information he received about the growing crisis and strongly influencing his response. They were William Bennett (conservative politician, commentator, and Secretary of Education from 1985 to 1988), Gary Bauer (Reagan's Deputy Under Secretary for Planning and Budget in the Department of Education from 1982 to 1987), and Pat Buchanan (senior advisor to Nixon and Reagan, and White House Communications Director from 1985 to 1987).

Buchanan's policy advice on AIDS was rooted in his conservative religious principles. In 1983, the year that 2,304 Americans died from AIDS-related illnesses, he said, "The poor homosexual—they have declared war upon nature, and now nature is exacting an awful retribution."[36] William Bennett, as Secretary of Education, flatly opposed providing students with lifesaving sex education about AIDS prevention. Gary Bauer went on to become the first president of the Family

---

[33] Ibid.
[34] Michael Bronski, "Rewriting the Script on Reagan: Why the President Ignored AIDS," *The Jewish Daily Forward*, November 14, 2003, http://forward.com/articles/7046/rewriting¬the¬script¬on¬reagan¬why¬the¬president/
[35] Ibid.
[36] Igor Volsky, "FLASHBACK – Buchanan: AIDS Is Nature's 'Awful Retribution' Against Homosexuality," *Think Progress*, May 24, 2011, http://thinkprogress.org/lgbt/2011/05/24/177440/buchanan-aids/.

Research Council, which was birthed by Focus on the Family and, even today, is arguably the most anti-gay public policy organization in the nation.

Paul Weyrich, the influential, religious-conservative activist, had seen the need for a new wedge issue to drive conservative voters to the Republican Party. He envisioned the political potential in blaming the AIDS epidemic on gays and their "immoral lives," and the disease became a platform on which to build the next revival among conservative voters.

C. Everett Koop, the bright star in the Reagan Administration

As has been mentioned, when Reagan was elected to the presidency, names of faithful members of the conservative right were submitted to his administration for possible appointment. Virtually all the suggestions were ignored—except the one to appoint C. Everett Koop as Surgeon General. As it turned out, Koop became the Surgeon General no one expected.

Koop had been the co-founder in 1975 of the Christian Action Council, the leading evangelical anti-abortion action group in the United States. As such, he'd been approached even before the election by Reagan's team. Koop, steeped in conservative thinking, writing, and speaking, was seen by the Religious Right as a strong leader in the Christian prolife movement and an ideal candidate for the office of Surgeon General. Democrats, meanwhile, were passionately opposed to Koop's nomination. Medical groups, public health groups, and women's right-to-choose groups pounded Congress over a period of eight months, objecting to Koop's appointment.

Even as his embattled confirmation hearings ensued, Koop was aware of twenty-six recorded deaths in a single month from Pneumocystis carinii pneumonia. Because he had only seen two cases of the disease in his forty years as a surgeon, he knew the deaths indicated the makings of an epidemic.

When his appointment was finally confirmed, Koop was convinced that he had a mandate to educate the American public about AIDS, for which there was still no cure in sight. But for the first four years of his term, not only was Koop prevented from speaking directly to Reagan about the epidemic, but he was also banned by his boss, Robert Schweiker, the Secretary of Health, from addressing the public about it.

When Margaret Heckler replaced Schweiker in 1983, she immediately asked a staff assistant about department priorities. Later, she recalled the conversation:

> I was quite surprised to learn from a conversation with David Winston, who had been a staff member of the Senate Health Committee under then-Senator [Robert] Schweiker, and who had served with Gov. Reagan at the Health Department in California . . . I asked his recommendations on the priorities I might set, and he said, "Oh, well, you must begin with AIDS." I said, "AIDS?" I had never heard of AIDS. "What is AIDS?" He said, "This is a disease that is killing young people, and the hospital wards in San Francisco are crowded—in fact, bulging." I said, "Well, I have never been briefed on this; I have never heard of it." I had just gone through the whole confirmation process, and it had never been mentioned.[37]

Immediately, Heckler attempted to approach Reagan for AIDS funding allocations, but never succeeded in speaking to him about it—though not for lack of trying. Reagan's priorities were economic stability and cutting the budget.[38]

---

[37] "Interview: Margaret Heckler," *Frontline*, January 11, 2006, http://www.pbs.org/wgbh/pages/frontline/aids/interviews/heckler.html.
[38] Ibid.

Koop later wrote, "At least a dozen times I pleaded with my critics in the White House to let me have a meeting with President Reagan."[39] Instead, Koop says of the issue, too many people "placed conservative ideology far above saving human lives."[40]

Similarly, Koop later stated, "Our first public health priority, to stop the further transmission of the AIDS virus, became needlessly mired in the homosexual politics of the early 1980s. We lost a great deal of precious time because of this, and I suspect we lost some lives as well."[41]

The AIDS crisis in America continued to grow at alarming rates while Reagan remained silent on the issue. Researchers, health care professionals, and doctors at the Centers for Disease Control and elsewhere were screaming for funding, yet Reagan remained silent.

On July 25, 1985, a hospital in Paris announced that the famous actor Rock Hudson, a close friend of Nancy and Ronald Reagan, had been diagnosed with AIDS; this news was reported widely, but still, Reagan remained silent.

Finally, on February 5, 1986, five years into the outbreak, on a surprise visit to the Department of Health and Human Services, unexpectedly Reagan said, "One of our biggest public health priorities is going to be to find a cure for AIDS."[42] Then he instructed Koop to prepare a report on the disease.

In drafts of the report, Koop advised condom usage to prevent the spread of AIDS. Knowing that Reagan's inner circle and domestic-policy advisors would delete any reference to condoms and sex education, Koop strategically guarded review copies of the drafts. At meetings, he handed out numbered copies and collected all of them at the conclusion.

---

[39] Holcomb B. Noble, "C. Everett Koop, Forceful U.S. Surgeon General, Dies at 96," *New York Times*, February 25, 2013, http://www.nytimes.com/2013/02/26/us/c-everett-koop-forceful-surgeon-general-dies-at-96.html?pagewanted=all.

[40] Ibid.

[41] Ibid.

[42] Carl M. Cannon, "Ronald Reagan and AIDS: Correcting the Record," *Real Clear Politics*, June 1, 2014, http://www.realclearpolitics.com/articles/2014/06/01/ronald_reagan_and_aids_correcting_the_record_122806.html.

Though Dr. Koop was pushed by White House aides to ensure that the final report would be morally judgmental of the gay community, he would not succumb to the pressures. His evasive strategy with the White House worked. On October 22, 1986, "The Surgeon General's Report on AIDS" was released. It was praised as "accurate, nonjudgmental, and comprehensive information on the HIV/AIDS epidemic, educating Americans in plain language about how the virus could and could not be spread and how individuals could protect themselves. The report said that the best protection against AIDS was abstinence and monogamy, but that for those who practiced neither, condoms were a necessary precaution."[43] Koop's prior detractors were stunned that the report was not the moral judgment on the gay community that they had expected.

Twenty million copies of the Surgeon General's initial report were distributed to local governments, schools, and doctors. In the introduction to the report, Koop pointed criticism directly at the Religious Right's attempt to blame AIDS on the gay community, writing:

> At the beginning of the AIDS epidemic many Americans had little sympathy for people with AIDS. The feeling was that somehow people from certain groups "deserved" their illness. Let us put those feelings behind us. We are fighting a disease, not a people. Those who are already afflicted are sick people and need our care, as do all sick patients. The country must face this epidemic as a unified society. We must prevent the spread of AIDS while at the same time preserving our humanity and intimacy.[44]

---

[43] Ronald Valdiserri, "In Memoriam: C. Everett Koop," February 27, 2013, http://www.aids.gov/podcast/podcast-gallery/#150783. Spoken and printed as a memorial upon Koop's death. Ronald Valdiserri, M.D., M.P.H., served as Deputy Assistant Secretary for Health, Infectious Diseases, and Director, Office of HIV/AIDS and Infectious Disease Policy, U.S. Department of Health and Human Services.

[44] Ibid.

Along with condom usage, the report advocated sex education and AIDS prevention education for students in the third grade and above. Immediately, Phyllis Schlafly of the Eagle Forum criticized Koop. She said it looked like the report "was edited by the Gay Task Force."[45] She also accused Koop of advocating for third graders to be taught how to engage in "safe sodomy."[46] Koop responded, "I'm not the Surgeon General to make Phyllis Schlafly happy. I'm Surgeon General to save lives."[47]

The Conservative Digest, founded by Weyrich associate Richard Viguerie, echoed Schlafly's exaggerated concerns, stating that Koop was "proposing instruction in buggery for schoolchildren as young as third grade on the spurious grounds that the problem is one of ignorance and not morality."[48] The National Review, founded by conservative William F. Buckley in 1955, wrote that Koop was "criminally negligent" in advocating the use of condoms.[49]

Dr. Koop was a disappointment to those who had put forth his name as a nominee and had advocated for his position as Surgeon General. His track record and strong performance as an abortion opponent had seemed to make him the ideal conservative candidate. Before his appointment, Koop had made no secret of his conservative religious leanings; in fact, he had spoken dismissively about "women's lib" and "gay pride," saying that both ideologies were anti-family. He was a conservative Christian raised in the Dutch Reformed Church who held staunch Calvinist views that the purpose of government was to uphold morality.

---

[45] Anthony Petro, "Koop's Crusade," *Slate*, 27 February 2013, http://www.slate.com/articles/health_and_science/medical_examiner/2013/02/c_everett_koop_and_aids_he_defied_and_collaborated_with_the_religious_right.html.
[46] Ibid.
[47] Ibid.
[48] William Martin, *With God on Our Side: The Rise of the Religious Right in America* (New York City: Broadway Books, 2005), p. 205.
[49] Ibid., p.205.

But during his confirmation hearings, Koop had assured the concerned Senate panel that he would not use his office to promote religious ideology, and he did not. In the struggle between public health and "morality," he saw it as his duty to protect public health. In the conflict between medical evidence and religious beliefs, Koop formed his opinions and took his directives based on medical evidence. He said, "My position on AIDS was dictated by scientific integrity and Christian compassion."[50]

Once he had encountered people living with AIDS, Dr. Koop made an intentional decision to distance himself from the non-compassionate ideology of those who had promoted him to the office. In the year following the Koop report, condom sales increased by 20%, thus decreasing the transmission of HIV and saving lives. Rather than positioning the spread of AIDS as something that could be stopped by preaching against it or outlawing "immoral" behavior, Koop's report had succeeded, at least for the most part, in dispelling the misunderstandings and myths that only gay men and drug users contracted HIV.

After informing public and medical officials of best practices with the initial October 1986 report, Dr. Koop launched the first nationwide HIV/AIDS education program and orchestrated the largest-ever public health campaign by sending a version of his report, called "Understanding AIDS," to all 107 million American households in May 1987. The pamphlet informed the public about HIV/AIDS transmission methods, clearly stating that HIV/AIDS could not be transferred through casual contact, but only through sexual contact, needle sharing, or contact with contaminated blood.

In the same month, on May 31, 1987, the President of the United States finally publicly spoke the word "AIDS" at the Third International Conference on AIDS in Washington, D.C. By then, over 36,000

---

[50] "The C. Everett Koop Papers: AIDS, the Surgeon General, and the Politics of Public Health," National Science Museum: Profiles in Science, http://profiles.nlm.nih.gov/ps/retrieve/Narrative/QQ/p¬nid/87.

Americans had been diagnosed with AIDS, and almost 21,000 had already died.

When Dr. Koop left office in 1989, the *New York Times* editorial board, which had previously weighed in against his appointment, praised him: "Throughout, he has put medical integrity above personal value judgment and has been, indeed, the nation's First Doctor."[51] Koop put medicine and science ahead of politics, holding his strong personal beliefs about homosexuality in tension with his duties as Surgeon General.

The face of AIDS becomes a child: Ryan White

While the televangelists were pointing at the "dirty gays" as a deserving target of God's punishment for anal sex, children who contracted HIV/AIDS through blood transfusions got caught in the public fear-filled frenzy. In December 1984, a gradual shift began to happen in the public face of AIDS.

Ryan White, a 13-year-old hemophiliac middle-schooler in Kokomo, Indiana, was diagnosed with the disease. He had contracted HIV years before in a blood transfusion and, once diagnosed, was given six months to live. He was one of the first hemophiliac children in the United States to suffer from AIDS. It is estimated that between 1979 and 1984, 90% of all hemophiliacs were infected with AIDS due to the contaminated plasma from Haiti in the early 1970s.[52]

When Ryan had recovered from the operation that led to his AIDS diagnosis, one-third of the parents and fifty teachers at his school reacted by signing a petition to ban him from attending. The family, guided by concerned legal counsel, challenged the Kokomo School Board for Ryan's right to attend public school. National media attention on the court battle helped expand the public conversation about AIDS and its transmission and catapulted the well-spoken young man into the

---

[51] "C. Everett Koop . . . Dies at 96," *New York Times*.
[52] http://www.hemophiliafed.org/programs/meetings-events/hemophilia-awareness-month/hemophilia-awareness-month-fact-day/.

spotlight. Celebrities began to socialize with Ryan White, helping to further de-stigmatize HIV/AIDS.

The family won on an appeal, and Ryan was allowed to attend school. But when shots were fired late one night into the family home, they made the decision to leave Kokomo and move to Cicero, Indiana. In August 1987, Ryan was welcomed to the high school there, where he remained a student until his death in April 1990, one month shy of his high school graduation.

Ryan White's life in the spotlight during the few years between his diagnosis and his death is partially credited with increasing public awareness and dissemination of accurate information about HIV/AIDS.

Also in 1987, utterly out of step with the changing public understanding about the causes and transmission of HIV/AIDS, Jerry Falwell delivered a message about AIDS on his national TV show. It was devoid of compassion and filled with damnation. Falwell warned that God was bringing the end of the sexual revolution through the AIDS epidemic. In his sermon "How Many Roads to Heaven?," Falwell stated, "[Gay men] are scared to walk near one of their own kind right now. And what we have been unable to do with our preaching, a God who hates sin has stopped dead in its tracks by saying 'Do it and die. Do it and die.'"[53]

By then, 20,139 Americans had died of AIDS-related illnesses. The Moral Majority opposed federally funded research to find a cure for AIDS. Rather, fundamentalist politicians and religious leaders called for punitive measures under the guise of fighting AIDS. Various people demanded quarantines, the reinstatement of sodomy laws, or nationwide programs to tattoo and mark people who had AIDS.

Interestingly, sexual and financial scandals erupted within the ranks of these vile televangelists during the very same time. Public distrust of televangelists increased, and they began to lose their dominant voice; even the Moral Majority lost its relevance and shut down in 1989.

---

[53] Nationally televised on Falwell's television show *Old Time Gospel Hour,* May 10, 1987.

Early Christian responses to epidemics

How a person contracts a disease should not be the barometer by which Christians determine their attitude toward the sick and needy. We are to reflect the same covenantal, unconditional posture of love and concern that God freely expresses toward His children, especially visible through His Son Jesus Christ.

Jesus' ministry exhibited a compassionate view of sickness, suffering, and poverty. He responded to the sick with humane acts intended to alleviate their suffering. He called His followers not to judge, but to emulate His merciful concern and sympathetic actions. Leprosy was the HIV/AIDS of Jesus' day; lepers were the social outcasts, often isolated and ignored. Jesus' example is clear. It is recorded in the Bible that He touched the afflicted with His hands and prayed for them. In the Gospels, we see Jesus repeatedly more concerned with reflecting the compassionate love of God than with dissecting illness and assigning blame.

Early records dating to less than two hundred years after Christ lived on earth document Christians, at risk to their own lives, caring for sick and dying people during extreme epidemic and pandemic conditions. Followers of Christ took seriously the words of Jesus recorded in John 13:34-35: "A new command I give you: Love one another. As I have loved you, so you must love one another. By this all men will know that you are my disciples, if you love one another" (NIV).

The Antonine Plague (165–180 AD), also called the Plague of Galen, was a pandemic now believed to be smallpox that was introduced to the Roman Empire by soldiers returning from Syria. Five million people died as it ran its course. In the following century, the Plague of Cyprian (251–266 AD) spread from Africa throughout the known world. It was transmitted person-to-person by physical contact and by touching or using clothing and items infected by the sick. Half of all people who encountered the disease died.

During each pandemic, government officials and the wealthy fled the cities for the countryside to escape contact with those who were infected. The Christian community remained behind, transforming themselves into a great force of caretakers.

On Easter Sunday in 260 AD, Bishop Dionysius of Corinth praised the efforts of the Christians, many of whom had died while caring for others. He said:

> Most of our brother Christians showed unbounded love and loyalty, never sparing themselves, and thinking only of one another. Heedless of danger, they took charge of the sick, attending to their every need and ministering to them in Christ, and with them departed this life serenely happy; for they were infected by others with the disease, drawing on themselves the sickness of their neighbors and cheerfully accepting their pains.[54]

The early Christians' dedication to caring for their neighbors as themselves during times of plague and sickness, whether the sick were believers or not, showcased the integrity of their unique message of love for others. These Christ-like actions had great social impact and attracted outsiders to the faith. This kind of selfless love caused an explosion of Gentile Christian congregations to arise alongside Judeo-Christian communities.

Two of my minister-friends recall the AIDS crisis.[55] D. Greg Smith[56] was ordained as a Roman Catholic priest in 1991 and came out and left the priesthood in 1999. He says:

---

[54] Rodney Stark. *The Rise of Christianity: A Sociologist Reconsiders History* (Princeton, NJ: Princeton University Press, 1996), 82.

[55] Personal stories included throughout this book were shared with me directly. Please see the "Acknowledgments" section for further details.

[56] Rev. Greg Smith will be ordained as an Episcopal priest in 2015 and blogs at http://dgsmith.org.

I was very involved with faith communities in the beginning of the AIDS crisis, and for the most part, I'm very embarrassed by the early response of churches to this disease. Most were very quick to judge the disease as God's punishment rather than seeing what it was: a wonderful chance to show God's love even in the face of death, disease and suffering.

This is a disease spread by people attempting on a variety of levels to be loved, to express intimacy and to connect with others. Like every other disease that's primarily transmitted sexually, we are very quick to show ignorance and judgment in order to avoid our own shame. Education and enlightened theology helps, but it's definitely a problem for biblical literalists who tend not to rely on science (or reality) to inform their faith.

And some still view it as God's judgment. I don't and have never felt that way. Our job as Christians is to jump into another's suffering and work to alleviate it, not walk by on the opposite side of the road.[57]

Greg is a licensed counselor; serves as the Director of AIDS Outreach in Bozeman, Montana; and lives with his longtime partner, Ken. He is a beautiful human being. "I have never doubted God's love for me, not for a second," Greg says. "As an ordained gay man living with HIV, I believe I represent an opportunity to help others love as Jesus did without reservation or hesitation. If they don't want to love me, that's okay. They can't stop me from loving them."

Rev. Gerald Green is a minister with the Unity Fellowship of Christ Church in San Diego. He worked in the African American community

---

[57] His reference is to Jesus' parable about the Good Samaritan, found in Luke 10:25-37.

in the early days of the AIDS crisis and has continued doing so for the past twenty-five years. He shares:

> As a person of faith and a minister of the Gospel, I wasn't too surprised at the response of the church at large and the black church in particular as it related to the onset of AIDS in the late '80s. I remember it like yesterday. I went to more funerals, memorials, and celebration of life services than I care to remember.
>
> My first knowledge of AIDS was when a good friend of mine in the entertainment business who danced professionally contracted the virus. One day he was vibrant and talking on the phone, and a couple of weeks later I was reading his eulogy at his funeral. I never thought HIV/AIDS was a punishment from God then [or] now. The churches in the black community where I came from refused to officiate and hold the funerals of those who had made transition from this expression to the next. Families were devastated because they had helped to build churches in their community, and when the institution they built turned their backs on them, we were all crushed. I had close friends who were musicians at churches for years, and once it was discovered they had AIDS, they would be thrown out and told they were an abomination.
>
> I went searching for answers, and God pointed me to the direction of a church in South Los Angeles called Unity Fellowship of Christ Church, founded by Rev. Carl Bean.
>
> Archbishop Bean founded the Minority AIDS Project in Los Angeles, the first organization of its kind in a community of

color, as well as being operated by people of color. Archbishop Bean, an openly gay man, knew he could not sit by without doing something to touch the lives of those suffering so they could know that God loved them and they could have dignity.

How might the Christian church as a whole have behaved in the earliest years of AIDS, not only in light of the Gospel, but also with reflection upon early church records of service to those in extreme epidemic/pandemic conditions? First, we missed it. We missed the opportunity to be Jesus with skin on. People living with AIDS were banished or estranged from their families and friends, and from housing, jobs, schools, and churches.

Many denominations and religious organizations holding a more compassionate, nonjudgmental view of people living with AIDS leaned toward education, needle exchange programs, and condom distribution and usage. But for the most part, they did not begin speaking up until 1987. The exception to the silence came from two organizations in 1983: The National Council of Churches of Christ and the Universal Fellowship of Metropolitan Community Churches (MCC) committed themselves to advocating and caring for people living with AIDS.

As the public became educated about HIV/AIDS, religious denominations announced official declarations and stances. In 1988, the 9 million member United Methodist Church, known for its long history of social activism, developed a policy called "AIDS and the Healing Ministry of the Church." The 5 million members of the Evangelical Lutheran Church in America were encouraged to support and participate in ministry to people suffering with AIDS. The Presbyterian Church (USA) and its 3 million members resolved that AIDS was an illness and "not a punishment for behavior deemed immoral."[58] They

---

[58] In 1994, the Presbyterian Church (USA), at its General Assembly, adopted a resolution entitled "To Meet AIDS with Grace and Truth," confessing that the denomination's response had been overdue.

promoted information to the membership to counter the cultural stereotyping of people with AIDS.

The face of HIV/AIDS today

According to statistics reported by UNAIDS and the World Health Organization, since the beginning of the global epidemic, almost 70 million people worldwide have been infected with HIV, and 35 million have died of AIDS-related illnesses. Sub-Saharan Africa, where one in twenty adults has HIV/AIDS, accounts for 69% of those living with HIV.

Women represent over half (52%) of all people living with HIV worldwide. Globally, young women between the ages of 15 and 24 are twice as likely to become infected with HIV as their male counterparts; in fact, for women of reproductive age worldwide, HIV/AIDS is the leading cause of death. Ninety-seven percent of all people living with HIV reside in low- and middle-income countries, particularly in Sub-Saharan Africa.

Global statistics paint a picture of a broad, far-reaching illness. HIV/AIDS is the leading cause of childhood death worldwide and the number one cause of death across all ages in Africa. In 2012, there were 3.3 million children living with HIV, the largest group in Sub-Saharan Africa, where over 15 million children have lost one or both parents to HIV/AIDS. Over 17 million children worldwide have lost one or both parents to AIDS.

In 2012, there were 2.3 million new HIV infections globally—most of which were transmitted heterosexually. In some countries, men who have sex with men, intravenous drug users, and sex workers account for the majority of new infections.

Most people living with HIV, or at risk of contracting it, do not have access to prevention, care, or treatment of the disease. There is still no known cure.

How I responded to AIDS

In November 2011, on the thirtieth anniversary of the first reported cases of a mysterious "gay cancer" in America, I went to the Nevada Museum of Art with my friend Dean to see the documentary *We Were Here*, produced by David Weissman. The film reflected deeply personal accounts of five people living in San Francisco when the disease soon to be known as HIV/AIDS first appeared.

For an hour and a half, I was mesmerized by stories eloquently told by eyewitnesses, survivors, and caretakers. Where was I while all this was happening? When people were dying and alone, where was I?

Feeling the shameful ignorance of so much profound pain and loss, I sank in my seat. After seeing *We Were Here*, I stayed awake till morning reading online about AIDS—dates, facts, stories, and science. Though I have hundreds of friends living with AIDS, I had never researched the topic before seeing the documentary. I took out a notebook and made a list of years and deaths from the epidemic. I had been completely removed from the crisis and need in the 1980s and 1990s. Now decades later, the impact of HIV/AIDS on the gay community pierced me.

Through the night, I wept in remorse, asking, "Where were you, Kathy?"

While people were dying and alone, where the heck was I? Why didn't I care? How could I not have noticed? First hundreds, then thousands, then tens of thousands of people died each year, and I went about my life. Isolated from the tragedy of people living with HIV, I got married, became a follower of Jesus Christ, raised and homeschooled my children, and led Bible studies.

At the height of the AIDS epidemic in 1993, Pastor Jerry Falwell said:

> AIDS is the wrath of a just God against homosexuals. To oppose it would be like an Israelite jumping in the Red Sea to save one of Pharaoh's charioteers. AIDS is not just God's

punishment for homosexuals. It is God's punishment for
the society that tolerates homosexuals.

Falwell's voice was the one I had heard and believed then.

A half-million Americans died of complications from HIV and I
don't recall feeling *any* compassion at the time. The space in me that
should have been occupied with kindness and empathy for people suffering from any deadly disease was instead filled with accusation and
disapproval.

Only once did the reality of the epidemic nudge against my insular
evangelical cocoon.

My husband and I were walking into our home as the phone rang. It
was 1988, and I had my newborn son in my arms. My husband reached
for the call. I listened to his side of the exchange; I understood that one
of his friends in New York City had died of the "gay cancer." My reaction
was dispassionate. I cared that my husband had lost a friend, yet I distinctly recall formulating judgments: People who died of AIDS got it by
having gay sex; gay sex was wrong and against God's plan; therefore, the
death was foreseeable and could and should have been avoided by not
following lust-filled desires. I am not proud of my behavior.

Since the beginning of the AIDS epidemic in 1981, 1.7 million
Americans have been infected with HIV, and over 650,000 have died of
AIDS-related illnesses. Of the 1.1 million Americans currently infected
with HIV, one in six do not even know they are infected.

In hindsight, we are better able to understand that ignoring HIV/
AIDS and placing a "morality" on it only served to spread the disease.
We were told that AIDS was a "gay disease," a punishment from God.
This was the message religious leaders were telling us at the onset of the
epidemic, and I still hear it spoken and see it written about frequently.

As a Christian, my response to HIV/AIDS in the 1980s and 1990s was
without excuse. I not only ignored the pain and death of people living
with AIDS, but I believed they "deserved" it. I had no understanding of

homosexuality with respect to human sexuality, and my religious views were constructed on what I had been told by religious and political leaders seeking to take advantage of my ignorance for the sake of their own corrupt (at worst) or misguided (at best) agendas.

PART III: SCIENCE

Chapter 8

The Myth of a Pink and Blue World

Sex, Gender, and Sexual Orientation

God made male and female

In the preceding chapters, we've explored the historical, cultural, and conjoined religious and political filters through which we view the lesbian, gay, bisexual, and transgender (LGBT) community. Finally, we're inching toward looking at the six passages of Scripture involving same-sex behavior. First, however, we need to better understand sex, gender, and sexual orientation. Since many of the Bible verses are rooted in male and female language, let's start with what the ancients believed about the creation of male and female.

In the fourth century BC, Aristotle argued that a woman was merely the fertile planting ground in which the male seed, containing all the ingredients needed to produce a human, grew. If the "heat" of a man's semen could overcome the "coldness" of the woman's body, a male child would form; in instances of failing male dominance, a female (of lesser value) would form.

Historically, a multitude of "abnormalities" in babies were thought to be the curse of God. In fact, in ancient Israel, those born with or acquiring defects, deformities, or illnesses were denied access to the temple area.[1] Babies born with both male and female genitals were thought to be mythical.[2]

We don't know much about "abnormal" births historically because medical records weren't kept until the 1800s. The little we do know and can find in various documents informs us that when babies were born with genitalia neither fully male nor fully female, they were categorized as "monstrous births."[3] The "monsters," it was believed, were sent by God as a divine warning and judgment on immoral behavior, such as a mother having "unclean and unnatural" sex during her menstruation. After all, God created only male and female, and the "monster" was surely God's punishment.

Three revolutionary breakthroughs happened in the 1870s that would eventually influence our understanding of sex, gender, and sexual orientation. Oscar Hertwig (1849–1922), a German zoologist, discovered that a human embryo was formed when a male sperm fertilized a female egg. Fellow German Walther Flemming (1843–1905) discovered that human cells had pairs of chromosomes carrying genetic code. And, as we discussed in Chapter 1, Karl Kertbeny noted and grouped people together by the sex to which they were attracted.

---

[1] Leviticus 21:18-21 (NIV) reads: "No man who has any defect may come near [the temple]: no man who is blind or lame, disfigured or deformed; no man with a crippled foot or hand, or who is a hunchback or a dwarf, or who has any eye defect, or who has festering or running sores or damaged testicles. No descendent of Aaron the priest who has any defect is to come near to present the food offerings to the LORD. He has a defect; he must not come near to offer the food of his God."
[2] Elizabeth Reis, "Intersex in America, 1620–1960," *University of Oregon Blog*, 415, http://blogs.uoregon.edu/healarts/files/2014/04/Hermaphrodites_Reis-24qs8ss.pdf.
[3] Ibid., 415.

God made male and female and . . .

The Bible says, "Male and female, he created them."[4] People often assume the verse says "male or female." This interpretation is really an oversimplification of God's design. The diversity of ways in which people are created is beginning to be understood as never before. Let's take a fresh look at sex and gender.

Did God make only male or female? Some folks have difficulty accommodating anything beyond the tidiness of "male plus female equals God's perfect will." But sometimes males are born with ovaries, female brains are placed in male bodies, and individuals are attracted to people of the same sex. These aren't defects or the curse of God for immoral behavior, as the ancients would have seen them; they are normal variations of human development.

"But," you may object, "an omniscient God knew and inspired the biblical writers to pen what they did." Of course God did. Though a full understanding of the diversity of human sexuality and the richness of God's creation only began to unfold over the last century (as has much of our knowledge of human development, psychology, and sexuality), it all fits beautifully into God's timeless truths and complex creation.

Here's where the challenge begins. Some people view science as scary, or as a threat to the truths in the Word of God, so they avoid scientific research and knowledge, or simply dismiss it. But science and faith aren't mutually exclusive. Both are necessary for thoughtful consideration of important theological questions pertaining to life sciences and human behavior, as well as to sex, gender, gender identity, and sexual orientation. Wading through some basic biology will give us a broader understanding and appreciation of the vastness of God and His design. For the sake of this discussion, I have simplified the complexity of the science. (If you'd like to go further and do more in-depth study, I have found that *Sex/Gender Biology in a Social World* [5] by Anne Fausto-

---

[4] Genesis 1:27 (NIV).
[5] Anne Fausto-Sterling, *Sex/Gender Biology in a Social World* (Oxford: Routledge), 2012.

Sterling, Professor of Biology and Gender Studies at Brown University, uses humor and excellent graphics to make biochemistry, neurobiology, and social constructs of gender accessible to most readers.)

For starters, some definitions will prove helpful: "Sex" refers to a person's biological status and is typically associated with male or female as indicated by physical factors: sex chromosomes, reproductive systems, gonads (ovaries and/or testicles), and genitalia. "Gender" is a set of social, psychological, and emotional traits influenced by societal expectations that classify a person as being male or female, or even somewhere along the spectrum from male to female.[6]

Every human cell has genes containing hereditary coding. The genes, either alone or in combination, express a person's physical traits. It is estimated that there are 150 different genes that influence height. So, if you ask, "Is there a gene for being tall?" the answer would be no, there is not just *one gene* for being tall, but that doesn't mean there is no genetic influence for height.[7]

In the past five years, scientists have discovered chemicals called epigenes which sit on top of genes (*epi,* meaning "on top of") and act like "on" and "off" switches. Epigenes don't change the genetic coding, but they can affect whether genetic code is expressed or not. Epigenes can be temporary and untraceable, or they may imprint a gene and pass the effects of the on-off switch from one generation to the next. Epigenes influence vast numbers of traits, including sex, gender, sexual orientation, and even disease. Geneticists are only beginning to understand the effects of epigenes.

Genes are arranged along strands of DNA on chromosomes. Humans have twenty-three pairs of chromosomes. The twenty-third pair determines whether a person is chromosomally male, designated as XY in genetics, or female, designated XX. When a sperm cell fertilizes an egg,

---

[6] Laura Erickson-Schroth, *Trans Bodies, Trans Selves* (New York: Oxford University Press, 2014), 614.

[7] Wayne Besen, "Real Scientists Debunk JONAH's Junk Science" (video), September 24, 2012, https://www.youtube.com/watch?v=bjCj7i87dM0#t=139.

the resultant embryo receives chromosomes from each parent. Right from the start, some of the genes from the parents may have been modified by the on-off switches caused by epigenes.

When the embryo's twenty-third chromosome is formed, most of the time it's either female XX or male XY, but in one out of 1,666 instances, it's not.[8] The cell may not divide properly; rather than carrying two Xs or one Y and one X, there may be extra Xs or Ys, or fewer Xs or Ys in the embryo. Besides XX and XY, other naturally occurring variations of the twenty-third chromosome include XXY, XO (the O indicates that neither an X or a Y is present), XXX, XXYY, and XXXY. The twenty-third chromosome is, therefore, not female XX or male XY; this individual is a third sex, or intersex.

So, it turns out, God created male and female, and intersex. Non-XX and non-XY chromosomes are only one way in which intersex people are created; there are others.

First, let's look at the most common way. Female XX embryos typically produce estrogen that stimulates the beginnings of ovaries from the fetal gonad. Male XY embryos typically produce male hormones called androgens that include testosterone and DHT. Male androgens shut down development of the female reproductive system, which is the initial "default" structure for every embryo. Male androgens begin to turn the undifferentiated fetal gonad into testes rather than the ovaries they otherwise would have become.

As early as between the eighth and the twelfth week of gestation, genes typically "know" to produce male hormones or female hormones that will work to differentiate the gonads into either testes or ovaries. Yet sometimes variations arise. Here's an instance where epigenes can modify the genetic messages which control appropriate levels of hormone production: While a fetus might be strictly XX or XY from a chromosomal standpoint, a female might develop testes, or both testes

---

[8] "How Common Is Intersex?" Intersex Society of North America, http://www.isna.org/faq/frequency.

and ovaries, and a male might develop ovaries, or both ovaries and testes. I know it sounds confusing! The external genitals can still appear strictly male or female, yet the person is neither male nor female, but intersex.

Is intersex common?

During the third month of gestational development, external genitals form; their formation is controlled by hormone production and levels. Depending on the measurements and standards used, one in every 1,500–2,000 births results in a baby born with ambiguous genitalia.[9] These babies are intersex.

So what exactly is intersex? Recall that sex is determined by chromosomes, internal reproductive systems, ovaries and/or testicles, and external genitalia. When at least one of those components is out of alignment with the others, a person is intersex. God created male and female, and intersex.

As mentioned above, until the 1900s, babies born with ambiguous genitalia were considered monsters and a curse from God for the mother's or father's immorality. We no longer view babies who are born intersex as defects or monsters because now we understand the science behind intersex births.

Before we see what doctors today advise for treatment of intersex babies, let's look at what was done with them between the 1950s and 2000, which led directly to the initial (mis)understanding of the concept of gender, and even sexual orientation.

Treatment of transsexuals and intersex people leads to discoveries about gender

Throughout history, there have been people who did not fit gender stereotypes. The Native American culture honored those recognized as both male and female as Two-Spirit people thought to possess great

---

[9] Ibid.

Walking the Bridgeless Canyon • 193

power.[10] The modern American culture, however, has seen things quite differently. Until the late 1940s, psychiatrists viewed people who wanted to change their outward expression to express the opposite sex as "mentally ill deviants."[11]

The science of understanding individuals who are born with their gender in conflict with their genital sex began in Europe. The earliest sex change surgeries took place in Austria and Germany in the 1920s. When sex changes became known through the American media, the public was immediately fascinated. In 1952, the *New York Daily News* announced: "Ex-G.I. Becomes Blonde Bombshell."[12] Twenty-six-year-old George Jorgensen (1926–1989), a former soldier in the Army, had undergone a sex change operation in Denmark and returned home as Christine Jorgensen.

New York City–based endocrinologist Dr. Harry Benjamin (1885–1986) was Jorgensen's doctor in the United States. Benjamin helped his patients bring their birth sex into alignment with their internal sense of being a man or a woman, even before gender was understood as something different from sex. This process of gender and sex alignment could never have been medically successful prior to the 1950s. What changed was that newly created synthetic hormones became widely available, and advancements were made in plastic surgery during World War II. Medical help became accessible for people who felt that their biological sex was not in accordance with their internal sense of identity.

Jorgensen had undergone surgery in Denmark to remove her testes and penis. Upon her return to New York City, she continued hormone therapy under the care of Dr. Benjamin, who also scheduled her for vaginoplasty, the creation of a vagina. The work was scheduled at Johns Hopkins Medical Center, where the earliest American sex reassignment surgeries were performed.

[10] "What Are Two-Spirits/Berdaches?" American Indian, First Nations, Aboriginal Two Spirit/GLBTQ Internet Resources, http://people.ucalgary.ca/~ptrembla/aboriginal/two-spirited-american-indian-resources.htm.
[11] Lynn Conway, "What Causes Transsexualism?" University of Michigan, April 7, 2003, http://ai.eecs.umich.edu/people/conway/TS/TScauses.html.
[12] *Trans Bodies, Trans Selves*, 508-509.

Jorgensen's transition was highly successful. She spent the rest of her life living publicly as a role model, educating and lecturing on college campuses. She summed up her transformation in a letter to her friends: "Remember the shy, miserable person who left America? Well, that person is no more and, as you can see, I am in marvelous spirits."[13]

Dr. John Money (1921–2006), a New Zealand–born psychologist and professor of pediatrics and medical psychology, was also on staff at Johns Hopkins from 1951 until his death in 2006. He assisted in many of the adult sex reassignment surgeries. While working in the Sexual Behaviors Unit, Money and his colleagues developed theories about behavioral traits and social conventions as they related to being either male or female. The behavioral differences had previously been referred to as "sex roles." Money wanted terminology to distinguish erotic and genital sex activities from typical male or female nonsexual activities. In 1955, he appropriated the word "gender," previously used to distinguish masculine and feminine nouns in some languages, to differentiate social roles from sexual roles.

Money creates protocol for intersex children

While progress was being made in the field of medicine and sex change surgeries, there were, unfortunately, some major setbacks when it came to decisions made for babies born with ambiguous genitalia. Prior to the 1950s, babies born neither 100% male nor 100% female were thought to have a birth defect. Sometimes, often without even discussing the birth oddity with the parents, doctors did "minor" surgeries to "correct" the infant's genital anomalies. Besides his work with adult genital surgeries, Dr. Money became a pioneer in the virtually unexplored field of infants born with ambiguous genitalia.

Despite the fact that there was almost no evidence of adults who had been born with ambiguous genitalia suffering mental health problems

---

[13] Christine Jorgensen, *Christine Jorgensen: A Personal Autobiography* (New York: Bantam Books, 1967), 105.

beyond the normal range, Money theorized that re-engineering the ambiguous genitalia of babies would shape them into happier, healthier adults. He further postulated that a person's internal sense of being, male or female, was not established until age three.

He had no evidence for this theory; it was simply a hunch. When asked about the gender of a child, Money said, "It seems that every child is born with some predisposition to go both ways. Which way it finally goes is determined by its environment."[14] Money popularized the "nurture over nature" argument with relation to gender. Though this theory has long since been dismissed in the scientific community, it persists to this day in some conservative circles where a person's—and in particular, a child's—environment is blamed as the reason a person might be gay or transgender.

Money and his colleagues combined the practical experience they had gained in overseeing adult sex reassignment surgeries and Money's "genderless before age three" theory to help create a "best practices" regimen for babies born with ambiguous genitalia. Routine surgeries by doctors to "correct" ambiguous genitalia on infants commenced on a wider scale because they thought this would fix the "problem."

If an infant's genitals were not clearly male or female, doctors were taught to make their sex-of-the-baby decision based on the length of the infant's penis. If the penis was longer than an inch, the baby was a boy. If the penis was shorter than an inch, surgery was performed to make the genitals look like a girl's. More girls were "created" than were boys because it was "easier to dig a hole than build a pole."[15]

Parents of these babies were instructed to raise the child as the sex and in the gender role correlating with the corrective surgery. Sometimes, when doctors performed "slight corrective surgeries" on infants, they never explained what the birth complications were or gave options to parents; they cut first and told later, if at all. At the time, this medical

---

[14] "Hopkins Pioneer in Gender Identity," *Baltimore Sun*, July 9, 2006.
[15] Morgan Holmes, *Intersex: A Perilous Difference* (London: Associated University Press, 2008), 148.

practice did not violate ethical standards. People didn't question doctors; they trusted medical professionals to make the best decisions for their children. Parents complied with "expert" advice.

Dr. Money fabricates and "proves" a theory about gender

Dr. Money wanted the fame of his "genderless until age three," "nurture over nature" theory to be solidified in a seminal research paper, but he needed the perfect case study. He got his break in 1967 from a tragic event in a family of Canadian farmers. Twin sons, born in 1965 to Janet and Ronald Reimer, had been suffering urination difficulties caused by non-retracting foreskins on their uncircumcised penises. When brothers Bruce and Brian were eight months old, their pediatrician recommended they be circumcised. During the procedure on Bruce, the machine used to cauterize his circumcision wound malfunctioned and his penis was burned to a stump beyond repair. Alarmed, the parents did not allow the procedure to be performed on Brian and took both children home.

Fourteen months later, Janet Reimer saw Dr. Money on a television interview where he was speaking about his extensive work with children born with ambiguous genitalia. He claimed that such an infant should undergo corrective surgery to make the baby distinguishable as either male or female. He said the child would become a well-functioning boy or girl and, hence, a healthy adult as a result of surgically altering the genitals and socially adapting the child to the gender role matching the external sex.

Concerned about Bruce's happiness and his future ability to function sexually as a man, Janet Reimer contacted John Money at the Johns Hopkins Medical Center. Money tried to persuade the Reimers to have 22-month-old Bruce undergo immediate sex reassignment surgery; they didn't go for it. As a step-down, Money recommended the removal of Bruce's penile stump and testicles and the introduction of an immediate regimen of female hormones. Additionally, Money instructed the parents to change Bruce's name to a female name, to never again speak about him as a boy, and to begin raising him as a girl.

The Reimers complied with several of Money's suggestions. They stopped short of vaginoplasty and the removal of his penile stump, but they did have Bruce's testicles removed, changed his name to Brenda, began to raise him as a girl, and exposed the newly named Brenda to exclusively female-gender activities and roles.

Money flew the family back to Johns Hopkins once a year to interview Brenda and her twin, Brian. The Reimers had no idea Dr. Money was writing a medical journal documenting the progress and "success" of Brenda's gender role reassignment. In his writings, Money referred to the study as the John/Joan case.

Brenda's gender reassignment was an utter failure. She never displayed any naturally typical feminine behaviors. Contrary to the overwhelming evidence of failure, Dr. Money continued to report the gender reassignment as a success. He wrote: "The child's behavior is so clearly that of an active little girl and so different from the boyish ways of her twin brother."[16]

As she approached the onset of puberty, Brenda's body began to masculinize and Money knew time was running out to perform a vaginoplasty. He told Brenda she would feel and look more like a girl and, to his purposes, act more like a girl. She consistently refused.

In 1978, Money made an aggressive effort to convince 13-year-old Brenda into surgery by inviting a transsexual[17] woman who had undergone adult corrective surgery to help coerce the child. The effort backfired. Brenda ran out of the appointment and told her parents that if they ever tried to force her to go back to Money, she would kill herself.

Faced with a suicidal 13-year-old, the parents ended the family silence and told Brenda and Brian the truth. Brenda, who had recalled

---

[16] Diane F. Halpern, *Sex Differences in Cognitive Abilities* (Psychology Press, 2013), 163.
[17] Transwomen were called transsexuals at the time.

distinctly feeling like a boy since age nine, immediately became David. As an adult, in retrospect, David remembered being happy at this point for the first time in his life. For twin Brian, the revelation triggered the onset of mental illness, which intensified over the years. When David grew older, he sued the pediatrician who had circumcised him for damages, got a penile implant, and married a woman.

Money's lies exposed

Outrageously, seventeen years later, Money was still reporting about the "successful" gender reassignment in medical journals! In 1997, at the age of thirty-two, David discovered that Money had been reporting lies about the supposed success of the John/Joan case. By then, Dr. Money's theory was established and had created "best practices" and medical standards that had been in use for four decades.

Not wanting another person to be destroyed by Money's theories, David encouraged his brother to participate in an exposé in *Rolling Stone* magazine detailing Money's false reporting. Soon after the story broke, Brian's mental illness worsened. He committed suicide by overdosing on his schizophrenia medication. Two years later, David Reimer, experiencing marital problems and never able to recover from lifelong depression, also committed suicide. Mother Janet Reimer blamed Money for the deaths of her sons and for using them as guinea pigs to test his gender theories.

In the United States, from the 1950s through the late 1990s, babies born with ambiguous genitalia were treated according to Money's assumption that gender was not inborn but could be nurtured by the child's environment before age three. Even when publicly exposed for lying, Dr. John Money never again commented on the case.

Fortunately, there have been other expert voices in the field of gender research. Beginning in 1972, Dr. Milton Diamond (1934–), a professor of anatomy and human sexuality, professionally challenged Money's "nurture over nature" gender theories. Diamond's research and findings could not get the necessary attention from the public to challenge Money's entrenched policies until after Money was finally exposed as a fraud in 1997. Now, however, Diamond and the Pacific Center for Sex and Society continue to produce well-respected research papers on sexuality, gender, transgenderism, and sexual orientation.

Besides a fascinating story, the John/Joan/David Reimer case highlights several issues of prime importance about sex and gender that can be applied to questions surrounding sexual orientation. First, the body of evidence collected over several decades from adults who underwent unnecessary and wrong gender assignment and sex reassignment surgeries teaches us that trying to match gender to genitals should not be a standard. Gender and genitals do not necessarily align. Gender is an innate trait established within the fetal brain.

Furthermore, the attempt to change what is natural and inborn in a person has devastating effects on lives. Rather than collect mental health information directly from adults who had been born with ambiguous genitalia, Dr. Money created theories based on his own flawed assumptions. Scientific research would not have validated Money's theories. The same neglectful methods had been used in the psychoanalytic community in dealing with gay men and women. Doctors talked *about* gay men and lesbians and decided how to "fix" them without talking *to* them or conducting any kind of fact-based research.

Without intentional malice, doctors invariably made incorrect decisions for four decades by following Money's protocol for assigning sex and gender to babies born with ambiguous genitalia. Corrective genital surgery was done in at least one in every thousand births.[18] Using even the most conservative estimates, at least one quarter of a million Americans now over eighteen years of age were subjected to these flawed, unethical, and *standard* practices. Many children were raised in genders unnatural to them.

---

[18] "How Common Is Intersex?"

Michael's story

This is the story of my friend Michael, who is in his late forties and is a medical doctor. He was one of the hundreds of thousands of children caught in the Money trap.

Michael identifies as male but was assigned female sex and gender at birth. Michael was born with no testes in his scrotum, a small vaginal opening with fused labia, and the opening to his urethra misplaced on the underside of his penile shaft. Because his genitals were ambiguous, initial chromosomal testing was done and he was diagnosed as an XX pseudohermaphrodite.[19]

Michael's parents were told to have his penis removed, consent to vaginoplasty, put him on hormones, and raise him as a girl. They agreed to a female gender assignment and hormone treatment, but not to female sex reassignment surgery, as it was then called.

Michael's chromosomes were tested again at age eight. He was diagnosed as 46 XY/XX mosaic male with male and female genitalia being raised as a female. Growing up, he was never at ease with his non–gender-conforming body. He felt very uncomfortable naked; he was very conscious that physically, he looked different from other girls, and he had always struggled with living as a girl. He preferred short hair and never wanted to wear feminine clothes. At the onset of puberty, he was attracted to females, yet the label "lesbian" did not make sense to him.

At sixteen, Michael asked his parents and doctor about his physical differences. Once he became aware of his intersex condition, he refused any further hormonal treatment.

Michael now lives as a man. His body is androgynous due to the intake of synthetic female hormones until age sixteen. He went to college and medical school as a female, so all his professional licensing is under his female name. In the past, potential employers assumed that

---

[19] "Pseudohermaphrodite" is an outdated term for a condition in which a person has the primary sex organs of one sex, but develops the secondary sex characteristics of the other sex. In Michael's case, he was born with an organ classified as a clitoris, yet had a scrotum, though without testicles.

he was transgender, and this prejudice has impacted his professional career. As an adult, he has suffered with trust and intimacy issues, depression, and thoughts of suicide. Past medical and social attempts to change Michael into a girl have had grave consequences on his life—consequences that still linger today.

Treatment of intersex babies today

There are thirty-one known intersex conditions, one of which is called XXY Klinefelter condition; one in one thousand babies is born with Klinefelter's.[20] Before the new standards, virtually all Klinefelter babies were raised as girls. Now, with the benefit of better research, two-thirds of Klinefelter babies are being raised as boys. That's quite a significant adjustment in standards and an important corrective concerning mistaken gender.

Only since 2004, through the work and education of intersex advocates, have the secrecy and shame been lifting off the intersex population and their families. In 2005, a group of pediatric endocrinologists recommended calling intersex conditions "disorders of sex development" or DSD. The most informative site I've found is Intersex Society of North America (ISNA).[21] The advocacy group associated with ISNA is Accord Alliance.

New medical standards of care for intersex babies were established in 2006. Somewhat reliable data is being collected to allow more informed conversations to take place at the birth of such babies. Because there is no way to know the gender of an intersex baby, experts recommend that intersex children be allowed to manifest their natural, innate gender, which may be witnessed as early as two years of age, usually by age three, and almost universally by age six. Not identifying a gender in an intersex baby may be socially difficult for parents, causing them

---

[20] Klinefelter Syndrome," Intersex Society of North America, http://www.isna.org/faq/conditions/klinefelter.
[21] Intersex Society of North America, http://www.isna.org.

uneasiness or even hostility on the part of others, but it can save the intersex person from a life of frustration, and mental and emotional anguish.

Transgender—when gender and sex are not in alignment

Misgendering tens of thousands of children over a half-century period has proven that people have an internal sense of gender. The positive outcome of the Money debacle is that it led to a body of knowledge about sex and gender that has added to our understanding of people whose sex doesn't align with their internal sense of who they are.

For 99.5% of people, biological sex and gender are aligned; the term for this is "cisgender." For the 0.5% whose gender does not match their sex, the term is "transgender."[22] The word "transgender" was coined in 1965 by psychiatrist John Oliven to differentiate between transvestites, those who for sexual arousal or emotional comfort dress in the clothing opposite to their birth sex, and transsexuals, those who have an internal sense that their gender is opposite to their birth sex and desire to express the internal sense in their dress and behavior. Although Oliven's intent was to differentiate the two concepts, the word "transgender" was picked up and used in the transvestite community, making it a confusing term until the end of the 1990s. The words "transgender," "transsexual," and "transvestite" were often used interchangeably for decades. "Transgender" evolved both into a larger umbrella term for many groups expressing gender variance,[23] and into the term for a

---

[22] Gary Gates, "How Many People Are Lesbian, Gay, Bisexual and Transgender?" The Williams Institute, April 2011, http://williamsinstitute.law.ucla.edu/research/census-lgbt-demographics-studies/how-many-people-are-lesbian-gay-bisexual-and-transgender/.

[23] *Cross-dresser* – A person who, either part- or full-time, dresses as the gender they were not assigned at birth. People cross-dress for a variety of reasons, including comfort, eroticism, and even shock value. A cross-dresser may be male, female, or intersex. A cross-dresser may have any one of a variety of sexual orientations.
Transvestite – A person who dresses in the clothing of the other gender, sometimes for sexual pleasure; the term is no longer in common usage.

specific group—those who experience dissonance between their birth sex and their internal sense of gender. The latter is the meaning I use throughout this book.

So, why are people transgender? Just as with those who are intersex, there is no single reason why about one in every thousand people is transgender.[24] Back to our basic biology lesson:

Researchers believe gender is likely established as a result of the release of hormones during fetal development once biological sex is set. This occurs in the fourth month when the brain circuitry is developing. Both genetics and hormones influence the fetal brain. The amount or lack of particular hormones released may be enough to establish the genitals of one sex or the other, but not enough to genderize the brain to match the sex. We don't know absolutely for sure how gender is established. What researchers do know is that the fetal brain is hardwired by the end of the fourth month of gestation and that gendering is part of that process.

When a baby is born, the doctor and family can know the baby's sex: male, female, or intersex. At that point, though, nobody can know the gender of the child. As babies develop into toddlers, they pick up cues from their environment and begin comparing themselves to peers and to adults. Unconsciously they begin wondering, "Who am I like, and who am I not like?"[25]

By age two, without the language skills to communicate it or the words to verbalize it, children know the difference between female and male. Researchers have created fascinating tests to prove just how much

---

Drag queen or drag king – A performance artist who has a stage persona often not part of their daily life.

Androgynous – A person who blends both male and female characteristics in their appearance.

Genderqueer – A person who does not stay within the confines of masculine or feminine dress; one who blurs the lines and often invents their own expressions of gender. People who identify in this group may also be termed "gender benders."

[24] "How Many People."

[25] Alix Spiegel, "Q&A: Therapists on Gender Identity Issues in Kids," NPR, May 7, 2008, http://www.npr.org/templates/story/story.php?storyId=90229789.

toddlers are aware of. By age five, a child knows if he or she belongs to male or female groups, and into which group he or she most comfortably fits. Most boys fit in with boys and men, and most girls know they "belong" with girls and women. However, not all children fit into the group corresponding with their biological sex. By age five, those who don't fit in are aware that something is "different" about them.

Lisa Salazar's story

When I set up the Board of Directors for Canyonwalker Connections Ministry, I intentionally asked Lisa Salazar, a Christian transwoman, to join me so I would have strong representation from the "T" in LGBT.

Lisa was born Santiago Salazar in the early 1950s in Colombia, grew up in California with the nickname Jim, and now lives in Vancouver, British Columbia. Ever since Lisa can remember, she felt a disconnect with her body:

> From my earliest memory, I felt something was amiss. I didn't like to see my private parts and avoided looking down when I was naked. I distinctly remember sitting in the bathtub in three inches of water and carefully laying a washcloth over my genitals to hide them from my eyes as I played with my bath toys. I surmise I could not have been more than three years old at the time.
>
> This feeling that something wasn't right wasn't based on me having seen a girl's body and deciding I had extra parts. I was probably ten years old before I ever saw an image in a textbook of what a girl's body looked like. By the time I understood what some of the anatomical differences were, I was already estranged from my body. So where did this disconnection come from, and what did it mean?

The few times I tried getting answers, I didn't have the language for it. The questions kept piling up inside, but I just kept my mouth shut.

My childhood prayers to wake up as a girl had been abandoned by high school, and I started to most fear that someone might find out how messed up I felt inside. I was careful not to say anything or ask any questions that could betray my secret struggle. I even worried when I had sleepovers with friends that I might talk in my sleep and say something and my life would be over. Adding to the confusion, I thought, "If I am really a girl, then I should be attracted to boys," but I wasn't [attracted] to boys.

When Jim was a junior at San Jose State, he became a Christian and believed that, with God's power, his internal struggle of feeling like a woman would finally come to an end. Despite his best efforts, those feelings never went away. Thinking it was an attack from Satan, Jim used his "thorn in the flesh" to draw closer to God.

When he fell in love with a young woman he met at a Bible study, it seemed as though his prayers to be "normal" were being answered. Five years into the marriage, and by then a father of two, Jim still felt his body was the wrong sex. The shame and burden of his struggle were overwhelming. He reasoned that the burden hadn't gone away because he hadn't shared the secret with his wife; so he did. Together they committed themselves over the next eight years to raising their sons while seeking God in earnest for healing.

In the early 1990s, Jim turned forty and, full of despair and shame, sought help from a psychiatrist, who recommended he go to the newly opened Gender Clinic at Vancouver General Hospital. Jim did not take the advice; as a Christian, he believed that God only created male or female. He chose to carry the burden for nine more years and constantly thought about death as a way to end the internal pain. Finally, Jim decided to go to the Gender Clinic, hoping that nine additional years of gender research had finally found a cure. Following a six-month evaluation, it was recommended that Jim undergo a regimen of hormones and genital reassignment surgery and live as a woman. Afraid of the social, religious, and familial costs, Jim again walked away.

Eight more years passed. The internal pain was intense. Jim was faced with a decision: transition or commit suicide. The psychiatrist assured Jim that, given the choice, people would rather he be alive as a woman than dead as a man. This time, Jim invested the time he needed to study the Bible in depth to reconcile his transition process with God's Word.

In 2007, unsure of when he would begin living full-time as Lisa, Jim began to disclose to family and friends about the changes to come. In early 2008, Lisa started hormone treatment and, six months later, began living full-time as a woman. By March 2010, Lisa had completed her surgical transition.

Lisa's wife, who had been supportive of Lisa's struggles, waited one more year before asking for a divorce. For her, the marriage was over; she wanted a husband. Had they stayed together, people would see them as a lesbian couple, which was a deal breaker for the woman who had married Jim. Lisa, who identifies as a lesbian, still loved her wife and would have preferred to stay married. Lisa has covered the details of the entire story in her book *Transparently*.[26]

More about transgender people

There are about 1.5 million transgender Americans, or approximately 0.5% of the population. Whereas 65%[27] of Americans know someone who is gay or lesbian, only 9%[28] know someone who is transgender.

---

[26] Lisa Salazar, *Transparently: Behind the Scenes of a Good Life* (Self-published, 2011).
[27] "Survey: A Shifting Landscape: A Decade of Change in American Attitudes about Same-Sex Marriage and LGBT Issues," Public Religion Research Institute, February 26, 2014, http://publicreligion.org/site/wp-content/uploads/2014/02/2014.LGBT_REPORT. pdf.
[28] Ibid.

Transgender adults and children are coming into self-awareness and becoming more public about their identity than they did in the past. Realization of transgender issues and the wider availability of resources is making it easier for parents to assist their children into gender and sex congruence at earlier ages.

As classified in 2013 by the American Psychiatric Association's *Diagnostic and Statistical Manual-5* (DSM-5), transgender people have a condition known as gender dysphoria. Until this most recent DSM revision, the diagnosis had been gender identity disorder (GID). Reclassification to gender dysphoria accomplishes two things: It recognizes the significant social distress associated with having the condition, and it helps decrease social, occupational, and legal stigmatization by eliminating the word "disorder." Although transgender people have a naturally occurring condition, keeping gender dysphoria listed as a condition in the DSM ensures that access to proper care under medical insurance plans is protected.

People assigned male at birth, but who more closely identify with being female, are known as transwomen, male-to-female, MTF, or, as some of my trans*[29] friends remind me, simply women. Conversely, people assigned female at birth, but who more closely identify with being male, are known as transmen, female-to-male, FTM, or, again, simply men. I've noticed that those in the trans* community who work to raise awareness often refer to themselves as transmen, transwomen, or transgender persons. Those who want to live a more obscure life simply identify as a man or a woman, dropping the modifier "trans."

Transitioning is when a person begins the process of expressing a gender not in alignment with their birth sex. Corrective surgery is referred to as genital reassignment, or reconstruction, surgery (GRS). In the past, it was referred to as sex reassignment surgery (SRS), but this term is not technically accurate. As we've learned, sex is a combination of chromosomes, reproductive systems, and genitals. Corrective

---

[29] "Trans*" is shorthand for "transman," "transwoman," and "transgender."

surgery for a transgender person doesn't change the sex chromosomes; therefore it is properly known as GRS.

Nonsurgical transitioning may be a person's only option or their personal choice. Not every transperson wants to go through or can afford GRS. Nonsurgical options include implementing a combination of any or all of the following: change of clothing, makeup, hairstyle, mannerisms, or hormone therapy. A birth male transitioning to a female gender expression may bind down his genitals, remove body hair, take estrogen, and grow a longer hairstyle. Others have their Adam's apple shaved and even their faces and chin line feminized. A birth female transitioning to a male gender expression will likely bind her breasts, begin taking testosterone, and cut her hair in a masculine style.

The way in which transpersons choose to physically express themselves is highly personal. Some elect to go through few external changes while others opt for more elaborate makeovers. For a transperson, trying to fall within the socially prescribed typical male or female gender expressions may be extremely difficult, if not impossible. The effects of a lifetime of other-sex hormones on the body are often irreversible. One of the major benefits of transitioning at a young age is to not be burdened by decades of "wrong" hormones coursing through one's body.

The trans* population suffers a disproportionately high rate of underemployment, homelessness, harassment, and family rejection.[30] Forty-one percent have had suicidal ideation or have attempted suicide.[31] Many do not have legal documents matching the gender in which they present. In some states, even getting documents changed from a person's birth sex to reflect their gender identity is not legally possible.

---

[30] Paul Guequirre, "Transgender Workers at Greater Risk for Unemployment and Poverty," Human Rights Campaign, September 6, 2013, http://www.hrc.org/blog/entry/transgender-workers-at-greater-risk-for-unemployment-and-poverty.

[31] Ann P. Haas and Philip L. Rodgers, "Suicide Attempts among Transgender and Gender Non-Conforming Adults," Williams Institute: American Foundation for Suicide Prevention, January 2014, http://williamsinstitute.law.ucla.edu/wpcontent/uploads/AFSP-WilliamsSuicideReportFinal.pdf.

Transetiquette

Although it is natural to be very curious when meeting a transman or transwoman, it's never polite to ask a transman or transwoman about their genitals. Would you think it acceptable if someone asked you about what is inside your underwear? If you are not a potential sex partner or a medical provider, the genitals of another human being, including someone who is transgender, are none of your business.

"Transgender" is an adjective, so "transgendered" is not the proper word; neither is it correct to call someone "a transgender." Also on the "no" list are several completely inappropriate words: "she-man," "she-male," and "tranny."

If you are unsure of a person's gender, it is polite to ask how he or she (or a variety of pronouns now emerging) would prefer to be addressed. The confusion involving gender identity is typically not on the part of a transgender person; they know how they identify. The only way to clear up your own confusion is to ask. A simple question can usually solve your discomfort; ask the same question you might ask any person: "What is your name?" Most transgender people select gender-specific names aligned to their new identity. Use pronouns associated with a person's gender identity; to do otherwise is highly insensitive and, frankly, mean-spirited.

When a person transitions, they might be attracted to the same sex as they were before their transition, or not. Once sexual-social restrictions are lifted off people who were previously closeted as trans*, they may feel more free to express who they are and to whom they are attracted. Which brings us to sexual orientation.

What is sexual orientation?

All people have a biological sex (male, female, or intersex), a gender (male, female, or along the spectrum from male to female), and a sexual orientation. Sexual orientation indicates the sex to which one is naturally attracted.

Sexual orientation is not a fully accurate term because it implies that orientation is only sexual; however, orientation includes emotional and romantic attractions along with sexual attractions. Sexual orientation has three components: sexual identity, sexual behavior, and sexual attraction. Most often, all three are congruent, but not always.

Sexual identity is a personal label an individual uses to describe his or her own sexual attractions. Sexual behavior is the manner in which people regularly express their sexuality. Sexual attraction defines the sex to whom one is naturally attracted. For the majority, all three are in sync. In Chapters 11 and 12, which focus on reparative therapy and mixed-orientation marriages, we'll read stories about people who label themselves heterosexual and engage in heterosexual behavior, yet have a homosexual orientation.

Professional, social, familial, or religious pressures can influence how a person chooses to identify sexually and express his or her sexuality.

Sexual orientation, and sexual attraction in particular, can be organized into general groups:

- *Heterosexuality* – Attraction to the opposite sex: male attraction to females, or female attraction to males. Heterosexual attraction occurs in about 95% of the population.
- *Homosexuality* – Attraction to the same sex: Male attraction to males, or female attraction to females. Homosexuality occurs in about 3.5% of the population, with 11%[32] of the population acknowledging at least some same-sex attraction and behavior.
- *Bisexuality* – Male attraction to both males and females, or female attraction to both males and females. Bisexuality occurs in about 1.8%[33] of the population.
- *Pansexuality* – Attraction to people of male or female sex, whether gender is male or female. A pansexual's attraction

---

[32] "How Many People."
[33] Ibid.

is not limited by either the sex or the gender of their partner. Pansexuality occurs in less than 1% of the population.

- *Asexuality* – Lack of sexual attraction to either males or females. Asexuals may experience romantic attractions without interest in sexual activity. Often, they participate in sexual activity to please their partners or to have children. Asexuality occurs in about 1% of population.[34] Asexuals may describe their own romantic attractions as heteroromantic, homoromantic, biromantic, panromantic, or aromantic.

All of these traits exist along a spectrum. All combinations and permutations are natural and to be expected as normal variations of human sexuality.

The science of sexual orientation

A rapidly developing body of knowledge strongly indicates that there is a genetic component to sexual orientation; however, there is more going on than just genetics.

Gendering and sexual orientation may be influenced by epigenes from the parents' chromosomal contributions. Recall from the beginning of this chapter that epigenes influence the quantity and type of hormones released during fetal development. As noted earlier, gender, and possibly sexual orientation, is likely established in the brain circuitry by the end of the fourth month of fetal development.

A 2014 study[35] of the DNA of over four hundred gay and straight men indicates that a section on the X chromosome, inherited from the mother, may influence sexual orientation. Other chromosome sections seem to be involved as well, but, as in the example shared earlier regarding tallness, there is likely not just one single "gay gene."

---

[34] "Research Relating to Asexuality," AvenWiki. http://www.asexuality.org/wiki/index.php?title=Research_relating_to_asexuality.

[35] Michael Bailey, "The Science of Sex and Attraction," American Association for the Advancement of Science in Chicago, Annual Conference, 2014.

Hormones in the fetal environment impact sexual orientation as well. Brain scans that have long indicated observable differences in the brains of heterosexuals and homosexuals have, in recent years, shown such differences *in utero*.[36]

The more times a woman becomes pregnant with a son, each subsequent son's chance of being gay increases by 33%.[37] The strongest theory behind this observation holds that the mother produces testosterone-blocking antibodies in response to carrying a male fetus. These testosterone blockers stay in her body and influence subsequent fetal sons, but not daughters. Hormones don't affect male and female fetuses in the same manner, so there isn't a similar increase in the likelihood of subsequent daughters being lesbians.

Most of the studies involving homosexuality have been conducted on men. Studies on the sexuality of lesbians are more recent. Researchers are discovering that sexuality is more fluid for women than it is for men.[38] Women tend to be more driven by relationships than by the sex of the partner.[39] In studies, even women who identify as strictly heterosexual respond to female sexual stimuli when posed in the context of relationship at higher rates than do strictly heterosexual men.[40] What is known about male sexuality cannot be directly transferred to female sexuality, whether heterosexual or homosexual.

One such example is the effects of testosterone on fetuses. Researchers know that a female fetus subjected to an excess release of testosterone in the fourth month of development has a greater chance of being a

[36] Kim Smythe, "National Geographic Explains the Biology of Homosexuality – Epigenetics" (video originally presented December 2008), posted to YouTube April 3, 2013, https://www.youtube.com/watch?v=H831wTEkSFE.
[37] A. Bogaert and R. Blanchard, "Homosexuality in Men and Number of Older Brothers," *American Journal of Psychiatry* 153 (1996), 27-31.
[38] "Lisa Diamond on Sexual Fluidity of Men and Women" (video), Cornell University, December 6, 2103, https://www.youtube.com/watch?v=m2rTHDOuUBw.
[39] Meredith Chivers, "The Puzzle of Women's Sexual Orientation – Why Straight Sexuality Isn't So Straightforward in Women" (video), WhomYouLove2012, October 17, 2013, https://www.youtube.com/watch?v=nSnywIol20A.
[40] Ibid.

lesbian than being heterosexual. Testosterone is measurable because it lingers in the baby's postnatal body. But testosterone in a female fetus doesn't *always* affect the developing girl, so something else is going on.[41] Likewise, measurable hormone inhibitors which block normal levels of testosterone absorption by a male fetus can create an environment where there is an increased chance that the male will be gay. Prenatal androgens that block testosterone absorption by male fetuses alter both the gait and vocal intonation of the adult male, who will likely identify as gay.[42]

Genes, epigenes, and hormones all influence sexual orientation. We just don't know the precise formula of the interaction and what the exact components are.

Brain neurology, however, is measurable. There are distinct differences in the brains of homosexual and heterosexual people of the same sex. The hypothalamus of a male homosexual brain has many similarities to a female heterosexual brain. Homosexual men, like heterosexual women, are generally more empathetic than are straight men, as well as being better with verbal fluency, spatial distances, and language skills.[43]

Conversely, lesbians, like heterosexual men, tend to hear lower-pitched sounds and, on average, throw objects (softballs, basketballs, footballs) better than heterosexual women.[44]

Eighty percent of youth who will later identify as gay or lesbian start displaying strong signs of gender-nonconforming behavior as early as age three.[45] Most children who will later identify as gay or lesbian know

[41] Sabrina Richards, "Can Epigenetics Explain Homosexuality?" *NeuroScientist News*, January 1, 2013, http://www.thescientist.com/?articles.view/articleNo/33773/title/CanEpigeneticsExplainHomosexuality/,

[42] *Sex/Gender Biology.*

[43] James Owens, "Gay Men, Straight Women Have Similar Brains," *National Geographic*, June 16, 2008, http://news.nationalgeographic.com/news/2008/06/080616-gay-brain.html.

[44] Joan C. Chrisler, *Handbook of Gender Research in Psychology* (Springer Science, 2010), 225-227.

[45] Eric Vilain, "Born This Way: Biological Tales of Sexual Orientation" (video), WhomYouLove2012, posted to YouTube October 9, 2013, https://www.youtube.com/watch?v=9MhzXaYOBDk.

between the ages of five and eight that they are different, but they don't yet know how. By puberty, they usually understand that they are attracted to the same sex. (We expand upon sexual orientation in gay and lesbian youth in Chapter 14.)

While there is no consensus as to the root cause of sexual orientation, it is agreed by all medical and health care professionals that orientation is not related to a child's postnatal social environment. In other words, there is nothing to indicate that parenting or early-childhood events, such as abuse, affect either gender or sexual orientation.

Feeling like outsiders and sensing that they should not talk about the differences they are experiencing often makes these children more vulnerable to abusers. While there is a higher correlation between homosexual orientation and becoming a victim of sexual abuse, the abuse does not cause homosexual orientation; rather, the orientation makes a child more susceptible to the abuse.[46] This scenario is frequently twisted backwards to say that childhood abuse leads to homosexuality.[47] This is patently false. The fact is that shamed children are easy and vulnerable targets for abusers.

The parts don't fit—or do they?

Throughout the history of human sexuality, "rules" about what people should and shouldn't do sexually with their partners, even their own spouses, were wrapped up in cultural and religious taboos. Many of those old prohibitions carry over to our lives even today, and we're largely unaware of the origin of the beliefs.

An interesting case in point affects every American male to some degree. The percentage of male circumcision in the United States over the last century is directly linked to beliefs and taboos surrounding

---

[46] "The Problem with the Belief that Child Sexual Abuse Causes Homosexuality, Bisexuality," Pandora's Project, 2009, http://www.pandys.org/articles/abuseandhomosexuality.html.

[47] "Facts about Homosexuality and Child Molestation," University of California, Davis, Psychology Department, http://psychology.ucdavis.edu/faculty_sites/rainbow/html/facts_molestation.html.

masturbation. In the 1870s, only one percent of American males were circumcised. By 1970, that number had risen to 90%.[48] The increase is totally attributable to taboo and myth. Circumcision was seen as a preventative measure to stop the "self-abuse" of masturbation with its threatened imaginary side effects of mental illness and sterility. Wrote Leslie Weatherhead in 1931:

> In olden days—not so very olden either—this practice was painted as the blackest of all possible sins. Anyone who practiced it was pretty sure of hell. Our grandfathers, including our medical grandfathers, if they did not avoid all reference to it, taught that it was not only a dreadful sin, but that also it had physical and mental consequences which were terrible, these consequences being regarded as the just punishment of God for human wickedness. It was said that the victim of this habit invariably brought disease upon himself and that if he did not speedily check it he would go mad. . . . The only hope of cure held out was said to lie in the exercise of the victim's will assisted by religious exercises of prayer and Bible reading.[49]

Similar prohibitions on sex acts—again, even between husbands and wives—have existed for centuries. For the most part, we remain unaware as to why we perceive some acts as "icky" and unnatural.

In the ancient world, sex was divided along two major axes: purpose (procreative or non-procreative) and role (active or passive). Immorality and "sin" were easily defined within those boundaries. In the 19th century, any sexual behavior not intended to lead to procreation, even

---

[48] "A Short History of Male Circumcision," http://www.whale.to/a/circumcision1.html.
[49] Leslie Weatherhead, *The Mastery of Sex through Psychology and Religion*, 1931. Cited in: Ralph Blair, "The Real Changes Taking Place in the Ex-Gay Movement," Evangelicals Concerned Inc., Fall 1986, http://ecinc.org/the-real-changes-taking-place-in-the-ex-gay-movement/.

within marriage, was considered by society to be immoral, and by the religious community to be sinful. Regarding the roles played (as we learned in Chapter 1), simply put, men who took the passive role in sex were disgraced. This concept is intrinsically connected to the low value placed on women. However, we (at least in the United States and many other countries of the world) no longer live in a culture where to be like a woman is contemptible, so the sexual taboos attached to patriarchal cultures have been disintegrating over time for both heterosexual and homosexual behavior.

Some non-procreative sexual acts commonly enjoyed today by heterosexual couples were taboo only sixty years ago. Sexual-social norms in general have changed dramatically in the past century. Today sex is seen as an opportunity to express affection, desire, comfort, bonding, love, and passion for one's partner. Sex isn't just about coitus for the sake of making babies anymore. A 2010 Indiana University study defined forty different ways in which people regularly engage in sexual practices.[50] Warning: If you are bothered by imagining or thinking about "gay sex," skip the next few paragraphs. The bottom line of this section is this: Sexual intercourse works just as well for gay people as it does for straight people.

What follows is a primer on human sexuality leading to better understanding of "gay sex," with much of it equally applicable to the "heterosexual lifestyle" for the sake of added heterosexual enjoyment. Let's start with an anatomy lesson.

All men, gay or straight, have a prostate, a walnut-sized gland located between the bladder and the penis and just in front of the rectum, an area of the body with an abundance of nerve endings. Stimulation of the prostate gland with a finger or the penis inserted into the rectum via the anus can be highly pleasurable and can lead to orgasm. It can be

---

[50] "Sex Practices National Survey of Sexual Health and Behavior," Indiana University, 2010, http://www.nationalsexstudy.indiana.edu/graph.html.

a safe practice between partners in loving sexual exchanges, caring for each other by using lubricants and condoms.

Not all gay couples engage in anal sex, and not all couples who engage in anal sex are gay. One-quarter of all heterosexual women under age forty participate in anal sex; the numbers vary across age demographics and ethnicity.[51] Likewise, many heterosexual men derive great pleasure from their female partners stimulating their prostate glands.

During the Victorian Age, and until the middle of the 19th century, women of social status typically did not participate in sex for pleasure. It was considered "vulgar."[52] Historically, heterosexual acts have been focused on male pleasure; women's sexual enjoyment came more into focus with the availability of birth control options. Whether a woman even had clitoral or vaginal orgasms was debated until Masters and Johnson "proved" in the 1950s that women experienced both.

Most women do not reach orgasm through coitus alone. Only one-third of women climax with coitus, another one-third with coitus plus additional stimulation, and another one-third only with stimulation other than coitus.[53] Two women having sexual contact with each other don't need a penis to reach orgasm. In fact, women have a higher chance of being pleased by other women because they rely on non-penile stimulation by their partners. Putting it plainly, the "natural way" of having male-female sex is typically more satisfying for heterosexual men than for heterosexual women.

How clever of God, the designer of human sexuality, to create the human body in such a way as to allow ample provision for mutually satisfying relationships between loving couples! Though used by many a preacher in the pulpit, the "male plug and female adaptor-cord analogy" is limiting, even for heterosexual couples. It describes one type of sexual interaction. Human sexuality is far more complex and beautiful than electricity.

---

[51] Ibid.

[52] *Marriage, a History*, 190.

[53] "Female Orgasm: Myth and Facts," The Society of Obstetricians and Gynaecologists of Canada, http://sogc.org/publications/female-orgasms-myths-and-facts/.

In terms of sex between same-sex partners, the objection that "the parts don't fit" doesn't make sense on even the most logical level. If the parts didn't work together, frankly, people wouldn't be putting them together. Gay sex not only fits—it works.

Human sexuality is far more elaborate than male and female and men with women. It is certainly more complicated than those who penned the words of the Bible or lived before the turn of the 20th century could have imagined.

Finally, we're ready to look at the passages of Scripture often used to create a Christian sexual ethic for lesbian, gay, bisexual, and transgender people, and for believers in general. Armed with some basic understanding about the biology and the science of sex, gender, and sexual orientation, we can allow the knowledge to inform us about the beauty and diversity of God's natural creation as it acts in harmony with the richness of God's spiritual recreation.

PART IV: THE BIBLE

Chapter 9

Same-Sex Behavior in the Bible
Looking at Passages of Scripture

Same-sex behavior in six Bible passages

We've explored the historical, scientific, and societal lenses influencing perspectives about people who are lesbian, gay, bisexual, and transgender (LGBT). Now it's time to look at Scripture passages directly referring to same-sex behavior in order to determine what these verses might have to say.

There are six biblical passages referring to same-sex behavior. Three are in the Old Testament—Genesis 19:1-13; Leviticus 18:22; Leviticus 20:13—and three are in the New Testament—Romans 1:26-32; 1 Corinthians 6:9-10; 1 Timothy 1:9-10.

In 1946, the creators of the Revised Standard Version (RSV) of the Bible were the first to translate Greek words associated with same-sex behavior as "homosexual." Some may argue that though prior translators and even those who wrote the original texts may not have known the word "homosexual," they used the language they did have to convey the concept of homosexuality. Doubtless, all six passages of Scripture depict negative views of males having sex with males, but can these verses be used as blanket condemnations of all forms of homosexuality, even long-term, monogamous relationships between equal-status partners? In order to answer that question, it's vital to understand what those referred to by the passages as engaging in same-sex behavior were doing and under what circumstances. Awareness of that context may inform our application of the texts to modern-day questions of moral and sexual ethics.

Let's look at the passages through the historical, social, and religious lenses of the times in which they were written, then investigate how they have been understood in the past, and finally, consider what the passages mean for us today. For a more detailed study of the passages, I recommend Dr. James V. Brownson's *Bible, Gender, Sexuality* and Matthew Vines' *God and the Gay Christian*.

What does Genesis say about same-sex behavior?

The story of Sodom and Gomorrah in Genesis 18-19 is a simple one. God was ready to destroy the cities and inhabitants of Sodom and Gomorrah because of their wickedness. God (called "the Lord" in this story) came, along with two angels in the form of men, to visit the home of Abraham, who lived far outside the cities. As the two men travelled on toward Sodom, the Lord engaged in negotiations with Abraham as to how many righteous inhabitants must be found there in order to save the city from destruction. Aware that his nephew, Lot, lived with his family in Sodom, Abraham bargained the number down to ten: He and the Lord agreed that if ten righteous people could be found, Sodom would be spared.

Meanwhile, as the two men entered the gates of Sodom, Lot, knowing of the possible dangers awaiting visitors who stayed in the town square overnight, invited them into the protection of his home. Late into the evening, the Bible says, all the men of Sodom surrounded Lot's house and demanded that he send the two guests out so the men of the city might have sex with them. The sex the men were demanding was not based on loving desire; rather, it was a form of gang rape intended to humiliate the guests.

In lieu of raping the visitors, Lot urged the crowd to take his two daughters. It's almost inconceivable to imagine a father doing such a thing. As is true with many passages of Scripture, this one needs to be understood within its own time and culture. In ancient cultures, women suffered low status. The rape of a woman, even one's own daughter, didn't compare to the humiliation suffered by a man if he were raped. Not satisfied with the offer of abusing the daughters, the men of Sodom persisted and demanded that the visitors come out of the house. Instead, the angels blinded the inhabitants of Sodom and quickly escaped with Lot, his wife, and his two daughters.

Though the Genesis 18-19 account never mentions what the sin was that was "so grievous" (18:20) as to lead to the destruction of Sodom, Ezekiel 16:49-50 does list sins of Sodom: arrogance, an uncaring attitude toward the poor and needy despite their own riches, and other "detestable things." In the thirteen mentions of Sodom and Gommorah after Genesis 19, same-sex behavior is never cited as the sin that caused the destruction of the city.

In the New Testament, Jesus mentions Sodom. As He sends His disciples out to preach, He alludes to the possible consequences that will be suffered by inhabitants of cities to which the disciples are going if they mistreat the visitors. Jesus warns in Matthew 10:14-15 (NIV): "If anyone will not welcome you or listen to your words, shake the dust off your feet when you leave that home or town. I tell you the truth, it will be more bearable for Sodom and Gomorrah on the day of judgment than for that town." Sodom is again mentioned in Luke 10:12 and in 2 Peter 2:6; no male-male sexual behavior is mentioned.

Sexual immorality *is* mentioned in Jude 1:7. The verse says that the people of Sodom had "given themselves over to sexual immorality and gone after strange flesh" (NIV). But the Greek words here, *sarkos heteras* or "other flesh," are thought by some commentators to indicate the flesh of angels, as the men of Sodom had tried to rape the angels.[1]

No Jewish writer specifies same-sex behavior as the sin of Sodom at any time over the 1,400 years following Sodom and Gomorrah's destruction. Philo, a first-century Jewish philosopher, was the earliest writer to directly connect the sin of Sodom to same-sex behavior. Philo writes of the inhabitants of Sodom in *On Abraham:*

> [A]s men . . . pursuing a great deal of intemperate indulgence of gluttony, and drinking, and unlawful connections; not only did they go mad after other women, and defile the marriage beds of others, but also those who were men lusted after one another, doing unseemly things, and not regarding or respecting their common nature . . . the men became accustomed to being treated like women, and in this way engendered among themselves the disease of females, and intolerable evil; for they not only, as to effeminacy and delicacy, became like women in their person, but they also made their souls most ignoble, corrupting in this way the whole race of man, as far as dependent on them.[2]

Philo's account is quite different from biblical texts referencing Sodom. Philo describes an overall orgy-like atmosphere of gluttony, drunkenness, and sexual excesses. The men of Sodom, driven by their lusts, had sex not only with their own wives, but with other men and their wives. Some men, Philo wrote, were "treated like women" (i.e., the penetrated, passive sex partner). As a consequence, according to the author, even their souls became like those of women—diseased, evil, and ignoble.

---

[1] James Brownson, *Bible, Gender, Sexuality* (Grand Rapids, MI: William B. Eerdmans, 2013), 42.

[2] "Early Jewish Writings," http://www.earlyjewishwritings.com/text/philo/book22.html.

Two other notable early Christian writers, Tertullian, in the second century, and St. Jerome, in the fourth century, did not link the sin of Sodom to same-sex behavior. St. Jerome, in fact, specifically echoed the prophet Ezekiel and identified arrogance and excesses of food and drink as the sins of Sodom.

Though no biblical texts explicitly connect same-sex behavior to the sin of Sodom, it was Augustine, a fifth-century theologian, who fixed the popular connection between the sin of Sodom and same-sex behavior. In referring to the men of Sodom, he decried those who took the passive role, writing that they were "corrupt and pervert their own nature by becoming inflamed with passion to make unnatural use of the thing which You [God] do not allow."[3]

Augustine also introduced to the church the imperative that sex, in order for it to be moral, had to be procreative.

What do Leviticus 18 and 20 say about same-sex behavior?

> Do not have sexual relations with a man as one does with a woman; that is detestable. (Leviticus 18:22, NIV)

> If a man has sexual relations with a man as one does with a woman, both of them have done what is detestable. They are to be put to death; their blood will be on their own heads. (Leviticus 20:13, NIV)

There is little doubt that the sexual behavior referenced in both of these chapters in Leviticus is not pleasing to God; neither was it acceptable to the Jews. Let's look at the overall context of the verses.

The two passages are contained in the Law God gave to Moses after the Jews left one pagan culture behind in Egypt and before they entered

---

[3] St. Augustine, *Confessions*, Book III, chap. 8.

another one in Canaan. The Law not only defined the way in which the Israelites were to serve God; it also established clear boundaries and prohibitions in order to keep the Jews holy, separate from, and undefiled by the surrounding cultures.

If a Jew broke any prohibitions in the Law, he or she was considered guilty of breaking the whole Law. Even though some Bible scholars group the Law's prohibitions into categories, there is no such distinction in the Bible. Today, we elevate some of the laws over others, supposing that they must still be kept while "lesser" laws can be disregarded. A few weighty injunctions once deserving of death or communal ostracism are completely disregarded by Christians today. These include the prohibition from engaging in sex while a woman has her period, the requirement that males be circumcised, and the law that forbade charging interest on loans. Furthermore, whether the prohibitions are grouped or not, the righteousness of believers is not dependent on their keeping of the Law, but on their faith in Jesus Christ.[4]

Still, there may be some who believe that parts of the Law must be followed by believers today, so rather than ignore the prohibitions as non-binding, let's try to understand the same-sex behavior described in Leviticus.

The verses clearly state that if a man has sex with another man, it is *toevah* and worthy of the death penalty. The Hebrew word *toevah*, which is most often translated "abomination," is found 117 times in the Old Testament. In most cases, it's associated with foreign, cultural, idolatrous, or religious practices. Old Testament scholar Phyllis Bird has shown how, by using the Levitical guidelines, God set clear boundaries to keep His people holy, separate from, and undefiled by pagan groups surrounding them. Bird explains that *toevah* "is not an ethical term, but a term of boundary marking" with "a basic sense of taboo."[5] Every

---

[4] Matthew Vines, *God and the Gay Christian* (New York City: Convergent, 2014), 78-83.
[5] Phyllis Bird, "The Bible in Christian Ethical Deliberation Concerning Homosexuality: Old Testament Contributions," in *Homosexuality, Science, and the "Plain Sense" of Scripture*, ed. David Balch (Grand Rapids, MI: William B. Eerdmans, 1999), 152.

facet of a Jew's life became a visible demarcation between himself and the pagan cultures surrounding him.

The ways in which the Israelites ate, dressed, planted fields, and trimmed their hair and beards were physical reminders of their distinct status as people of God. Their lives were governed by orderliness. Ambiguous things were deemed an abomination and taboo; fish with legs (crustaceans), clothing woven from more than one fabric, and fields planted with two kinds of seeds all blurred the sense of order and boundaries and were thus considered impure.

The Israelites' extreme sense of separateness kept them from doing *anything* that would even remotely resemble how the pagans looked or what the pagans did. Same-sex behavior, whether in situations of personal lustful excess or of ritual and worship, was a common pagan practice and, therefore, strictly forbidden for the Israelites.

Some have argued that the central issue of the Leviticus 18:22 injunction is the "unfittedness" of body parts between two people of the same sex. Notice, however, that while there *is* a Levitical prohibition against men or women having sex with animals, there is no prohibition against women having sex with women. Further, the Bible, in its totality, is absolutely silent on any imperative about body parts fitting together in a "proper" way. Until the late 19th century, the social and religious focus on how people participated in sex remained centered on two key issues: what role a person took in the sex act (active or passive), and whether the sex act was procreative or non-procreative. That's it; people in the ancient world simply did not think of sex in terms of what anatomical parts fit together.[6]

The Levitical prohibitions involve same-sex behavior in a pagan culture where a man taking the sexual role of a woman was degrading. The Israelites were told to remain separate from all behaviors resembling

---

[6] "Dr. James Brownson – Gender Complementarity" (video), The Reformation Project, September 19, 2013. Retrieved July 5, 2014, https://www.youtube.com/watch?v=k1f0KD-B0Z8.

those of the pagans, lest they become like them or appear to be one of them.

And again, Christians today are not subject to finding their righteousness by keeping the Law; our righteousness is found in the atoning work of Jesus which we claim through faith.

What does Romans 1:26-27 say about same-sex behavior?

The first part of Paul's letter to the church in Rome deals with the universality of sin, our inability to gain a right status before God through our own merits, our subsequent need for a relationship with God through Jesus, and the consequences of a life lived outside of submission to God. Not only was it difficult to express in detail what salvation in Christ meant, but Paul was further challenged by having to communicate Christian doctrine to two very different audiences: the Jewish Christians and the Gentile Christians.

The ethics of the Jewish converts to Christianity were rooted in their understanding of sin and righteousness as revealed in the Law of Moses. Even if they kept the whole Law, Paul told the Jews, they would never be righteous enough on their own without placing their faith in Jesus as an intermediary to a saving relationship with God.

Paul couldn't use the same line of reasoning with the Gentile Christians because, not only did they *not* know the Law, but their ethics were grounded elsewhere. The prevailing philosophy of the Greco-Roman world at the time was Stoicism. A moral and ethical stoic life was one where an individual lived in harmony with his or her society and wider world, including the natural world. What one person did affected the whole of society. Self, society, and world were very interconnected.[7]

For a Stoic to be in complete harmony with nature was akin to a Jew keeping the whole of the Law. Neither aspiration was fully possible all the time, and even if they did come close to perfection, it would still

---

[7] *Bible, Gender, Sexuality,* 244-247.

not be enough to be righteous before God. Whether one was a Jew or a Gentile, regardless of one's attempt at good living, without God, one's ethics disintegrated into immorality.

Immorality to a Gentile was different than immorality to a Jew. Paul couldn't prick the conscience of the Gentiles by writing to them about breaking the Law; he had to use words, scenarios, and principles from ethical foundations that *they* understood.

We see the use of the words "nature" and "natural" several times in Romans 1 as Paul directly addresses the Gentiles. While we may think of "nature" and "natural" as referring to the biological and physical world today, that's only a small piece of what those words meant to the Romans in the first century. For one who followed Stoicism, to be in harmony with nature, or to act naturally, meant keeping a moral convergence of *all three of these:* individual self-control, compliance with social-sexual norms, and sexual acts for the purpose of procreation. Conversely, the Gentiles would have understood that disharmony with nature, or acting unnaturally in a state of sexual impurity, meant being lustful, defying the male-dominant social and sexual norms, and participating in non-procreative sex. With the groundwork laid of what the Gentiles saw as *nature, natural,* and *sexual immorality,* we can understand the masterful way in which Paul appeals to them beginning in Romans 1:18.

Paul starts by writing that, even if an individual does not have knowledge of what Christians today call the Old Testament, God has made Himself plainly known in creation since the beginning of time. Every person is given a choice to either glorify and thank Creator God, or reject Him. Beginning in verse 21, Paul describes the life of those who reject God. Near the end of chapter 1, Paul describes those who reject God *in terms the Roman Gentiles would understand:*

> Because of this [their rejection of God], God gave them over to shameful lusts. Even their women exchanged natural relations for unnatural ones. In the same way the men also

abandoned natural relations with women and were inflamed
with lust for one another. (Roman 1:26-27, Thompson Chain
Reference NIV)

Every behavior in Romans 1:26-27 is counter to the natural harmony
of moral stoic behavior. In the scenario Paul depicts, both the men and
women have abandoned self-control, are driven by lust, and are participating in sexually impure acts. All the behaviors are called "shameful"
because they are lustful, outside the male-dominant social and sexual
norms, and not procreative.

Let's stop here for a moment and examine gender hierarchy in the ancient world with its extreme form of dominance of male over female. The
structure of extreme male dominance is so unlike our culture today; it's
easy to miss why the sexual activities in verses 26-27 were so shameful if
we don't recognize that first-century gender hierarchy is at play.

In the ancient world, men dominated while women submitted in *all*
areas: in the relationship between husband and wife, in the family, in
the culture, in intellectual arenas, in government, and, most certainly
important in the context of Romans 1, in sex.

Men were the active participants in sex, the penetrators. Women
were the passive participants in sex, the penetrated. Also, the social
value of a woman was far beneath that of a man. So, when a man either
voluntarily took, or was placed in, the sexual role of a woman as the
penetrated partner, his entire social and personal status was degraded
to that of a woman.

Further, when a man abandoned his self-control and was driven by
his lust, he was found to be acting like a woman. Men, it was believed,
were able to control themselves, yet women were unrestrained in their
passions.[8] Even if a man maintained the active role of penetrator, in
losing self-control, he had become like a woman.[9]

---

[8] Ibid., 236.
[9] Ibid., 245.

In verses 26-27, we've already seen loss of self-control and disregard of sexual roles. Add non-procreative sex to this scenario, and *everything* going on countered the Stoics' sense of morality and harmony with nature.

Nature/Natural = self-control + social-sexual norm compliance + sex acts intent on procreation

Unnatural/against nature = lust + defiance of male-dominant social-sexual norms + non-procreative sex

Because Romans 1:26-27 is the only passage in the Bible *possibly*—but not necessarily—containing commentary on lesbian sex, we need to examine it more closely. The verses describe the women as *"their* women," or the men's wives. While we don't know exactly what the women were doing, we do know it was outside the bounds of what the Romans would have considered natural. Again, *natural* dictated both an active male penetrator and procreative sex.

Bible scholar Dr. James Brownson suggests that the women may have participated in non-procreative sex acts.[10] New Testament scholar Bernadette Brooten argues that the statement that "women exchanged natural relations for unnatural relations" means "women exchanged the passive, subordinate sexual role for an active autonomous role."[11]

Unnatural female sex in the Greco-Roman world could have been any one of the following behaviors: sex with a man where the woman takes the dominant position, non-procreative sex with a man or another woman, or even solo masturbation. Using Romans 1:26-27 to construct a wholesale condemnation of lesbian relationships is certainly not a strong position from which to build a case. We simply

---

[10] Ibid., 244.
[11] Bernadette Brooten, "Paul's Views on the Nature of Women and Female Homoeroticism," in *Immaculate and Powerful: The Female in Sacred Image and Social Reality*, ed. Clarissa Atkinson (Boston: Beacon Press, 1985), 63.

can't tell from the passage what the sexual behavior was. We do know that whatever the acts were, they were motivated by lust, not love, and do not illustrate the affection between two women in a committed Christian relationship.

Finally, what timeless message might we find in Romans 1:26-27? To the Gentiles, an immoral life was one in disharmony with nature as they understood the concept. Their perception of out-of-control sexuality doesn't translate into our culture.

We don't live in a culture where every area of life from relationship to government is structured within a gender hierarchy of extreme male dominance and female submission. It's not disgraceful or degrading for a man to take a "submissive" cultural role "like a woman," or to be under the authority of a female boss or leader, or to participate in tasks, such as child-rearing, that were historically seen as women's work. Positive and negative emotions and intellectual endeavors aren't defined along the lines of one's sex. Couples, including heterosexual couples, regularly engage in non-coital, non-procreative sex without the burden of cultural or religious shame that would have certainly been attached to it at the time of Paul's writing.

The wide availability of contraception since the 1960s has affected sexual freedom for women even inside marriage. Sex is not just for making babies; it is like "marriage glue" and has a component of pleasure for both partners. These would not have been significant aspects of a first-century view of sexual acts.

The scene in Romans 1:26-27 was considered so bad because men and women had challenged social-sexual male-dominance roles and participated in non-procreative sex, neither of which is immoral in our culture. Romans 1 also addressed those who had rejected God and fallen into a life of sexual impurity and excess. So, what might out-of-control sexual immorality equivalent to that of Romans 1:26-27 look like to us? Surely it would include sex acts driven by out-of-control lust and concern for self-satisfaction in fleeting relationships—and straight and gay both get caught in that net!

Before wrapping up the examination of Romans 1, let's note that verse 27 speaks of the "due penalty" that befalls those who reject God. The due penalty *as understood by the Roman Gentiles* was a life devoid of self-control and filled with excesses leading to personal and social dishonor and shame. As we saw in Chapter 7, many of the televangelists in the 1980s and 1990s declared that God Himself had sent the "due penalty" of HIV/AIDS on the gay community because they were engaged in same-sex behavior. The words "due penalty" have been, and still are, taken out of context and used as a condemnation against people living with or who have died of HIV/AIDS. The following was spoken by Jerry Falwell in 1987, when 20,139 Americans had already died of AIDS:

> God says . . . that homosexuality is a perverted and reprobate lifestyle. God also says that those engaged in such homosexual acts will receive "in their own persons, due penalty of their error." He's bringing judgment against this wicked practice through AIDS.[12]

And the misuse of this scripture continues today. The following was spoken by David Barton, conservative Christian historian, on the radio broadcast "WallBuilders Live," on May 15, 2013, when over 641,000 Americans had died of AIDS-related causes:

> Romans 1:27 is one of the reasons we'll never find a cure for AIDS . . . because the Bible says "men committed shameful acts with other men, sexual acts, and received in themselves the due penalty for their error."

---

[12] Jerry Falwell, "How Many Roads to Heaven?" sermon on The Old Time Gospel Hour television show, May 10, 1987.

What do 1 Corinthians and 1 Timothy say about same-sex behavior?

There are two more passages in the New Testament associated with same-sex behavior. They are 1 Corinthians 6:9-10 and 1 Timothy 1:9-10. The passages contain two Greek words, *arsenokoitai* and *malakoi,* crucial to understanding the intent of the verses, yet challenging to translate into modern-day English. Consequently, not all English Bibles agree on how the words *malakoi* and *arsenokoitai* should be translated. Many translations, such as the NIV below, combine the two distinct words into one word. We'll see why this is problematic.

Here are 1 Corinthians 6:9-10 and 1 Timothy 1:9-10 with *malakoi* and *arsenokoitai(s)*[13] inserted:

> Do you not know that the unrighteous will not inherit the kingdom of God? Do not be deceived. Neither fornicators, nor idolaters, nor adulterers, nor homosexuals [*malakoi*], nor sodomites [*arsenokoitai*], nor thieves, nor covetous, nor drunkards, nor revilers, nor extortioners will inherit the kingdom of God. (1 Corinthians 6:9-10, NKJV)

> We also know that the law is made not for the righteous but for lawbreakers and rebels, the ungodly and sinful, the unholy and irreligious, for those who kill their fathers or mothers, for murderers, for the sexually immoral, for those practicing homosexuality [*arsenokoitais*], for slave traders and liars and perjurers—and for whatever else is contrary to the sound doctrine that conforms to the gospel concerning

---

[13] Greek has five cases for nouns; two such cases are nominative and dative. When a noun is the subject, it is in the nominative case. When it is the indirect object and modified by "to" or "for," the noun is in the dative case. In 1 Corinthians, the Greek word stem *arsenokoites* is written in the nominative case, *arsenokoitai*, because it is the subject. In 1 Timothy, the word describes for whom the law was written and thus is in the dative case; hence, *arsenokoitais*.

the glory of the blessed God, which he entrusted to me. (1 Timothy 1:9-10, NIV)

Let's start with *arsenokoitais* in 1 Timothy 1:9-10 before we move on to 1 Corinthians 6:9-10, where both *arsenokoitai* and *malakoi* are used. *Arsenokoites* was rarely used in Greek writings. Paul seems to have coined it from two words: *arsen,* meaning male, and *koites,* meaning bed. Some have speculated that the word Paul used comes directly from, and has the same meaning as, *arsen* and *koiten* in the Greek translation of Leviticus 20:13: "males who lie with males." The Hebrew words *arsen* and *koiten,* used to describe events 1,600 years before Paul, suggest pederasty, or men having sex with young boys.

As used by Paul in the first century, *arsenokoitai likely* means pederasty. Pederastic relationships, inherently abusive and exploitative, are not equivalent to committed, loving, and monogamous same-sex relationships today. To say that they are would be like saying sex trafficking of young girls is equivalent to marriage.

But how can we verify the essence of *arsenokoitais* in this passage? The only way to get closer to the intended meaning is to find it used in context in other texts around the same general time period—in this case, the first century. This, too, is problematic. *Arsenokoites* is found in fewer than one hundred writings over a period of six hundred years, and in most cases it is in lists which don't provide narrative clues. Most frequently, *arsenokoites* was associated with money and exploitative sex; for example:[14]

- In the *Sibylline Oracle,* a collection of writings from the second to the sixth centuries, *arsenokoites* was listed along with stealing, lying, and murder.

---

[14] Dale B. Martin, *"Arsenokoites* and *Malakos*: Meaning and Consequences," *Biblical Ethics & Homosexuality: Listening to Scripture,* edited by Robert L. Brawley (Louisville, Kentucky: Westminster John Knox Press, 1996), 120-122.

- In the *Acts of John*, a document dating from the second century, *arsenokoites* appeared in context with robbery, cheating, and sex with shrine prostitutes.
- In all translations of nonbiblical texts prior to the 1500s in which *arsenokoites* was used, it was most closely connected to exploitative sex for money.

English translations of the Bible have used the following words (not an exhaustive list) to represent the concept of *arsenokoitais:*

- bugger (1557)
- liers with mankind (1582)
- sodomites (1735)
- abusers of themselves with mankind (1885)
- those who abuse themselves with men (1890)

The closest meaning of *arsenokoitai* over five hundred years of translation was men who took the active role in nonprocreative sex. *Arsenokoitai* did not define what we would call the sexual orientation of a person; it indicated the *role played* in the sexual act.

A curious shift began to happen for the first time in the late 1940s: *Arsenokoitai* was translated in the 1946 Revised Standard Version (RSV) of the Bible as "homosexual." This meant that the translation changed the meaning of the original word from a condemnation of *any kind of man who played the dominant role in sex with another male* to a condemnation of *one* specific kind of man—a gay person.

After the RSV translated *arsenokoitai* to "homosexual," the floodgates opened. *Arsenokoitai* was soon translated variously:

- pervert (1962)
- sexual pervert (1966)

- sodomite (1966)[15]
- those who practice homosexuality (1978)

These changing translations directly reflect the evolving perceptions of gay people in the culture surrounding the American translators of the Bible.

Recall that the late 1930s saw the beginning of discrimination against "sexual inverts" by medical professionals, law enforcement, and the mainstream culture. By the 1940s, the government joined in with deliberately discriminatory policies. By the 1950s, the Lavender Scare was in full swing and the "sex pervert" paranoia began sweeping the country. By the late 1970s, when the conservative Christian community turned its full focus on "the homosexuals," the word *arsenokoitai,* without benefit of any additional historical information or biblical scholarship, came to be translated, almost universally in English versions of the Bible, as "homosexual."

In the culture in which *arsenokoitai* originated, the meaning was closest either to pederasty or to a man engaged in exploitative sex with a male with some sort of trade or money involved. Such relationships were not and are not equal-status relationships; one partner has power, while the other is being used and degraded. Furthermore, *no one* knows the fully nuanced meaning of *arsenokoitai,* but it is clear from all its contexts that *it does not refer to women in any way.* Yet, when *arsenokoitai* was mistranslated to "homosexual," it immediately, by definition, came to include women as well as men. The translation shift of *arsenokoitai* from men who engage in exploitative sex with males to "homosexual" referring to both men and women appears to have been "prompted not by criteria of historical criticism"—a respected form of literary scholarship—"but by shifts in modern sexual ideology."[16]

---

[15] In 1735, "sodomite" meant those who participated in non-procreative sex. In 1966, the word meant gay men.

[16] *Biblical Ethics & Homosexuality: Listening to Scripture,* 119.

Now to *malakoi,* which is paired in context with *arsenokoitai* in 1 Corinthians 6:9-10. *Malakoi* is easier to translate because it appears in more ancient texts than *arsenokoitai,* yet it suffers other complications when translated to modern English. Older translations for *malakoi* are:

- weaklings (1525)
- effeminate (1582, 1901)
- those who make women of themselves (1890)
- the sensual (1951)

Then, just as happened with *arsenokoitais,* there was a radical shift over just a few decades. Following cultural stereotyping of gay people, *malakoi* was translated as follows:

- those who participate in homosexuality (1958)
- sexual perverts (1972)
- male prostitute (1989)

So, how did *malakoi* shift from its association with character traits to association with specific kinds of people performing sexual acts?

The answer lies in another Greek word, *malakos,* which means "soft." A modern reader might consider *malakos* to highlight the finer qualities of a woman and perhaps then assume an association with "softer," more feminine men. But this is an ancient word with ancient meanings.

Malakos is associated with the traits of women as women were seen in the ancient world: morally weak, given to unnatural vices, lazy, unchaste, lustful, whorish, impure, and taking a submissive role in sex. *Malakos* was used to characterize men who lived lives of decadence; partook in excesses of food, drink, and sex; were weak in battle; prettied themselves for sexual exploits with women; or even were simply too bookish. Additionally, men who fell deeply in love with women and lost control of their passions or neglected their business pursuits were thought to be effeminate.[17]

Malakos and "effeminate," although they did in part describe men who took the role of a woman in sex, encompassed traits beyond just sex roles. *Malakos* and "effeminate" described a disposition associated with all the negative traits assigned to women.

The ancient system and culture of patriarchy, where men ruled, and gender hierarchy, where men dominated women, form an inextricable backdrop to the meanings of *malakos* and "effeminate." In those historical social structures, the *worst* way one could treat a man was to treat him as if he were a woman, and the *worst* thing a man could act like was a woman.

The historical meaning of *malakoi* presents a modern translational problem because the most consistent and best historical translation of *malakoi* really *is* "effeminate"—but not our modern understanding of "effeminate." So when the 1552 Douay-Rheims Bible and the 1901 American Standard Version translated *malakoi* as "effeminate," the word still included the sense of all the ugly traits thought to be associated with women; it had nothing to do with gay men. *Nothing.* Today "effeminate" means "having or showing qualities that are considered more suitable to women than to men."[18] The modern word doesn't carry the baggage of ancient negative views of women. But Paul was not writing to a world where women were of equal status to men, a world where to be a woman, or to be like a woman, was to be honorable, or to behave honorably. In light of all this, the best modern translation of *malakoi* would include in its meaning an indulgent or excessive disposition which *may* at times include sexual excess.

By now it should be clearer why translating *malakoi* as "homosexual" is completely inaccurate. There are several translators and modern Bible commentators who compound these inaccuracies by further asserting

---

[17] Ibid., 128-129
[18] Merriam-Webster Dictionary, http://www.merriam-webster.com/dictionary/effeminate.

that *malakoi* refers to the passive partner in gay sex and that *arsenokoitais* describes the active partner in gay sex. This appears to be a highly biased translation of words to suit modern conservative presumptions.

Translations based on theology or ideology?

The structure of this book examines how systems interconnect and influence one another, whether those systems are medical, cultural, religious, and political, or in the case of Bible translations, a combined linguistic-cultural ideology.

No system, whether science, culture, politics, or religion, operates in a vacuum. Obviously, those who translate the Bible live in and are influenced by their own culture. In the late 1940s, gay people became the scapegoat of the culture and the legal system. Consistent with what was happening in the culture and legal system, *malakoi* and *arsenokoitai(s)* came to indicate the two partners in gay sex.

Neither word had ever been associated with sexual activities on the part of women. The only association with women had been an extensive list of unfavorable female characteristics from ancient cultures to the 19th century.

A quite unfortunate and significant shift in translating *malakoi* and *arsenokoitai* occurred in 1971, when the English editors of The Living Bible combined the two Greek words *malakoi* and *arsenokoitai* into the *single* English word "homosexual." The publishers and compilers of The Living Bible took it upon themselves to effectively ban lesbians from the kingdom of God with a new version of 1 Corinthians 6:9-10. This may well be the worst case of a lack of scriptural faithfulness in all the different translations of *malakoi* and *arsenokoitais*.

The Living Bible editorial team was dominated by evangelical, Southern Baptist, and Assemblies of God pastors and theologians, all conservative voices.[19] Over 40 million copies of the English version

---

[19] Michael Marlowe, "The New Living Translation," *Bible Research*, http://www.bible-researcher.com/nlt.html.

of The Living Bible have been sold. It was revised and updated to the New Living Translation (NLT) in 1996. In the updated New Living Translation, *malakoi* and *arsenokoitais* have been retranslated as "male prostitute" and "those who practice homosexuality," respectively (the latter still includes lesbians). As of March 2014, the NLT is the top-selling English language Bible.[20]

Transgender people and Deuteronomy 22:5

There is a single verse in the Bible frequently used to shame the transgender and transsexual communities and those who express their gender in a variety of ways. It is located in one of the books of the Law between a verse about helping a fallen ox and instruction on how to treat a mother bird and her young. Deuteronomy 22:5 (KJV) states:

> A woman shall not wear that which pertaineth unto a man, neither shall a man put on a woman's garment; for whosoever doeth these things is an abomination unto the LORD thy God.

It would be simple to brush away Deuteronomy 22:5 altogether, saying that it is part of the Law and therefore no longer relevant to modern Christians. After all, cisgender Christians, whose sex and gender are in alignment, no longer adhere to this prohibition either; women wear pants, men wear kilts, and clothing styles are more influenced by culture than religion. Rather than simply ignore or dismiss the verse, it is more useful to try to understand what the verse means in the context of the culture in which it was written.

First, even among Jewish rabbis, there is no agreement as to what this verse means precisely; there is, however, general agreement that it does not refer to those who cross-dress or to transgender people who wear

---

[20] "CBA Best Sellers," *Christian Booksellers Association*, March 2014, http://biblebook-shelf.weebly.com/blog/march-2014-bible-bestseller-lists-cba.

clothing more aligned with their gender identity.[21] The three predominant possible meanings of this verse have one commonality: wearing the clothing of the other sex with the intention to deceive. One interpretation proposes that the phrase "that which pertaineth to a man" refers to a sword or other pieces of his weaponry. In other words, a woman should not be given weapons and sent to war. It is also similarly suggested that this verse means that a man should not dress in the clothes of a woman to hide among women, particularly during a time when he should be soldiering.

The final two predominant arguments are in line with the general instruction found throughout the Jewish Law to keep things separate: types of seeds in a vineyard (Deuteronomy 22:9), an ox and a donkey when plowing (Deuteronomy 22:10), and wool and linen in clothing (Deuteronomy 22:11). Men and women in ancient Israel (and in some sects even today) were regularly segregated, thereby limiting their interaction. This argument is supported by the discourse on marriage and adultery that follows Deuteronomy 22:5 in Deuteronomy 22:13-30.

The intent of the law, in this last interpretation of the verse, is to prevent men and women from mixing by deceitful entry into the segregated space of the other sex with the intent of committing adultery. In the verse, *adultery* is what is called an abomination unto God.[22] Cross-dressing is not strictly and always forbidden in the Law; it was specifically permitted beginning in the 16th-century Code of Jewish Law that allowed men to dress as women and women as men for the Jewish feast of Purim for the purpose of celebration, as opposed to with the intent to deceive and commit adultery.[23]

The interpretations of the verse are diverse, and while many conservative Christians have tried to use the verse to condemn transgender

---

[21] Rabbi Jon-Jay Tilsen, "Cross Dressing and Deuteronomy 22:5," Congregation Beth El-Keser Israel, http://www.beki.org/crossdress.html.

[22] Ibid.

[23] Rabbi Sylvia Rothschild, "With Increasing Joy, We Explore Our Dark Side: Purim Thoughts," rabbisylviarothschild, March 2. 2014, http://rabbisylviarothschild.wordpress.com/2014/03/02/with-increasing-joy-we-explore-our-dark-side-purim-thoughts/.

people who wear clothing opposite to their birth sex, most Jewish legal discussion of the verse centers on the intention of deception.[24]

Deception, however, is not the motivation of transgender people wearing the clothing of the gender with which they identify. When transgender people wear the clothing of their internal gender, they are trying to decrease their emotional and mental stress by bringing their outward appearance into congruence with their gender identity.

Scripture clearly says . . .

In February 2013, over a weeklong period, I attended a local church to listen to several presentations given by an "ex-gay" leader.[25] One evening, the ex-gay leader spoke to a room filled with over two hundred teens aged twelve to eighteen. He presented his dramatic testimony and shared stories of extreme abandonment and sexual abuse in his childhood that led, he said, to same-sex temptations in his teen and adult years.

By submitting his life to Jesus, he claimed, he was able to "leave the homosexual lifestyle" and be set free from all gay temptations. He offered 1 Corinthians 6:9-10, additionally using verse 11 as "proof" that God could indeed change homosexuals to heterosexuals, "And that [homosexuals / *malakoi* / *arsenokoitai*] is what some of you were. But you were washed, you were set free, you were justified in the name of the Lord Jesus Christ and by the Spirit of our God."

The way in which he understood 1 Corinthians 6:9-10 either condemned him to hell or provided a means of escape from his homosexuality. Upon submission to Jesus, he believed, he had been washed clean and set free from his same-sex attractions. "The Bible is crystal clear about 1 Corinthians 6:9-10," he told the teenagers.

At the end of the evening, I sat at the back of the room and off to the side watching the crowd of teens leave the fellowship hall. If my gut

---

[24] "Cross Dressing and Deuteronomy 22:5."
[25] Kathy Baldock, "Ex-Gay Kent Paris at Summit Christian Church, Nevada," *Canyonwalker Connections*, February 2012, http://canyonwalkerconnections.com/ex-gay-kent-paris-at-summit-christian-church-nevada/.

instincts were right, I saw at least eight gay kids leaving the meeting. They all appeared quite despondent. They'd been told they were going to hell because "the Bible is crystal clear about 1 Corinthians 6:9-10."

I, too, once thought the Bible was crystal clear on the meaning of Romans 1:26-27, 1 Corinthians 6:9-10, and 1 Timothy 1:9-10. As I began to meet gay and lesbian Christians who embodied the Spirit of God and were involved in committed, long-term intimate relationships, my understanding of the verses was challenged. My friends professed their faith and showed changed lives. How could I question their testimony and witness?

Could it be that the sexual behaviors portrayed between men, and perhaps between women, in Romans 1:26-27, 1 Corinthians 6:9-10, and 1 Timothy 1:9-10 do not portray Christians in committed, same-sex relationships?

Even if you are not ready to accept the insights I have offered, can you, perhaps, consider that your understanding of the passages might not be "crystal clear"?

Unless you are *sure* of God's condemnation of the gay, lesbian, bisexual, and transgender community, can you, in good conscience, continue to use the beautiful Word of God as a weapon of destruction and a barrier to the throne of God? I encourage you to prayerfully consider the impact of how these verses have been translated in the past almost-seventy years.

I often think about those kids leaving the youth meeting in 2013. There was a boy who looked to be about thirteen years old walking with his mother. I watched them. They were silent as they exited. The mother appeared steeped in shame; she couldn't look at anyone, not even her own son. The boy, with his downcast eyes and slumped shoulders, seemed completely dejected.

I can only begin to imagine how many nights he has lain in his bed in the dark begging God to make him straight, sometimes wishing God would just take him rather than shame his family. He must have sat there in agony for two hours listening to the speaker tell him he could stop being gay while playing the internal tapes over and over: "Lord, I have *tried*. I have *begged* You to take this away. And You haven't. I can't change. So, now, I'm going to hell."

Believing what we have been told is true has caused immeasurable damage, and it continues today.

Chapter 10

Creating Families
Historical and Civil Marriage and the Case for Christian Same-Sex Marriage

Some gay people dreamed about getting married

Ted Hayes was born in 1931 in Memphis, Tennessee, and grew up in East Tennessee, ground zero for fundamentalist Christianity. After serving in the Korean War, he earned a degree in chemistry at the University of Chattanooga. When he announced to his family that he was going to enter Southern Baptist Theological Seminary, his mother was disappointed that he wasn't going to use his degree for a lucrative career.

Ted had a secret. He knew he liked boys the way other boys liked girls. He had known since he was eight years old that he experienced life differently, and he knew he had to keep it a secret—after all, it was Tennessee in the 1930s and 1940s.

Ted went to Southern Baptist Theological Seminary in Louisville, Kentucky, and graduated in 1966. "It was a different time in the Baptist Church then. The love of God and the love of Jesus were evident." Ted worked hard and avoided eligible women wanting to date and marry the minister of education. To cover up his secret, he told them, "I can only be involved in one thing at a time. For now, that is serving God."

The technique worked until 1971, when, while serving in Jacksonville, Florida, Ted was strongly attracted to a fellow male staff member. The Southern Baptist Convention was in the infancy stages of the now full-blown fundamentalist takeover. A core group of fundamentalist leaders created and enforced the "Bible inerrancy" litmus test. They asserted that every printed word of Scripture was directly from God. Theological moderates had allowed for errors by human participants in the work of God, holding that the Bible did, indeed, contain all truths necessary for life and salvation, yet needed to be read in context. But now a concerted and organized effort was being made to replace the leadership of all boards, councils, and seminaries with fundamentalist Baptists.

Ted recalls a "witch hunt" targeting the removal of gays in the mid-1970s. The stress of the possible discovery of his attraction to men and the disgrace it would cause took a toll on Ted's health. While serving the Jacksonville church, he was hospitalized for three months. Once out of the hospital, he fell into a severe depression. He knew he couldn't tell anyone he was gay; desperate, he took enough pills to commit suicide. Knowing Ted had been sick and had just been released from the hospital, a friend stopped by to visit, found him, and took him to the emergency room. The action saved Ted's life.

Ted then entered counseling to deal with the stress of hiding for his whole life as a gay Christian man in the south. Sure that he would be "discovered," Ted left the ministry and went back to school to earn a doctorate in counseling. He still hadn't come out to his family.

The person who finally forced Ted out of hiding was Anita Bryant. Her anti-gay campaign was sweeping across America in 1978, and Christians were rallying together to fight the dreaded "gay invasion." Ted wrote to his hometown newspaper and likened Bryant's attacks on the gay community to Hitler's attacks on the Jews; the letter to the editor was published, with Ted's name in print for all—including his family—to see. That weekend, Ted went home for Christmas dinner, and, out of earshot of his dad, his mother asked him, "Ted, why did you write that? Now everyone will think you are a homosexual."

Ted replied, "Well, Mother, I am." She was stunned. "If you had told us sooner, we could have gotten you some help," she said.

Ted was forty-seven years old when he finally came out to his family. After his mother's response, the family reacted the way many families do—they didn't talk about it. Two years later, when the news of Anita Bryant's divorce was all over the news, Ted overheard his mother say, "Well, that bitch finally got what she deserved." From then on between Ted and his parents, it was all good.

Ted moved to New Mexico in 1981 to work as a counselor and decided to look for a partner in the gay newspaper *The Advocate*. He noticed a personal ad by a man named Jack Waite, and wrote to him.

Jack Waite had known as a boy growing up in Montana in the 1920s that he was gay. As Ted told me, "In those days, in Montana or Tennessee, you could have gotten beaten to death for being gay." When Jack was barely out of his teens, he moved from Montana to Hollywood, California, where he met Harry, an entertainer who played the piano and was as interested in Jack as Jack was in him. The two became a couple and relocated to New York after World War II. They spent thirty-nine happy years together, until Harry's death in 1979.

Jack sifted through the 200-plus responses to his personal ad and narrowed it down to four. Ted was one of those four, and after the two met, Ted became the finalist. Imagine the joy and sense of wonder for Ted to feel loved by someone and to love in return! At the age of fifty-two, for the first time, he was hugged and kissed by someone he loved and who loved him back. He and Jack were perfect for each other; they eventually moved in with one another in New York and were together for twenty-six years. "I was blessed," Ted says about Jack. "I could truly say that I loved him more each day than the day before."

Jack and Ted never dreamed that marriage would be a possibility for them, but when Massachusetts became the first state to legalize same-sex marriage in 2004, they decided that when the right came to their home state of New York, they would tie the knot and "make it official." This plan suddenly took on a sense of urgency when Jack was diagnosed with terminal cancer.

While the hearings were going on in the New York Legislature in Albany, Ted made an appointment to petition his state senator, leaving Jack at home with a caretaker. Ted never got to meet with the senator; the latter cancelled, saying he had a conflict and did not offer to reschedule. Three days later, on May 2, 2009, Jack Waite died at the age of ninety-five.

In June 2011, marriage equality came to New York State. Ted was very emotional—elated that his state was finally treating people like him as equals, but aching with sadness because Jack was not around to see it.

I asked Ted about the long-ago times when he was young and closeted: "Could you ever have imagined marriage equality available in your lifetime?"

He replied, "No, it is mind-boggling what has happened in the past ten years."

Ted ended our conversation with two insights: First, the anti-gay sentiment now found in churches has replaced the love Ted experienced while in seminary and serving churches in the 1960s and early 1970s. He feels this is the result of the "the tail wagging the dog," or a few people controlling the conversation.

The other thought is a challenge for all readers: "The trouble comes when we use the Bible to confirm our biases rather than to confront them."

The shifting definition of marriage

Across cultures, marriage is a social union or civil contract establishing rights, benefits, and obligations between spouses, and sometimes includes families. This union or contract can be recognized by a community composed of family and peers, a tribe, an organization, a religious group, and/or a state.

Marriage in the form we know it today is often touted as a timeless institution. Yes, God did begin with Adam and Eve in Genesis 2. But "traditional marriage" fell apart by Genesis 4. Cain had a wife, but as two of a *very* small number of people on earth, surely they were *closely* related. Throughout the Bible, several kinds of marriages are described and blessed: a man and a woman, a man and his concubines, a man and his brother's widow, a man and a woman and her slaves, a man and many women, a soldier and his prisoners of war, and a rapist and his victim. In all forms of these many biblical marriages, women were property of the man.

In ancient Rome, the "traditional family" consisted of a man, his wife, and female and male slaves with whom the husband could have sex. When the Roman Empire collapsed, the Roman Catholic Church was the only stable political entity capable of taking its place. The rule of the Roman Catholic Church was challenged by leaders of smaller kingdoms and fiefdoms all over Europe who desired the advantages of the Church's growth and political power.

In order to squelch the challenges and keep the power centralized at the Vatican, Pope Leo III appointed Charlemagne as the first Holy Roman Emperor. New rules for marriage were constructed to ensure that powerful and wealthy men could not expand their economic and political reach by marrying several wives and annexing the land and wealth that came with such marriages. Marriages were subject to the pope's approval and became restricted—no polygamy, no divorce, no remarriage, no marrying members of one's own family—and illegitimate children could not inherit the wealth of the patriarch. In effect, the new marriage regulations ensured that powerful and wealthy men could not expand their holdings either by divorce and remarriage, or by taking several wives and annexing the property that came with such economic and/or political moves. Marriage between one man and one woman ensured fewer threats to the supremacy of the Holy Roman Empire.[1]

Marriage has not *always* been a religious rite or sacrament. In the 13th century, it was in the infancy stages of becoming a Roman Catholic sacrament. By the 15th century, marriage was fully considered a Christian sacrament. By the 16th century, it was required that marriages be performed publicly in the presence of a priest. The Catholic Church "owned" marriage until the Protestant movement when the Church of England challenged the Catholic Church's authority, and civil marriages began.

Until the mid-1500s, priests were allowed to marry and amass wealth and land just like anyone else; such property passed to a priest's wife and children upon his death. But starting in 1563, married priests were restricted from saying mass.[2] This policy change, in effect, stopped priests from marrying, so upon their death, any wealth they had was passed to the church.[3]

New opposition to the Church came in the 17th and 18th centuries when the thinkers of the Enlightenment challenged religious and traditional teaching on many topics, including the status of women and the matter of arranged marriages. Over the next century, marriage unions based on love and romance, rather than economics, began to emerge.[4]

Though marriage as a union of two (or more) people has existed since Genesis 2, the structure, purpose, legal status, and place of religion in the agreement has shifted constantly through time, across cultures, and even within the Christian church itself.

Since the 1780s, marriage in the United States has been a civil contract granting legal status to a couple during a public civil marriage

---

[1] Stephanie Coontz, *Marriage, a History* (New York: Penguin Books, 2005), 94.

[2] James Bone, "Catholic Priests May Be Allowed to Marry amid Papal Changes," *The Faith Times*, September 12, 2013, http://www.thetimes.co.uk/tto/faith/article3866516.ece.

[3] Paul Vitello, "On Eve of Retirement, Cardinal Breathes Life into Debate on Priestly Celibacy," *New York Times*, March 21, 2009. http://www.nytimes.com/2009/03/22/nyregion/22egan.html?pagewanted=1&_r=1&.

[4] *Marriage, a History*, 177-191.

ceremony performed by agents of the state. Marriages performed by priests or pastors are accomplished by clergy acting as agents of the state.

Before advocacy for same-sex marriage, the last major challenge to marriage laws in the United States came in the 1960s. Laws against interracial marriage, or miscegenation laws, had been in effect for nearly three centuries. According to many religious conservatives, it was a sin, as well as a crime, for a white person to wed a person of African ancestry. As mentioned in Chapter 5, a Bible account sometimes referred to as the "curse of Ham" (Genesis 9:18-27) was understood to mean that all Africans, who were thought to be Ham's direct descendants, were cursed to be forever subservient to others and kept separate from other races. Hence, no intermarriage allowed. Though today this theology has been forgotten, or denied,[5] as recently as the late 1960s, various states still restricted marriage between a white person and a member of another racial group, primarily blacks.

Additionally, a dozen states forbade a white person to marry a Native American; one state banned such legal unions until as recently as 1959. In a dozen states, white people were banned from marrying Asians. Nine states banned whites and Filipinos from intermarriage. Curiously, some states banned white people from marrying Native Hawaiians.

In 1958, Mildred Jeter, a 19-year-old woman of African American and Native American descent travelled with Richard Loving, a 25-year-old white man, to Washington, D.C., to get married. Their home state of Virginia did not allow interracial marriage, but they were in love and wanted to get married. The Lovings had the full blessing of their marriage from their close-knit families. Though several other interracial couples lived in their isolated community, someone tipped off the county authorities about the Lovings' marriage, illegal in Virginia. The local police raided the Loving home in the middle of the night, hoping

---

[5] David Mark Whitford, *The Curse of Ham in the Early Modern Era: The Bible and Justifications* (Burlington, Vermont: Ashgate Publishing, 2009), 2.

to find the couple having "illegal" sex. There was no "crime" going on; they were sleeping. Mildred showed the police their marriage certificate, yet the couple was immediately arrested for "cohabiting as man and wife, against the peace and dignity of the Commonwealth."[6]

The trial judge in their case, Leon Bazile, found the couple guilty and stated in his decision:

> Almighty God created the races, white, black, yellow, and red, and he placed them on separate continents. And but for the interference with his arrangement there would be no cause for such marriages. The fact that he separated the races shows that he did not intend for the races to mix.[7]

In lieu of serving a one-year prison sentence, the Lovings were ordered to leave Virginia; they moved to Washington, D.C. After five years of living apart from their families, unable even to visit Virginia as a couple, Mildred wrote a letter to Attorney General Robert F. Kennedy, asking for his help. Kennedy's office referred the Lovings to the American Civil Liberties Union (ACLU) in 1964.

After a series of appeals in the lower courts, *Loving v. Virginia* made it to the United States Supreme Court in 1967. The justices ruled that Virginia's and twelve other states' statutes against interracial marriage violated both the Due Process Clause and the Equal Protection Clause of the Fourteenth Amendment. Chief Justice Earl Warren wrote the opinion for the unanimous court decision, outlining the importance of marriage: "Marriage is one of the 'basic civil rights of man,' fundamental to our very existence and survival," he stated.

---

6 Claire Guthrie Gastañaga, "Loving Day – Celebrating the Freedom to Marry," *American Civil Liberties Union of Virginia,* June 12, 2013, https://acluva.org/13299/loving-day-celebrating-the-freedom-to-marry/.

7 Ibid.

Eleven years later, in 1978, the Supreme Court reaffirmed marriage as a basic American right under the Equal Protection Clause: "The right to marry is of fundamental importance for all" (*Zablocki v. Redhail*).

At the time of the landmark *Loving v. Virginia* case, the following were the four main arguments against interracial marriage:

- All interracial relationships, even committed, long-standing ones, were considered illicit sex rather than loving marriages and, thus, morally wrong.
- Interracial marriage was contrary to the will of God.
- Interracial marriage was "unnatural."
- The right to legislate marriage should belong to the states, not the federal government.[8]

The major objections voiced by marriage equality opponents today are uncannily similar to yesteryear's cries against interracial marriage:

- A moral wrong should not be a civil right or a "special right."
- Marriage was created and defined by God as between one man and one woman, and cannot be redefined.
- Marriage between two people of the same sex violates natural law.[9]
- Popular vote should not be trumped by federal legislation.

Additional arguments are also heard about same-sex marriage:

- Let them have civil unions; it's good enough.

---

[8] Peggy Pascoe, "Why the Ugly Rhetoric Against Gay Marriage Is Familiar to This Historian of Miscegenation," *History News Network*, April 19, 2004, http://hnn.us/article/4708.
[9] "10 Reasons Why Homosexual 'Marriage' Is Harmful and Must Be Opposed," *TFP Student Action*, http://www.tfpstudentaction.org/politically-incorrect/homosexuality/10-reasons-why-homosexual-marriage-is-harmful-and-must-be-opposed.html..

- Religious leaders will be forced to perform same-sex marriages in their churches.
- Same-sex couples cannot procreate.
- Same-sex marriage will destroy the "sanctity of marriage."

That marriage is a civil right of fundamental importance for all American citizens has already been addressed—nearly half a century ago.

The long road to marriage equality

Though the first state to pass marriage equality laws was Massachusetts in May 2004, the quest for same-sex marriage actually began long before that—forty-five years ago, in fact, just a few years after the *Loving v. Virginia* decision. In December 1968, Rev. Troy Perry, founder of the Metropolitan Community Church (MCC) in Los Angeles, performed the first public same-sex "holy union" in the United States. In 1969, Rev. Perry sued the State of California for recognition of the civil rights of a couple from MCC, Neva Heckman and Judith Bellew, on the grounds that the couple had been together for two years and thus fit the definition of a common-law marriage, for which California State law did not specify genders. The suit was dismissed, and Perry continued to marry couples in his church.[10]

The earliest successful same-sex marriage took place in Minnesota as the result of an oversight. Jack Baker met James McConnell in 1966 at a Halloween party in Norman, Oklahoma. Not long afterward, Baker, a U.S. Air Force veteran, was fired from a job on the Air Force base for being gay. The couple relocated to Minneapolis, where McConnell worked at the University of Minnesota library and Baker studied law. They applied for a marriage license in Hennepin County in 1970.

The application was blocked by the district attorney, whose ruling was supported by the Minnesota Supreme Court, which stated: "The

---

[10] "Early MCC Marriage Equality History," *Metropolitan Community Churches, http://mccchurch.org/overview/history-of-mcc/.*

institution of marriage as a union of a man and a woman, uniquely involving the procreation and rearing of children within a family, is as old as Genesis."[11] The court decision did not deter Baker and McConnell, who were determined to get married.

In 1971, McConnell changed his name to a gender-neutral name, Pat Lynn McConnell. Jack and "Pat" moved to another Minnesota county and, after a waiting period, appli ed for, and were granted a marriage license. A sympathetic Methodist minister married the pair. The county judge, thinking the case wasn't worth pursuing, allowed Baker and McConnell to remain legally married.

Baker and McConnell are now in their seventies and have been together for over forty years. McConnell is retired from the university library, and Baker has had a career as an attorney and successfully ran for Minneapolis City Council and a judgeship. When marriage equality came to Minnesota in 2013, the couple opted not to get married. "We are already legally married," Baker said.[12]

Opposition to marriage equality also began over forty years ago. In 1973, the same year the American Psychiatric Association declassified homosexuality as a mental illness, the citizens of Maryland passed a statute banning same-sex marriage. As of this writing, thirty-one states have such bans in place, in the form of either a constitutional amendment or a state law. Every one of these laws is currently being challenged.

The laws are being challenged under the decisions in the *Loving v. Virginia* and *Zablocki v. Redhail* cases, declaring marriage an American civil right. Specifically, the challenges are grounded in what is often called the Due Process Clause of the Fourteenth Amendment, which says that states may not deprive persons of life, liberty, or property

---

[11] Patrick Condon, "Jack Baker and Michael McConnell, Couple in 1971 Minnesota Gay Marriage Case, Still United," *Huffington Post*, December 10, 2012, http://www.huffingtonpost.com/2012/12/10/jack-baker-michael-mcconnell-minnesota-gay-marriage_n_2271573.html.

[12] Ibid.

without due process, and the Equal Protection Clause, which ensures that "No State shall . . . deny to any person within its jurisdiction the equal protection of the laws."[13]

Some have argued that the "wish of the people" is being ignored by judges overriding state laws, statutes, and amendments; however, no group of people, not even the majority, has the right to withhold the civil rights of any other group.

In 1967, *only 4% of Americans* approved of interracial marriage,[14] yet the Supreme Court dismissed the desire of 96% of Americans who did not support it in order to preserve the rights of the minority. As of 2013, approval for marriage equality was well over the 50% mark, and is increasing by about 2% each year.[15] Public opinion on marriage equality in the United States has shifted rapidly in recent years, largely due to relationships. As more lesbian, gay, bisexual, and transgender people come out and we in the straight majority get to know them, support grows nationwide for their access to marriage, a civil right of fundamental importance for all Americans. There is a strong likelihood that the United States will soon join the other seventeen countries[16] of the world that extend marriage rights to same-sex couples.

Marriage equality and religious liberties

Marriage equality is not an affront to the religious liberties of Christians. Pastors can choose to marry, or not to marry, *anyone* based on any criteria they or their church set; this has always been true. Every state that

---

13 14th Amendment to U.S. Constitution, *Library of Congress*, http://www.loc.gov/rr/program/bib/ourdocs/14thamendment.html.
14 Frank Newport, "In U.S., 87% Approve of Black-White Marriage, vs. 4% in 1958," *Gallup Politics*, July 25, 2013, http://www.gallup.com/poll/163697/approvemarriage-blackswhites.aspx.
15 Nate Silver, "How Opinion on Same-Sex Marriage Is Changing, and What It Means," *New York Times*, March 26, 2013, http://fivethirtyeight.blogs.nytimes.com/2013/03/26/how-opinion-on-same-sex-marriage-is-changing-and-what-it-means/?module=-Search&mabReward=relbias%3As.
16 Netherlands, Belgium, Spain, Canada, South Africa, Norway, Sweden, Portugal, Iceland, Argentina, Denmark, France, Brazil, Uruguay, New Zealand, Britain, and Luxembourg.

has passed laws allowing same-sex marriage has also spelled out clergy's freedom of choice to perform, or not perform, marriage ceremonies.

The right of clergy to speak in condemnation of same-sex marriages is likewise protected. Most Christians could not imagine speaking as offensively as the members of the Westboro Baptist Church have been known to do; however, even *their* rights to free speech are protected.

And while it is important to note that people with business licenses are obligated under the laws of their jurisdiction not to discriminate against any member of the public who wants to do business, churches and church-affiliated organizations with the correctly filed tax status can turn away same-sex couples if they so choose.[17]

Forty years ago, when Bob Jones University was stripped of its tax-exempt status as a result of its racial-segregation policies, conservative Christians and politicians attempted to deflect attention from what the administration viewed as their "right to discriminate." They claimed that their religious liberties had been violated. Today, conservative Christians and politicians are doing the same thing: attempting to deflect attention from their discriminatory views, whether anti–gay marriage stances or anti-transgender policies,[18] by repositioning the issue as a matter of religious liberty being threatened.

---

[17] In 2007, a New Jersey judge ruled against a Christian retreat house that refused to allow a lesbian couple to have their civil union ceremony performed on the premises at a beachfront pavilion. The property owner, the Ocean Grove Camp Meeting Association (OGCMA), is affiliated with the Methodist Church but is not a church. The organization applied for a "Green Acres" tax exemption from the State of New Jersey Department of Environmental Protection. The tax exemption required that Ocean Grove be used as a facility open to the public on an equal basis. In exchange for the tax break, the OGCMA agreed. This case was presented by Alliance Defense Fund (now, Alliance Defending Freedom) as a religious liberties issue. It never was such; it was a tax status issue, just as the Bob Jones University case was in 1970. Source: Deacon Greg Kandra, "Will Churches Be Sued Over Gay Marriage?" *Patheos*, June 27, 2013, http://www.patheos.com/blogs/deaconsbench/2013/06/will-churches-be-sued-over-gay-marriage-its-already-happened-and-a-judge-ruled-church-teaching-irrelevant/.

[18] Kate Tracy, "Gordon College Loses City Contract, Gets Accreditation Scrutiny," *Christianity Today*, July, 14, 2014, http://www.christianitytoday.com/gleanings/2014/july/gordoncollegelosescitycontractgetsaccreditationscrut.html/?paging=off.

It is important to note that not every Christian denomination holds the same views as most evangelicals and other conservative Christians. The members of denominations that support marriage equality want *their* religious liberty to perform marriages for same-sex couples as part of what they believe God calls them to do.

Even recognizing that marriage is a civil right may be challenging for some Christians as they seek to balance what they believe the Bible says about marriage with their understanding of the civic responsibility not to withhold rights from a minority group. As a concession, some feel more open to civil unions in lieu of marriage. The problem lies in the fact that civil unions are not equal to marriage; they extend fewer than two hundred benefits, protections, and responsibilities to couples, while civil marriage offers over one thousand legal benefits, protections, and responsibilities.[19]

LGBT Christians seek the blessing of Christian marriage

David Evans-Carlson, a Child and Youth Mental Health Clinician from the Midwest, was raised in a devout Seventh-Day Adventist (SDA) home. Most of his family is currently involved in SDA ministry work and leadership. In 2011, at the age of twenty-seven, David legally married Canadian Colin Evans-Carlson, then thirty-three, a clinical counselor, evangelical Christian, and former attendee of Columbia Bible College in British Columbia. Canada legalized same-sex marriage nationwide in 2005, so David and Colin's marriage is fully recognized.

I met the couple several years ago when they first started dating. I was walking down a corridor at a conference, rushing from one workshop to another, and passed by these two young men sitting on the floor holding hands and laughing. I walked backwards and bent down to talk with them. "I *need* to know you two," I said. "You are beautiful together.

---

[19] "Overview of Federal Benefits Granted to Married Couples," *Human Rights Campaign*, http://www.hrc.org/resources/entry/ an-overview-of-federal-rights-and-protections-granted-to-married-couples.

Tell me who you are." Their mutual love and respect radiated from them as we spent some time in conversation.

David says the following of their relationship:

> Colin and I grew up in Christian homes and were active in our churches. Gay people were thought to be people who didn't care about God. If they cared about God, they certainly wouldn't be gay. As men who had accepted Christ and identified fully as Christian, it was difficult for each of us in earlier years to begin to realize that we ourselves were gay.
>
> Within the Christian church, it was thought that straight people fell in love and gay people were reduced to a sex act. So falling in love with Colin was an amazing, surprising, and life-giving experience. We shared a love for each other and love for God that bonded us together deeply.
>
> What we wish churches and fellow Christians understood is that Colin and I want to be held to the same standards of love and commitment that other married, straight couples in the church are held to. We want to be held to our vows of faithfulness and fidelity. We want to be supported and prayed for when times are tough. We want to raise our children in community to love Jesus.
>
> Marriage brings a certain universal weight and understanding to a relationship. It is not just a "boyfriend" passing through, but something substantial and permanent. Our families could see that the other man was their son or brother's husband for life. We are building a home now.

> Marriage provides this beautiful space for our whole selves to be opened up in a context of love and acceptance. My husband knows all about me—the good, the bad, and everything in between—and he still looks at me with love. There is something so divinely redemptive about this kind of covenant love. It is a love I wish for all people to be blessed with, both gay and straight, within the context of marriage.

Both Colin and David grew up in devoutly Christian homes. Their marriage is legally recognized, but these Christian men desire even more the blessing of their church community, and to have their marriage, and future family, enriched and nourished among people in the Christian faith.

Is Christian marriage available to couples like David and Colin? There are denominations that would welcome this couple and their family. Not all Christian denominations oppose marriage equality; in some states, the pressure to strike down same-sex marriage bans is coming from denominations themselves. Some denominations support marriage equality as part of their doctrine or policies. These include the Presbyterian Church USA, the Evangelical Lutheran Church in America, the Episcopal Church USA, the Metropolitan Community Church, the Society of Friends (Quakers), and the United Church of Christ.[20] Gay members of these denominations are gaining access to both legal marriage and the chance to celebrate their wedding in their church. For instance, the United Church of Christ (UCC), a progressive Christian denomination with over a million members and 5,100 local churches, has officially blessed the unions of same-sex couples since 1993. In April 2014, UCC leaders filed a court case in North Carolina, claiming that the religious liberties of the UCC were being infringed upon because they were not allowed to wed same-sex couples there.

---

[20] David Masci, "Where Christian Churches, Other Religions Stand on Gay Marriage," *Pew Research*, June 18, 2014, http://www.pewresearch.org/facttank/2014/06/18/wherechristianchurchesstandongaymarriage/.

The United Methodist Church, more welcoming than many denominations, is wrestling with the issue by regions and by countries. Many Independent Baptists also affirm the rights and inclusion of gays and lesbians. Though in a handful of mainline denominations, pastors who affirm or perform same-sex marriages are still being defrocked, some are being reinstated[21] as the issues come to be understood more clearly.

David Farmer and his partner are in a relationship strengthened and upheld by both a legal marriage performed in California and a union blessed within their faith community. I met David through my association with The Reformation Project.[22] David, a 56-year-old conservative Baptist, lives in Springfield, Virginia, with his partner and husband, Ron.

> We've been together for twenty-two years. I never entertained the thought that marriage would be possible in my lifetime. Even when it was not yet legal, we made our commitment to each other early in the relationship. In 1995, we held a commitment ceremony officiated by an ordained Southern Baptist minister to express our covenant to one another in the presence of God and our close friends. We were legally married again in 2008; however, our 1995 ceremony is [what we consider] our true marriage.
>
> I wish I had known early in my life that same-sex marriage would be possible. I might have not given up on organized religion for a period. Nonetheless, God had a plan for me, and I found the perfect person to spend my life with, and

[21] Kathy L. Gilbert, "Update: Frank Schaefer Reinstated as United Methodist Pastor," *United Methodist Church*, June 24, 2014, http://www.umc.org/newsandmedia/panel-ordersschaeferscredentialsrestored. Accessed June 30, 2014.

[22] The mission statement of The Reformation Project, founded by Matthew Vines in 2012, is "to train Christians to support and affirm lesbian, gay, bisexual, and transgender (LGBT) people. Through building a deep grassroots movement, we strive to create an environment in which Christian leaders will have the freedom to take the next steps toward affirming and including LGBT people in all aspects of church life." http://www.reformationproject.org.

together, we found our way back into a fulfilling church life. My church, Ravensworth Baptist Church, would officiate a same-sex marriage today if it were legal in Virginia. It may be legal soon because a judge struck down the state's ban on marriage equality and civil unions.

I am hopeful that more churches will open their hearts on this issue. I pray that more pastors and congregations discern [the] Scriptures and rightly place the six or seven passages mentioning same-sex activity in [the] cultural context in which they were written. I pray that the Holy Spirit will move them to become inclusive.

David and Ron made a commitment before God and their friends over two decades ago and have entered a legal civil marriage. Though not sanctioned within the Southern Baptist Convention, David and Ron consider their marriage to be a Christian marriage.

What is Christian marriage?

Most conservative Christians look to Genesis 2, as well as the words of Jesus and Paul, as the standard to which they adhere for Christian marriage. The first biblical account of marriage is the story of Adam and Eve in Genesis. Eve was created as a "helper suitable for" Adam. Genesis 2:18 states clearly *why* Eve was created—to fill Adam's loneliness: "It is not good for the man to be alone" (NIV). When God brought Eve to Adam, Adam said, "This is now bone of my bones and flesh of my flesh; she shall be called 'woman,' for she was taken out of man" (Genesis 2:23, NIV).

"One flesh" is repeated several times in the Old Testament. When Laban greeted his nephew, Jacob, Laban said, "Surely you are my own bone and my flesh" (Genesis 29:14, ESV). David's messengers were instructed in 2 Samuel 19:12-13 to remind the elders of Judah of the "flesh and blood" connection he had with them. "One flesh" is also used in Judges 9:2, 2 Samuel 5:1, and 1 Chronicles 11:1. In all cases, the commonality is covenant relationship.

In the Genesis creation story, Adam and Eve join in a covenant relationship unique from their relationships with any of the other creatures on earth; it is one of primacy and intimacy. Genesis 2:24 (NIV) says, "For this reason a man will leave his father and mother and be united to his wife, and the two will be one flesh." The leaving indicated here is not a physical leaving. In the ancient world it was the wife who left her family, not the husband. What the man leaves behind is the primary bond he has had with his family to create a new primary covenant with his wife.[23]

In Matthew 19:1-12, Jesus spoke about marriage in response to a question the Pharisees posed about divorce: "Is it lawful for a man to divorce his wife for any reason?" (v. 3, NIV). Jesus calls to his listeners' minds the covenantal one-flesh relationship between Adam and Eve and says that the marriage covenant is not to be broken.

Paul, too, spoke strongly against divorce. In Ephesians 5:21-33 we discover the purpose of Christian marriage, which helps us understand the strong admonitions against divorce.

> Submit to one another out of reverence for Christ. Wives, submit yourselves to your own husbands as you do to the Lord. For the husband is the head of the wife as Christ is the head of the church, his body, of which he is the Savior. Now as the church submits to Christ, so also wives should submit to their husbands in everything.

> Husbands, love your wives, just as Christ loved the church and gave himself up for her to make her holy, cleansing her by the washing with water through the word, and to

---

[23] Dr. James Brownson, *Bible, Gender, Sexuality* (Grand Rapids, MI: William B. Eerdmans, 2013), 88.

present her to himself as a radiant church, without stain or wrinkle or any other blemish, but holy and blameless. In this same way, husbands ought to love their wives as their own bodies. He who loves his wife loves himself. After all, no one ever hated their own body, but they feed and care for their body, just as Christ does the church—for we are members of his body. "For this reason a man will leave his father and mother and be united to his wife, and the two will become one flesh." This is a profound mystery—but I am talking about Christ and the church. However, each one of you also must love his wife as he loves himself, and the wife must respect her husband. (NIV)

Paul tells us that marriage, though a "profound mystery," is the picture of Jesus' sacrificial death for the Bride.[24] Jesus, in His death, gave everything for the Bride. The one-flesh covenant between Christ and the church is both unconditional and sealed with the blood and death of Jesus. "One flesh" echoes the covenant relationship seen first in Genesis 2:18, 22-24. Sacrificial love, modeled by Christ's giving everything for His Bride, is retold in the witness of Christian marriage. "Just as Christ loved the church and gave Himself up" is the high standard of selfless giving two Christians joined in marriage are to follow.

Through His death and perfect sacrifice, the eternal covenant between Christ and His Bride, the church, is unbreakable. *This* is why God says He hates divorce (Malachi 2:16). When Christians divorce, the beautiful image that bears witness to God's unconditional covenant with His people and to Christ's sacrificial love is damaged.

Before we move on to look at other conditions of Christian marriage, we need to challenge ourselves on an important point: Can two people of the same sex join together in a covenantal, sacrificial, one-flesh,

---

[24] Rev. 21:910.

unbreakable bond reflecting the selflessness of Christ and the eternal promises of God to His people?

We may not understand the "profound mystery" of Christ and His Bride or of two people joined in marriage, for now we "see through a glass darkly."[25] But there is a richness and spiritual dimension at play when two people are joined together covenantally and sexually.

In 2004, San Francisco Mayor Gavin Newsom directed the city clerk to begin issuing licenses to same-sex couples. Over a period of twenty-nine days, until the ceremonies were halted, four thousand couples from all over the United States went to San Francisco to be legally married. Connie Barker, now fifty-five, from Marin County, and her partner, Jan Heard, took the opportunity to marry.

> Honestly, at this point, I really don't believe that human beings get any kind of vote at all on what does or doesn't constitute a marriage. To me, it's just as simple as this: The covenants being entered into by same-sex couples in courthouses and churches all over the country and around the world either are or are not real before heaven. The unions so joyfully attested to by thousands and thousands of happy families and communities both here and abroad either are or are not righteous, godly, and holy. We as human beings only have it in our power to change the human institution to rightly or wrongly reflect the spiritual reality. And when we make things on earth more like what they are in heaven, powerful things happen.

In state after state and country after country, scenes like those from early 2004 in San Francisco have repeated themselves. Beaming couples wait eagerly at courthouse doors, then emerge a few hours later absolutely glowing—and with

---

25 1 Cor. 13:12 (KJV).

a new and palpable sense of boldness about their own equality, a boldness as much spiritual as legal—the law really only seals the deal.

LGBT people are being changed by that; I know I was. In fact, I'm not sure which has surprised me more, how much the world has changed since 2004, or how much I have. What took place those few days, and on so many, many days since, is both sacred and powerful. It was a massive act of corporate municipal civil disobedience, a whole community coming together to do what human law and custom had long said wasn't right, or even legal. It was driven by what that community had lived and seen over decades—our own experience had already convinced more of us than anyone had any idea that, before any God worthy of the name, marriage was not only right, but necessary.

And heaven blessed it! Power went out from that time and place, it most assuredly did! Suddenly, it wasn't just a political calculation or a theoretical argument anymore. Instead it was about thousands and thousands of people unexpectedly finding ourselves changed in ways we'd never anticipated, and thinking things like, "Wow, maybe the church has got this right—maybe civil marriage is holy and sacramental!" And asking things like, "WHY was I EVER willing to settle for LESS than this . . . for myself, or anyone else??!!!"

Agitate, legislate, and adjudicate as much as you like against something as spiritually powerful and blessed as that. You'll only likely end up doing what Gamaliel warned the Council about in the book of Acts: opposing a move of God. You won't be able to stop it.[26]

Whether they understand it or not, that's what the people who oppose same-sex marriage are now up against.

How do you curse what God has blessed? How do you undo a sacramental change in somebody else's soul?

I first heard Connie's powerful message while we sat having lunch together. I'd never thought about *the spiritual power in civil marriages*. The beauty of the spiritual dimension was so unexpected, I asked Connie to tell me the story twice!

The gay and transgender communities have for too long been denied the deep spiritual dimension afforded in coming together, not only before community and families, but before their faith communities. People *have* agitated, legislated, and adjudicated against the joining together of two people who are simply asking to share in the sacredness of what the majority already has.

Is there a biblical imperative for procreation in Christian marriage?

Returning to Genesis, the natural flow of the covenantal relationship between Adam and Eve led to procreation. However, procreation was not defined as a condition of their one-flesh covenant.

In the creation story, "God blessed them and said, 'Be fruitful and increase in number'" (Genesis 1:22, NIV). It was a *blessing* pronounced upon humankind, not a commandment. In the Genesis 2 creation story, Eve was created because "it is not good for the man to be alone" (Genesis 2:18). There is no mention of procreation as the purpose of

---

[26] See Acts 5:29-39, in particular vv. 38b-39.

Eve's creation; rather, her purpose was to provide a suitable companion and helper, because it is not good for one to be alone.

Likewise, in the Ephesians 5 definition of marriage, there is no mention of procreation. Although sexual intercourse may create children, procreation is not the sole reason for the gift of sex. The Bible never names procreation as a condition of marriage.[27] Sex is more than baby-making; as we've said before, it's "marriage glue." Marriage bonds are deepened and strengthened through the intimate and exclusive sexual relationship.

Though not a requisite for marriage, procreation was, of course, highly valuable in the Old Testament world. Logically, for the human race to flourish, the first two people had to be fertile and mutually attracted. Furthermore, the small tribe of Israelites and their bloodline needed to be preserved to ensure the birth of Jesus as prophesied. The question becomes, though, does the man-and-woman relationship of Genesis 2 become the norm, or standard, for *all* people, *all* the time?

In the New Testament, God's family is grown not through procreation but by faith and by people becoming new followers of Jesus. In Mark 3:31-35, a crowd gathered around Jesus, squeezing out His mother and brothers. Someone went to Jesus to tell Him, "Your mother and brothers are outside looking for you." Jesus replied, "Who are my mother and my brothers? . . . Whoever does God's will is my brother and sister and mother" (NIV).

Consider, too, that no society has ever denied marriage to infertile people. Nor have marriages been nullified for not producing children. The Bible never requires procreation of a married couple. There are numerous biblical examples of infertile women and couples, yet the fact of infertility never invalidates their marriage or their value in God's eyes.

What's more, sex between a man and a woman is not the only way to create a family. Adoption, surrogacy, artificial insemination, step-parenting, grandparenting, and legal guardianship are just some of the

---

[27] *Bible, Gender, Sexuality*, 89.

ways our society provides for children to be nurtured by people who love them and will take responsibility for them.

As of 2013, as many as six million children and adults in America had a gay or transgender parent. An estimated 39% of individuals who are part of same-sex couples have children at home with them. About one-third of lesbians and one-fifth of gay men have children.[28]

For those who care about the protection of families and children, consider this: A substantial number of gay parents in the United States have children living with them; they would like to provide their children with a family built on the foundation of a loving marriage recognized in both civil and Christian spheres. For no other reason than that these parents make up half of a same-sex couple—no matter that it's a loving, committed relationship—access to this foundation of family is denied them.

Suzanne Lindsay, a 41-year-old English teacher and Sunday school director from Baltimore, Maryland, drives a minivan, has two kids, and is married to her wife, Shannon.

> When I told my father, who is a Lutheran minister, that I was going to marry my girlfriend of five years, I didn't expect him to perform our ceremony, but I expected him to be present. He threw words at me like "abomination" and such. We haven't spoken since.
>
> My future wife just wanted to get married. Anywhere. I wanted to be married in a church. My faith summoned it. We worshipped in two to three churches a Sunday trying to find a church to have our ceremony. But, more importantly, we were trying to find a church home. We knew that one day we would have children and that raising them in church was important to us.

---

[28] "LGBT Parenting in the United States," *The Williams Institute*, February 2013, http://williamsinstitute.law.ucla.edu/research/censuslgbtdemographicsstudies/lgbtparentingintheunitedstates/.

272 • Kathy Baldock

We found our church home, First and Saint Stephens United Church of Christ. We were married in 2006 in a ceremony that our minister called "conservative" because we wanted a sermon, and communion, and we sang three hymns.

We've baptized our two children in our home church, [and we] nurture them in Sunday school, church festivals, and regular fellowship. It has been a blessing to our family!

Complementarity: The "need" for two different parts that fit together

You'll frequently hear or read the word "complementarity" used to support the "one man and one woman" standard of Christian marriage. In its simplest form, as used by the church, complementarity means two distinct parts coming together to form a more complete whole. There are three basic uses of complementarity: the reuniting of two parts of the human—male and female—to form the complete Adam as he was before Eve was taken from his side, the coming together of two opposite genders for gender fittedness in both marriage and service in the church, and the coming together of male and female for anatomical (sexual) fittedness in marriage.

But where does the word "complementarity" come from? Where can the principle be found in the Bible? Finally, should it be applied to same-sex couples?

By the mid-1980s, feminism from American culture had made its way into conservative Christian circles. Women aspired to join the ranks of leaders, teachers, and preachers in church organizations, and they wanted more equality within the family structure. Regarded as "Christian feminists," they began challenging the church's organizational patriarchy that placed men in the dominant roles and women in the supportive roles, as well as questioning marriage gender hierarchy, which assumed male dominance and female submission. These two principles had been firmly entrenched in conservative churches.

At a 1987 joint conference of the Evangelical Theological Society (ETS) and the Council for Biblical Manhood and Womanhood, a committee of evangelical and Southern Baptist leaders gathered in Danvers, Pennsylvania, to discuss the problem. In a thinly veiled attempt to "stop the spread of Biblical [sic] feminism,"[29] the committee drew up the Danvers Statement, which affirmed: "Distinctions in masculine and feminine roles are ordained by God as part of the created order, and should find an echo in every human heart."[30] The document not-so-subtly reinforced patriarchy and gender hierarchy, and softened the appearance of power structures by calling the pattern "complementarity"—a word they invented to fit their purpose of dealing with Christian feminists. Complementarity asserts that only through men and women working together in churches and marriages, in separate but equal gender roles, are we able to see the full image of God.

The committee members signed the document, and complementarity was born.

Though the "problem" of women seeking full parity in the church and in the home was temporarily solved, complementarity is less than generous to those of us who are single. According to this ideology, without joining our lives to another person, we can't reflect the image of God. Fortunately, this understanding is ultimately unsupported by Scripture, because Jesus, as a single man, was the full image of God (Colossians 1:15).

Nonetheless, in 1987, complementarity took its place in Christian tradition as a "timeless" biblical principle asserting and defining the importance of maintaining gender roles in church leadership and

---

[29] Randall Balmer, *Encyclopedia of Evangelicalism* (Waco, Texas: Baylor University Press, 2004), 170.

[30] "The Danvers Statement on Biblical Manhood and Womanhood," December 1987, p. 2, item 2. http://keithwalters.files.wordpress.com/2008/07/thedanversstatementon-biblicalmanhoodandwomanhood.pdf.

organization, and in marriages, where the truth of the principle should "echo in every heart."[31]

The differences in gender roles in churches and marriages remained the focus of complementarity through the 1990s; however, something started to change. Several dynamics within the gay community prompted a growing interest in obtaining more widespread legal rights for marriage.

Initially, lesbian feminists hadn't been interested in marriage, an institution so long associated with patriarchy. However, as more lesbian couples decided to use artificial insemination to create families, there was a mini "baby boom" among lesbians.[32]

In a widely publicized court case in 1993, a Virginia court decided to take away Sharon Bottoms' two-year-old son and give custody of the child to Bottoms' mother because, the judge explained, her lesbian "conduct is illegal, a Class 6 felony in the Commonwealth of Virginia."[33] In an amazing dismissal of Bottoms' parental rights, the judge further stated that Bottoms was "an unfit parent" because "it is the opinion of this Court that her conduct is immoral." The Virginia Supreme Court rejected the original decision, but Bottoms had to share parental rights with the grandparents.[34] This was most certainly a call to the lesbian community regarding the need for protections for their families.

In the male gay community, AIDS had killed tens of thousands of gay men. Few partners had the legal protections they needed to care for or make health care decisions for their dying partners. Families regularly cut the surviving partner out of medical decisions and funeral arrangements, and unprotected by spousal leases and mortgages, gay survivors often lost their apartments and homes.

Large numbers of gay and lesbian couples began to recognize the lack of legal protection for their families and partnerships and the need for

---

[31] Ibid.
[32] George Chauncey, *Why Marriage?* (New York: Basic Books, 2004), 105.
[33] Ibid., 107.
[34] Ibid., 107.

legal sanctioning of their relationships. Early talk about marriage rights didn't go unnoticed by the conservative religious and political right.

Members of the Council for Biblical Manhood and Womanhood, acutely aware of the already eroding walls of division between gender roles, feared that if they did not hold on tightly to complementarity, such erosion might lead to increased tolerance of homosexuality and, in time, same-sex marriage.[35]

In the late 1990s, complementarity began to take on the imperative of anatomical differences as an additional "God-ordained" requisite for a couple to fully reflect the image of God in a marriage. This suggests an obvious question: Is there any biblical record that lists anatomical differences as a condition of marriage?

Marriage is described in the Bible as the union of a man and a woman, but what about body parts? In Genesis 2 and Ephesians 5, the descriptions of marriage are inherently bound in male/female, husband/wife language. You won't find, nor should you expect to find, affirmation of monogamous, committed, equal status, same-sex marriages in the Bible. Can we, however, lift biblical truths about marriage out of the culturally bound language of male and female and still preserve core principles of Christian marriage as a reflection of our covenant with God? Especially considering what we have learned about sex having more than just procreative purposes and the various ways human anatomy *can* work for the sake of sexual pleasure apart from the limited means of a penis inserted into a vagina, can we truly and rationally use supposed anatomical "fittedness" as a sensible argument against same-sex marriage? As we saw in the previous chapter, the Bible, in its totality, is silent on any imperative about body parts fitting together in a "proper" way. People in the ancient world simply did not think of sex in terms of what anatomical parts fit together.[36]

---

[35] "Egalitarianism and Homosexuality," *The Council on Biblical Manhood and Womanhood,* http://cbmw.org/uncategorized/egalitarianism-and-homosexuality/.
[36] The Reformation Project. (September 19, 2013) Dr. James Brownson Gender Complementarity (video), https://www.youtube.com/watch?v=k1f0KD-B0Z8.

Using Galatians 3:28, we understand that the boundaries between Jew and Gentile, free and slave, and male and female will not exist in eternity and, in fact, are not to persist in the church on earth either, where we "are all one in Christ Jesus." The spiritual segregation between Jewish and Gentile Christians was eliminated in the first-century church. We are consciously working toward abolishing slavery worldwide. And, while women are moving toward equal status in some cultures faster than in others, male-female hierarchies will not exist in the heavenly kingdom of God. Though one day, we'll experience it more fully, the kingdom of God is present *now* in the lives of the disciples of Christ.

In Matthew 6, Jesus instructed us to emulate His prayer to His Father: "Your kingdom come, Your will be done, on earth as it is in heaven" (v. 10, NIV). We are told to pray for God's kingdom to come more fully to earth even now. In God's kingdom, *all systems of hierarchy will be gone.*

Everyone will be equal.

Believers are to continually work toward—not against—that for which we pray. Those who act to thicken and maintain the hierarchical divisions of slave/master and male/female are doing so in *direct opposition* to the explicit Word of God imploring us to eradicate division and oppressive power structures.

The doctrine of complementarity was originally created to restrain Christian feminism in 1987. The "biblical imperative" for anatomical differences was tacked onto the meaning of complementarity in the late 1990s to give "scriptural" basis to fencing gays and lesbians out of Christian marriage.

Christian marriage for transgender individuals

As we saw in Chapter 8, biology is not clean-cut in dividing male and female; intersex and transgender people exist. What should we do with those who don't fit into the pink and blue boxes of gender and anatomical differences as required by the doctrine of complementarity? Intersex and transgender people can't be ignored in the conversation about legal or Christian marriage.

They, too, seek to form loving, committed, legally protected marriages blessed by God and their faith communities.

Marriage being restricted to a man and a woman may or may not affect transgender people who wish to enter legal unions. In the majority of states, a transman (FTM) who has a female birth certificate may only be allowed to marry a man. Likewise, a transwoman (MTF) with a male birth certificate may only be allowed to marry a female.

While any person can legally change their name, this procedure does not automatically change gendered documents like birth certificates. There is no nationwide standard as to how this situation is handled. In some states, a transgender person must undergo "surgical treatment" in order to change their birth certificate. This is problematic, partly because the extent of surgery is often not clearly defined, and partly because the decision of what and how much a transgender person chooses to transition is personal, and often impacted by finances.

Transgender people may not be in your social circle, but they make up about one-quarter of a percent to one percent of the population. Therefore, legal and Christian conversations about marriage must include intersex and transgender people.

Again, Christian marriage is a one-flesh, sacrificial, selfless, and loving covenant agreement between two people. According to this definition, it is not restricted by gender or anatomical parts.

Will you consider both civil and Christian marriage for LGBT couples?

Just as many little girls grow up dreaming of their wedding day, so did Wendy Wilson and Abby McMillen.

One summer, I was honored to be part of a team of educators, theologians, and pastors who spoke to the congregants at St. James Episcopal Church, Bozeman, Montana, about extending marriage blessings to the gay and lesbian couples in their body. Before I spoke, Wendy pulled me aside. She and her partner Abby hoped their home church would accept and bless same-sex unions, yet she was tentative and concerned; she didn't want to cause tension in the membership. In Wendy's words:

> My partner and I have been together for twelve years. We live and love in a committed, working relationship that is full of joy, but like all relationships, we don't always agree. In fact, that we don't always agree is what makes us a great couple. We are each other's check and balance. In June of 2013, when the Supreme Court ruled that the federal government would recognize same-sex marriages performed in states where same-sex marriage is legal, regardless of the couple's state of residence, my partner and I were in instant agreement: We would get married. Because it seemed so unattainable, we'd only ever casually discussed marriage.

> We dreamed of getting married the way all girls do! Ours would be like something right out of "Annie Get Your Gun." We imagined a wedding in a big church with bridesmaids and flower girls. We started making plans.

> We live in Montana, a state where same-sex marriage is not yet legal. We are lucky to be part of a surprisingly supportive community. In August of 2013, our church announced an educational series to discuss the topic of same-sex blessings. The Episcopal Church had provided a same-sex blessing liturgy for a couple of years, but each parish must democratically approve the use of the liturgy before the priest can perform the blessing. Over the period of several months, our congregation met to listen to different opinions, insights, and arguments both for and against the topic.

My partner and I love our church family, and while we have been fully accepted and embraced by the parish as a whole, the last thing we wanted was to offend anyone by our desire to marry. We were delighted and humbled when—after fourteen weeks of panels, speakers, proper deliberations, and casual chats—our vestry voted 14–1 to accept the same-sex liturgy.

Our priest can now perform the blessing, [albeit] not a wedding ceremony. Even though we had gone to New York and gotten legally married in December 2013, we were united in a ceremony at our church in the spring of 2014. It was important to us that we have both federal and legal recognition of our union and the blessing of God and our church family. We had bridesmaids, a bridesman, and flower girls. And the pretty dresses we grew up imagining. Family and friends surrounded us. We danced the night away. It was a dream come true. We are proud to be making history in the state of Montana and in our great United States, but, most importantly, we are committed to God and to each other, forever.

The question of extending civil marriage for same-sex couples has been building over the last forty-five years. As a nation, we are headed toward granting federal rights and protections for same-sex married couples within the next few years.

But for Christians, the issue of same-sex marriage is not just about civil rights; it is more complex because to deny civil rights to a group of people is at odds with a doctrine of justice. There is no biblical precedent that validates the intentional discrimination of a group of people. To the contrary, we are prompted by our faith to do away with injustice and inequality.

The LGBT community is legally a class of people and, by law, is due the protection and extension of civil rights accorded every class of people. Civil rights cannot be withheld simply because a group, whether the minority or majority, does not want to extend rights to another group. Popular vote has never dictated civil rights in America. So, on the most basic question of same-sex marriage, does withholding the right to civil marriage align with your personal Christian principles not only as a citizen of the United States but also as a citizen of the kingdom of God?

Part V: LGBT Christians and Their Allies

Chapter 11

Trying to "Fix" Gay People?

The Futility of Reparative Therapy

The beginning of ex-gay ministries in the Christian church

As gay people started coming out of closets that had been created by a culture of fear built upon poorly researched psychoanalytic theories, almost immediately, the church shoved them into another shame-filled closet built of previously dismissed but recycled psychological ideas, this time aligning them with the Holy Word of God. The Christian reparative therapy movement began in California, a hotbed of Christian movements in the late 1960s and the 1970s.

Melodyland Theater in Anaheim, California, had featured big-name entertainment in the 1950s, such as Liberace, Jimmy Durante, and Connie Francis, but had fallen into decline. When the property went up for auction in 1960, Pastor Ralph Wilkerson bought it, altered the name slightly, and started what would become one of the largest and most influential evangelical Christian churches in the country.

The church was well known for its innovative use of toll-free hotlines to help people in distress. There were hotlines for addictions, financial needs, and divorce; whatever help people needed, the people of Melodyland were there to offer.

In the early 1970s, Michael Bussee, a gay man married to a woman, was studying for his counseling degree and working the hotlines. Bussee explains that when it came to gay callers,

> . . . the other hotline workers were trying to exorcise demons out of people, or they told the callers they were probably gay because they had been molested. I knew all this was wrong, from not only my own story, but from my education. We [the gay people answering the hotlines] were disturbed that there were support groups for all kinds of issues and nothing for gay people, so we began to field the calls coming in on the hotline from gay people and do the follow-ups. No one had been telling them that God loved them. All we wanted to do was reach out, affirm, and evangelize them. There was no junk science or politics attached to it.[1]

Wanting to offer a more loving response to homosexual callers and church members, Bussee, Gary Cooper, and Jim Kaspar formally organized a group they named EXIT (Ex-Gay Intervention Team) to offer hotline counseling, prayer groups, Bible studies, follow-up phone calls, and workshops.

Bussee realized that the *only* resource on homosexuality in the sizable Melodyland Christian Center bookstore was a very demeaning "Chick Tract,"[2] a cartoon-style publication portraying gay people as pedophiles. Bussee asked the bookstore manager to keep a look out for appropriate and helpful books on the topic.

---

[1] Kathy Baldock, "Back to the Start of the Real Roots of Exodus," *Canyonwalker Connections*, October 2012, http://canyonwalkerconnections.com/back-to-bondage-the-restored-hope-network-exits-exodus/.

[2] "Chick Tracts" are created and published by Jack Chick and depict a variety of Christian issues in comic book style.

One day, Bussee noticed *The Third Sex,* by heterosexual street preacher Kent Philpott,[3] on the bookstore shelves. He realized that there were people in other parts of the country doing Christian work with the homosexual community and decided it was time for them to gather and meet one another.

In September 1976, Bussee arranged a conference that drew sixty-six attendees. Before the conference concluded, the conference-goers decided to form a board to work toward future yearly get-togethers. Bussee, Kaspar, Frank Worthen (co-founder of Love in Action, San Rafael, California), Robbi Kenney (Outpost Ministry, Minneapolis, Minnesota), and Ron Dennis, who had a small ministry in Nevada, were elected to the board. Gary Cooper, who years later became Bussee's partner and husband, had been instrumental in EXIT and was a founder of the new group, but was not on the board. Cooper was not yet "out." In searching for a name for the new umbrella organization encompassing this group of ministries, Kenney suggested "Exodus International," and it stuck.

While Bussee was involved with Exodus International from 1976 through 1979, there was no call for reparative therapy;[4] no introduction of recycled faulty, non-scientific junk psychology; and no joining with political causes. For a time, Exodus International remained faithful to its original mission: to reach out in love, evangelize, and provide a space for gay people to share mutual support.

It was during this time that Anita Bryant solidified her Save Our Children campaign in in Dade County, Florida. Bryant began joining forces with conservative Christians and asked if some board members of Exodus International would join her in her cause. They declined. Politics was not yet part of Exodus International's mission.

California clinical psychologist Dr. Joseph Nicolosi approached Exodus International about exchanging referrals. Bussee recalls reviewing Nicolosi's work on reparative therapy and knowing even then

---

[3] Kent Philpott, *The Third Sex*, Logos International, 1975.
[4] Reparative therapy is also called conversion therapy, and includes a range of treatments aimed at changing sexual orientation from homosexual to heterosexual.

that it was junk science. Exodus declined any association with Nicolosi. Nicolosi later became a founding member, along with Dr. Charles Socarides, of the National Association for Research and Therapy for Homosexuality (NARTH).[5]

Other Christian reparative therapy ministries

Love in Action (LIA) was founded in 1973 by Frank Worthen, John Evans, and Kent Philpott, author of *The Third Sex*. Philpott's book contained six testimonials from men claiming that faith in Jesus had changed them into heterosexuals. Within one year of the book's publication, all six men recanted their stories, but Philpott, himself a lifelong heterosexual, continued to produce the book. He is currently writing an updated version.

Philpott still "ministers" to "struggling homosexuals" in San Rafael, California. Cofounder Evans left LIA after his best friend, John McIntyre, in despair over his continuing homosexual orientation, committed suicide. Evans later said, "They're destroying people's lives. If you don't do their thing, you're not of God; you'll go to hell. They're living in a fantasy world."[6]

Founders of LIA, believing that homosexuality is a sexual addiction (something no addiction expert believes), combined theology, celibacy, and behavioral modification to "cure individuals of their sinful addiction to homosexuality."[7]

Seventh-Day Adventist Colin Cook founded another prominent reparative therapy ministry, Homosexuals Anonymous, in 1979. Cook was a public face of reparative therapy, often seen on television praising

---

[5] NARTH announced an organizational name change in August 2014. They are rebranding as Alliance for Therapeutic Choice and Scientific Integrity.
[6] Michael Ybarra, "Going Straight: Christian Groups Press Gay People to Take a Heterosexual Path," *Wall Street Journal*, April 21, 1993, http://www.skeptictank.org/hs/gaycurg.htm.
[7] Spoken by Frank Worthen in a keynote address when recounting the history of Love in Action at the Restored Hope Network Inaugural Conference, September 2012, Kathy Baldock, "Back to the Start," September 2012, *Canyonwalker Connections*, http://canyonwalkerconnections.com/back-to-the-start-the-real-roots-of-exodus/.

the success of his own change to heterosexuality, until he was caught in 1986 giving nude massages to gay clients he was "counseling." Cook took a short hiatus but returned to anti-gay advocacy in 1992 to help Focus on the Family in its fight to amend the Colorado Constitution with the passage of Amendment 2. (Amendment 2 prevented any city, town, or county in Colorado from taking legislative or judicial action to recognize gays as a protected class of people.[8] In effect, it allowed for the legal discrimination of gay Coloradans.)

Love Won Out was founded in 1998 as an outreach ministry of Focus on the Family, led by ex-gay[9] John Paulk and his ex-lesbian wife, Anne. The couple appeared in a $600,000 nationwide ad campaign proclaiming freedom from homosexuality. The effort was sponsored by fifteen Religious Right organizations, including the Christian Coalition, the American Family Association, the Family Research Council, and Focus on the Family. With few voices challenging the claims of ex-gays, Christian change therapy took the stage. The Paulks even appeared on the front cover of *Newsweek* with the words "Gay for Life? Going Straight: The Uproar over Change Therapy" emblazoned on the cover.[10]

John Paulk came out as gay in 2013 and apologized for his part in promoting reparative therapy, admitting that he has always been gay.[11] The couple is divorced, and Anne continues in Christian ministry with Restored Hope Network, working to "heal" homosexuals.

---

[8] Amendment 2 passed by popular vote 53%–47%. Supporters of withholding protection from gay individuals asserted that gays want "special rights." The vote was overturned in 1996 in a 6–3 Supreme Court decision in *Romer v. Evans,* which stated that the Amendment targeted homosexuals based on animosity.

[9] "Ex-gay" is the term used for a person who, having once identified as gay, no longer does so.

[10] Gabriel Arana, "My So-Called Ex-Gay Life," *American Prospect,* April 25, 2012, http://prospect.org/article/my-so-called-ex-gay-life.

[11] John Paulk, "To Straight and Back," *Politico Magazine,* June 19, 2014, http://www.politico.com/magazine/story/2014/06/life-as-ex-ex-gay-paulk-108090_Page2.html#.VBTvoVYxGuc.

Yet another reparative therapy ministry called Desert Streams/ Living Waters was founded in 1980 in Santa Monica, California, by Andy Comiskey. It continues offering 20-week programs to "deal with" homosexuality today.

Flawed theories + behavior modification + the Bible = damage

Frank Worthen and other Exodus International leaders and member ministries began to change their direction and philosophy in the late 1970s and the 1980s to more closely align with reparative therapy theories. Reparative therapy, originally introduced by psychoanalyst Sandor Rado in 1940, operates under the premise that people with same-sex attractions need to restore broken family relationships and dynamics in order to "fix" their orientation and become heterosexual. The family relationship break, it is thought, causes a person to seek out unhealthy interactions with a member of the same sex. By finding the root cause of the disruption, it is theorized, heterosexuality can be restored. That was Rado's assumption, which had already been disproven and disavowed before it was adopted by Exodus International and similar Christian ministries in the late 1970s.

The real problem was not just the application of bad psychotherapy; it was what happened next that has caused unimaginable damage to gay, lesbian, bisexual, and transgender Christians over the past thirty-five years, and counting. Christian reparative therapy ministry leaders added a spiritual dimension to "fixing" sexual orientation.

Based on their interpretation of Romans 1:24-32, homosexuality was an open, willful rebellion against God, resulting from a childhood wound. Using a creative interpretation of 1 Corinthians 6:9-11, reparative therapy leaders claimed that homosexuality could be fixed. Paul's phrase "Such *were* some of you" in 1 Corinthians 6:11 (KJV) was repurposed and reinterpreted to mean that gays could change their sexual orientation. Rado's 1940s theories, since disproven, were revived and given a Christian twist. A new Christian industry was created in the 1970s to "fix" homosexuality by the power of Jesus.

It wasn't just flawed theories; it was people's lives

Jesus states in Matthew 7:18 (NIV), "A good tree cannot bear bad fruit, and a bad tree cannot bear good fruit." The testimony of those who have been subjected to reparative therapy, or change ministries, whether in their churches or outsourced by their churches, is overwhelmingly conclusive that these ministries bear bad fruit. The level of destruction inflicted by such ministries on the gay and transgender Christian community and their families can never be fully known.

Before I became involved in the lives of gay Christians, I had only heard the testimonies of ex-gays. I assumed those stories were the norm, but they are *not*. Following, I share the stories of some of my friends who have tried to change their sexual orientation.

Growing up gay and in a Christian home in the 1960s was difficult for Lee Walker, now 60, who lives in Houston, Texas. He was raised in a strong Baptist home. His father led him through the Baptist "Roman Road"[12] to salvation when he was eight.

> I entered kindergarten in the 1960s, a turbulent decade both for the country and for this little Baptist boy who soon realized he was attracted to other boys. I didn't have a label like "gay" or "homosexual" to put to it, but I had been called a sissy once or twice. In my early teens, in the mid-1960s, I heard a lot about "queers," so I cautiously looked it up in the dictionary. I remember the horror dousing me like a bucket of slime when I read the definition. I thought, "Dear God, that's me."

---

[12] The "Roman Road" is an evangelism technique that uses verses from the Book of Romans to explain that all have sinned and need God for salvation, how to receive that gift, and the results of salvation.

Even in my early years, I had fully internalized the message from the church and society that I was defective at best, and a perverted abomination at worst. As the nation struggled with political and social upheaval, I struggled to keep the closet door shut. I constantly repented and prayed for deliverance. Shame and guilt met me at every turn—the nonstop background noise to my life. My faith in Christ was an intrinsic part of my core by now. I could no more separate myself from God than I could rid myself of these "evil thoughts." I privately prayed and silently repented continually.

For a decade, Lee's life was a steady struggle over his sexual attractions. He'd internalized the shame and guilt. He knew he was a Christian, but didn't know how to get rid of his "horrible defect." Lee had heard about the successes of other gay people finding "deliverance" from homosexuality. He sought help from an ex-gay ministry to change his attractions.

In time I found that, at my core, nothing whatsoever had changed. When I got the wake-up call of a lifetime—getting diagnosed with HIV in 1996—I stopped to re-evaluate everything I'd believed or been taught about homosexuality. By fully accepting reality instead of what I'd always been taught by others, I finally came to accept the reality that I was both gay and Christian. It was not until early middle age that I finally accepted [that] my orientation is how I am wired. God didn't hate me. He loves me. He is extravagantly in love with me, as I am with Him. I wish I could have known all this as a little boy in the trailer park.

Lee has a compassionate and caring heart. He is gifted with godly wisdom, kindness, and strength. After a full career in Christian theatre, he has just graduated from the Houston School of Theology and is on his way to working as a counselor. Lee's desire is to help gay and transgender people overcome the effects of the shaming and destructive messages about homosexuality from both the culture and the church.

Jerry Reiter, 57, from Palm Springs, California, was raised in a Catholic home with his six siblings. His father was a firefighter and amateur boxer. Contrary to the "sissy boy" theories of the prominent psychoanalysts of the 1960s, Jerry—who boxed, was good in sports, and was close to his dad—turned out to be the gay son. Jerry's younger brother, on the other hand, refused to fight, did not participate in team sports, and was close to his mother. He is the straight son. When Jerry hit puberty, he knew he was "different."

> When I was twelve years old and in eighth grade, I started having these funny "butterfly in the tummy" feelings around certain guys. I didn't think of this as sexual until an older boy said to us junior-high boys, "Ya know those girls you think are really icky right now? Well, someday you are going to look at them and get this electricity going right through you and get a feeling like you've got butterflies in your stomach." I almost fell over. He was describing what I experienced, all right, but I was sure I was the only person in the entire world who felt this for someone of the same gender. That was very scary.

> In the library, I looked up "homosexuality" and found out it was a crime, a mental disorder, a sin, and a grave moral evil. I wanted to talk with my dad about this but had no clue how to bring it up.

One night in the summer of 1969, the news was covering homosexuals rioting at the Stonewall Inn in New York City. I asked Dad, "What do you think of those people—homosexuals?" He called them every horrible name and said they were worse than animals. No surprise—I did not tell him I might be one of those monsters.

At the age of fourteen, Jerry met some "Jesus people" and became a born-again Christian. He joined the charismatic movement, and the butterflies for boys remained.

My feelings of attraction were growing in intensity, but I didn't act on them. I fell in love with a guy that year for the first time, though I did not realize that was possible. Sounds strange, but I had no clue two people of the same sex could fall in love. He was in love with me, too. We were together as much as possible. We did not do anything, though, but it was driving us both crazy.

Jerry was willing to do anything to have the kind of marriage and family he saw in his parents' relationship. So at the age of sixteen, with some of his own money and without the knowledge of his family, Jerry entered gay conversion therapy because he was terrified that he might "act on" his attractions and let both God and his family down. Under the weight of fear and shame, he even considered suicide.

A friend of mine beat me to it. He was about my age and his father found a magazine with naked guys in it. The father called my friend every kind of dirty name you could call a gay person. [My friend] ran upstairs and took his father's shotgun out and blew his brains out. The dad felt terrible, but never told anyone outside the family why his son killed himself. [My friend's] cousin told me what had happened. I realized how devastating suicide was to family, friends, the entire community.

Thinking his homosexual demons could be "cast out" with prayer and fasting, several times Jerry went without food for up to a week while praying intensely. Then, through another friend who was also trying not to be gay, Jerry heard about Exodus International. The group was meeting at Melodyland Christian Center in Anaheim, led by Michael Bussee. Jerry spent twenty-two years in Exodus, as well as similar Christian ex-gay fellowships and counseling, only to learn that nobody was actually changing from homosexual to heterosexual.

Jerry's local ex-gay chapter leader died of AIDS. This was fifteen years *after* he had supposedly become ex-gay. Still, no one acknowledged that he must have contracted the virus even as he was continually preaching the miracle of his "change" from gay to straight.

Jerry says, "Ex-gays are more likely to have unprotected sex since they must not admit, even to themselves, they need protection." Many of them have had, or do have, wives at home and could not, or cannot, hide condoms. Jerry observed all the hypocrisy within the ex-gay movement. The ex-gays were more involved in unsafe, promiscuous sex than were the gays they preached against, Jerry realized. None of this made any sense to him.

The seemingly impossible demands of reparative therapy were conflated as demands of God. Over the past thirty-five years, untold numbers of gay Christians have turned from God in their "failure" and "inability to please God," who, they were told, could not accept them as a gay person. Some felt so rejected and depressed that they turned to self-destructive behaviors, including suicide; some went deep in the closet to try to fit in at church; some became vehemently opposed to all things religious; some decided to seek God in other religions, or no religion; and very few individuals were able to find a church community in which they could worship and serve God without being rejected.

Michael Watt, 48, who lives in Memphis, Tennessee, had read several books and tried several programs to try to stop being gay before he entered a five-month program with the organization Love in Action.

> My journey into the reparative therapy arena began in my mid- to late twenties. I purchased books from my church bookstore, my neighborhood Christian bookstore, Focus on the Family, and Exodus International. I devoured these books, hoping that I would learn something that would help me not be gay. Because of what I read in these books, I believed that I was broken.

> In my late thirties, I began an intense five-month discipleship program at a ministry called Love in Action in Memphis, Tennessee. I was told I was broken emotionally, and that my same-sex attractions were due to my unmet emotional needs resulting from inadequate relationships with my father and with my male peers while growing up.

> For the next six years, I did everything I could to have my "unmet emotional needs" met in a healthy manner. I formed men's Bible studies and small groups; I spent more time with my straight male friends; I limited my time being "one of the girls" with my female friends, and tried to get interested in sports. I did everything by the book, hoping my attractions would redirect themselves toward women. I dated a wonderful, godly woman for almost two years. Absolutely nothing worked. I was still attracted to men.

> I had a gaping hole in my life that no straight man or woman would be able to fill. I wanted to connect intimately to the heart of another man. Trying to do everything possible for

almost thirty-two years to not be gay just sucked the life out of me. At the age of forty-six, I finally accepted the fact that I am gay, and have always been gay.

Michael continues:

Since accepting that I am gay, I am at peace for the first time in my life. All of the inner turmoil and anguish has vanished. My family and my friends have noticed this change in me. My relationship with Christ is no longer based on my performance. My acceptance from God is no longer wrapped around my trying to be straight.

I once believed that I had to choose between being gay and being a Christian, that I had to reconcile my faith with my sexual orientation first. For me, I needed those years to do that. Decades of processing my sexual orientation through a reparative therapy mindset made me feel shame. I do get angry at times. I grieve the lost years and what could have been, had I accepted that I am gay earlier.

When I was twenty-six, I fell in love with my best friend. I often wonder what would have been, had he and I both had the freedom to be who we are at a much earlier age. I wonder if he and I would [now] be celebrating twenty-two years together. Instead, I am approaching the age of fifty and still single.

Darlene Bogle, 70, and her life partner, Becky, live in San Jose, California. They are a blessing of "extra mothers" in my life. Darlene was an Exodus International ministry leader and counselor for over fifteen years. She authored two "I am no longer a lesbian" books for Exodus

International, was their television and seminar spokesperson, and counseled hundreds of Christian clients "struggling with homosexuality."

When Darlene was growing up in a small town in Washington State, she knew by high school that she was a lesbian. She experienced a sexual relationship with a girl, yet had no framework to define the experience or label it. Darlene attended a "holiness church," went to a Christian college, and fell in love with Linda at age eighteen. She thought she would be with Linda forever, but was conflicted because she didn't understand how, as a Christian, she could be attracted to women. She thought there was something wrong with her and desperately wanted to please God, so she tried to date boys.

Linda went home over the Christmas break, and Darlene was planning to visit her. But Linda's mother called Darlene right after Christmas; Linda had committed suicide.

Darlene was devastated. She left college and went to Los Angeles to work with the Teen Challenge ministry.

> I figured if I could minister to others with drug/alcohol/addiction problems, then I wouldn't have to think about my own attractions. It didn't work because I was attracted to many of the masculine women we brought into the center.

> I left after six months and returned to college. I was a friend with the Dean of Women. She felt I needed spiritual deliverance from demons. She took me to see several well-known deliverance ministers. They prayed with me, but I remember one of them telling me, "You aren't ready" and "I can't help you."

> I read the Bible constantly and thought I was okay. I began to shut down my feelings. I didn't speak to anyone about my attractions. Denial didn't work. Not having an outlet to talk

about my feelings only made me a powder keg that would eventually explode. I learned to lie about who I was.

Darlene joined the Army and settled in California. She prayed, and submitted to several more deliverance ministries. She was telling more lies to cover up who she was.

Then I heard about Exodus International and how they had the answer to heal homosexuality. I joined them. Because I had so much "truth," I became a leader.

For almost fifteen years I taught, spoke nationally, and was on television proclaiming freedom from homosexuality. Depression and denial eventually betrayed me. I knew in my heart that what I craved was not a strong hairy chest of a man, but the soft embrace of a woman. I felt that I had failed as a leader but, more importantly, [that] God had failed me by not healing my sexual attractions. I'd written a book telling the world I was healed and [that] there was hope for change, but it wasn't really my truth.

I met a woman (Des) who was Christian and lesbian. I couldn't deny my attraction to her. We talked for hours, and a change began to happen at my core. God hadn't been able to change me because that was how He created me. I was falling in love.

My church, Exodus staff, and many Christian colleagues told me I was wrong and making a choice to sin, yet I experienced a new freedom and joy as I embraced who God had made me to be. It took time, but I was no longer failing God, and He was affirming me.

Now, I've become stronger in my faith. I use every opportunity to share God's love with all His children. I'm no longer conflicted, and have a great peace in knowing that all the stuff I went through to be accepted wasn't necessary or required by my God who loves me just as I am! The freedom to share how to be whole and loved unconditionally is worth the condemnation of right-wing religious leaders who tell me I'm leading others to hell by my proclamation of inclusion. I love to tell the Story of Truth!

Darlene and Des were together until the day Des died of cancer. Darlene is well known in the ex-ex-gay[13] ministry arena. Since leaving Exodus International in 1991, Darlene Bogle and Michael Bussee (who had left in 1979) have been actively working to counter the falsehoods underlying reparative therapy.

Christian reparative therapy ministries close down worldwide

Love in Action (LIA) was the oldest ex-gay ministry, the flagship of the entire ex-gay movement, founded in 1973. LIA had a full-time residential program where gay men and women could stay for intensive treatment. Its executive director of twenty-two years, John Smid,[14] resigned from his post in 2008. He said he had "never met a man who experienced a change from homosexual to heterosexual."[15] During his time at LIA, Smid spent eleven years on the Board of Exodus International.

He shares the following:

[13] "Ex-ex-gay" is used to describe gays who have undergone reparative therapy to "no longer be gay," then have come out again as gay.
[14] John Smid, *EX'D OUT: How I Fired the Shame Committee* (Self-published, 2012).
[15] John Smid, "Where Is the Repentance?", *Grace Rivers*, October 7, 2011, http://www.gracerivers.com/gays-repent/.

So often people will say someone needs to "repent" from homosexuality. It is something that actually cannot be repented of; people are, or they are not, homosexual. It is an intrinsic part of their being (or personally, my being).

One cannot repent of something that is unchangeable. I have gone through a tremendous amount of grief over the many years that I spoke of change, repentance, reorientation, and such when, barring some kind of miracle, none of this can occur with homosexuality.

Yes, there are homosexuals who make dramatic changes in their lives as they walk through the transformation process with Jesus. I have heard story after story of changes that have occurred as men and women find the grace of God in their lives as homosexual people. But I'm sorry, this transformation process may not meet the expectations of many Christians. I also want to reiterate here that the transformation for the vast majority of homosexuals will not include a change of sexual orientation. Actually, I've never met a man who experienced a change from homosexual to heterosexual.

In 2013, Smid left his longtime wife and fell in love with a man. John and Larry now live happily together in Texas.

LIA gave up its name in 2012 and handed over its files to a Christian sex addiction ministry calling itself Restoration Path. Their website is geared toward sex addictions in general and homosexuality in particular.

Additionally, several international reparative therapy organizations originally established to "fix" gay people have changed course. The group Courage was essentially Exodus United Kingdom. In 2002, after fifteen years in ministry, its leader, Jeremy Marks, announced that *he had never seen one client*, including himself, change sexual orientation. Today the renamed organization, Courage UK, is gay-affirming.

For many years, New Directions had been the Exodus affiliate in Canada. In 2007, under the leadership of Wendy Gritter, they, too, changed their stance and direction, acknowledging that sexual orientation is not a choice.[16] New Directions' position on LGBTQ Christians is now as follows:

> We consider the question of faithful discipleship for LGBTQ Christians to be a disputable matter. Therefore, we honour the autonomy of each individual to discern and clarify their convictions and values and encourage them to live in alignment with them—trusting that the Holy Spirit is more than able to lead and guide. When people are living in congruence with their conscience before God, we have seen good fruit in both the lives of those who are celibate and those who have covenanted with a life partner.[17]

In January 2012, Alan Chambers, who had been the president of Exodus International since 2001, attended the Gay Christian Network (GCN) conference at the invitation of Justin Lee, the GCN founder. Chambers took part in a panel discussion with Gritter, Marks, and Smid, moderated by Lee. The conversation was strained, yet transparent. Chambers was publicly challenged about Exodus International's policy encouraging reparative therapy counseling for minors.[18] Two hours into the exchange, Chambers admitted:

---

[16] Wendy Gritter released her book, *Generous Spaciousness: Responding to Gay Christians in the Church,* in May 2014. Some of her work is profiled in Chapter 15.

[17] Wendy Gritter, letter to Kathy Baldock, August 6, 2014.

[18] Kathy Baldock, "Alan Chambers and the Message of Exodus at the Gay Christian Network Conference," *Canyonwalker Connections,* January 2012, http://canyonwalkerconnections.com/alan-chambers-and-the-message-of-exodus-at-the-gay-christian-network-conference/.

The majority of people that I have met, and I would say the majority meaning 99.9% of them, have not experienced a change in their orientation or have gotten to a place where they could say that they could never be tempted or are not tempted in some way or experience some level of same-sex attraction. I think there is a gender issue there; there are some women who have challenged me and said that [referring to themselves] my orientation or my attractions have changed completely. Those have been rare. The vast majority of people that I know will experience some level of same-sex attraction.

Exodus International eventually shut down in May 2013. At the final Exodus International conference, Chambers offered a public apology for the harm done to gay people and their families through the practice of reparative therapy.[19] Chambers himself admits to ongoing same-sex attractions.[20]

The news that Exodus International had shut down forced Living Waters Australia's leader, Ron Brookman, to consider the status of Australia's major ex-gay ministry. Brookman said Living Waters would need to redouble their efforts to pick up some of the slack left by Exodus International. Instead, the ministry's numbers dwindled so drastically in the following months that the organization was visibly in trouble. The final straw came when nobody would step forward and say, "I am no longer gay. Pick me as the new leader." Thus, when Brookman stepped down, there was no one ready to take over leadership of the organization. Living Waters shut down permanently in April 2014.

---

[19] Kathy Baldock, "We Have Asked Gay People to Change; Now, It Is Time for the Church to Change," *Canyonwalker Connections,* June 2013, http://canyonwalkerconnections.com/we-have-asked-gay-people-to-change-it-is-time-for-the-church-to-change/.
[20] Audrey Barrick, "Wife of Former Homosexual Alan Chambers Says She Never Doubted Marrying Him," *The Christian Post,* January 17, 2014, http://www.christianpost.com/news/wife-of-former-homosexual-alan-chambers-says-she-never-doubted-marrying-him-112897/.

Even before that, Evergreen International, the largest Mormon ex-gay ministry in the world, founded in 1989,[21] had shut down on January 1, 2014.

After forty years of failure, the damage continues

Before Exodus International closed down, but as it was trying to decide how to move forward, several of its former affiliate members regrouped and formed a new umbrella organization, Restored Hope Network (RHN). I attended RHN's inaugural conference in September 2012 and published a detailed report of the two-day event on the Canyonwalker Connections blog.[22] RHN, its member ministries, and its proponents[23] support a therapy model that combines behavior modification and spiritual submission. The model is a variation of the long-discarded theories of the 1950s about the root causes of homosexuality: blaming homosexuality on an overbearing mother/weak father, or on sexual abuse, but now adding rebellion against God as an additional cause, with faith in Jesus as the cure. Ministries of this type operate largely unchallenged and unquestioned by conservative churches that regularly entrust their LGBT members to such programs.

This is essentially a replay of the dynamics that existed between the isolated psychoanalysts from the 1930s to the 1980s and the other mental health experts who interacted with homosexuals outside of therapeutic situations. This time, however, Christian ministries reside

---

[21] Trudy Ring, "Mormon 'Ex-Gay' Group Shuts Down, Absorbed by Other Organizations," *The Advocate*, January 3, 2014.

[22] Kathy Baldock, "Back to Bondage: The Restored Hope Network Exits Exodus," *Canyonwalker Connections,* September 2012, http://canyonwalkerconnections.com/back-to-bondage-the-restored-hope-network-exits-exodus/.

[23] The reparative therapy techniques and theology of RHN are supported by members of their Board of Reference: Matt Barber, Liberty Counsel; Michael Brown, FIRE School of Ministry; Donald Carson, Trinity Evangelical Divinity School; Dr. James Dobson, Family Talk; Dr. Albert Mohler, Southern Baptist Theological Seminary; Joseph Nicolosi, Alliance for Therapeutic Choice and Scientific Integrity (formerly NARTH); Ray Ortlund, The Gospel Coalition; Janet Parshall, Moody Radio host of "In the Market"; Mat Staver, Liberty Counsel; and others, http://www.restoredhopenetwork.org/index.php/who-we-are/board-of-reference.

in the "ivory tower," ignoring the testimony of LGBT Christians and information gathered from medical and psychological experts over the past thirty years in the fields of human sexuality, sex, gender, and sexual orientation.

In 2009, the American Psychological Association, in a 130-page study,[24] reported the harm done to people who have undergone reparative therapy. It is currently against the law in two states, New Jersey and California, to subject minors to reparative therapy treatment by a licensed health care professional. More and more states are introducing similar laws, and a nationwide bill is in the works in Congress.

Every major medical and mental health organization in the United States has issued a statement condemning reparative therapy. It has not proven to change the sexual orientation of anyone, and it harms many. Following are statements against sexual orientation reorientation by three American professional mental health organizations:

- *American Psychiatric Association:* "In the last four decades, 'reparative' therapists have not produced any rigorous scientific research to substantiate their claims of cure. Until there is such research available, the APA recommends that ethical practitioners refrain from attempts to change individuals' sexual orientation, keeping in mind the medical dictum to first, do no harm."
- *American Psychoanalytic Association:* "Psychoanalytic technique does not encompass purposeful efforts to 'convert' or 'repair' an individual's sexual orientation."
- *American Psychological Association:* The APA resolves to "affirm that same-sex sexual and romantic attractions, feelings, and behaviors are normal and positive variations of human sexuality."

---

[24] "Report of the American Psychological Association Task Force on Appropriate Therapeutic Responses to Sexual Orientation," *American Psychological Association*, August 2009, http://www.apa.org/pi/lgbt/resources/therapeutic-response.pdf.

Every major medical and psychological organization in the United States is against "corrective methods" for both sexual orientation and gender identity.[25]

"But I've met healed homosexuals!"

You might be wondering, "What about the healed homosexuals who have come to speak at my church?" While it is important to honor another's testimony and journey with God, including their story of change, it is equally important to respect the overwhelming body of evidence and the witness of gay and transgender Christians for whom such treatment has been destructive.

The testimonies of ex-gays who claim they are no longer gay are usually dramatic. Their stories are not indicative of all gay people, and are often fueled by guilt and shame. For instance, John Paulk, considered the ex-gay poster boy for many years, shared pictures of his life as a former drag queen during his young adult years. The stark contrast from drag queen to a married father of three earned him hundreds of interviews. These types of stories make the best testimonies from church pulpits. You would be quite pressed to hear an undramatic testimony of an ex-gay person who grew up in a normal home with great parents.

When you listen to the testimony of a person who says he or she no longer "lives in the lifestyle," or is "no longer homosexual," especially in church-presentation settings, consider what he or she may or may not be saying.

---

[25] American Academy of Pediatrics, American Psychological Association, American Psychiatric Association, American Medical Association, National Association of Social Workers, National Association of School Counselors, National Association of School Psychologists, American Academy of Physician Assistants, American Academy of Family Physicians, American College of Obstetricians and Gynecologists, American College of Nurse Midwives, American Counselors Association, American Medical Student Association, World Professional Association for Transgender Health, American Academy of Family Physicians, American Public Health Service Association, National Commission on Correctional Health Care, American Physical Therapy Association, and the World Health Organization.

When closely questioned, almost all ex-gays admit they still experience same-sex attractions, rather than opposite-sex attractions. Some consciously limit time with close friends of the same sex, admitting that they do so to keep from being sexually tempted. Most ex-gay ministry leaders don't acknowledge the existence of bisexuals. It can "complicate" testimonies. Yet, some ex-gays, including some high-profile leaders, have admitted that they are bisexual and currently live with an opposite-sex spouse.

Many ex-gays practice "positive confessions" when speaking of their orientation. Speaking what you hope for is a kind of spiritualized "fake it 'til you make it." They speak about their sexual orientation in faith of what God *will do* and *can do*, not about what their current reality is. "God has healed me" is an example of positive confession. It may or may not be a statement of fact. Listen closely to the words used in their testimonies. There are "former homosexuals" who profess one thing publicly, yet privately tell the truth about their enduring same-sex attractions.

When asked about same-sex sexual temptation, they may flippantly offer, "Well, of course I am tempted—aren't most people tempted?" But by which sex are they tempted—the same sex or the opposite sex? There are no reports of sex scandals involving an ex-gay and someone of the opposite sex. There have been many such scandals involving ex-gays and someone of the same sex.

Ministry leaders and clients who leave the reparative therapy industry attest to the use of deceiving language regularly. An ex-gay with a spouse and children is not evidence of heterosexuality, or a move from same-sex attraction. In Chapter 12, you will read stories of people in mixed-orientation marriages.

Recall from Chapter 8, sexual behavior may not be the same as sexual orientation. The two terms shouldn't be confused. There is sexual identity, sexual behavior, and sexual attraction; most times they all align toward one sex. I have asked scores of gays and lesbians how they can perform sexually with a person of the opposite sex. The most common answer: "I fantasize *a lot* while having sex with my partner."

Sexual orientation is a complex human condition, however, and because of religious beliefs, obligations, vows, or social pressure, some gay, lesbian, and bisexual people may choose to remain in mixed-orientation marriages.

What about celibacy for gays?

As the harsh and ineffective reparative therapy model winds down, a *seemingly* kinder approach is being introduced in churches, especially in churches with younger populations. *"Everyone* is welcome here," they boast. *Everyone*—all political parties, the rich, the college student, the divorced, the young, the old, and . . . the homosexuals. The "welcoming" stance is likely conditional for those who are gay, though. You are welcome, but . . .

While church leaders may accept that people have a natural sexual attraction or gender identity that cannot be changed, church policy may state that gay people must control their natural desires and not act sexually or romantically upon their attractions and, further, should commit themselves to lifelong celibacy.

This "you can be gay, but don't act on it" approach may be genuinely offered as a compromise position, with "kindness" keeping gay congregants coming to church, engaged in community, celibate, and sitting on the sidelines.

Though it appears to be a gracious accommodation, imposing celibacy on a person and acknowledging simultaneously that they will have an unchangeable lifelong struggle with temptation doesn't hold up to Christian history or biblical scrutiny.

First, abstinence before marriage, or chastity, is not the same thing as celibacy. Celibacy implies that you will never have an intimate relationship and, for a gay or lesbian person, that he or she will never marry someone of the same sex. Marrying a person of the opposite sex is, of course, a possibility, but that makes two people in a marriage who will suffer an unnatural mismatch. Celibacy throughout church history has been viewed as a spiritual gift or calling, not a condition forcefully imposed on another person without their consent. Revisiting Romans 1:18-32, you may recall that the passage states that the same-sex sexual behavior in question was driven by lust. So is it a biblical stance to tell gay Christians it's okay to not "act on it" while acknowledging that they will experience desire?

In Matthew 5:21-22, 27-28 (NIV), Jesus says:

> You have heard that it was said to the people long ago, "You shall not murder, and anyone who murders will be subject to judgment." But I tell you that anyone who is angry with a brother or sister will be subject to judgment. . . . You have heard that it was said, "You shall not commit adultery." But I tell you that anyone who looks at a woman lustfully has already committed adultery with her in his heart.

Christian principles teach that anger is just as sinful as murder and lust as sinful as adultery. If having a homosexual orientation is considered a sin, then according to the Scriptures, having unchanging, lifelong same-sex desires is also sin because having the desire is spiritually equivalent to participating in same-sex sexual acts.

According to the words of Jesus, there's no wiggle room or distinction between lifelong lust and desire on the one hand, and taking action on such desires on the other. Because God looks at our hearts and not just our actions, I don't get an extra jewel in my crown for hating my enemy and *fantasizing* about ruining him, yet not actually *doing* it.

If you firmly believe that Romans 1 refers to people with a homosexual orientation, and to committed, monogamous, same-sex relationships, and condemns the latter as wrong, then you must also hold that even lifelong, same-sex *desire* is wrong.

That's a radical thought!

Requiring gay Christians to remain celibate may be birthed of a genuinely caring, pastoral heart; however, it appears not to hold up scripturally. It is merely a side stop on the journey to truly grappling with the Scriptures and understanding how committed gay Christians fit into our churches.

In summary, reparative therapy for change in sexual orientation was disavowed over four decades ago by major professional mental health organizations. All major professional medical associations agree that sexual orientation change therapy does not work. Most experts, along with people who who have gone through the change-therapy process, say it is harmful.

With the best of intentions, well-meaning pastors, ministry leaders, and fellow Christians still direct LGBT Christians toward reparative and change-therapy programs. They are motivated by what they believe is love for gay and transgender people, but to the LGBT person, it is not a loving action. Good ministries will produce good fruits. To see whether the motivation is love or not, all we need do is look at the fruit. If something brings love and life, it is good. If it yields fear and damage, it is bad. Overwhelmingly, reparative therapy undermines the emotional, psychological, physical, sexual, and spiritual health of gay, lesbian, bisexual, and transgender people.

There is yet another widespread consequence of the denial that gay and lesbian Christians exist in the world and in our churches, and of the insistence upon "fixing" them: mixed-orientation marriages. We'll look at this phenomenon next.

Chapter 12

Gay People Marry Straight People—Now What?

Looking at Mixed-Orientation Marriages

The invisible repercussions of denying the existence of gays and lesbians in churches

In the past, when gay and lesbian Christians in conservative faith communities were honest and open about their sexual orientation, they were typically faced with three options:

- If church doctrine declared a homosexual orientation to be incompatible with Christianity, gays were asked or pressured to leave the congregation.
- If the church had associations with a reparative therapy ministry, gay Christians were directed toward such ministries to get help with their "homosexual struggles."
- If church policy allowed for homosexual orientation, but not "practicing homosexuals," gay Christians were expected to commit to lifelong celibacy.

Though some of these options are changing, this limited menu of choices created, and in many places continues to create, immense problems often invisible to outsiders.

Given these choices, it is not surprising that gay and lesbian Christians who wanted to remain in their conservative churches frequently didn't come out. If they wanted to get married and have a family, the most acceptable option was marriage to a person of the opposite sex.

Marriage between a gay spouse and a straight spouse is called a mixed-orientation marriage. Although there are no reliable estimates as to the number of mixed-orientation marriages in the United States, it is believed that between one and two million people are involved in such relationships.[1]

You may have never heard about mixed-orientation marriages; they're rarely discussed, especially in Christian circles. If a church has several hundred members, at least one or two mixed-orientation couples are likely within the fellowship.

A person with a homosexual orientation decides to enter a mixed-orientation marriage for a variety of reasons. Some believe their "homosexual struggles" are temporary, a curiosity, or a phase they are going through, and that it will not be permanent. Many gays and lesbians in the past, especially during their younger years, lacked the language or understanding to acknowledge their attractions even to themselves, much less to others. This is particularly applicable to people over forty. They believed, and were often directly told by religious and ministry leaders, that their "homosexual struggles" would disappear when they entered into heterosexual marriage. Gay Christians *believed* these lies by the hundreds of thousands.

What is known anecdotally is that more gay men enter into mixed-orientation marriages than do lesbians, because society and the church place a higher premium on masculinity and patriarchy. It's tougher for

---

[1] Amity Pierce Buxton and Lisa B. Schwartz, "Straight Spouses Speak Out: Implications for Gay and Lesbian Marriage," *California Journal of Health Promotion* 2 (2004). http://www.cjhp.org/Volume2_2004/SpIssLGBT/24-31-buxton.pdf.

men than for women to come out as gay, which has led them, in higher numbers, to enter into mixed-orientation marriages.

Believing they might be able to suppress their natural orientation, gays have married straight people. The overwhelming majority of gays who married straight spouses *genuinely* did feel sincere love for their spouse when they got married. Because sexual orientation has three components—sexual identity, sexual behavior, and sexual attraction—people can sometimes juggle two of those balls in the air for a time, but not for long. The romantic high early in a relationship and the sexual-behavior masquerade can help one turn a blind eye to natural orientation, but it can rarely be sustained.

The best way to understand the complexities and pain involved in mixed-orientation marriages is to let those involved in them tell their own stories. All of the following stories involve individuals who identified as Christian when they got married.

Ex-gay ministry leaders in mixed-orientation marriages

Chad Boone, a 47-year-old gay man from Jacksonville, Florida, was married to his wife for over twenty years and fathered three children with her. Chad grew up in a small town where he felt like he was different from his peers because of his attraction to other guys. He was occasionally teased about it, which only drove him deeper into the closet, hiding his true feelings and emerging sexual orientation.

For years, Chad had relationships with both men and women, yet pushed aside any notion that he might *be* gay. He hoped his relationships with men had just been "a phase," and believed marriage would "cure" him of homosexuality. Six months into his marriage, Chad told his wife about his attraction to men. He also told her she was the love of his life and he only wanted to be with her. He was being sincere.

The couple joined an evangelical charismatic church where homosexuality as a sin, and its damning consequences were regular topics of preaching. Chad was okay with that; after all, he had left *that life* behind. But over time, life's pressures increased, and it became harder to keep his sexual orientation suppressed. Chad began to lead a double life, participating in gay chat rooms and viewing gay porn online.

Chad and his family next moved to a new church home where homosexuality was addressed more openly. Although it was still considered a sin at the new church, it was considered something he could deal with through reparative therapy. Chad participated in an ex-gay ministry branch in his church. He was confident that his homosexuality could be managed and possibly cured. He was hopeful that with hard work, he might be able to lead a fulfilled straight life.

> I jumped in with both feet and got involved in leadership, planning, and teaching. I went on experiential healing weekends and sought reparative counseling to set me "straight." Through my network, I found men in other groups. On the "down-low," we stayed connected online. We were all too embarrassed to talk about our sexuality openly outside the online groups. This created a great sense of shame for me.

> Once again, I was keeping my dirty little secrets and leading a double life. I knew that if my church friends and extended family found out, I would surely be rejected and alone. I kept my secret hidden. It looked good on the surface. With the support of my wife, I stayed involved in ex-gay ministry for almost ten years. Together, we even reached out to other couples that were in our same situation.

When Chad turned forty, he began to question the integrity of his duplicitous life. His hidden life didn't line up with his ministerial life, and he knew his sexual orientation had not changed. He still longed for a soul connection with a man. The emotional isolation drove him even deeper into reparative therapy and, consequently, into depression. He became desperate.

> I went to bed at night asking God to heal me or not let me wake up the next day. Frustrated that my prayers were not being answered, I felt trapped in my marriage. I started drinking hard liquor, and lots of it, just to cope. I tried drowning my pain for a couple of years. Eventually, my wife kicked me out of the house for the last time. I was alone and desperate. I got into a 12-step recovery program, and with God, my sponsor, and others, I came face to face with many fears, hang-ups, and bad habits. I had a spiritual awakening, too: "I am gay. I am me. I am loved. I can be whole just as I am."

> I heard God ask me, "What is the most loving thing you can do?" I answered, "To set myself and my family free." They deserved to be free to love and be themselves, too. Nobody in my family was happy with a dysfunctional, depressed husband and father.

> Since that moment, it has been an honest journey for me. My wife and I have been separated for almost two years. I miss her, and even more, I miss seeing my kids every day.

> Some days I feel deep sadness. Some days are okay. It's been a grieving and letting-go process. My wife has been the only one in my life who has shown me unconditional love. Sometimes I ask myself, "Was I a fool to walk away?" At the end of the day, I can't forfeit who I am or Whose I am. I know without any doubt that I am loved, forgiven, and free. My wife deserved no less.

My sobriety, sense of self, and integrity all depend on my ability to be authentic and open about who I am. The aching pain I felt deep in my chest for so many years is gone. The codependency I had on others to make me feel and look acceptable is dissolving.

Living alone and starting over has its difficulties, but it's an authentic journey now. We're only as sick as our secrets. No more secrets. I am happy in life again and finding purpose in helping others. Life is getting better, one day at a time.

Chad's story is not unusual. Beginning in the 1970s, Christians in conservative churches who "struggled with SSA (same-sex attraction)" were regularly directed to reparative therapy programs to find the "root cause" of their homosexuality.[2] Once the root cause was uncovered and dealt with, they were assured, their homosexual desires would disappear. The "positive confession" movement was thriving in Christian circles in the 1980s and 1990s. If "homosexual strugglers" confessed their sin of homosexuality and claimed to be healed by faith, they were assured that God would oblige and heal them. Usually, the internal struggle and guilt lifted for a season; sexual behavior was often suppressed, but sexual attractions didn't change.

When Jerry Reiter of Palm Desert, California, now 57, was a young man, he sought the counsel of his priest at the Franciscan University. The priest, who had a counseling degree, assured Jerry that he could "cure" him of his "unwanted feelings." Gay men were routinely told that if they took the next step and married a woman, God would "bless them with heterosexuality."

---

[2] Kathy Baldock, "The Real Roots of Exodus," *Canyonwalker Connections*, October 2012, http://canyonwalkerconnections.com/back-to-the-start-the-real-roots-of-exodus/.

The priest encouraged me to marry a woman. He assured me that "those other feelings" would diminish and go away in time if I stayed married. Studies since have shown that the opposite is true. Same-sex attractions increase the longer a gay man is married to a woman.

Many pastors and Christian counselors continue to advise gays and lesbians to marry someone of the opposite sex. I was convinced [homosexuality] was just a temptation to be overcome. I even tried to get "deliverance from the demon of homosexuality." My sexual orientation never changed.

My family's reaction to my homosexuality was a huge part of my struggle. I knew they would never accept me as I really was. I also wanted a family of my own, but when I was young, marriage to someone of the same sex was unthinkable. It was hard even for gays and lesbians to imagine it for themselves. We thought it would never happen.

Jerry married a woman, had two sons, and became part of an ex-gay ministry. He played the public role model of a "former homosexual" and travelled to other churches to show that gay people could change orientation. Meeting homosexuals "healed" of their struggles encouraged people in the churches he visited. But it was a sham performance.

Several of those who were publicly claiming to be heterosexual were privately talking about sexual experiences with men. Even though Jerry knew they were being hypocrites, they kept up the charade so others would stay strong and "leave homosexuality." Eventually, Jerry's marriage ended and his former wife remarried. Jerry had a part in her remarriage; he introduced her to her new husband. "We are friends now, and the love remains," says Jerry.

"When I get married, my attractions will change"

Lynn Golden, now forty-five and living in Greensboro, North Carolina, grew up in Sioux Falls, South Dakota. When she was twelve, her friends were crushing on boys. She taped posters of hot male icons on her bedroom walls, trying to develop her own interest in guys, but it didn't work. She was interested in girls. She *knew* she had to keep it hidden from friends and from people at church.

At nineteen, Lynn got a glimpse of her future in a vision. If she married a man, it looked like "darkness, gloom, hopelessness, despair, and extreme mental and emotional anguish." Still, the social and religious pressures against being a lesbian were so strong. Lynn thought marrying a man was the only way for her to please God and the church; she opted for a life of suffering in silence. She didn't tell her future husband, Dale, about her sexual attractions toward women, and at age twenty-one, she married him.

He noticed that though Lynn made time to be with her women friends, she didn't make efforts to spend time alone with him. Lynn never initiated physical or verbal affection with Dale. He accused her of having affairs, but she wasn't having affairs. After eight years of marriage, and with two sons under age seven, Lynn could no longer handle the mental anguish of living a lie and pretending to be heterosexual; she told Dale she was gay.

Together, the couple decided that Lynn hadn't tried hard enough on her own and that she should try reparative therapy resources to get some additional help. She sought out both Exodus International and Seventh-Day Adventist Kinship to try to change her sexual orientation. She worked on herself for *another decade.* Lynn says:

> I prayed over and over again for God to change my sexuality, and all I got was silence. During all this time, while I was in the closet and struggling with my sexuality, I endured loneliness—deep loneliness—insomnia, self-hatred, and

suicidal thoughts. I would spend my nights begging God to just kill me so that I could just get this life over with.

December 17, 2009, I almost got my wish. After a near-fatal car accident, I decided to go directly to God and ask Him what He thought of my sexuality.

Suddenly, information that I had never seen seemed to come my way. I learned what the Bible says and doesn't say about sexuality. I felt like God assured me that He saw my sexuality as a non-issue. It was time for me to tell Dale the truth and to set him free to find a woman who could love him as a wife should; he needed the kind of love that I could never give him. I came out to him again in 2012.

I've told many people that living as a heterosexual feels like walking with my shoes on the wrong feet. I was able to do it, but I felt so unnatural, and it was painful and extremely uncomfortable living the heterosexual lifestyle when every part of me just wanted to be with the woman of my dreams.

Lynn is now married to Linda, the woman of her dreams. I met the two of them in Charlotte in August 2013. The joy and love they have with one another is unmistakable; it's obvious they "fit." Lynn says:

I feel vibrantly alive. I don't want to die anymore. My self-hatred is gone. I have such incredible peace and deep inner joy at sharing life with and being married to Linda. We have a spiritual connection unlike anything I ever thought possible with another human being.

Everything is so natural and is so right. She is my "suitable" helpmate. My connection with God is even deeper and more profound now that I have embraced every part of who He made me to be, and it is so easy to love others more deeply. My life is filled with living color.

This is what gays are missing when they are kept in the closet. They are being deprived of this kind of love. I am so grateful that I allowed myself to question God directly about my sexuality, and that I listened for His response.

I was accused so many times of being selfish for leaving my marriage. However, my ex-husband, who is still my close friend, is on cloud nine in love with his soul mate, whom he would have never met had we stayed together. I could have held his life back from the joy he feels now if I had stayed with him. Instead, I cut those chains and allowed us both to have wings.

Even after entering a mixed-orientation marriage, most gay men and lesbians don't readily share information about their sexual orientation with their spouses. Overwhelmingly, they have believed that in marrying a person of the opposite sex, their natural attractions would change over time.

Jonathan Shinn, 34, from California, was raised in a loving, nuclear, and intact Christian home. Even in his early memories, he knew he'd been attracted to guys, but he kept it a secret. He wanted what his parents had: a loving marriage and a family. He thought if he centered his life on God and faith, did the right things, and got married, he'd stop being gay. He thought the struggle and pain would go away. Jonathan says:

It was all in vain. I wish I had been honest and transparent. There's power in truth. I wish I'd seen that before wrecking someone else's life in an effort to do the "right thing." I got married, finished graduate school, and had two children.

I dragged someone else into my unresolved pain. I tried denial, prayer, and therapy. None of it worked. I hurt my wife deeply in the process. Whether my intentions were pure or not, I still deceived someone. She didn't deserve to be the collateral damage from my problem. With good cause, she left me. It was the hardest thing that I've ever been through.

In the end, it was the best for both of us and, ultimately, even our children. I have a new, honest, and real faith in God that does not rely on my performance or life circumstances. To young people thinking that you can keep this secret forever—don't try. It will more than likely eat you alive.

Christian ministry workers hiding in mixed-orientation marriages

To avoid gossip and speculation about their sexual orientation, it's not uncommon for gay Christian ministry workers to marry a person of the opposite sex. Angie Campbell, 44, from South Bend, Indiana, shares:

I have been doing my best over the last twenty years to live the life I thought I was supposed to live, a life that everyone told me—and I believed—was pleasing to God. I love God with all of my heart, and displeasing Him or doing anything to damage my relationship with Him is something I have never wanted to do.

I tried so hard growing up to be like the other girls. I put the posters of guy rock stars on my wall, dated boys, and did everything I could to fit the image of the "normal girl." But it was just never me. When I finally realized and admitted to myself as a teenager that I was gay, I felt like I finally fit somewhere.

I have always had a deep love for God from as long as I can remember. I grew up writing poems about Him and the Bible. I had an awareness of His presence and respect for Him that kept me out of a lot of trouble growing up. I never felt convicted about my sexuality, even though everyone in my sphere of influence condemned it.

Over the years, I've struggled with severe anxiety. I got it into my head that maybe this was God's judgment against my sexual orientation. Maybe all the Christians were right and I was wrong after all. I don't know why I never studied what the Bible says or searched it out for myself, but I didn't.

I went to Bible college to pursue my passion of worship music. I soon became the project of a couple of well-meaning, wonderful ladies who were trying to transform me into a "woman of God" with dresses, makeup, and by changing the way I walked. I met a kind, wonderful young man that I enjoyed being with—as a friend. He adored me, which was filling a hole in my heart of needing attention and acceptance, as well as helping me fill this new role in life that I thought I was supposed to be in as a woman.

Despite feeling in my heart that the Lord was telling me not to go through with the marriage, I married him anyway. I was so uncomfortable in this role from the moment I said "I do." I did sincerely love him. Out of my love for him and commitment to our marriage, I was able to overcome my feelings for a while. I've tried to make it be more for years, [but] it was always just a friendship [type of] love on my end.

After sixteen years of marriage and one child, Angie could no longer keep the balancing act together. In 2012, she had to admit to her husband that she was miserable. Keeping up the image of being a worship leader and a powerful woman of God was killing her. Under the stress, she had lost thirty pounds in two months. Angie didn't want to embarrass her husband, but they were both extremely unhappy and needed to be honest. With this new level of acceptance before God, Angie spent time trying to find the roots of what might have caused her to be a lesbian. She began to do some online searches and came across Kori Ashton's website.[3] Angie was immediately attracted to Kori's story.

Like Angie, Kori had been a worship leader for several years. Raised in a devoted Christian home, Kori was dismissed from Bible school after falling in love with the dean's lesbian daughter. She went back into the closet, got into reparative therapy, and travelled around the country leading worship for Exodus International conferences. Eventually, Kori accepted that God had made her gay and left Exodus, thinking she was also leaving behind the opportunity to ever lead Christian worship again.

In December 2011, I attended the Gay Christian Network conference, where Kori led worship for the first time in many years; she cried a lot that weekend. Kori had begun the journey into a full and authentic life, which now includes her wife, Becky, and son, Andrew. With a desire to help other lesbian Christians, Kori created a website that includes a link to my website, Canyonwalker Connections.[4]

---

[3] http://lesbepure.com.
[4] www.canyonwalkerconnections.com.

From Kori's site, Angie found mine and wrote me a desperate email very late one night in 2013. I wrote back to her immediately and suggested she attend a special ministry weekend with Pastor Tony Roberts at Bishop Randy Duncan's New Life Community Church[5] in La Porte, Indiana, near her home. Angie went, and there she found an accepting and supportive church home that, to her delight, even allowed her to lead worship.

One of the standard recommendations I give people who contact me is to get involved with the online support community at the Gay Christian Network (GCN).[6] Angie signed up and began exchanging encouragement with other Christian lesbians. Almost immediately, she got a private message on the GCN forums from a woman in New Zealand named Ariel.

Fast-forward to today: Angie is at peace, her health has improved, her anxiety issues are becoming a thing of the past, and she lives in New Zealand with Ariel. After Angie's teenaged daughter met Ariel and saw the two women interact, she wrote to the New Zealand immigration bureau on behalf of her mother:

> I enjoyed being with Ariel, and she and my mom and I had a lot of fun together. My mom and Ariel are the single most romantic couple I've ever seen. They are loving, kind, and generous to each other, and to me. They are perfect! I never would have guessed that my bland, boring, brown-loving mom could ever be with a fun, energetic person like Ariel.

Chet de Rouen, 44, from Gilbert, Arizona, grew up in rural Louisiana. He had never heard the word "gay" as a young man. He was aware, however, that he liked boys at an early age. At his Assemblies of God college, he finally did hear the word "gay," and he knew it fit him. After college,

---

[5] New Life Community Church, La Porte, Indiana, http://www.nlcch.org.
[6] www.gaychristian.net.

he went on to become a pastor. Because he was sure, through prayer, fasting, and reading the Bible, that he would overcome his "gayness," he never told his wife about his sexual attractions.

> The first five years of my marriage were pretty blissful with very little desire for men. However, sex always felt awkward and unfulfilling. I never felt that I truly pleased my wife. It was embarrassing and humiliating at times.

> The second five years began to get rocky, but it was manageable. I used my diagnosis of low testosterone to compensate for my lack of sexual desire with my wife.

> The final four years were hell. I became depressed, anxious, and planned my suicide on several occasions. I wanted to make it look like an accident so the shame for my family would be minimal. The pressure built to an unmanageable level, and I began to seek the sexual attention of men.

> It was my first sexual encounter with a man that finalized [that] I was, in fact, gay and that sex with my wife would never be what it was intended [to be] between a married couple. It was a great risk in coming out. I knew I could lose my wife, kids, family, and church. I was a minister with the Assemblies of God denomination, so this was not going to go well in any aspect. I knew it would destroy everything that I thought was real, honest, and true.

> I came to my wife and got honest with her. I'm one of the lucky men who received grace and mercy from his spouse. We cried together and began to make plans to end our almost fifteen-year marriage. I had wanted nothing more

than to be a husband and a father with a nice job, home, carpool, neighborhood, pets, a red front door, and a white picket fence out front. I was devastated. I knew that I had forever hurt my wife, and the guilt was almost too much to bear. I fell back into depression and suicidal planning. She stood by me and held me up. Unfortunately, she lost most of her friends as well. They were shocked, surprised, and angry that she didn't put me to the curb, take away my children, take all the assets, and leave me to "get what I had coming." She was the closest thing to Christianity that I had ever seen in my life. Even our immediate family members posted evil things about us on Facebook.

Currently, my relationship with God is incredibly fragile. I'm surely not the person that I used to be. I doubt that God is real. I doubt that the Bible is inerrant or relevant for me today. The thought of going into a church sends me into an anxiety attack.

Chet says of his family today:

Christa is the only woman I have ever loved. It hurt us deeply to dissolve the marriage. Nonetheless, we both embraced it as the most honorable thing we could do for each other and our children. I now see a happier and healthier woman with self-worth and self-esteem.

Straight spouses suffer

Most gay people I know who have been, or are, in mixed-orientation marriages care for their spouses deeply. The potential of eventually hurting them can keep gay spouses in the marriage even though the straight spouse suffers in other ways. A spouse in a mixed-orientation marriage rarely gets the appropriate romantic, emotional, and sexual care he or she deserves.

Gay spouses quite often elect to come out when their children are raised and the partners are empty-nesters. It is then that the sense of lifelong, profound emptiness and longing to be with a person of the same sex can be overwhelming and even crushing to the gay spouse. Contemplating the life they've robbed their spouse of, along with their own loneliness and deception, slowly destroys them from the inside. Most gay spouses eventually experience a life-or-death urgency to come out. Many times, freedom for the gay spouse becomes a gift for his or her straight spouse as well.

Bruce Strine, 62, from Westminster, Maryland, knew he was same-sex attracted from an early age, yet he married a woman when he was twenty-four years old.

> Before we got married, I shared with my wife that I struggled with same-sex attraction. We both naïvely thought that once we got married, those desires would go away. If anything, it confirmed to me that I was gay. Sexual intimacy with my wife felt awkward and unnatural. During the last twenty of our thirty years of marriage, there was no sexual intimacy.

> We are separated now and will eventually divorce. After we separated, I told my wife that my deepest regret is that I was unable to meet her emotional and sexual needs. My question for anyone who is gay and thinking about marriage to someone of the opposite sex is: "Will you be able to meet his or her emotional and sexual needs?" If the answer is "no," it would be unfair to the other person to pursue marriage.

How is church leadership responding to mixed-orientation marriages?

Outside the Christian church, there are nationwide support groups for people in mixed-orientation marriages. These groups acknowledge that mixed-orientation marriages are rarely viable; thus, their primary counsel to those who find themselves in such a relationship is to get a divorce.

The largest of these groups, the Straight Spouse Network (SSN),[7] was founded in 1984 by Bonnie Kaye, M.Ed., who had been married to a gay man. Since beginning the organization, Kaye has used her knowledge and personal experience to counsel over 70,000 women and hundreds of gay men[8] in mixed-orientation marriages.

In contrast to SSN's counsel, church leaders, with little understanding of homosexuality and rare experience with mixed-orientation marriages, often advise couples to stay married. Using the flawed premise that sexual orientation is akin to "fixable" behaviors like substance abuse or adultery, many church and ministry leaders tell gay spouses to submit their natural sexual attraction to Christ for healing and preservation of the marriage.

Straight women in mixed-orientation marriages are regularly praised by church leaders as "suffering servants": *"God will give you the strength you need. If you are patient and pray, God will turn this around."* God is indeed all-powerful; however, homosexuality is a normal part of His creation, and all experts agree that fully homosexual people cannot be transformed into fully heterosexual people.

The conservative Christian church is *completely* failing mixed-orientation couples during a time in their lives that is probably leading to the end of their marriage. Rather than ministering to them with compassion and support, the church lays even more guilt, shame, and futile

---

[7] www.straightspouse.org
[8] Bonnie Kaye, *Straight Wives: Shattered Lives,* Vol. 2 (British Columbia: CCB Publishing, 2011), 3.

expectations on these couples. The added burdens often drive both the spouses and their children away from church.

I met Emily Reese when we were guests on a local radio talk show to discuss homosexuality in conservative churches. Emily grew up in a religiously conservative family in Iowa. She met her husband, Devon, while he was attending the University of Missouri–Kansas City. They met and fell in love when they worked as servers at Applebee's. Several months before their wedding, friends warned Emily of their strong suspicions about Devon's sexuality.

> One night, after a party, a friend came to me and said, "Emily, Devon is gay. You cannot marry him. I hate to be the one to tell you, but you need to know, honey." Well, I reacted with anger because Devon had come to me before they could tell me about an event at a bar the previous evening. I told our friend something to the effect: "That's not true. He already told me everything. He already came clean, so don't tell me any lies."

> My friend rolled his eyes, knowing it was a lost cause, and said, "Okay. I'm telling you he's gay. It's your life. Don't say you weren't warned." At that point, I wouldn't have wanted to believe it anyway. We were already engaged and had the wedding planned.

After the birth of their first child, Emily and Devon moved to Nevada. They attended a strong nondenominational Bible church where Devon was a lay youth pastor. Without Emily's being aware, Devon had contacted Exodus International years before for help to "fix" his homosexuality. It hadn't worked. Ten years into the marriage, under stressful circumstances, Devon finally came out.

Emily approached her church leadership and close church friends for help. Leadership offered her a set of tapes on homosexuality, approaching it as a fixable behavior.

They also suggested she join a home group as a precaution to keep herself from falling into adultery. When divorce became inevitable, members of the church leadership, including a small group of trusted friends, blamed Emily for not sticking with the marriage.

> Because my solution and my handling of it didn't fit within their paradigm or Christian ideals, it was more comfortable for them to blame me and reject me than face the fact that maybe, just maybe, they were wrong and needed to evaluate their own ideas on homosexuality.

After offering no constructive help, church leadership and her confidantes prayed for Emily and Devon and "released them to the world." Over the next three years, the couple worked through the divorce devoid of support from their church family.

Emily was diagnosed with an aggressive colon cancer after the divorce and the family grew closer as Devon and his partner—now his husband—took over full-time parenting of the three children so Emily could focus on healing.

> At that point I accepted Devon for who he was, who he is, and who he will become. This is my stance of what "unconditional love" means. I can look back without bitterness. I certainly hope that others can learn from my experience because the betrayal was horrible. It took me nearly a year and a half to accept the truth that Devon wasn't making a "choice." He didn't want to be gay. He was torn.

I can honestly say that I'm glad I didn't believe that he was gay before I married him because we wouldn't have had our three beautiful children. I wouldn't have gotten to change, in so many ways, for the better. I would still be stuck in the "love the sinner, hate the sin" mentality.

I've stopped going to church altogether and, for a while, threw the baby out with the bath water. I understand that loving, same-sex relationships are not what God is referring to in the Bible. Now I am more comfortable praying, reading the Bible, and believing in Jesus' words, especially the Letters in Red. I really know now how to love unconditionally without strings attached or an agenda to change someone else. The empathy that I gained for others by our marriage is a gift. I wouldn't change a thing about my life and our marriage.

Emily is a talented blogger who is now reaching out to other straight spouses and offering the help and hope that were absent in her time of need.[9] We had occasion to go back to the church in which she and her husband served in ministry to listen to an ex-gay leader tell youth and adults that sexual orientation can and should be changed.[10] It was hard for Emily to listen to and to witness the ways in which the leaders of her old church continued to promote reparative therapy as a viable option.

During the question time, Emily submitted a written question asking how they would help a person who came to them admitting that they struggled with homosexuality. The pastor's answer was the same near-futile response gay people and their families have been hearing for decades: "We would love the sinner and hate the sin and minister

---

[9] Emily's blogsite: http://samesidessupportforstraightspouses.wordpress.com/.

[10] Kathy Baldock, "Speaking Up Against Ex-Gay Kent Paris at Summit Church Then . . .," *Canyonwalker* Connections, February 2012, http://canyonwalkerconnections.com/speaking-up-against-ex-gay-kent-paris-at-summit-christian-church-then/

to their needs." It was the same response that had failed Emily, Devon, and the children.

Neither Emily nor Devon nor their children attend church any longer. Church leaders did not minister to their needs; they tried to fix what was not broken, shamed them when they did not comply, and caused further damage to each family member's individual relationship with God.

The leaders of Mark's church failed him, too. Mark knew he was attracted to boys at an early age, but there wasn't anyone he could talk to about it. During puberty, when he innocently told a boy he loved him, the word got back to his family. Rather than talk to Mark about the situation, they shamed him and let him know that what he had done was *not okay*. Mark was prepared to hide his sexual orientation for the rest of his life. As an adult, he married Cheri and had three children.

I know Mark well; he is one of my hiking buddies. He is a giving man. If anyone needs help or an answer in technology or computers, Mark is the go-to person. He has been a valuable member of several congregations, partnering to build churches and running the media teams of large worship communities.

> I never wanted anyone to know I was gay. I really thought I would die without anyone ever knowing. However, I was outed; I didn't get a chance to think of the cost of coming out. Now, except for a few close family members, they all hate me.

When the leadership of Mark's church found out he was gay, he was made to feel uncomfortable enough to leave. The next two churches he visited while looking for a new church home had "heard about" him, and he was not welcome there either.

Mark and his family no longer attend church. Cheri says they have suffered "alienation, judgment, abandonment from family and church."

Understanding rejection, Mark and Cheri host bimonthly open conversation and dinner parties. "We're an assortment of people caring for one another in mutual respect; we've become a church of sorts," Cheri explains. It is in this style of fellowship that Mark and Cheri live out authentic and open Christianity.

Stay married or get a divorce?

Some couples in mixed-orientation marriages, such as Mark and Cheri, choose to stay together. The decision each couple makes and their reasons for doing so vary. Sometimes the spouses are each other's best friends; they deeply love one another and don't want to lose the connection.

Other reasons for staying together may include financial and emotional security for the spouse and children. Even with the best of intentions, this may not be viable. Wesley T. urges the gay partner to consider the future for children in mixed-orientation marriages:

> It doesn't make sense to me to build a family unit knowing that the likelihood of it remaining intact is worse than the already dismal marriage-to-divorce statistics. What doesn't make sense to children is the fact that one parent is gay and that they now have to live in two homes, travel back and forth, and share holidays.

> I believe in doing no harm, or the very least possible. To me, it is knowingly causing harm, or at best, an unnecessary disruption to a child's life. I would strongly discourage the gay person and the straight one from marrying each other. I use my own past experience in a mixed-orientation marriage as a reference. If they still choose to get married, I would then suggest that they never have children to spare them the pain of the likely future divorce.

Wesley is correct in his assessment of the probability of failure of mixed-orientation marriages. Within the first three years of the discovery that one spouse is gay, 20% of mixed-orientation marriages fail. In the end, only about one in four couples remains married. It is estimated that about 20% of gay men in the United States are in mixed-orientation marriages.[11] Until we as a society, and subsequently as the church, allow people to marry a person of the sex and gender to which they are naturally attracted, marriages will be unfairly burdened by mixed orientations.

The heterosexual partner is often forgotten in the mixed-orientation–marriage dynamic, and it is usually a wife. For most of her marriage, she has likely struggled with feelings of extremely low self-confidence, believing she is neither sexually attractive nor desired by her husband. She frequently thinks she is physically, emotionally, or intellectually inferior. She may even believe she doesn't deserve her husband's attention.

When he finally does come out, there is often a feeling of relief expressed as "Oh, it's not *me*." But profoundly painful trauma and the devastation of loss of identity usually quickly follow. The straight spouse's ability to trust people and self is undermined. He or she wonders, "What else in our lives wasn't true?"

Some partners are completely surprised when their spouse comes out. Gloria J., from Illinois, had just celebrated her twenty-first wedding anniversary with her husband. Two weeks later, her husband confessed to an affair with a man.

> I didn't know what to do, what to say. I couldn't wrap my head around it. I began looking back to see what I had done to cause this. My husband explained that he had struggled with same-sex attraction before we met. He thought that by marrying me, I would be able to fix him. I never suspected

---

[11] Laura Compton, "Two Decades of Mixed-orientation Marriages," Mormons for Marriage, January 8, 2011, http://www.mormonsformarriage.com/two-decades-of-mixed-orientation-marriages/.

anything. Looking back to the time before we were married, he touched on the subject briefly, but dismissed it as something from puberty. He never expressed that this was an ongoing struggle.

After the sudden shock and many tears, overwhelming fear struck. *What was I going to do, where would I go?* "What about our family [and] daughter? How are we going to explain this to our church family, friends, and immediate family? Who do I talk to?" I suddenly realized that I had no one to talk to about this. I felt alone.

When the gay spouse comes out, he or she may feel a sense of euphoria and even relief for the first time in years. At the same time, the heterosexual spouse may be utterly devastated. Mark's wife, Cheri, recalls:

The emotional cost was huge. Finding out someone I had spent so many years with was gay and I didn't know about it made me feel as if I had possibly misunderstood everything else in our relationship. I felt as if I didn't belong anywhere. It was almost as if the world had shifted somehow, and I hadn't caught up. I was disoriented, to say the least.

As our situation became known, many family and friends either rejected us or judged us. Our children are young adults now. Their friends don't seem to care or act any differently toward us. I hope this [is] a sign of a new generation. The most hurtful group of all was the church.

As many spouses in mixed-orientation marriages discover, church leaders are ill-prepared and rarely offer wise advice to couples struggling in mixed-orientation marriages. Most couples in mixed-orientation marriages report extreme disappointment in the way in which they were treated by church leadership. Note that both gay and straight spouses in the situations shared above expressed anger at ill-informed pastors who told them what to do and, worse, presented the solution as if they were speaking the will of God. Chet, the former Assemblies of God pastor, said:

> I began to resent God, church, and anything regarding Christianity. "Hate" would be an honest word. I felt I [had] failed God and He surely hated me. In fact, I was sure of it. His "children," my former church friends, confirmed that God had no place for me in their church unless I turned back to God or became celibate. I became a miserable human being.

There is no single solution that works for every mixed-orientation marriage. Whereas secular counsel, for the most part, suggests the couple work quickly toward separation and divorce, conservative Christian leaders, especially the people who support reparative therapy models, recommend that couples stay together. Ultimately, the best resolution remains with the couple. Cheri offers:

> Each couple's situation and resolution is different. There is no right or wrong way to walk this path. What is required is love and honor for one another. The greatest gift the gay spouse can give the straight spouse is being completely honest about their orientation. Many couples choose to end their relationship, but others, like us, move forward.

> Finding a nonjudgmental counselor with no agenda who can support both spouses is critical. Online information

and support is available for the straight spouse. It should be carefully considered though. There are wounded, bitter people who distort information. Give each other plenty of time. If you can, don't make any radical changes right away. Finally, be kind to yourself and surround yourself with the people and activities that bring you peace.

Spouses who have been involved in mixed-orientation marriages seem to agree that it is important for the gay spouse to come out and be honest with their partner about their orientation. The dishonesty of living a lie usually takes a toll on the emotional and physical health of both partners. Gloria J., the heterosexual spouse of a gay man, says:

> To the men and women who are struggling in a relationship with the opposite sex (married or single) and believe they are gay or question their orientation, I would plead with them to share their heart with the one they are in a relationship with. If single, please do not marry with the belief that the person you marry will be able to "fix" you.

> Be honest with your struggle. Talk it through and seek counsel if needed to help sort through your thoughts and feelings. Trust me, it is better to be honest with the person and risk the relationship than to marry, have children, and then come out. For the one who is married, as difficult as it is, be honest, share your heart, share your struggle with your spouse. Seek counsel on how to move forward.

Mark L., 59, from Houston, Texas, was married to his wife for twenty-seven years. Together, they made the decision to divorce. Mark's former wife is remarried, and Mark married his partner a few years ago. Mark and his husband are involved in a reconciling United Methodist

Church where their marriage is fully supported by the congregation. He offers this advice:

> When I read about younger gay Christians who struggle with social acceptance in their families and faith communities and they express the idea of intentionally entering into a mixed-orientation marriage, my heart breaks.

> I see my 19-year-old self, determined to gut it out for God, placing my own emotional health, as well as [that of] others (the spouse, the kids), into an untenable position that almost certainly leads to eventual heartbreak and pain. I do and say what I can to dissuade people from making this choice. However, as I understand all too well, the need for acceptance is so very strong.

> I pray that the continuing growth of visibility and acceptance of the gay-Christian phenomenon will help fewer and fewer people to take that route of entering into mixed-orientation marriages.

Pastoral and congregational response to mixed-orientation marriages

If you're a straight Christian in a conservative church, it's highly likely that you aren't aware of the frequency with which mixed-orientation marriages take place. About twelve years ago, I went to a gay friend's fortieth birthday party. It was the first time I became aware of the prevalence of such marriages. I sat with a local psychology professor, and we chatted about mixed-orientation marriages. The husband of a friend, a longtime deacon at a megachurch in my town, had just been arrested for soliciting a male police officer in a sting operation at a park restroom.

The professor pointed at the men at the party and rattled off bits of their stories. "He was once married, . . . used to be married, . . . married, . . . was married . . ." Thinking of my female friend's plight, I asked, "And what's happened to the wives?"

"Collateral damage," he said. "They're the largest single group of wounded people that no one talks about or cares about. The husband comes out to his freedom in who he is, and the wife is left stunned and broken and shamed with no one to talk to. Someone needs to care about these women."

While conservative churches offer and facilitate care groups for people with an array of needs, from divorce to addiction to bereavement, the spouses in mixed-orientation marriages are typically abandoned or expected to navigate the difficulties on their own. Occasionally, the "successful" couples who are still together are displayed for all to see as evidence of the "power of Christ" to change sexual orientation, but when their marriages break up, they are shuffled away and shunned.

As mentioned earlier in this book, in September 2012, I attended the inaugural conference of the Restored Hope Network (RHN),[12] the newly formed and more stringent reparative therapy umbrella ministry that replaced Exodus International[13] when it closed down.

Of the approximately 140 attendees, about half appeared to be in mixed-orientation marriages. An RHN leader spoke from the stage and encouraged the "ex-gay" partner to follow God by submitting their sexuality to Him and, further, encouraged the couples to stay married. The speaker was being far less than transparent. Her own marriage was in the initial stages of divorce. This fact was not public information; however, I was aware of it. It was disheartening to witness more

---

[12] Kathy Baldock, "Back to the Closet: Restored Hope Network on Homosexuality – Part III," *Canyonwalker Connections*, September 2012, http://canyonwalkerconnections.com/back-to-the-closet-restored-hope-network-on-homosexuality/.
[13] Kathy Baldock, "We Have Asked Gay People to Change; Now, It's Time for the Church to Change," *Canyonwalker Connections*, May 2013, http://canyonwalkerconnections.com/we-have-asked-gay-people-to-change-it-is-time-for-the-church-to-change/.

disingenuous "hope" being dispensed to the mixed-orientation couples in attendance.

Of course, there are couples who have managed to navigate their own expectations for marriage with a spouse who is naturally inclined to the same sex. They create and live within their own paradigm of what marriage is. Additionally, there are bisexual people who are able to find satisfaction in a relationship with a male or a female, allowing them to conform to the church's traditional opposite-sex requirements regarding marriage. For the most part, however, the outside mask of mixed-orientation marriage covers what is falling to pieces behind closed doors.[14] Couples aware of their orientation differences generally "keep up appearances" in churches. This behavior is both expected and supported, while honesty about the situation is rarely encouraged.

For over ten years, Chad, who shared some of his story earlier in the chapter, led ex-gay support groups for men in mixed-orientation marriages. At the time, he was leading a double life, as were many other ministry leaders. As we talked over coffee, I asked him, "In those ten years when you led mixed-orientation marriage groups, how many couples did you think were in healthy, mutually beneficial heterosexual-type marriages?" As if going through a mental Rolodex, he hesitated. I expected him to give me a number, or a percentage of those he had worked with. Then he answered, *"None. Not one couple. None."*

The stories I've presented here are those of Christians—all people known to me. They are, or were, people deeply committed to Christ. These stories are typical, and every one of them represents a tough situation. Many of the gay spouses faced utter despair, even to the brink of suicide. Before judging what people *should* have done, it is important to consider, which is better for a child or family—a gay parent, or a dead one? This is not an exaggerated possible outcome.

---

[14] Zoe Schlanger, "Can Gays Convert?" *Newsweek*, May 1, 2014, http://www.newsweek.com/ex-ex-gay-pride-249282.

The systemic problem of mixed-orientation marriages has been created by a gross lack of understanding about what homosexuality is, and what it is not. It is important to understand that being gay is not just about sex, just as being heterosexual is not just about sex. Sexual orientation is about basic human connections, which are natural to each person.

Gay people, like straight people, want to find a relationship in which there is comfort, transparency, and intimacy. Most gay people, like most straight people, want to get married and start families. Gay people, like straight people, often want to remain in the faith communities and denominations in which they were raised. For the most part, when gays and lesbians come out in conservative churches, they are robbed of the opportunity for and the blessings of these things. They cannot date, get married, or begin families in a traditional way; instead, they are pressured to lie, hide, and deceive themselves and their mate.

A growing number of open and affirming congregations are established each year, providing gay Christians with new options. Still, some gay people want to stay in the churches and denominations where their families have attended for years, or maybe generations. We've stripped away these beautiful and enduring family legacies from many gay and transgender Christians.

People with homosexual orientations are frequently treated by church leaders as if they have behavioral problems (adultery, substance abuse, and pornography are most frequently cited as the equivalents). They're told to get help, "just stop," and "submit to Christ." A person cannot "just stop" having a homosexual orientation any more than a heterosexual can "just stop" being heterosexual. When they fail to change, they experience shame, depression, thoughts of suicide, and feelings of loneliness. Their focus turns to changing their outside actions and performing in hopes of pleasing God and those around them. In the end, it's futile for the gay person, and the spouse and family are cheated of an emotionally engaged partner and parent. The whole family begins crumbling on the inside in silence and isolation.

Jesus warned the teachers of the Law to stop laying unfair hardships on others: "They tie up heavy burdens and lay them on men's shoulders, but they themselves are unwilling to move them with so much as a finger" (Matthew 23:4, NASB).

Denying the existence of gay people and the needs of mixed-orientation couples in churches only adds another layer of shame onto a couple and family already drowning in it. Most gay people in mixed-orientation marriages have spent decades pleading with God to change them. They know every Bible verse associated with same-sex behavior, and they've probably studied them in Hebrew and Greek. Many have tried reparative therapy, fasting, and deliverance—repeatedly—and they are still gay.

People in crisis often turn to their home groups or Bible study groups, yet on this issue, there is shame attached. The wife of a gay man feels like she is sexually insufficient; the same holds true for men married to lesbians. The straight spouses are stuck with no one to confide in except pastoral staff.

Pastors may not know all the answers about how to best minister to couples in mixed-orientation marriages, but as pastors, they do know how to care for and love people. Without further information, they can, at minimum, do that.

Beyond acceptance, how might the conservative church respond to the needs of those in mixed-orientation marriages? The steps are basic, yet monumental for most conservative church leaders. The foundation lies in an investment of time in studying the six key passages of Scripture used to create a religious sexual ethic for gay people.

Additionally, no matter where you may find yourself along the spectrum from affirming to non-affirming, tools are available to help you understand what homosexuality is and is not. Peeling away stereotypes and myths may help leaders to minister to those in mixed-orientation marriages from the point of *reality*, not from unrealistic expectations. It is easy to imagine what "they" should do, but to personalize the burdens we unconsciously lay upon others, imagine this scenario: As a parent, would you support one of your own children marrying a spouse who has undergone reparative therapy? We often expect others to walk a path we are not willing to recommend to our own loved ones.

You have likely seen a "poster couple" for successful mixed-orientation marriages. As Lynn put it so well, a person can go through life with their shoes on the wrong feet and manage, but it is a constant strain. Gay people can try to curb sexual activity, but not participating in same-sex sex does not reflect a change in orientation. Sexual orientation is deeper and more complicated than simply to whom one is romantically attracted, or with whom one has sex. Sexual orientation also encompasses emotional connections, affection, and comfort.

The Bible is *not* a handbook on human sexuality or sexual orientation. Leaders must look elsewhere for sex education. I suggested this recently to a straight pastor friend, who stiffened and rocked back in his chair in surprise. My recommendation was not just unexpected; it was an enormous shift for him to even consider. Pastors are not required in their training to take courses on human sexuality, yet they are expected to dispense advice to their flock on diverse topics involving sexuality.

What's happening outside church walls is happening inside church walls. It is all part of the human experience. Ignorance and lack of education about sex, sexual orientation, gender identities, and human sexuality in general have led to harmful assumptions and poor pastoral counsel.

At the very core of conversations about gay and transgender Christians' inclusion in churches are people who typically know next to nothing about what homosexuality or transgenderism is, yet they have been making the policy decisions for churches and denominations.

A positive and simple step toward understanding human sexuality might include *requiring* church staff members to take an entry-level college class on the topic. Although it could make for an interesting class dynamic between college students and pastors, it might also be quite intimidating for the latter. Perhaps inviting an expert on human sexuality to do a church staff training session would offer a more comfortable setting. However such education might be accomplished, effectively ministering to the real suffering of those in mixed-orientation marriages is part of the pastoral call.

When one person in the marriage is intersex or transgender

Just thinking about the needs of congregational members in mixed-orientation marriages can be overwhelming. Not only are there gay and lesbian congregants in most churches, but if a church has more than about a thousand participants, statistically, there are surely intersex and transgender members among them. Counseling a couple in which one person is cisgender (the term for those in whom sex and gender identity match) and the other is intersex or transgender adds a layer of complexity in mixed–gender identity marriages that pastors rarely encounter.

Let's imagine the "simpler" of the two situations as an example to illustrate the pastoral challenge: Susan and Lance have been members of your church for decades. They attend weekly and have raised their children in Sunday school. Susan has always felt that she sees life through an uncomfortable, almost unbearable filter—she feels like she is a man on the inside. An emergency medical procedure sends Susan to the hospital, where she gets an MRI, followed by a chromosome test. Susan's DNA reveals she is chromosomally a male.

Together, Susan and Lance make a decision to honor Susan's lifelong urgency to present and live as a male. She transitions to male. How might they be received when they come to church as a same-sex couple?

As with mixed-orientation marriages, same-gender couples (when one spouse is transgender and the other is cisgender) and their families face difficult decisions and are in need of support from their pastor, congregation, and friends, who likely have little understanding about transgender or intersex conditions.

Finally, speaking to a mixed-orientation or same-gender couple: If your church leadership is unwilling or unable to understand sexual orientation or gender identity, you will not likely receive compassionate, informed care there. Do not seek help from Christian reparative therapy ministries. The unreasonable expectations and burdens they place upon the gay, transgender, or intersex spouse, and hence, on their spouse and family, may become unmanageable.

There *are* Christian counselors educated in human sexuality who *can* speak from godly wisdom. Seek them out and *interview* them. If they use a model expecting the gay spouse to change or alter orientation, or the trans* spouse to ignore their gender identity, move along and find another therapist. The counselor doesn't even need to be local to you; Skype is a wonderful tool used by many therapists. Keep going until you find a counselor who can help you navigate the unique complexities of mixed-orientation and same-gender marriages.

Chapter 13

They Did Not Leave Church When the Church Left Them

The Beginning of the Gay and Transgender Christian Movement

Rev. Troy Perry, founder of the Gay Christian Movement

As gay people started coming out of the closet in the late 1960s, they found there were few spiritual refuges that would welcome them as congregants, let alone leaders. Though a handful of ministers in San Francisco felt compelled to stand alongside the gay community for justice and human rights,[1] for the most part once gay people came out, they were put out. No denomination had a policy that welcomed gays into fellowship.[2]

---

[1] Jaweed Kaleem, "Unearthing the Surprising Religious History of American Gay Rights Activism," *The Huffington Post,* June 28, 2014, http://www.huffingtonpost.com/2014/06/28/gay-religious-history_n_5538178.html.
[2] The Metropolitan Community Church was the first, in 1968, to welcome LGBT people, followed by the United Church of Christ in 1973.

When Troy Perry (1940–) was a young man in Florida, his elderly aunt told him, "Troy Jr., you are called to ministry, but it won't be in the church you are in [now]"—that is, the Pentecostal church. By age fifteen, Perry was already a licensed Baptist preacher, but in those days, one could not be ordained unless one was married, so at just eighteen, he married a preacher's daughter. The couple relocated to Illinois, where Perry fathered two sons and attended Bible college at the Moody Bible Institute.

But while pastoring a small Church of God congregation, Rev. Perry secretly started having sexual relationships with other men. Although it may seem strange to us today, in the early 1960s, Perry did not understand that he was gay.

> Pentecostals didn't preach about sex and would have never even used the word "homosexual." Homosexuality was not a separate act but something *heterosexuals* did, versus being "queer" or "sissies," and I *knew* I wasn't a sissy. When I sinned, I did what Pentecostals do. I prayed for forgiveness.[3]

Once his affairs were discovered, Rev. Perry was asked to leave the church. The family moved to Santa Ana in Southern California, where he began pastoring another church.

In the process of preparing for a sermon one day, Rev. Perry visited a bookstore in search of information. While there, he spotted a male "physique" magazine and was surprised by his sexual response. Sheepishly, he asked the bookstore clerk if she had any information about homosexuality. She offered Perry a copy of *The Homosexual in America: A Subjective Approach,* by Edward Sagarin.[4]

Sagarin, a married homosexual, was a professor of sociology and criminology at City University, New York, who wrote under the pseudonym

---

[3] Scott Bloom, dir., *Call Me Troy* (Frameline, 2007).
[4] Donald Webster Cory, *The Homosexual in America: A Subjective Approach* (New York: Greenberg, 1951).

Donald Webster Cory. For its time, the book is a surprisingly excellent work with a positive view of homosexuality. It was published in 1951 directly on the heels of the first Kinsey Report (1948), and contains personal and anecdotal information as well as research that helped assure homosexual men that they were not alone.

For Perry, the book was an eye-opener; he found there were millions of men like him. Perry finally understood that he was gay. He hid the book under his mattress for a time, but then decided to speak to his wife. As he broached the subject, she interrupted: "Does this have anything to do with the book I found under the mattress? Do you think you are a homosexual?" Perry said "yes." The two agreed to divorce, though it ripped Perry to pieces. "I loved her, and I loved my kids."[5]

Perry was expelled from the pulpit again. This time, he moved away from ministry, got a job in retail, and was soon drafted into the military (1965). After two years of service, he returned to Los Angeles, where, following a failed love affair, he attempted suicide.

It was a desperate and oppressive time for the homosexual community in Los Angeles. The police walked into gay bars and arrested customers just for being there. When a close friend was arrested for patronizing a gay bar, Perry's sense of justice was awakened. He felt he could help fight the constant persecution if he could organize and empower gay people by helping them rediscover their religious roots. It was a revolutionary idea in the late 1960s.

Gays were not welcome in mainstream churches, yet Perry had a vision of creating a spiritual refuge. He placed a small ad in *The Advocate*, a magazine whose target audience is the LGBT community, inviting gay people to join him for a worship service in his living room. Twelve people showed up, and the Metropolitan Community Church (MCC) was born.

The group grew immediately; they rented meeting places and kept outgrowing them. Within three years, MCC swelled to over a thousand

---

[5] *Call Me Troy.*

members and moved into an old movie theater. They grew again, and purchased and renovated an old church.

It didn't take long for MCC to become a regular target of violence, picketing, and even arson. People were outraged at the idea of a gay church, so they tried to burn it down. Not only did the members rebuild the local MCC meeting place, but they began expanding into other cities and states as well.

In 1969, Perry became the first minister to apply for same-sex marriage licenses for members of his church and began performing same-sex unions. Even members of the gay community thought Rev. Perry was foolhardy and overly hopeful in his early pursuit of marriage equality. Perry also led the first Gay Pride Parade in Los Angeles in 1970, publicly opposed Anita Bryant and the Briggs Initiative seeking to ban gay and lesbian teachers in California, and helped organize the National March on Washington for Lesbian and Gay Rights in the late 1970s.

Perry and his partner, Philip De Blieck, have been together since 1985. They were legally married under Canadian law at the Metropolitan Community Church of Toronto in 2003. They went to Canada because marriage equality was not yet available anywhere in the United States. Upon their return home, they sued the State of California for recognition of their marriage and won. The State appealed, and the ruling was overturned. But after many twists along the way, marriage is now legal in California for LGBT citizens.

I met Rev. Perry in 2008 at the twentieth-anniversary conference of The Evangelical Network (TEN), a group of gay-affirming Pentecostal and evangelical churches and member ministries.[6] Several of the original members of the organization had returned for the milestone celebration. During one of the sessions, Rev. Perry spoke in his lovely, courteous Southern manner.

When lunchtime came, I went to his table and asked if I might speak with him. He pulled a chair out, invited me to sit, and turned to face

---

[6] The Evangelical Network, www.t-e-n.org.

me. Rev. Perry was fully attentive, but I couldn't speak. I started to cry. During my non-affirming years outside of the gay Christian movement, I'd heard of Rev. Perry and the MCC churches. I'd made ugly, disrespectful remarks and judgments about Perry and had spoken of MCCs as non-Jesus, non-Bible, "church lite" alternatives to "real" Christianity. After hearing Perry speak, I felt ashamed.

Rev. Perry, concerned about why I was consumed with emotion, tried to console me. I blubbered, "I am so sorry I judged you. Will you forgive me?" He gently held and patted my hands. "It's okay, darlin'. I forgive you." Rev. Perry, a man who has graciously faced protracted opposition, oppression, and injustice, then smiled and changed the mood. "Darlin', tell me about yourself and why you are here." We sat and chatted. A few years later, I ran into Rev. Perry and his husband during the parade lineup for San Francisco Pride. He called me over, and we chatted again.

God called and anointed a very good and courageous man to lead the gay Christian movement starting in 1968. Rev. Troy Perry has been a strong, passionate, and tenacious man of God and a pioneer for political and social justice for over forty-five years. His life is beautifully depicted in the documentary *Call Me Troy* (2007).

Lonnie Frisbee, hippie preacher and leader of the Jesus People Movement

The "Jesus Movement" began in California at the same time Rev. Perry was establishing the Metropolitan Community Church in Los Angeles. The late 1960s was a time of radical cultural change in the United States, with the onset of the feminist, anti-war, and hippie movements. Within the hippie counterculture, there was a Christian element dubbed early on "the Jesus Movement," and its members were known as "Jesus freaks" or "Jesus people."

Jesus freaks emerged with a countercultural eagerness to return to Bible basics—simple living, miracles, signs and wonders, healing, and prayer. Three major church movements—Calvary Chapel, the

Vineyard, and Harvest Christian Fellowship—were birthed as part of the Southern California Jesus Movement. The intersection, commonality, and key to the massive explosion of all three was one man: Lonnie Frisbee (1949–1993).

Frisbee, born in Costa Mesa, California, was awarded an art scholarship to the Academy of Art in San Francisco at the age of seventeen. He dropped out of high school and moved to that city, where he got caught up in the 1967 Summer of Love that hit the Haight-Ashbury neighborhood. Over 100,000 mostly young people converged on San Francisco. Hippies, anti-war activists, and feminists gathered in communal living, amid heightened sexual experimentation.

Frisbee, who had become a Christian at the age of eight,[7] now became a self-described "nudist, vegetarian hippie" and a regular drug user. He had been dabbling on the edges of Christianity in various forms of spiritualism. When Frisbee got high, his version of "turn on, tune in, drop out" was unlike that of some of his friends. Rather than engaging in mysticism and the occult, Frisbee read the New Testament. On one visit to his old hangout in the mountains near Palm Springs, he returned to one of his favorite spots up in the waterfalls. He stripped down, got in the water, and screamed up to heaven, "Jesus, if you are really real—reveal yourself to me!"[8] Frisbee said the atmosphere changed. "At 18 years old God was calling me to serve Him. It blew my mind—but I was definitely saying—'Yes, Lord.'"[9]

Frisbee was bewildered as to why people weren't living and believing the way the early Christians had, especially those in the Book of Acts. Why weren't people getting healed and seeing miracles? He took his passions to the beaches and started to preach.

Early hippie street missionaries from a Christian outreach called The Living Room, located in the Haight, helped Frisbee understand the Bible

---

[7] Lonnie Frisbee and Roger Sachs, *Not by Might nor by Power: The Jesus Revolution* (Santa Maria, California: Freedom Publications, 2012), 28.

[8] Ibid., 50.

[9] Ibid., 51.

better and asked him to join the group. Soon, he quit art school, abandoning his scholarship, and moved north of San Francisco to Novato, where he lived in a Christian commune called The House of Acts. From that base, Frisbee started taking month-long trips down to Southern California to preach on the beaches and by his old familiar hangouts, the waterfalls in the canyons.

One day he preached to a young runaway, Connie, and baptized her in a pool of water. She'd been a severely rejected child who thought she would never be loved,[10] so she appreciated Frisbee's growing attention. When he asked her to marry him, Connie initially rejected his proposal because she felt no romantic feelings for Frisbee and knew that he had homosexual attractions. Fuming with disappointment, he stayed away. Hating the feeling of Frisbee's rejection, and despite her misgivings, Connie gave in and married him in 1968.[11] They made Novato their home base.

Frisbee continued hitchhiking around California, telling people about Jesus. As he passed through Costa Mesa one time, he crossed paths with Pastor Chuck Smith Sr. Smith had been pastoring a small, formerly charismatic Foursquare Gospel church called Calvary Chapel, which had grown from twenty-five to eighty people in three years. He was in the process of building a small chapel on the property to accommodate the growth.

In passing, Smith had mentioned to his daughter that he wanted to meet a "real" hippie in person. His daughter's boyfriend had once given Frisbee a ride, knew where to find him, and brought him to Smith's home. Immediately impressed by Frisbee's faith and charisma, Smith invited him to come live in the chapel while it was still being built.

Within a week of moving into the chapel, Frisbee's beach preaching netted thirty-five new converts. Plans changed and the chapel was

---

[10] Matt Coker, "The First Jesus Freak," *OCWeekly*, March 3, 2005, http://www.ocweekly.com/20050303/features/thefirstjesusfreak/.

[11] Ibid.

transformed into House of Miracles, a live-in rehab center and ministry of Calvary Chapel. Frisbee also started leading Bible studies there.

Within a short time, several thousand people were attending Frisbee's weekly gatherings. They were being drawn off the beaches to join in worship and hear him speak. Pastor Smith began construction on a larger church, but in the meantime, services were held under a tent.

Undeniably, God was using Lonnie Frisbee in unique and magnificent ways to birth the Jesus Movement. Between 1968 and 1971, Frisbee brought several thousand new Christian converts to Calvary Chapel. Thousands of people began attending midweek services under a tent. Later, Frisbee said:

> I would share and preach, and maybe Marsha Carter would sing "Come to the Water." She wrote the lyrics in minutes one day. The Lord just downloaded it supernaturally. It became our signature song for revival. It became famous all over the world. It is the Jesus People tribute to our King. Marsha would sing like an angel.[12]

(We'll learn more about Marsha Carter shortly.)

Frisbee preached wherever he could; over five hundred people were being baptized each month. In some of his initial testimonies given at Calvary Chapel, Frisbee talked about his earlier days in the gay scene. By the age of fifteen, he had been hanging out in the Laguna Beach gay bars. Typical of the positive confession movement of the time, if a person denounced same-sex behavior, stopped participating in same-sex behavior, or verbally confessed change, they were considered "no longer homosexual." Once his "sin" was confessed and he publicly rejected "the homosexual lifestyle," Frisbee was told to never speak about it again in his testimonies.[13]

---

[12] *Not by Might*, 86.
[13] "An Exclusive Interview with David Di Sabatino, Director of *Frisbee: The Life and Death of a Hippie Preacher*," *Christian Nightmares*, 2013, http://christiannightmares.

Knowing that the Frisbees had a mixed-orientation marriage, we can understand the difficulties they faced in light of the previous chapter. Three years into the relationship, Connie told Pastor Smith that her marriage was in shambles. Even though Smith knew Frisbee had been/was gay, he responded by reminding her that it was the price she needed to pay for being married to a man so greatly used by God. Smith laid out the priorities Connie needed to abide by: God first, ministry second, and family third. He added that she would just have to stay married and deal with it.[14]

Still, God continued to use Frisbee to bring tens of thousands of young people into Calvary Chapel. Frisbee was always out preaching at the beaches, and he even went to local high schools at lunchtime to preach. During such a lunchtime preaching session at Newport Harbor High School in 1970, a student in at the back of the gathered group was heckling him. Frisbee recalled:

> Little railing accusations from a brat came flying at me. He said rude things and then began to mock openly. And the Lord said to me, "Stretch forth thy hand, and with the authority I've placed on your life—you bring him down."[15]

Frisbee called the young man to the center of a prayer circle, stretched out his hand, and the young man fell limp on the ground under the power of the Holy Spirit. That young man was 17-year-old Greg Laurie, future founder of the Harvest Christian Fellowship in Riverside, California, and Harvest Crusades. Laurie now pastors one of the largest churches in the United States, yet *never* speaks of Lonnie Frisbee in his conversion story.[16]

---

tumblr.com/post/64657227995/an-exclusive-interview-with-the-director-of.
[14] Ibid.
[15] *Not by Might*, 124.
[16] "The First Jesus Freak."

Frisbee became an enigma to those around him. He was said to party hard on Saturday nights, and to preach harder on Sunday. Despite his inconsistent behavior, hundreds of people would come forth in response to his call to conversion and baptism.

The Frisbees' marriage became more distant and strained. Frisbee looked for spiritual guidance and confided in Bob Mumford, leader of the fledgling Shepherding Movement. The Shepherding Movement of the early 1970s was a highly controversial charismatic movement where "sheep" fully submitted their lives to the "shepherd." Essentially, every decision was dictated by one's spiritual leader. Mumford, one of the original founders of the movement, invited the Frisbees to Florida to help them get their marriage in order.

Mumford told Frisbee it was time to leave the ministry, get a regular job, settle down, and have kids. Frisbee complied. He got a haircut, put on suits, and got a job, submitting to yet another leader who didn't acknowledge that he was gay. Frisbee continued to try to hide and deny his homosexuality, but when he was caught in an affair with a man, he was out once again.

The information of Frisbee's continued gay relationships didn't reach Pastor Smith, who invited the Frisbees to come back to Calvary Chapel, where he walked in with his haircut and his three-piece suit and was asked to run the tape ministry. The renewed working relationship didn't go well with Pastor Smith, however. When Smith realized that Frisbee's homosexuality had not "gone away," as he had once thought, their friendship ruptured.[17]

Things also didn't go well with Connie, who had an affair with another pastor. The Frisbees got divorced, and they both left Calvary Chapel.

By 1977, John Wimber, another Calvary Chapel pastor, had also parted ways with Pastor Smith and had helped a man named Kenn

---

[17] John G. Turner, "They Got High on Jesus Instead." *Christianity Today*, July 11, 2013, http://www.christianitytoday.com/ct/2013/july-web-only/gods-forever-family-they-got-high-on-jesus-instead.html.

Gulliksen establish Vineyard Christian Fellowship. Wimber wanted to focus more on healings and the supernatural manifestations of the Spirit than did Smith. After Frisbee's expulsion from Calvary, he also wanted to focus on spiritual and demonstrative manifestations, along with evangelism. In 1980, Wimber invited Frisbee to preach at his church.

During his first night preaching, Frisbee invited everyone under twenty-one years old to come forward to the altar. Witnesses claim that as soon as the kids got next to Frisbee, they fell to the floor. Some of the older churchgoers walked out of the sanctuary in disgust. But Wimber was excited; he had been praying to see the presence of God.[18]

The next day, Wimber was called before the church elders to explain what had happened. Before he could finish telling the story, Frisbee burst into the meeting, walked directly to the most critical of the elders, and yelled, "You need to have the experience of God!" The elder shook uncontrollably and fell to the floor under the power of the Holy Spirit.[19]

The converted Vineyard youth created another ripple of Jesus freaks in Southern California. Kids in junior high and high school were witnessing to their friends and baptizing them in pools and hot tubs. Within six months, Wimber's Vineyard church, with the help of Frisbee's preaching, teaching, and praying, exploded from 500 to 2,500 in attendance. Thus began the Vineyard Church movement.

While having lunch with Wimber one day, Pastor Smith's son, Chuck Smith Jr., asked Wimber how he had been able to reconcile working with a homosexual—meaning Frisbee. Wimber had not known that Frisbee was gay. Smith Jr., who had received a phone call from the pastor of a man who had confessed to a six-month affair with Frisbee, filled him in. The next day, Wimber asked Frisbee to leave the Vineyard Church.

In his later years, speaking about his life, Frisbee admitted to his "sin of homosexuality,"[20] though he never considered one sin greater than

---

[18] "The First Jesus Freak."
[19] Ibid.
[20] Ibid.

any other. His sexuality had largely been an open secret, overlooked or conveniently ignored by leadership in the early years of his ministry. He said, "My critics will jump on [the] confession of faith that I made at twenty-two years of age because of my future failures, but I want to mention that it is a lifelong process that we go through."[21]

Frisbee was trying to figure out his sexual orientation in the early 1980s in a Christian environment. As we've seen in the stories in the past two chapters, even gay people themselves often didn't realize they were gay or what that meant. After being pushed out of the church, Lonnie Frisbee, one of the finest and most gifted evangelists of a generation, moved back to Florida. When he was invited some years later to preach and teach in Sweden, Denmark, and South Africa, revival followed him wherever he went.[22]

When asked in 1992 why he thought God had used him in such powerful ways, Frisbee said:

> I stand in total awe every time the Lord touches our lives, every time He reveals His loving kindness toward us. Every time He uses me. Believe me, I am the least likely candidate for what the Lord has done with me. I look back and the only explanation I can offer is that since I was a little child, I have desperately needed God. I had nothing or no one to turn to except God. He responded to my cries with a plan and a divine purpose for my life.[23]

The Jesus Movement lasted about a decade and assimilated young evangelicals nationwide into the revival. Thousands of these converts are pastors and leaders of parachurch organizations today.[24] The revival began with the most unlikely of people—a gay hippie who many said

---

[21] *Not By Might*, 104.
[22] "Interview with David Di Sabatino."
[23] Ibid., 14.
[24] "They Got High."

looked like Jesus Himself. God anointed and called Lonnie Frisbee to birth a Holy Spirit movement within the hippie counterculture.

The leaders of the Calvary Church and the Vineyard Church movements wrote Frisbee out of their official histories in the very early years. As for Harvest Christian Fellowship, even raising the name of Lonnie Frisbee to Greg Laurie is said to be strictly *verboten*.[25] Harvest Christian Fellowship currently offers a reparative therapy ministry called New Creation[26] on their campus, using 1 Corinthians 6:9-10—and verse 11: "and such were some of you"—as the scriptural basis "to reach out to those in the homosexual lifestyle or those who struggle with same-sex attraction." Frisbee was said to have been hurt by those who turned their backs on him, but he did forgive them.

Lonnie Frisbee died of AIDS in Florida in 1993, at the age of forty-three. His life story is told in the documentary *Frisbee: The Life and Death of a Hippie Preacher*.[27]

Marsha Stevens-Pino, the "Mother of Modern Christian Music"

Marsha Stevens-Pino's, née Carter (1952–), father had been a pastor before she was born. By the time she was an adolescent, both of her parents, "though upstanding citizens and recognized in the community for service,"[28] were emotionally absent alcoholics often leaving Marsha to care for her younger sister, Wendy.[29] As a young teenager, Marsha realized she was having different feelings about boys than other girls did.

> I went to the school library first, and then to the public library, trying to figure out if I had that "disease." One book

[25] "The First Jesus Freak."
[26] New Creation, http://www.harvest.org/church/ministries/newcreation.html.
[27] David Di Sabatino, dir., *Lonnie Frisbee: The Life and Death of a Hippie Preacher* (Passion River, 2008).
[28] Rev. Sylvia Pennington, *Ex-Gays? There Are None* (Hawthorne, CA: Lambda Christian Fellowship, 1989), 365.
[29] *Ex-Gays?*, 365.

which I found said to talk to your pastor or school nurse if you thought you had it. I wasn't going to speak to the pastor who would, in turn, tell my parents, so I went into the school nurse's office three times but couldn't bring myself to talk to her. I was upset and wrote a whole bunch of suicide notes, got my father's gun, took it to school, and told everybody it wasn't their fault.[30]

Everyone around Marsha thought her "big secret" was that she was pregnant; confused herself, she refused to tell anyone the truth. She was sent to the school psychologist, who wrote her parents "a really cold, brutal letter"[31] telling them what had happened: "Just to inform you that on May 14 your daughter tried to kill herself at school."

In order to drown her homosexual feelings over the next three years, Marsha got into drugs. When she was sixteen and in her junior year of high school, her brother, newly converted to Christianity, came home from college and invited her to an event at the beach. Thinking it was a party, Marsha joined him, only to be disappointed to discover that it was a Calvary Chapel service. The gathering was a new experience for her; she had never heard anyone talk about Jesus as if He were alive. Not long after, in June of 1969, Marsha attended an evangelistic outreach on the beach. Pastors Smith and Frisbee were speaking at a restaurant, along with Pat Boone. Boone was showing a video interview that kept cutting back and forth between him talking to college kids about Jesus and girls in white go-go boots singing "Who's trippin' down the streets of the city . . . ?" Marsha said of the meeting:

I thought it was very silly and dismissed it. If Jesus was that cool, why did He need girls in go-go boots singing pop songs to make him palatable? Frisbee was the one who stood up

---

[30] Ibid., 366
[31] Ibid., 366.

and said almost exactly that. "Well," he said, "I understand you are trying to reach young people, but I think what young people want is just the truth. And I think if we told the truth about Jesus and who He is, we wouldn't need any dancing girls to keep us kids tuned in." I loved him! The next week, we met near the beach on the cement-poured basement of what would become Calvary Chapel—no walls or roof.

I even helpfully brought in the ashtray from my car so we could smoke and not mess the place up. No one yelled at me. Someone just said, "I think it would be really cool if we could keep this space really respectful. I'm not going to smoke in here." We all want to be cool, heaven knows, so no one smoked.

That week, Chuck talked to us about choices and at the end we all prayed. By that I mean that everyone went around the room and each person pitched in a sentence or two to God. They were very conversational. It got to me, and I froze before I blurted, "Dear God, please accept me into Thy fold!" Mercifully, no one laughed, and even God got the idea.

Marsha accepted Jesus and "prayed for the Holy Spirit to give [her] the power to be a witness for Jesus." During the prayer, Marsha "felt like a little kid sitting in Jesus' lap." In the experience, Jesus then took her "by this river of water" and told her that every night, as she buried her head under her covers in a home with alcoholic parents, He had been there. Marsha felt that Jesus said to her, "I was there every night, I felt every teardrop, that's why I died."[32]

When Marsha tried to communicate the spiritual encounter to other people at church, she found that the best way to do it was in a song.

---

[32] Ibid., 368.

She used the only four chords she knew on her guitar in a song that she wrote in minutes. Marsha shared the song with Wendy, then dragged her little sister along to church the next week to help her sing it; 14-year-old Wendy got saved too.

Marsha started a group called Children of the Day with Wendy and two friends, Peter Jacobs, a loner who had been kicked out of his home and lived in a shack down the street from the Carters, and Russ Stevens, who played bass in a band and sang tenor. They were just four teenagers who became Christians and wanted to sing about their love of Jesus and the new life they had.

When she was only sixteen, Marsha wrote the well-known, beautiful worship song "For Those Tears I Died," also known as "Come to the Waters":[33]

> Jesus said, "Come to the water, stand by My side
> I know you are thirsty, you won't be denied;
> I felt every teardrop when in darkness you cried
> And I strove to remind you that for those tears I died."

The Encyclopedia of Contemporary Christian Music says of this song: "It is an absolute masterpiece that expresses adolescent piety better than any other Christian song ever written—and yet it evokes imagery of baptism and liberation that even technologically mature adults appreciate."[34]

With a tone much like that of the group Peter, Paul & Mary, Children of the Day established another point of connection for youth in the Jesus People movement. Creating a new form of Christian music mirroring the popular music of the day was a revolutionary concept. Inaugurated at Calvary Chapel, Children of the Day became the first musical group in the contemporary Christian music movement. Their initial album,

---

[33] Marsha Stevens, "For Those Tears I Died," EMI Christian Music Group, 1969.

[34] "Children of the Day," Mark Allan Powell. *The Encyclopedia of Contemporary Christian Music* (Peabody, MA: Hendrickson Publishers, 2002), 165.

released in 1971 on the first Christian rock and folk label, Maranatha! Music, was financed by a $900 loan from Pastor Smith.

Maranatha! Music was started as a nonprofit music outreach from Smith's Calvary Chapel. Because of Marsha's contribution to the major shift in Christian worship music, she is widely known as "the mother of contemporary Christian music."

Believing that when she "became a Christian, [she] became a different person [who] no longer thought about homosexuality," at the age of nineteen ,[35] Marsha married band member Russ Stevens. While Children of the Day travelled the world leading worship until 1979, the Stevens' marriage evolved into a platonic relationship. The couple did have two children together, but after two years of counseling, they decided they were better friends than spouses and got a divorce.[36] In her late twenties, drug-free, and becoming more honest about her feelings, within a year of the divorce, Marsha came out as a lesbian. She stated later, "The feelings that I had when I was fourteen were suddenly on the surface."[37] Immediately, Marsha was shunned by Calvary Chapel, and by the administration and parents of the Christian school her children attended.

Once it became known to the greater Christian community that Marsha was a lesbian, worship leaders in churches across the country started tearing copies of "Come to the Water" out of their church hymnals. When Marsha's partner Winky's daughter died of congenital heart disease, Marsha's former fans and supporters told her it was God's vengeance on her "lifestyle" and that her children would be next to die.[38] Maranatha! Music even stopped paying her royalties, justifying the action by saying she had broken a contractual clause. As they saw it, coming out as a lesbian was tantamount to publicly renouncing her faith. It's difficult to find third-party accounts in the annals of contemporary

---

[35] Ibid., 371.
[36] Ibid., 373.
[37] Ibid., 373.
[38] "Marsha Stevens," *Encyclopedia of Contemporary Christian Music*, 871.

Christian music that include interviews, music reviews, or even references to Stevens-Pino's contributions. For being a lesbian, she has been all but written out of contemporary Christian music history.

Typical of LGBT Christians in the late 1970s, Marsha did not know any other lesbian Christians. She had heard of, but avoided, the Metropolitan Community Church, believing "it was probably a quasi-religious group that did a lot of social work" and not "real Christians."[39] But then Marsha and Winky found an MCC congregation near them and began participating in it during their early years together. Today, Marsha is an ordained lay evangelist with MCC.

In 1987, Marsha founded a music ministry she named Born Again Lesbian Music (BALM), which she and her wife, Cindy, now run together.[40] Although her audience is limited to those in affirming churches, Marsha Stevens-Pino continues to use her gifts of writing, singing, and playing Christian music. Stevens-Pino is still widely dismissed by conservative Christians, often accused of no longer being a Christian and of turning her back on Jesus. But her Christian witness testifies otherwise. I met Marsha in 2008. Grace and the fruits of the Holy Spirit *ooze* out of her, and her music continues to witness to a close personal relationship with Jesus Christ.

God had not left His gay children

God called Troy Perry to preach at the age of fifteen. He called Lonnie Frisbee to begin the explosion of the Jesus People movement, including the Calvary Chapel, Vineyard, and Harvest Christian Fellowship movements, at the age of nineteen. And God called 16-year-old Marsha Stevens-Pino to usher in contemporary Christian music.

Did God know they were gay? Of course He did.

God entrusted and anointed these three, and countless other gay Christians, at a pivotal time that included both the Jesus Movement and

---

[39] *Ex-Gays?*, 381.
[40] BALM Ministries, http://balmministries.net.

the gay liberation movement. But, discarded by traditional churches and hippie Christian movements alike once they came out as gay, some entered reparative therapy, many were joined in mixed-orientation marriages, and all had to find their faith-footing again.

God looks to the margins to use the foolish and unlikely to confound those who think they know what God says, wants, and does. God chooses the lowly, the despised, and the discarded to bring about His will.[41] By discarding so many LGBT men and women of God, the Christian church has lost out on the full, rich diversity and spiritual gifts of countless Christians over the past forty-five years or more.

Their love of God overcomes the rejection of the church

Many gay pastors, ministry leaders, and church members did not survive the rejection and excommunication prevalent in conservative American churches: instead, they left the faith altogether. Let me introduce you to a few pastors and ministry leader-friends who persevered and who are doing great work in the gay and transgender Christian community.

Pastor Dan Burchett, 61, was raised in the Assemblies of God church. He knew at puberty that he was attracted to boys and not girls. He likens the realization of his sexual orientation to clinging to the edge of a cliff in sheer dread. If he let go, he would lose everything; yet, holding on in silence was terrifying.

The son of a pastor, Dan didn't speak to *anyone* about his attractions—except to God. He was gripped by dread, fearing someone might find out. As a young man, he hoped he could manage his attractions and ignore his sexuality by marrying a woman who loved God the way he did. Against all rational thought, he did just that. He couldn't even be honest with himself, much less muster the strength to tell his wife about his attractions.

---

[41] 1 Corinthians 1:26-29.

The extreme isolation that pushed him into marriage didn't go away. Finally, he couldn't endure the deception any longer. Pastor Dan says:

> I believed I was risking everything I valued in speaking of my sexual orientation openly to my wife, my family, and people in ministry. I had accepted that I was going to lose everything I valued: my marriage, my ministry, and my reputation. I was in so much pain I simply could no longer pretend any of it mattered. The emotional cost was bankrupting me.

Pastor Dan eventually told his wife. Even today, when he talks about it, his regret for the anguish he put her through is visible on his face. Because of his honesty, he did lose everything—his marriage, his ordination, his reputation, his friends, and his ministry.

After several years of emotional and professional turmoil, Pastor Dan was hired as the head pastor of Open Door Ministries in Long Beach, California.[42] He now leads a congregation of gay and transgender Christians, as well as a growing number of straight allies and parents of gay children. Many of Open Door's members are refugees from reparative therapy programs and larger churches and ministries where they maintained a "straight appearance" as they served.

Pastor Maria Caruana, 56, leads Freedom in Christ (FIC) Evangelical Church[43] in San Francisco. The members of FIC have been an important part of my personal journey as an advocate for the gay and transgender Christian community. After my first Gay Christian Network conference in 2007, longtime FIC member Ed Ness glued himself to me and answered my numerous theological questions—even some downright dumb ones! Ed invited me to events, gatherings, and special services

---

[42] Open Door Ministries, http://www.greateropendoor.org.
[43] Freedom in Christ Evangelical Church, http://www.ficcsf.com.

at FIC, where I met Pastor Maria. They came to be like family to me, loving and including me as family does.

For sixteen years, Pastor Maria has led the gay and transgender Christians of FIC. She was raised as a Catholic, but did not participate in the Catholic Church. Not seeing peace or godly love in her family, she felt abandoned by God. Through friendship with a lesbian Christian, Maria became a believer. She says:

> When I realized that God did exist and loved me enough to die for my sins, it didn't matter that I was a lesbian. All that mattered was that God was real and He loved me enough to die for me.

> It is sad that church doesn't share the gospel anymore. They don't share the good news; they share bad news: shame, guilt, and humiliation. The church needs to get back to the gospel. I'm blessed to be the pastor of a Bible-based church in the "gayest" city in America. I've met so many LGBT people who want to and do have a relationship with God, but our services aren't packed.

> We're challenged because so many gay and transgender people believe they can't have a relationship with God. The community has been told that God hates them, wants nothing to do with them, that they're an abomination and going to hell. They're afraid of being hurt further. They don't have any use for a God who has no use for them. My biggest challenge is righting the wrongs done by the Christian Church.

> I consider myself a fundamentalist Christian. I believe in the fundamentals of the faith, yet that's a dirty word for

the LGBT community. It's a constant challenge to gain the right to be heard by the community once they know you're a Christian.

For over twenty years, the members of Freedom in Christ Evangelical Church have been a constant witness to the gay and transgender communities in San Francisco. I've worked with them at street festivals and places traditional churches rarely would venture. As Pastor Maria says, with her thick Brooklyn accent, "We go where Jesus would go. These people need Jesus, too."

At FIC, transgender Christians of color, gay men, lesbians, and drag queens worship God alongside one another. Pastor Maria is a strong and godly leader and has been with her wife, Terrie, a pastor at City of Refuge in Oakland, for over twenty-three years.

Pastors Randy Morgan, 42, and Johnny Layton, 41, lead New Covenant Christian Church,[44] a vibrant Pentecostal LGBT community in Atlanta. Pastor Randy knew at the age of ten that he was called into Christian ministry. He recalls having a "very distinct, supernatural encounter with Jesus Himself." By the age of thirteen and at the height of anti-gay preaching during the AIDS crisis (mid-1980s), he knew he was "gay—real gay."

Even though Pastor Randy was attracted to guys, he didn't understand his attractions, nor could he label his feelings as "homosexuality." Rather, he tried to ignore them and deny that he was gay. When the attractions kept getting stronger, he was sure he was being demonically oppressed. He sought out the help of older ministers to lay hands on him and cast the demons out. The more he tried to escape his attractions, the more God said to him, "Son, you are fearfully and wonderfully made."

I first heard that when I was about sixteen, and I knew it was undeniably God. However, I kept telling Him, "God, Your theology is wrong. God, I am horribly and terribly

---

[44] New Covenant Christian Church, Atlanta, Georgia, http://www.newcovenantatlanta.com.

made." My wrestling ended much the same way Jacob's did in Genesis. I would never walk the same after I finally gave in to Him. It was years later before I could be honest. Even though I had never even acted on those feelings, I felt incredible shame and guilt because I believed I had done something to rebel against God.

Young, gay, and called by God . . . I didn't know anyone who could mentor me to make sure that all aspects of my life would be balanced. I felt like I had to choose between God and my sexual orientation. I chose the thing that mattered—God. Then all of the suppression rose to the surface, and I finally came out. It was excruciating at first. I had to leave my spiritual household of faith. It was an entirely painful event at the age of twenty-one. It was 1994.

Soon after I came out, I met Johnny Layton. We are celebrating twenty-one years together. Johnny's faith helped me heal from the wounds of rejection. Together we started New Covenant Church in 2000. Because of the complementary nature of our life together and our anointing, God has done amazing things in our lives. Johnny and I are both in full-time ministry together, overseeing the New Covenant Church of Atlanta and the Covenant Network. The Covenant Network[45] is a growing, thriving, Spirit-filled ministry that works with hundreds of people globally to establish churches and ministries that are Spirit-filled, Word-based, and affirming toward all people.

For those of us who are called by God and gay, the mainstream church is missing out on a tapestry of gifts and

---

[45] New Covenant Network, http://thecovenantnetwork.com.

callings. So many of our women and men have gifts that God has placed in them, but the church is afraid of what they don't understand. I'm so thankful that God created me gay. He has shown that the Word of God can be transmitted through a gay man! God uses earthly vessels to get His message of love and power into the earth. He uses unique vessels. The LGBT community is a unique vessel.

Pastors Randy and Johnny host a large conference each summer for over three hundred lesbian, gay, bisexual, and transgender Christians and allies who worship in the charismatic/Pentecostal style.

Kevin Diaz, 50, of Lafayette, Colorado, rose to prominence in the parachurch and megachurch worlds. During his work with the Continental Singers (1987–1994), Kevin became the National Talent Director, overseeing the annual recruitment of twenty-three touring music teams. Additionally, he travelled on eight tours through all fifty states and thirteen countries. Kevin continued his ministry work with Promise Keepers (1994–1999), where he was instrumental in executing the live programming for over fifty stadium and arena events. He served as the Event Program Director and, eventually, the Director of Program Services, all while living as a closeted gay man.

As a child in his native Arizona, Kevin behaved like the other boys— roughhousing, getting dirty, building things, and exploring—yet he knew he was "different." Typical of young gay boys in the 1970s, he had no language or role models to help him sort out the internal differences. As he came into puberty, Kevin was confused by the fascination his friends had with girls. Because he noticed that boys who were suspected of being attracted to boys were the targets of ridicule, he kept the confusion to himself.

Throughout his teen years, Kevin awaited the "magical moment" when his attractions would "naturally" turn to girls. For years, he had been praying and believing God would do this for him.

I had such great hope in the months leading up to my birthdays. I fantasized about how it would feel to be attracted to the opposite sex and imagined the great relief it would bring, knowing I was finally "normal." My prayers intensified during the months before each birthday. The hope of God giving me the gift of "normalcy" was exciting and exhilarating. It was just like waiting for Christmas morning or finally being able to start our trip from Phoenix to Anaheim for our summer Disneyland trips! I expected to wake up the morning of my birthday, or shortly thereabouts, and feel more male and attracted to women.

Kevin waited on his sixteenth birthday, then on his eighteenth. Every year near his birthday, he repeated the hope-filled ritual. His twentieth, twenty-first, twenty-fifth, and thirtieth birthdays passed. There was no change. His prayers of anticipation turned to resignation; he was "broken" and "defective." He needed to figure out how he had come to be homosexual, so he went through the typical Christian checklist. Could he blame his attraction to men on parenting? No, he had wonderful and involved parents. Had he ever been sexually abused or "recruited"? Again, no.

Kevin learned to shut his brain off when he felt attracted to males. Though suffering profound isolation, he never attempted to fill the emptiness by dating women. I asked Kevin how he managed to pull *that* one off. He is a nice-looking, well-mannered, talented, and polite Christian man. Surely he attracted the attention of plenty of women. His response is one I've often heard. He told the people around him that he had chosen to do one thing well, and his focus was on serving God. Although he had excellent friendships with women, he did not want to become involved in an empty and dishonest courtship.

Of his work with Promise Keepers and experiences that followed, Kevin shares:

As I worked directly with the stadium platform speakers within the Promise Keepers organization, I found myself terrified to work alongside these men of God. I believed that at any moment, with 50,000–60,000 men looking on, I might be exposed by a word the Lord could give them in the middle of the conference. Back in my hotel room, I was on my knees pleading and begging the Lord to change me and protect my secret. I didn't want my same-sex attractions exposed because it would bring shame on God's ministry.

Proverbs 13:12 speaks of deferred hope making the heart sick. I lived this, intimately and daily. I wrestled with the meaning of Matthew 7:9-11 because it seemed as if God was not giving me good things. I asked and begged to be given bread—correction and healing from my same-sex attractions. I saw the Lord's answer as a stone, a snake—no change, and the undeniable feelings of attraction to men. Now I know that God wasn't answering my prayers with snakes and stones. He had already answered my prayers with goodness; it was there all along. I just could not see it.

Isolation and loneliness became my way of living. I maintained celibacy but not because of a gifting of celibacy. I never spoke of my attractions—never. Not to anyone, ever. Survival demanded secrecy that I was attracted to men. I never took the risk of coming out.

I intentionally removed myself from ministry as a way of transitioning into a life where I could live honestly and sincerely. In late 2006, I was drawn back to asking God for help with my attractions. For the first time, my prayers took a dramatic shift. Out of sheer desperation, I finally asked God the only question that I hadn't explored. I asked, "Father, since You won't heal me or change me, show me why You haven't healed or changed me." It had never dawned on me to ask this question. The process of accepting my same-sex attraction as being natural or given began during that period. I did internet searches and I mustered the courage to purchase *Stranger at the Gate: To Be Gay and Christian in America,* by Mel White.[46] White was a ghostwriter for Billy Graham, Jerry Falwell, and Pat Robertson, and a filmmaker, producer, and director of fifty-three Christian documentaries.

What caught my attention about the book was the author—a Christian man very similar to me. He was involved in ministry throughout his life. I couldn't believe what was written in a book review. It said that White was a man with same-sex attractions and a Christian. Impossible! It was like trying to visualize a square circle. I didn't believe that being a Christian and having same-sex attractions could be congruent. When the book arrived, I completely devoured it. White's words and his life journey cracked open the door of hope for me. I was astounded that someone else in ministry had gone through what I was trying to fight in solitude. I wasn't alone! For the first time I wasn't alone!

At the age of forty-two, Kevin started the difficult process of reconciling his sexuality and his faith. He started on a year-and-a-half-long "firestorm of research and study." One evening, after reading, he screamed, "Is it possible, Lord? It just might be possible. I think it's possible to be gay and Christian!"

---

[46] Mel White, *Stranger at the Gate: To Be Gay and Christian in America* (New York: Plume, 1994).

Kevin and I talked long into a July night when I visited him. We chatted until almost 4 a.m. He is a supremely gifted man.

What I have come to know, without doubt, is that the LGBT Christian community has been endowed with a unique richness from God. The abundance of musical and creative talent in the gay community is well known. There is also a bounty of empathetic, gracious, and merciful people among them.

Many fail to recognize the loss to conservative churches of almost two generations of excellent pastors, leaders, and servants. We have a generation of young gay, lesbian, bisexual, and transgender Christians growing up in our churches now. How shall we treat them?

Chapter 14

The Next Generation of Gay and Trans* Christians

Nurturing Their Christian Growth

Flawed theories applied to gay adolescents in the 1970s and 1980s

The history of medical and mental health research concerning gay youth is a very short one, dating back just over forty years. In 1952, Evelyn Hooker had challenged the methods of her peers in the American Psychological Association (APA) who had believed that homosexuality was a mental illness. Yet, twenty years later it was still classified as pathological in the *Diagnostic and Statistical Manual* (DSM-5), the "bible" for the practice of psychiatry in the United States.

Not until February 1972 was an empirical study involving gay adolescents published in a medical journal.[1] The research focused on sixty

---

[1] Thomas Roestler and Robert W. Deisher, "Youthful Male Homosexuality: Homosexual Experience and the Process of Developing Homosexual Identity in Males Aged 16 to 22 Years," *Journal of the American Medical Association*, 1972, http://jama.jamanetwork.com/article.aspx?articleid=340984.

young gay men, ages 16 to 22, from the street-hustler community in Seattle. All of the participants lived in crisis situations. Not only had they had many more sexual encounters than average, but they suffered a range of behaviors atypical of the general teenage population, including high truancy rates, poor academic records, high levels of substance abuse, elevated numbers of suicide attempts, and a wide range of emotional problems.[2] The findings of this single study, conducted on runaways, prostitutes, and juvenile delinquents, stood for the next fifteen years as the sole research effort concerning the mental health of gay male adolescents. Being young and gay became intrinsically linked with being "troubled."[3]

For the average gay teen questioning his or her sexual attractions and feelings, there was no information to help sort out the confusion. The few gay or transgender characters depicted on television or in the movies were shown in a negative light, amid shame and secrecy, or as the object of ridicule. (Such would be the case until the late 1990s.) Often, the young LGBT person's only available information was in the books hidden beneath the mattress in his or her parents' bedroom.

As we noted earlier, *Everything You Always Wanted to Know about Sex but Were Afraid to Ask* was a top-selling book during the sexual revolution of the late 1960s and 1970s. The chapter on male homosexuals is absurd by our standards,[4] yet it was read by over 150 million people and widely respected as the truth. After reading a few paragraphs, when gay youth couldn't identify with the image portrayed, in utter horror they'd say, "That is *not* me; I don't want to be anything like that!" or "I must not be gay."

When the gay liberation movement began in the late 1960s, gay adolescents likely heard their parents speaking in disgust about "those people." The fear of being "like that" or like "those people" shamed gay

---

[2] Ritch Savin-Williams, *The New Gay Teenager* (Cambridge, MA: Harvard University Press, 2005), 56.

[3] Ibid., 55.

[4] Refer to quotes in Chapter 4.

adolescents into silence and, frequently, extreme internal isolation. There was just *no* information available for them, or about them.

In the late 1970s, when the Religious Right merged with the New Right, the verbal and political attacks on the gay community became more pronounced, especially within conservative Christian homes. *The Gay Invasion,*[5] by William D. Rodgers (1977); *The Unhappy Gays,*[6] by Tim LaHaye (1978); and *Listen, America!,*[7] by Jerry Falwell (1981) were all popular titles consumed by the Christian market. The severity of the contemptuous attitudes in these books and others from the period cannot be overemphasized. In many Christian circles, especially during the height of the AIDS crisis (1981–1995), regular tirades from televangelists added to the vilification of the gay community. It was a devastating time to be young, gay, and Christian.

It is inconceivable to imagine that for almost fifteen years, the 1972 study of runaways, prostitutes, and juvenile delinquents stood as the benchmark regarding the lives of gay youth.[8] The first national symposium addressing the medical, psychological, and social needs of gay youth was held in Minneapolis in 1986. However, the discussions remained focused on at-risk gay youth and issues affecting them: homelessness, prostitution, substance abuse, mental health issues, and sexually transmitted diseases. There were no experts on adolescent development or psychology in attendance at the conference.

The following year, Dr. Gary Remafedi, a pediatrician, conducted a study involving just twenty-nine gay adolescents.[9] Again, almost the entire sample group suffered homelessness, prostitution, substance abuse, mental health issues, sexually transmitted diseases, and/or HIV/AIDS. Not surprisingly, Remafedi concluded that "the very experience of acquiring a homosexual or bisexual identity at an early age placed the

---

[5] William D. Rodgers, *The Gay Invasion* (Denver, CO: Accent Books, 1977).
[6] Tim LaHaye, *The Unhappy Gays* (Wheaton, IL: Tyndale House, 1978).
[7] Jerry Falwell, *Listen, America!* (New York: Bantam Books, 1981).
[8] *New Gay Teenager,* 56.
[9] Ibid., 54.

individual at risk for dysfunction."[10] Like Bieber, Bergler, and Socarides[11] before him, Remafedi formed theories about the entire gay adolescent population based on his observations of a very limited number of study participants in crisis situations. The flawed paradigm—that gay youth were "troubled" youth—remained intact through the 1980s.

During the entire decade of the 1980s, a total of only forty articles[12] and studies dealing with gay adolescents appeared in medical and mental health publications; the focus was always on at-risk youth. Suicide among their ranks was particularly highlighted in the bulk of the articles. The first adolescent-focused publication that dedicated an entire issue to the topic of adolescent gays and lesbians was *High School Journal* 1993.[13] Four years later, an article about gay youth finally appeared in the *Journal of Research on Adolescence*, the flagship publication of adolescent research.[14]

We need to be mindful of the fact that, until the 1990s, not even the *experts* realized there were normal kids, doing normal kid things, growing up in good homes, who just happened to be gay. It's easier, then, to understand how the many gay people whose stories we've heard could have been aware they were "different" without knowing exactly what that meant in terms of their sexual orientation. Accurate information about and for gay adolescents was sorely missing. Anti-gay books portrayed extreme characterizations that didn't resonate with young gay people. And there was a distinct lack of visible positive gay role models in the culture, and certainly within the Christian church.

---

[10] Ibid., 54.
[11] See Chapter 2.
[12] *New Gay Teenager*, 58.
[13] J.P. Elia, "Homophobia in the High School: A Problem in Need of a Resolution," *High School Journal*, no. 77 (1993): 177-185. The *High School Journal* publishes research, scholarship, and reviews critical to the field of secondary education. Founded in 1918, it is the oldest peer-reviewed academic journal in education.
[14] The article, written by Ritch Savin-Williams, was entitled "The Disclosure to Families of Same-Sex Attraction by Lesbian, Gay, and Bisexual Youths." Society for Research on Adolescence publishes the *Journal of Research on Adolescence* and focuses on policy research issues; it was founded in 1984. http://www.sra.org/.

Today, as they reflect upon their past, almost three-quarters of gay men and two-thirds of lesbians say they knew they were "different" as children.[15] Many were made to feel ashamed in a culture heavily biased toward heterosexuality. Even as children, gay youth recognized that gay people in general were the target of mocking and name-calling. They feared being hurt or bullied, and they didn't want to bring shame on their families, so they kept their differentness a secret. In each personal story we've seen so far, once teens figured out they were different, they remained silent initially. Sometimes they kept the secret till their late teens. Sometimes they kept it for decades. Sometimes they kept it through a heterosexual marriage.

I've frequently heard comments like "There were no homosexuals when I went to school. This coming-out as a teenager is all a *new* thing." And that may well appear to be true. I asked my mother if she knew of any gays in the 1940s, when she was a young woman growing up in New York City. She had to think about it for a while. She does not recall anyone using the word "homosexual" about themselves or other people. She does recall one particularly gentle teenager named Billy. With the understanding and awareness my mother has gained over the past few years, she believes that Billy was gay. He never dated, yet always got along well with the young women. Mom remembers him as unusually kind. When her family didn't have the money to buy her a cheerleading sweater, Billy lent her his yellow sweater for the year so she could be a cheerleader. She remembers him teasing her about making sure not to leave permanent "bumps" in his sweater (from her breasts)! Billy was a bit of a loner who never fit in. He tried to enter the priesthood after high school, but was rejected by several orders of priests. Billy committed suicide before he was twenty years old.

When I graduated from high school in the New York Metropolitan Area in 1974, none of my fellow students were out of the closet as LGBT.

---

[15] WhomYouLove2012, "Born This Way: Biological Tales of Sexual Orientation" (video), Eric Vilain, October 9, 2013, https://www.youtube.com/watch?v=9MhzXaYOBDk.

Of course, I now know of several of my former classmates who are gay or lesbian, and one who is a transwoman. When my youngest child attended a large high school and graduated in 2005, no student came out during those four years. Recently, I spoke at a Gay-Straight Alliance (GSA) meeting at the high school my children attended. The room was packed with about forty students, mostly LGBT. The president of the GSA was a nerdy and delightful young lesbian who aspires to be a geneticist. She was also the school valedictorian. Yes, the times *have* changed, and the secrecy and shame that have plagued gay youth for generations are lifting.

Finally, research involving typical LGBT youth

Research on healthy gay and transgender youth has been going on for less than three decades. While the internet allows gay and transgender youth to search out reliable information on their own, now nationwide programs and organizations are available to support the coming-out process: The Trevor Project; the Gay, Lesbian & Straight Education Network (GLSEN); PFLAG National[16] (Parents, Families and Friends of Lesbians and Gays); and the Gay Christian Network (GCN). Positive gay and transgender role models on television; in movies, music, sports, politics, leadership, and the arts; and, yes, in faith communities have become more vocal and visible. Unlike their predecessors, gay youth today are better able at an earlier age to understand their feelings and attractions.

For the most part, boys figure out they are gay earlier than do girls. This happens at about age ten for boys and twelve for girls. The average age at which youth label themselves as gay is fourteen. Typically, they come out to someone by age seventeen. The first person they share their secret with is usually a close friend with whom they feel safe—not

---

[16] Formerly known as Parents and Friends of Lesbians and Gays. PFLAG is now Parents, Families, and Friends of Lesbians and Gays, or PFLAG National.

usually with a parent. Among those who tell a family member, twenty is the median age.[17]

Gay youth offer a variety of reasons why they hesitate to come out to their families. In an extensive study of over 10,000 LGBT youth,[18] 30% say their family is homophobic or transphobic, while another 19% are scared of their family's reaction. Ten percent are simply not ready, and 10% don't feel they have the ability to talk to their family about their orientation. Finally, 16% of gay youth don't come out to their family for religious reasons; they have heard condemning messages about what God thinks of gay and trans*[19] people and choose to keep their attractions and/or gender identity a secret.

Coming out to a parent can feel very risky to a gay child. The very last love a child is willing to "risk" is the love of their parent. This was true for Missa Borah,[20] a 20-year-old gay Christian from Illinois.

> When I realized I was gay, my first thought was, "My parents are going to be so disappointed." At that time, I felt that I would rather be closeted my whole life than disappoint my parents. I wish I had talked to them about it the moment I realized I was gay so that they could love and support me. Instead, I waited for three years to tell them. By then, my whole town knew. I didn't realize how willing they would be to learn more about sexual orientation. My church had been silent on homosexuality. For LGBT kids, by default, churches are a place of non-acceptance. When gay youth see a church go out of their way to support the LGBT community, that speaks volumes to us. It draws people in.

---

[17] "A Survey of LGBT Americans," Pew Research Social and Demographic Trends, June 13, 2013, http://www.pewsocialtrends.org/2013/06/13/a-survey-of-lgbt-americans/.
[18] "Being Out," Human Rights Campaign, 2012, http://www.hrc.org/Youth#.T9D4KOJYtvd.
[19] "Trans*" is frequently used as shorthand for "transman," "transwoman," and "transgender."
[20] Missa blogs at www.missaborah.com.

Affirming churches should be loud and proud and let the LGBT community know they support them.

Missa's mom, Jena Borah, 51, of Charleston, Illinois, is typical of most Christians in conservative churches. Even after thirty-five years as a disciple of Jesus, she had never studied the subject of homosexuality, simply because she "didn't need to." She believed what her Bible teachers and leaders told her about homosexuality and Scripture. She had never even met an openly gay person until Missa, her youngest daughter, came out on the day her parents dropped her off at college when she was eighteen.

Missa had been seeking God about her sexual orientation for a long time and had come to peace with Him. Jena told Missa that although she did not understand it, she would try. For the next year, Jena did not tell anyone that Missa was gay. Jena spent the time doing what she had never done for herself—searching the Bible about homosexuality, while listening to the Holy Spirit.

> I had always thought being gay was a choice, but after hearing from Missa and many other Christian gay people who have tried for years to change, I realize that people are born with a sexual orientation, just like I was. My daughter never even knew a gay person growing up. Her life was full of homeschooling, church, and missions work. She realized she liked girls the way her friends liked boys in about third grade.
>
> Gay people think God hates them. Kids who grew up in the church and then realize they are gay are afraid, confused, and hurt. Missa and I went to the Gay Christian Network conference in January. Over seven hundred LGBT people, their friends, and families gathered together. We sang worship songs, listened to sermons, and attended workshops.

> I felt the power of the Holy Spirit there like I haven't felt in a long time. Missa had a spiritual revival there. When she came home, she started a Bible study group for LGBT believers and their friends. We have up to ten mostly straight college students attending. They are hungry for the Word of God. They thought Jesus wasn't for them, but now they are so thankful to be in a safe place to learn about Him and grow in their faith.

Though Jena Borah may not have understood exactly what she needed to do to keep Missa safe and feeling loved, her instincts led her to a series of healthy and loving responses when her child came out to her.

Healthy and damaging responses to LGBT youth

The premiere researcher and lecturer on the health care needs of gay adolescents is Dr. Caitlin Ryan, director of the Family Acceptance Project,[21] based at San Francisco State University. Dr. Ryan has worked on LGBT health and mental health issues for over forty years. She began doing research and social work specifically with gay youth in the 1990s.

Dr. Ryan has been acknowledged by the American Psychiatric Association, the American Psychological Association, and the National Association of Social Workers for her valuable contributions and groundbreaking research. She is widely recognized for her expertise on gay youth suicide prevention and family acceptance and rejection issues for gay youth across a broad spectrum of ethnic and religious diversity.

Dr. Ryan and her research team have established a list of over one hundred positive and negative behaviors families use in reaction to their gay or transgender child. Researchers have analyzed how the behaviors affect adolescents or teens as they grow into young adults. They have quantified the risk of suicide, depression, substance abuse, and HIV and STDs. Positive outcomes, such as healthy self-esteem and a

---

[21] The Family Acceptance Project, www.familyacceptance.sfsu.edu.

hopeful sense of the future, were also evaluated. A family's response to their young gay or trans* child, whether positive or negative, has dramatic implications on the life of the child as he or she becomes an adult. Even the actions of *well-meaning* Christian parents, if they encourage or force orientation change therapy on their child, lead to detrimental effects in the future. Family rejection of gay and trans* young people has profound implications that place them at high risk of physical and mental health problems as they grow into young adults. Compared to gay and transgender youth who are not rejected by their families, highly rejected young people are:[22]

> eight times more likely to attempt suicide;
> six times more likely to suffer high rates of depression;
> three times more likely to use illegal drugs and alcohol; and
> three times more likely to become infected by HIV and other STDs.

Supportive behaviors promoting the well-being of a gay or transgender child include:[23]

> talking with your child about their LGBT identity;
> expressing affection;
> providing emotional support to your child;
> advocating for and protecting your child from mistreatment;
> for families of faith, attending affirming events/churches;
> advocating for your child within your faith community;
> connecting your child to positive role models;
> welcoming your child's partner into your home and lives;
> and speaking to them positively of their future.

---

[22] Dr. Caitlin Ryan, "Supportive Families, Healthy Children," *The Family Acceptance Project*, 2009, 5.
[23] Ibid., 9.

When 21-year-old Canadian Emilee Friesen came out, her parents incorporated all these supportive behaviors to help their daughter navigate what is, for so many youth, a difficult time. Emilee is a twin, a hockey goalie, and an embalmer who is following in her parents' steps in the family's funeral business.

> I knew my mom thought being gay was okay. I knew that my dad loved and accepted his gay sister. Still, I was terrified of coming out to them. I was afraid that it would be upsetting if their own daughter were gay. I came out to a few of my friends before I came out to my parents. Some of them said, "Are you sure? How do you know?"

> I was leading worship and teaching Sunday school. I knew that would stop once I told my pastor. I started building a wall, anticipating the reaction of my pastor and church. I wasn't able to hear the messages at church anymore. Eventually, I did come out to my pastor. The elders met with my parents and [me] and told me I could come on Sundays and sit in their pews. They said they wouldn't kick me out, but sitting in the pews was all I'd be doing.

> Sitting just made my walls grow higher than ever. My story would be very different had my church just let me keep playing drums once a month on a Sunday morning. My view on churches in general would be different had my church let me keep serving.

Emilee is trying to find her way back into church. When she goes home to her parents, she goes to church with them at their new, welcoming church.

Her mom, Eunice Friesen, 45, lives in Grande Prairie, Alberta, Canada. When Emilee came out to Eunice, it was a "non-issue." Eunice thought she would lose friends from church, and she did. But for her, there was never any shame or embarrassment in having a gay daughter.

> I was relieved when Emilee decided to come out to our church leadership because I knew it was difficult for her not to be authentic at church. Sadly, our church stripped Emilee of any place of service in the congregation, and to this day, that is a great heartache for me.
>
> The summary dismissal of her as a valued, contributing Christian pains me. My husband and I were supportive of inclusion before Emilee came out. It bothers me that some of my Christian friends think that we are only affirming because of our child. My biggest regret is not having been more vocally supportive of the LGBT community within my faith community before my daughter came out.
>
> I believe the conservative church is beginning to shift and that pressure is coming from the pews. It's exciting to see the tide of change coming from theological leaders, too, as they grow in understanding of how Scriptures relate (or fail to relate) to the contemporary LGBT community.
>
> It has been a blessing to watch my daughter grow rapidly since coming out. She can be herself now. In her newfound comfort, she has excelled socially and professionally. I am so very proud to be her mom!

How is the church responding to

gay and trans* youth?

In recent years, Dr. Ryan has been working with leadership of The Church of Jesus Christ of Latter-Day Saints (LDS) to create best practices to keep gay Mormon youth safe while they stay engaged in the faith with their family.[24] Tragically, among conservative Christian churches there has not been similar movement to assimilate Dr. Ryan's research into practice or policy. Rather, the more prevalent attitudes in conservative churches continue to include attempts to diminish same-sex attractions while shifting gay youth toward their "heterosexual potential"[25] or forcing them into lifelong celibacy.

The theories of Catholic psychologist Dr. Joseph Nicolosi (1947–) are at the core of the reparative therapy model used within conservative churches to address same-sex attractions in both adults and adolescents. Nicolosi and others who promote similar theories believe that disruption in a child's healthy relationship with the same-sex parent, most often caused by an over-involved and intrusive mother, or a distant or detached father,[26] creates an internal sense of "incompleteness" about their own maleness or femaleness. Nicolosi calls the incompleteness "gender dysphoria." (Using the term "gender dysphoria" in this manner takes on an entirely different meaning from the one used and understood by every major mental and medical health professional group in the United States. Correctly used, "gender dysphoria" refers to the condition suffered in the non-alignment of gender and biological sex, a transgender condition.)

---

[24] Joseph Walker, "New Booklet Targets LDS Families of Homosexual Youth," *Deseret News*, June 15, 2012, http://www.deseretnews.com/article/865557584/New-booklet-targets-LDS-families-of-homosexual-youth.html?pg=all.

[25] Kathy Baldock, "Back to Bondage: The Restored Hope Network," *Canyonwalker Connections*, October 2012, http://canyonwalkerconnections.com/back-to-bondage-the-restored-hope-network-exits-exodus/.

[26] For public discussion with parents of gay youth at their conference, see: Kathy Baldock, "Back to the Closet: Restored Hope Network on Homosexuality," *Canyonwalker Connections*, October 2012, http://canyonwalkerconnections.com/back-to-the-closet-restored-hope-network-on-homosexuality/

Nicolosi's theory supposes that gay people develop a high degree of mental anguish resulting from their gender incompleteness, which in turn drives them to have sex with a same-sex partner in order to complete their own maleness or femaleness.[27] Though no professional mental or medical health association in the United States supports this theory or the reparative therapy treatment associated with it,[28] Nicolosi claims a 66% success rate in converting gay people to straight.[29]

From Dr. Ryan's research, we have seen how damaging non-acceptance can be to gay teens, yet variations of reparative therapy are the most common methods used by Christian ministries with gay adults and adolescents alike. By his own admission, over 60%[30] of Nicolosi's historic patient load has been gay youth under eighteen years of age, half of whom are from religious families.

In recent years, two states, New Jersey and California, have made it illegal for a licensed therapist to try to change the sexual orientation of a minor. In California, an organization called the National Association for Research and Therapy of Homosexuality (NARTH)[31] sued the state for the right to treat gay youth with reparative therapy.[32] In 2012, NARTH

---

[27] Dr. Joseph Nicolosi, "Biblical Sexual Ethics Workshop" (public conference call), *The Salt and Light Council*, July 8, 2014.

[28] Reparative therapy is not endorsed by any of the following organizations: American Academy of Pediatrics, American Psychological Association, American Psychiatric Association, American Medical Association, National Association of Social Workers, National Association of School Counselors, National Association of School Psychologists, American Academy of Physician Assistants, American Academy of Family Physicians, American College of Obstetricians and Gynecologists, American College of Nurse Midwives, American Counselors Association, American Medical Student Association, World Professional Association for Transgender Health, American Academy of Family Physicians, American Public Health Service Association, National Commission on Correctional Health Care, American Physical Therapy Association, or the World Health Organization.

[29] "'Ex-Gay' Leader Joseph Nicolosi Claims 66% Success Rate; Stephen Fry Says He Looks Gay," *On Top*, October 15, 2013, http://www.ontopmag.com/article. aspx?id=16694&MediaType=1&Category=4#.

[30] Ibid.

[31] NARTH is currently rebranding itself as Alliance for Therapeutic Choice and Scientific Integrity (ATCSI).

[32] Michael Gryboski, "Group Sues California Over Bill Banning Reparative Therapy for Gay Teens," *The Christian Post*, October 2, 2012, http://www.christianpost.com/news/

lost its case. In an additional blow, the Supreme Court declined to hear an appeal.[33]

Though licensed therapists are banned by law from using reparative therapy with gay and trans* youth, pastors, staff, and lay ministry leaders are not.[34]

Resources for Christian parents of gay and transgender children

If you are the Christian parent of a gay or transgender child, be diligent in researching sexual orientation or gender identity, adolescent development, psychology, science, and the Bible so that you can make informed and wise decisions about how to best engage your child within your family and faith. *How you handle your gay or transgender child will affect his or her adult life.*

A number of organizations are available to support you: The Family Acceptance Project's website[35] contains valuable research and resources to help strengthen families and youth during the coming-out process. PFLAG National (Parents, Families, and Friends of Lesbians and Gays)[36] is the largest organization in the United States for friends, families, and allies to join with LGBT people for education and advocacy. (See Chapter 4 for the story of its beginnings.) Over 350 chapters nationwide hold monthly meetings. Local and national conferences are held yearly. Christian parents are warmly received and can find excellent support within local PFLAG chapters.

---

group-sues-calif-over-bill-banning-reparative-therapy-for-gay-teens-82555/.

[33] David S. Joachim, "Supreme Court Declines Case Contesting Ban on Gay 'Conversion Therapy,'" *New York Times*, June 30, 2014, http://www.nytimes.com/2014/07/01/us/supreme-court-declines-case-contesting-ban-on-gay-conversion-therapy.html.

[34] Here is a list of reparative therapy ministries associated with Christian churches and denominations, as well as parachurch organizations involved in reparative therapy ministry: http://canyonwalkerconnections.com/avoid-christian-reparative-therapy-ministries/.

[35] Family Acceptance Project, http://familyproject.sfsu.edu.

[36] PFLAG National, www.pflag.org.

FreedHearts[37] is another lifeline of support for the LGBT community and families dealing with faith issues. Founder and blogger Susan Cottrell has authored *Mom, I'm Gay – Loving Your LGBTQ Child without Sacrificing Your Faith*.[38] Through the FreedHearts organization, Christian parents of LGBT children are connecting on Facebook in rapidly growing regional support groups for mothers or fathers; to become involved, contact Cottrell through the FreedHearts website.

Kim Pearson is the Training Director and co-founder of TransYouth Family Allies (TYFA).[39] When her teenage child came out as a transgender male, it spurred Pearson's interest in education and advocacy. TYFA is the only national organization supporting, educating, and advocating exclusively for gender-variant and transgender children. Pearson, who educates various groups and in schools, is the leading expert in the United States on adolescent transgender issues. If there are 500–1,000 students in a school, there is at least one transchild among them in need of support and protection.

Young gay and transgender Christian role models

What has been sorely lacking for gay and trans* youth within conservative churches in past decades is positive role models. In Chapter 13, we saw that LGBT Christians who came out in the past had few options other than to stay in their churches and hide their sexual orientation, or come out and leave their faith communities. However, with the growing witness of LGBT Christians who are coming out and remaining engaged in Christianity, this is changing quickly.

I know hundreds of remarkable young LGBT Christians who are leaders in their denominations, churches, and communities, and who are working toward inclusion in conservative Christian environments.

---

[37] FreedHearts, www.FreedHearts.org.
[38] Susan Cottrell, *Mom, I'm Gay – Loving Your LGBTQ Child without Sacrificing Your Faith* (Austin, TX: FreedHearts, 2014).
[39] TransYouth Family Allies, www.imatyfa.org.

Nick Norton is a 20-year-old Catholic college student from Detroit, Michigan. He has attended Catholic schools since kindergarten and is now working within his denomination to foster understanding about sexual orientation as it intersects with faith. Part of the success of his process in coming out as a gay Christian had to do with finding a trusted mentor.

> I came out as gay to a Catholic priest. The entire process enriched my life. I gained so much: a deeper love for myself, a more honest relationship with the church community, and a stronger spiritual core. I wish I had known how much weight would be removed from my shoulders once I came out, and what a powerful voice I would develop. One piece of advice I would give to young Christians in conservative environments is to always be safe! Be careful about who you pick as a faith mentor. Never let anyone tell you that you aren't welcome in church.

Tim Rosenberger is a 20-year-old from Lakewood, Ohio, where he grew up attending a Lutheran Church–Missouri Synod congregation. He is an American Studies student at Georgetown University and Vice-Chair of the D.C. Federation of College Republicans.

> For a long time, I felt that being faithful required a deliberate decision to choose my faith over being gay. Many of the Christians I most respected—my family, friends, and church—did not support my decision to come out. The deterioration of those relationships put a great strain on my relationship with Christ. As I surrendered myself more fully to God's will, I saw things improve. I formed incredibly strong relationships with people who supported my entire person while affirming my faith. I would encourage others

facing the decision to come out to surrender to God's grace. He will sustain and strengthen you. In affirming yourself as His complete creation, you will walk more closely than ever with Him.

Devin Kennamer is a 23-year-old native of Henagar, Alabama, and a graduate of the University of North Alabama, who works in marketing in Birmingham. Devin was homeschooled from kindergarten through high school and has, until recently, attended one church throughout his life—Grace Presbyterian Church in Fort Payne, Alabama. The leadership of his childhood church is displeased with Devin, who will not agree that the Bible condemns homosexuality.

> When I told my parents that I was gay, I wasn't scared that my parents would no longer love me; that was never in question. I was homeschooled through all of my years under the supervision of my church, Grace Presbyterian (PCA) in Fort Payne, Alabama. I attended summer Bible camps, and even worked as a Junior Counselor. I was always involved in church activities and mission trips, but my orientation was never really a question. It was obvious! I simply tried to ignore it. I had never met other people that were like me, so I was fearful that I could never live as gay and Christian. It was simply not an option.

> God never left my side through this struggle; He was always there. I went through very scary and dark moments where I didn't feel like eating, couldn't sleep at night, and was nervous about what other people would think. When I came out as gay and Christian, I lost the respect of some people. Some think you can't hold a high view of the Scriptures and be gay. I consider myself very conservative in my view of

the Scriptures. In my mind, without doubt, if I were born heterosexual, I would not be as close with Christ as I am today. Through my struggle of begging God to answer the question "Why?", I got so much closer to God than I could ever imagine. Growing up in church, it's easy to get numb to God's love and mercy.

Megan Rhinehart is a 29-year-old entrepreneur and e-commerce professional who graduated from Baylor University. She was very involved with Reformed University Fellowship in college and now attends an Anglican Mission church in Atlanta. Megan understands well the shame laid on gay youth. Now free of such restrictions, Megan lives her faith in a vibrant way, engaging those around her to share the Gospel.

Coming out is the painful process of shedding shame that doesn't belong. It is painful! But what is on the other side is worth it. As I let go of shame, I began to become alive to my dreams, my passions, my style and new community. These are oddly wrapped up in my sexuality, and they are the best way I know how to worship God.

My advice is to Google everything. Don't assume a pastor or ministry leader knows what is right. Don't assume it will get better as others become more accepting. It only gets better as you draw boundaries, stand up for yourself, and take a risk at romance. I am hopeful the Church will begin to change as we press into how queer relationships reflect God's nearness to us in Christ.

Matt, who is in his early twenties and is from Los Angeles, graduated from a Christian university. Matt is a gay African American Christian who doesn't have his family's emotional support for living his life authentically. In fact, one parent actively speaks out on the other side of this issue.

For some youth, additional pressure to conform to heterosexuality comes from within their ethnic or racial group. There is systemic resistance within the African American community about accepting that homosexuality is just as present among blacks as among whites. Such resistance encourages turning a blind eye to homosexuality and forces a substantial percentage of gay African American men to pretend to be heterosexual and to "go on the down-low." ("The down-low" is a term meaning that people hide their sexuality while secretly engaging in same-sex behavior.) Consequently, heterosexual African American women are experiencing the greatest percent increase in new HIV cases. Similar family pressures are experienced by Latino and Asian gay youth, in particular those from Christian families. Matt is from a very conservative Christian family.

> When I came out as gay and Christian, I risked uprooting everything that I knew in my life. I grew up in the church and went to private Christian schools, including college. I feared that my family would isolate and reject me and that my friends would leave me. I was also concerned about living a life that was wrong in God's eyes, so I thought about staying in the closet. If I had, nothing in my life would have changed. But the cost of living a lie and not being honest with myself was to risk a life of destruction. I decided to be honest with myself, and I suddenly felt free.

> My journey in coming out started with seeking God more for help and comfort. I got closer to Him. I am serious about my faith. Coming out caused me to dig deeper to justify myself to those who have questioned me. I wish I had known that being gay wasn't a sin. I grew up thinking that

my existence was shameful, even though I had the cleanest record in the book. No one should have to grow up in shame and live a life where they think that faith is justified by their works. I am getting stronger.

It takes a special person to be queer and Christian; stay strong. Know that God loves you no matter what. Seek Him, and He will show you the way.

Roman Catholic Mateo Williamson, 23, is a native of Phoenix, Arizona, and a microbiology student headed toward medical school. He hopes to be able to work to combat the health disparities faced by sexual and gender minorities. Mateo is a transman.

As a young transman who grew up in the Catholic Church, it is important to me to never forget the pain I felt about the apparent clash between my faith and inner truth. Fully embracing who God made me to be was never an option in my mind until I reached the end of my rope at the age of twenty. I struggled with the thought that I was broken and had failed in my lifelong attempt to embrace the gender that society expected of me. Because I viewed God as an extension of the church that had trouble accepting me, I also felt that perhaps I was a disappointment even to God.

This began to change when I met other transgender people and was able to see Christ so present in them. I was moved by their journeys and the beauty of their determination and will to rise from the ashes. To me, transition was very symbolic of a resurrection.

> When I reached that point of surrender and self-accep-
> tance, I was given new life. My hope is that Christians all
> over the world will begin to see the beauty in transgender
> people and how their stories can enrich our faith lives.

Gay and transgender Christians who attend conservative and fundamentalist Christian colleges and universities suffer extensive challenges
while hiding their orientation in non-affirming and/or even overtly
anti-gay environments. Jeffrey Hoffman, 43, from New York City, is
a board director of SafetyNet,[40] an organization that equips and em-
powers LGBT students and alumni from institutions of higher learning
where religion plays a significant role. I receive an alarming amount of
mail from LGBT students and alumni from fundamentalist Christian
colleges who have been conditioned to fear their sexuality. When they
"fall," they are consumed with fear and shame. Gay and transgender students from faith communities that instill hyper-loyalty in their student
populations are pushed near to the point of suicide. SafetyNet exists for
these students and alumni. Currently, SafetyNet operates at over ninety
Christian colleges and universities, either openly or underground.

Jeffrey knows well how traumatic it can be for LGBT people to
hide in such environments; he grew up in the Bob Jones Academy and
University system.

> I was eight years old when I first saw a man naked in the
> Bob Jones University gym locker room and experienced
> my first crush. I was perhaps nine when my Sunday school
> teacher molested me. I was ten when Bob Jones III told an
> Associated Press reporter that gay people should be stoned
> to death "as the Bible commands," and only a tween when
> I heard him declare that "AIDS is God's punishment" from
> the chapel pulpit.

---

[40] SafetyNet, http://onesafetynet.com.

As a teen, my gay secret was my solitary, unspoken burden. I cried myself to sleep praying for God to take it away and make me straight. At eighteen, I finally heard God saying that I am His beloved child, but I struggled for six more years to accept myself fully in an affirming church.

I daily talk to people whose experiences mirror mine. Some days it seems nothing will ever change: fundamentalists continue pushing LGBTQ folks out of the church and writing us out of the gospel. But then someone will tell me she read my story and God changed her mind. That's when I catch a glimpse of God's great kingdom coming to earth, the kingdom of love and light.

Resources for LGBT Christians

A positive environment for LGBT youth is the Gay-Straight Alliance (GSA) Network.[41] GSAs are student-led organizations found in growing numbers of schools, colleges, and universities. GSAs promote education and safe schools for all students, regardless of sexual orientation, gender identity, or expression. Each club has a teacher-advisor, holds regular meetings, and is open to any students who support the mission of creating safe and supportive environments. As we have seen, it is not unusual for LGBT students to not be out to their own families. GSAs provide a needed place where they can feel accepted and safe.

Research has found that LGBT students in schools with GSAs are subjected to less bullying and discrimination, and experience less suicidal ideation.[42]

---

[41] Gay-Straight Alliance Network, www.gsanetwork.org.
[42] "Gay-Straight Alliances in Schools Reduce Suicide Risk for All Students," *The University of British Columbia UBC News*, January 20, 2014, http://news.ubc.ca/2014/01/20/gay-straight-alliances-in-schools-reduce-suicide-risk-for-all-students/.

LGBT Christians of all ages can find excellent online support with Gay Christian Network (GCN).[43] GCN was founded in 2001 by Justin Lee as a safe online community for gay, lesbian, bisexual, and transgender Christians and their families and allies. The website has dozens of forums categorized by denomination, region of the country, interests, and general sharing. GCN is an ecumenical organization embracing a wide range of theological beliefs, from conservative to progressive Christianity. "Side A" Christians, those who do not believe homosexuality is a sin, interact safely with "Side B" Christians, who believe God loves gay people but does not condone homosexual activity. The organization hosts a conference each January. The 2014 conference had over seven hundred attendees, 10% of whom were families and allies of the LGBT community. I've been involved with GCN since 2007 and serve on the Advisory Board.

There are now welcoming organizations, ministries, and programs for most denominational backgrounds, as well as a growing list of welcoming churches worldwide. Those organizations can be found at Canyonwalker Connections—Resources—Welcoming Church Programs, Ministries, and Organizations.[44] The persistent witness of older LGBT Christians from over four decades is now increasingly joined by the vibrant witness of younger LGBT Christians. Unlike those before them, young gay and transgender Christians have information, positive role models, strong biblical arguments, and relationships with straight Christians willing to stand alongside them for equality in churches.

Let's see where you might fit in.

---

[43]   Gay Christian Network, www.gaychristian.net.
[44]   Canyonwalker Connections, http://canyonwalkerconnections.com/welcoming-church-programs/.

Chapter 15

Making the Christian Church Safe and Welcoming for LGBT Christians

Those Who Advocate for Inclusion

Where are you and where is your church along the path to inclusion?

The landscape of the American Christian church is shifting because many of us have established relationships with gay and transgender friends and family members.

Relationship changes things. When we love and respect a person, any *issue* related to him or her becomes more *human* and more personal. As lesbian, gay, bisexual, and transgender (LGBT) individuals come out, more of us are being challenged to re-examine our belief systems and stereotypes.

It is no longer a question of *if* you or your church home will engage the questions surrounding faith, sexuality, and gender; it is a question of *when*. Twenty years ago, only one in four people reported that they had a family member or a close friend who was lesbian, gay, bisexual, or transgender;

now that number has tripled.[1] The church has never been faced with this issue as it is now. At no point in history could our ancestors in the faith have imagined that there would be people who are exclusively same-sex attracted, profess faith in Jesus Christ, and desire equal status in the Christian church. This is a new frontier for Christianity, and we can meet this challenge with productive Christ-like attitudes.

Australian author Anthony Venn-Brown knows what it's like to be at the inner core of denominational life, as well as cast to the outer edges. Based on his own life's journey and on years working with churches, he has identified a progression of stages that congregations must move through in order to become safe and welcoming for LGBT Christians.

After twenty-two years of trying to change his sexual orientation, and after sixteen years of marriage, Venn-Brown, a former Assemblies of God pastor and international speaker, came out as gay in 1991. Immediately, he lost his position as a respected pastor at a popular megachurch and his reputation as a speaker at international conferences. Venn-Brown's autobiography, *A Life of Unlearning*,[2] tells openly and honestly of his struggle to conform to heterosexuality in the conservative Christian world, his coming out as a gay ordained minister, and the consequences.

In 2011, Venn-Brown founded Ambassadors & Bridge Builders International[3] and began doing reconciliation work with churches from that vantage point. Over time, he has noted that every church is at a certain stage of openness to LGBT attendees and members. He cites the following stages churches go through along the journey from extremely unwelcoming to fully inclusive:[4]

---

[1] David Briggs, "Homosexuality and the Pews: Seven Signs Influencing Congregational Acceptance of Gays and Lesbians," *Public Religion Research Institute*, February 26, 2014, http://blogs.thearda.com/trend/featured/homosexuality-and-the-pews-seven-signs-influencing-congregational-acceptance-of-gays-and-lesbians/.

[2] Anthony Venn-Brown, *A Life of Unlearning* (Sydney: New Holland Publishers, 2004).

[3] Ambassadors & Bridge Builders International, http://gayambassador.blogspot.com.

[4] Anthony Venn-Brown, "Issues for Churches to Work Through to Become a Welcoming and Affirming Church" (workshop handout), 2009.

Aversion: One of the first hurdles to overcome for some heterosexuals or faith communities is their aversion to even thinking about same-sex behavior, in particular sex between men. Rather than thinking about gay people as humans, they view them primarily in the context of a sex act.

Negativity or hostility: A rejection of people based on the assumption that they are the enemy. We've exposed the root causes of many negative LGBT stereotypes in previous chapters. A shift in attitude to an intentional desire to see the image of God in those not like us will help move a congregation or believer to the next step, which is . . .

Deconstructing negative stereotypes about LGBT people: Stereotypes such as that all gay men are promiscuous and secretly want to be women and that lesbians are anti-men can be countered by having conversations with LGBT individuals and couples.

Creating safety: Making LGBT people feel truly welcome in your church by creating a safe place for worship and for open dialogue that does not seek to change their orientation. Many LGBT believers have come out of churches where conditions have been placed upon them to change. Addressing this concern directly will help create safety.

Learning and studying: Conducting an open study of the six passages of Scripture used to create modern ethics regarding homosexuality. Most LGBT Christians have worked through these verses, whereas most heterosexual Christians have not.

The Canyonwalker Connections blog[5] has a list of books (including detailed reviews) that may match your community's level of commitment. They range from reading individuals' testimonies to more formal

---

[5] Canyonwalker Connections, http://canyonwalkerconnections.com/canyonwalker-connections-qr-page/.

study; in particular, I highly recommend these thoughtful, intelligent, and grace-filled books:

- *Torn: Rescuing the Gospel from the Gays-vs.-Christians Debate,*[6] the personal story of GCN president Justin Lee
- *Bible, Gender, Sexuality,*[7] by Dr. James Brownson, a New Testament professor for over thirty years who revisited the Scriptures when his own son came out
- *God and the Gay Christian,*[8] by Matthew Vines, a young scholar who spent several years studying in order to understand how his sexual orientation aligned with his conservative views of Scripture

Deliberating: Openly discussing church policy regarding celibacy, service, membership, and issues related to gay believers.

Considering federal rights: Having open conversations about how state-recognized and, potentially, federally recognized marriages might affect your congregation.

Accepting: Fully welcoming committed gays and lesbians in relationships on an equal footing with those in heterosexual relationships.

Affirming: Allowing LGBT Christians' use of the full range of their God-ordained gifts in service within the faith community.

---

[6] Justin Lee, *Torn: Rescuing the Gospel from the Gays-vs.-Christians Debate* (New York: Jericho Press, 2013).

[7] James V. Brownson, *Bible, Gender, Sexuality: Reframing the Church's Debate on Same-Sex Relationships* (Ann Arbor, MI: William B. Eerdmans, 2013).

[8] Matthew Vines, *God and the Gay Christian* (New York: Convergent Books, 2014).

They've left your churches

About one-half of LGBT Americans have no affiliation with a faith community, compared with only one-fifth of Americans in general.[9] Of gay and trans* people who are religiously affiliated, most identify with mainline Protestant faiths,[10] and almost one-quarter of the LGBT population identifies as born-again Christians.[11] A number of denominations now welcome and/or affirm LGBT Christians, including the United Church of Christ, the Episcopal Church, the Disciples of Christ, the American Baptist Church, the Alliance of Baptists, the Evangelical Anglican Church in America, the Society of Friends (Quakers), the Evangelical Lutheran Church in America, the Presbyterian Church (USA), and the United Methodist Church.[12] These denominations comprise about 70% of the almost five thousand congregations in the United States that welcome LGBT people.[13] Clearly, LGBT Christians are attending and participating in churches. Those who assume that someone cannot be both gay and Christian ignore the fact that LGBT Christians are already openly worshipping God in fully inclusive denominations in the United States, and in some degree of secrecy within the other 45,000-plus Christian denominations worldwide.[14]

---

[9] Candace Chellew-Hodge, "Nearly Half of LGBT People Claim No Religion," *Religion Dispatch*, June 18, 2014, http://religiondispatches.org/nearly-half-of-lgbt-people-claim-no-religion/.

[10] Matthew Brown, "Survey: Gay and Lesbian Population Has Unique Religious Profile," *Deseret News*, June 15, 2013, http://www.deseretnews.com/article/865581728/Survey-Gay-and-lesbian-population-has-unique-religious-profile.html?pg=all.

[11] "Spiritual Profiles of Homosexual Adults Provide Surprising Insights," Barna Group, June 20, 2009, https://www.barna.org/barna-update/article/13-culture/282-spiritual-profile-of-homosexual-adults-provides-surprising-insights#.VB-wlEsxGuc.

[12] "Affirming Congregations," GaycCurch.org, http://www.gaychurch.org/affirming-denominations/.

[13] Jaweed Kaleem. "Gay-Friendly Churches and Houses of Worship Growing, According to National Congregations Study," *Huffington Post*, November 13, 2013, http://www.huffingtonpost.com/2013/11/13/gay-friendly-churches_n_4268975.html.

[14] "Status of Global Missions, 2014, in the Context of AD 1800–2014," Gordon Conwell Theological University, http://www.gordonconwell.edu/resources/documents/StatusOfGlobalMission.pdf.

Outside the mainstream, increasing numbers of fully affirming non-denominational churches are being planted and growing. LGBT pastors and their allies have been establishing churches that reflect Baptist, Pentecostal, Evangelical, Roman Catholic, and a variety of other faith roots. While in some geographic areas, particularly in the south or more rural areas, LGBT Christians have fewer options available, their church choices are increasing as this revival grows.

For those who are too geographically distant or otherwise unable to attend a local house of worship, many affirming churches host online services, making them universally available. Anyone with access to the internet can do an online search for "LGBT-affirming churches in [geographic area]." Additionally, a list of over 7,500 welcoming churches in forty-seven countries is available at GayChurch.org.

It's encouraging to witness so many vibrant, fully affirming churches popping up in the least expected of places. For example, in the midst of a swath of highly anti-gay Christian congregations between suburban Raleigh, North Carolina, and Greenville, South Carolina, sits a community of mature gay Christian believers in a small town outside Hickory, North Carolina, led by Pastor Dave Thomas. The congregants of Abundant Grace Church in rural Granite Falls join me each year at Charlotte Pride to reach out to the festival-goers and stand against vitriolic street preachers in a Wall of Love.[15] Nearby in more urban Charlotte, thirteen churches welcome LGBT congregants. Wherever God calls His LGBT people into or back to ministry, they are establishing churches, often in unlikely places—where they are most needed!

Over the years, I've met thousands of LGBT Christians who, for countless reasons, have silently slipped out of churches or even left Christianity altogether. The most obvious impetus for the exodus is condemning messages constructed from faulty interpretations of those six passages of Scripture we examined in Chapter 9.

---

[15] Kathy Baldock. "Wall of Love at Pride Charlotte: Standing against Hate in Love," *Canyonwalker Connections*, August 2012, http://canyonwalkerconnections.com/wall.

Even if your church home uses, or seems to use, a kinder tone, if there is condemnation just below the surface, LGBT people who have been battered by judgment since childhood will hear it. Many congregations proudly believe they have established welcoming and positive environments simply because their pastors are not preaching negative messages about homosexuality; however, it's not that simple.

Subtle, and often unintentional, cues scream loudly into the souls of LGBT Christians seeking safe places to worship and serve. They have left churches—even "kind" churches—for a variety of reasons. Some reasons are listed below; however, there are many others as well:

Insensitivity to their journey with Jesus: There's an assumption that LGBT people have not "done the work" or have not read some or all of the six passages in the Bible dealing with same-sex behavior. Rest assured, by the time they come out, they have likely been reflecting on these verses for over a decade. Pointing them out *one more time,* as if they have somehow missed them, indicates a lack of understanding of the journeys and testimonies of LGBT Christians. You may have heard a testimony from a person who says they are no longer gay. Yes, God *can* do anything, but for person after person, years—often decades—of begging, prayer, therapy, exorcisms, and support have not altered people's sexual orientation. Trying and failing to become straight often results in self-hatred. LGBT Christians frequently call it "exhausting" to continually validate their personal salvation, testimony, and understanding of Scripture to non-affirming Christians.

Similarly, having their testimony dismissed: Many conservative Christians ignore or discount the testimonies of LGBT Christians as "experiences" and "stories" that are inherently less valid than the testimonies, experiences, and stories of straight Christians.

Inability to conform to the unreasonable expectation of orientation change: No matter how hard they try, LGBT Christians cannot stop being gay or transgender. They may leave church believing they are disappointing God and their Christian family.

Stringent, inflexible views and the unwillingness to hear other views: The insistence of particular biblical interpretations as "truth," without dialogue or consideration that there may be other faithful ways to view Scripture. It excludes and denies the personhood and testimony of LGBT believers when a superior value is placed on only one interpretation, rather than understanding that we all see the Scriptures through filters. *All* of us use filters to interpret the Bible.

The un-Christ-like witness of fellow believers: Some struggle with the image of God as One who created them gay or transgender and then allows so much damaging hatred to spill from His followers.

Extreme frustration, loneliness, and isolation: This is often the experience of LGBT Christians who hide their sexual or gender identity in churches that do not accept "the homosexual lifestyle."

Denial of opportunities to serve the body of Christ: The inability to freely use their God-given gifts in faith communities can be frustrating.

Lack of resources: Some gay Christians are unable to reconcile their sexuality and faith without outside help. The task seems insurmountable and overwhelming. It can be easier to just not deal with it.

Lack of godly same-sex role models: Within predominantly straight churches, this means few or no healthy same-sex relationships to emulate, little or no encouragement for gay or trans* people's Christian walk, and a lack of mature LGBT Christians to mentor them.

An absence of allies and advocates: Many LGBT Christians are exhausted by being an agent of change in their churches without the help of straight Christian allies to stand with and for them in the face of injustice.

Potential for divisiveness: Some LGBT Christians do not want to cause internal church conflict over sexual orientation and gender identity issues, so they leave.

They don't want to leave their/your churches

Why not just let LGBT Christians go to affirming churches and leave you alone with "your church"? For the most part, people stay in churches and denominations that are part of their family's legacy of faith. Most of us are comfortable with the tenets and worship style of our past and have established deep roots in our churches.

Whether they are growing up in the church and coming to awareness that they are gay or transgender, or have been hiding and longing to come out for a long time, LGBT Christians have few options. They can hide their sexual orientation and/or gender identity, along with their intimate relationship if they are in one; hide their orientation and marry a spouse of the opposite sex; come out as gay and remain celibate in a supposedly more "progressive," yet still non-affirming congregation; leave and find a welcoming church; or leave formal church altogether.

Only recently have new options become available. Although some LGBT Christians feel they are called to remain in non-affirming churches and engage their leadership with the possibility of policy change, if church leadership is not willing to take part in genuine dialogue that truly honors the heart and spirit of LGBT believers, it may be time to consider a permanent move out of the congregation. Such environments, in the end, stifle spiritual growth.

Not only are these difficult—even traumatic—choices for gay and transgender believers to make, but the rest of the church is losing out.

Sadly, most of us do not even realize it. Over the past half century, we've lost the diversity and richness of the gifts and insights LGBT believers offer the body of Christ. It's not possible to see the fullness of the image of God when we exclude the stories, witness, blessings, and gifts of a whole segment of His children.

Moving toward including LGBT Christians in conservative churches

You may be a member or a pastor of a church you call "welcoming." In progressive evangelicalism, welcoming most frequently means that hospitality is extended to gay and transgender people. But beyond that, there are usually conditions and restrictions placed on how they live their lives and where they may serve.

I've had many meetings and conversations with pastors of "welcoming" churches. Initially, they assure me that *everyone* is welcome to come to their services and join their community and programs; on further exploration, it becomes apparent that they put conditions on their welcome.

Once LGBT people get in the front doors of "welcoming" churches, they are rarely treated equally to heterosexual congregants. The definition of "welcoming" matters to gay and transgender Christians. What *you* mean by "welcoming" and what LGBT Christians view as welcoming may be very different. You need to consider the following questions:

At what level are LGBT people able to participate and serve in your church? In what ministries are they included, and just as importantly, from what ministries are they excluded? Can they be worship leaders, work in the children's ministries, or lead Bible or home study groups? Sidelining LGBT Christians to duties such as ushering and staffing the coffee bar is not an open-service policy, unless those are places where the individual *chooses* to serve. Will gay and transgender people be restricted in their service and fenced out of using their gifts in the congregation, whether by a written or an unspoken policy?

Do gay, lesbian, and bisexual Christians who want to become part of your church family need to "repent" for their sexual orientation? Do you expect them to change at some unspecified future time? Is there an assumption or hopeful attitude that they will come to no longer identify as gay? Will you direct them to a reparative therapy program? Is the goal to "fix" them? Will you encourage lifelong celibacy and discourage any same-sex relationships?

Some say gay and transgender Christians need to place their "identity in Christ." So do heterosexual Christians, yet heterosexuals can also be in committed intimate relationships. If your church is not going to support the committed same-sex relationships of LGBT congregants, be honest about that. Bait-and-switch is deceptively un-Christ-like and serves to push gay and transgender believers *farther* away each time the deception happens.

What version of the Bible does your church officially use? Some versions, as seen in Chapter 9, include poor and inaccurate translations of key verses. If your sanctioned translation includes the word "homosexual," you *will* offend gay congregants. There are more accurate translations that do not use the word "homosexual."

If your church is a membership church, can LGBT Christians become members?

If LGBT people are in a committed relationship, will they be welcome as a couple? Will they be permitted to interact with the same level of affection commonly acceptable for heterosexual couples in your congregation? Can they touch arms, hold hands, or sit closely in worship or times of prayer? As marriage equality becomes more widespread state by state, how will you treat same-sex couples who are legally married?

How do you treat transgender people?

Pastors and ministry leaders who have reconsidered their stances

Danny Cortez, 47, of La Mirada, California, is a graduate of Biola University and has been the teaching pastor of a small conservative Southern Baptist Conference (SBC) church for the past sixteen years. He started a journey of moving toward an affirming stance several years ago when a young lesbian in his congregation asked him to watch *Through My Eyes*.[16]

Through My Eyes is a documentary produced by the Gay Christian Network featuring young LGBT Christians telling how and when they came to the realization that they were gay, and talking about the reactions of their families and churches. There is no additional commentary; it is simply the compelling words of two dozen young LGBT Christians telling powerful stories.

After seeing it, Pastor Danny began searching for information on the issue of homosexuality and Christianity. Over the span of three years, he came to an affirming stance.

One day, on his way to dropping off his son, 15-year-old Drew, at high school, Pastor Danny told Drew he had changed his mind on the matter of same-sex marriage. At that moment, feeling safe to do so, Drew came out to him as gay.

I met Pastor Danny and his wife, Abby, at the 2014 Gay Christian Network conference.[17] No other church within the SBC has yet moved to a position supportive of LGBT Christians. Pastor Danny says:

> "We fear what we do not know." These are the words I heard from a young transgender woman who grew up in the church. She lives in the reality of people being afraid of her.

[16] Justin Lee, dir., *Through My Eyes* (Gay Christian Network, 2009); DVD available for purchase at https://www.gaychristian.net/store/through-my-eyes-dvd.
[17] Kathy Baldock, "Pastor's Kid Comes Out and Family Stands with Him," *Canyonwalker Connections*, February 2014, http://canyonwalkerconnections.com/pastorskidcomesoutandfamilystandswithhim/.

She is treated by Christians like a person with leprosy. She is marginalized and made to feel shame. Unfortunately, the church has been moved by fear rather than love whenever LGBT brothers and sisters confront us.

What the church desperately needs is the courage to seek to understand the real-life struggles that the LGBT community faces. As Dallas Willard stated, "Understanding is the basis of care." Without our willingness to understand, we will be misguided into thinking that we are showing love when in reality, we are not.

Unless we repent, we will miss our calling to care for those who have been oppressed for too long.

Pastor Brett Glanzmann is one of the teaching pastors at a large evangelical church in Sparks, Nevada, where he has been on staff for over eighteen years. He was a youth pastor during his first five years of employment. When one of the youth in his group came out to him, Pastor Brett responded by going through a reparative therapy book with him.

Over the next fifteen years, a half dozen more young men came to his office to talk to him about their homosexuality. Rather than giving potentially harmful advice, Pastor Brett just decided to listen, "seeking to understand rather than be understood." Two years ago, one of his family members made an office appointment with him and came out as gay.

When the issue becomes a person, as it did in my case and in the lives of many others, we are forced to revisit scriptures we were once "sure" about.

I find it difficult to dialogue openly about LGBT issues in the Evangelical Church for several reasons. The first is the high value placed on certainty. More than anything, many evangelicals need to be right. They need to know without a doubt that they are on God's side of an issue. They often state that the Bible is "abundantly clear," even when it is not.

Evangelical Christians have difficulty living in the tension of an issue even though that is where the greatest amount of spiritual growth occurs. Rather than live in the tension of open dialogue where we might learn from one another, people will fall on one side or the other—either keep LGBT people out of our church, or simply affirm everything. When straight and gay people have to work out their faith side by side, there is discomfort. However, it's the only way to learn and grow.

To engage in healthy dialogue, we need to see people as people, not as black-and-white "issues." When my family member came out, I was forced to look beyond the issue to the heart of the person God made him to be. The transformation for me came through getting to know LGBT people who love God. I pray that more people in the church have such an experience!

Kelly and Bryan Lee, both 38, are on the staff of Lakeside Church, an affirming, nondenominational church in Minneapolis, Minnesota. Kelly was raised Roman Catholic and Pastor Bryan grew up Southern Baptist and has a Master of Divinity degree from Bethel Seminary. They are high-school sweethearts, married for over eighteen years, and the parents of two small children. They actively educate on LGBT inclusion, and Kelly serves on the board of the local PFLAG chapter.

By standing in solidarity with our LGBTQ brothers and sisters, we, as straight advocates, have the potential to help break the chains of fear and anxiety that bind many non-affirming Christians. Over the years, we've developed deep relationships and trust with many non-affirming Christians. As we've shifted to an affirming stance, we've also developed deep relationships with LGBTQ folks. This places us in a good position to open a door to truth by personally refuting the inaccurate beliefs and generalizations that many non-affirming Christians naively hold in their ignorance. We're able to use the platform of trust to share the stories and voices of LGBTQ folk who are otherwise often shut out. The truth has power to break the bondage of fears and anxieties born out of ignorance and lies.

Ruth Cooper, 55, is a minister and founder of Above ALL Names, a ministry of reconciliation. She lives in Royal Palm Beach, Florida, with Barry, her husband of thirty-six years. They have five children and numerous grandchildren. For several years, Ruth has had access to the legislators on Capitol Hill. She facilitated and hosted non-partisan prayer gatherings for legislators. In recent years, Ruth has become a strong voice of affirmation and prophecy in affirming churches.

For many years I prayed and cried out for not only the heart of God toward others, but the eyes of a Creator that sees value in all humans. This brought me to an encounter with a young man who was dealing with his sexual identity. My family and I befriended him. He had gone to church leaders seeking for answers, and he got judgment instead. Watching him struggle broke my heart. I realized that this was not an isolated case. Religion has been the culprit of wars and demonizing all that is not within its circles or its opinions.

As a straight minister, I realized that all my past relationship within church walls was just that—the past. My
spiritual journey had changed. I started to question what
I believed and found myself hiding in the closet trying to
cover up my changing beliefs. I had so many questions to
ask of God. My ministry suffered. That did not matter; the
rewards of giving, loving, and encouraging those that God
so loved [are] irreplaceable.

My dear gay friend is now a pastor and has been instrumental in my life. The gay community and affirming churches
have shown me the true unconditional love of God, and
the experience, though bumpy at times, has been good. My
prayer is that organized religion will change and become
affirming sooner than later. There is a world in need, and we
have been commissioned to bring hope.

There are many people and organizations professionally equipped
to guide congregations through dialogue to create safer and more
welcoming environments for LGBT believers. In her book, *Generous
Spaciousness: Responding to Gay Christians in the Church*,[18] Wendy
VanderWal-Gritter, Executive Director of New Direction Ministries[19]
in Canada, provides an excellent resource for leaders of conservative churches and those who engage the issue of welcoming LGBT
Christians. Wendy, who once led a Canadian-based Exodus ministry
that supported reparative therapy, guides the reader along a neutral
journey of question-asking to discover his or her own moral ethics
based on Scripture.

For almost a decade, Wendy has guided church and ministry
groups through the transition of becoming more genuinely welcoming

---

[18] Wendy Gritter. *Generous Spaciousness: Responding to Gay Christians in the Church*
(Ada, MI: Brazos, 2014).
[19] New Direction Ministries, www.newdirection.ca.

environments for LGBT believers. Her gentle and wise approach helps leaders discover the path that most resonates with their particular Christ-centered theology.

Ordinary Christians who have become affirming

As we remove the lenses and filters through which we interpret the Word of God, we discover for ourselves the meaning of the six passages of Scripture involving same-sex behavior. Frequently, a conflict arises between strong traditional Christian beliefs and a motivation to investigate another point of view. In my case, when I met Netto, her life and integrity challenged the stereotypes I had accepted as true about gay people. When I realized the stereotypes were wrong, I was faced with a decision about how to reconcile what I had been taught with what I saw in the lives of LGBT people.

Then I met gay and transgender Christians who professed faith in Christ and whose lives (though not their orientation) were changed as a result, and they clearly exhibited the fruits of the Holy Spirit. I came to know, love, and respect them. At that point, I was ready to challenge my deeply entrenched beliefs. To be clear, I was not challenging my beliefs about *God;* I was challenging my beliefs about *what people told me those six passages of Scripture meant.*

You might be facing a choice, too. *What's going to happen if you lay your beliefs surrounding this issue down on the table and look at them from every angle?* Is what you think the truth? The information in this book might help you to better answer that question now. Ask yourself, how does my belief about a person line up with what I've been told are biblical truths?

It's okay. Really, it is. We can set aside "knowing" and risk being uncomfortable for a while. As Pastor Brett said, lots of us do not like "living in the tension." *We need to know.*

This messy space is called "cognitive dissonance." It can be horribly uncomfortable for folks who want answers *now.* There might even be a temptation to run back to what's comfortable and surround yourself with all the people who have not ventured out into this new frontier.

All of us who are allies and advocates have experienced these feelings. Whatever each person's motivation, at some point he or she took that first uncomfortable step. What makes these ordinary people extraordinary is that they kept walking forward, even in the discomfort; they walked forward until they got answers. Most lost friends; some lost their reputation, their job, or a position of leadership. But all gained characteristics of Jesus that now shine through their lives.

Ryan Kenji Kuramitsu, 21, is a popular blogger[20] and a college student studying social work and Spanish at the University of Illinois, where he was also once a member of Campus Crusade for Christ (Cru). He works at a refugee center, as a resident advisor, and doing community service to end human trafficking.

After his parents divorced, Ryan was raised in both Roman Catholic and conservative evangelical churches. When his mother came out as a lesbian, he was forced to address and research a subject he never thought he would face. When he eventually came to an affirming stance, "folks got more upset about my blog post on homosexuality than about the fact that I had just discovered sex trafficking going on where I live. Defending the 'biblically sound' view of homosexuality superseded both trafficking and maintaining our friendship[s]."

Indeed, when he came out on his blog as affirming of the LGBT Christian community, almost all of his Christian friends turned on him. His Cru Bible study leader met with him on New Year's Eve and pleaded with him to "re-submit to authority," commit to meeting with staff four times a week, read "nothing but the Bible for the next sixteen weeks, and not post on [his] blog, Facebook, or Twitter until summer."

---

[20] Ryan blogs at www.arealrattlesnake.com.

One of the things I didn't do when I began this journey of reconciliation was count the cost. I never really considered all of the precious, privileged things I would lose when I came out as supportive of queer Christians. Over the past few years, I've lost a lot more than I ever thought I could. But it's not anything near what my LGBT friends have been through, and I am so grateful for their examples, for their grace and patience. I've worked with many campus ministries, and it is clear to me that my generation still has miles and miles to go when it comes to justice and equality for the LGBT community. But there is hope. Things are changing, for good, and I am also very grateful for the lessons I've learned, and for the many relationships I've built in this time.

Mother of three heterosexual adult children and wife of a pastor, Canadian Betsy Johnson, 53, has attended conservative churches for over thirty-five years. When reflecting on her life a few years ago, she wondered why she was not making a significant difference as a follower of Christ. Betsy is a thinker and a journaler; she sought God for an answer. She sensed Him whispering to her to reach out to gay people with a message of unconditional love. Although she was not comfortable with people's "gayness," God told her to let Him handle it. She realized that the love she had previously extended to others had been conditional.

That was Betsy's epiphany. She tried something new; she tried loving others without boundaries. Betsy says, "It was like getting saved again after thirty-five years."

The power of being a straight advocate is [that] I have no hidden agenda. I'm not doing it because I needed to come to terms with my sexuality, or because I have a gay kid and need to reconcile my faith. I'm an advocate because love dictates that I stand for the rights and freedoms of all people.

I believe there is far too much tradition, it's way too political, and that most "Christians" are just not interested in doing the hard work (and it is hard work) of revisiting the teachings that have led them to believe homosexuality is sin. However, I do believe God is working outside the walls of the church. Many LGBTQ people will come to know the love of Jesus as a result of new affirming communities being started and populated by people like me who simply can no longer tolerate the un-Christ-like attitudes of traditional churches toward LGBTQ people. God will find a way to reach the people that He loves, regardless of what the church is or isn't doing.

Betsy has since left her congregation of twenty-five years. She does one-on-one work with LGBT people who find her and need her loving, attentive, and empathetic approach. Working with the gay and transgender community has changed the way she sees God, others, and life.

Native-born Venezuelan AnaYelsi Sanchez,[21] 29, belongs to a nondenominational Christian church and is a trained anti–human trafficking activist, artist, and community organizer living in Orlando, Florida. When she came out as affirming to LGBT Christians, she lost her job as the Director of Communications and Development for a faith-based anti-trafficking agency.

I'm not involved in LGBTQ issues. I'm involved with LGBTQ people. They are my friends, my confidantes, and my inspiration. I can't imagine sharing their lives and not [being] willing to fight on their behalf. It would make for a

---

[21] AnaYelsi blogs at www.browneyedamazon.com.

fractured relationship, and I'm too greedy for that. I want it all. My job as an ally is to stand in the tension and to amplify the voices of LGBTQ people. I've lost friendships, and even jobs, as I've grown in boldness. It's little to sacrifice compared to what my LGBTQ friends have endured, and honestly, if ever there was something to sacrifice for, it's the people I love.

Lisa Bohn,[22] 40, teaches theatre at Arkansas State University in Jonesboro. She is married and the mother of two young sons. Lisa grew up in Chapel Hill, North Carolina, where she attended a Baptist church. She is now a member of an Episcopal church that welcomes gay and transgender congregants.

My work as a straight ally in the church has most certainly had an impact on my faith. I had stayed away from Christianity for a long time. The way the biblical "truth" had been previously presented to me—yelled at me, preached at me, thrown at me—didn't seem like [the] true nature of the loving and merciful God.

It was when I encountered Matthew Vines' video,[23] Kathy Baldock's work, and The Reformation Project[24] that I realized it was possible to be both completely affirming of the LGBTQ community as well as truly, honestly, and proudly Christian. I think my position as a straight ally is potentially very powerful, as I have no personal "agenda" in terms of working toward inclusion.

---

[22] Lisa blogs at http://theheartdivide.wordpress.com/.
[23] Matthew Vines, "The Gay Debate: The Bible and Homosexuality" (video), March 10, 2012, https://www.youtube.com/watch?v=ezQjNJUSraY&feature=share.
[24] The Reformation Project, www.reformationproject.org.

Michele Grabbe is an "ordinary" mom of three extraordinary children in rural Belgrade, Montana. She was raised in a conservative Christian environment in West Texas. She had no intentions of becoming an activist for *any* cause until her middle child and only son, Jakob, came out as bisexual.

Now, Michele is the president of the local PFLAG group. Her husband, Sean, is Training Officer with the Bozeman Fire Department, and Michele's mom, Rosie, is the secretary at a local Episcopal church. As a family, they have made significant inroads in their community and church through education on issues of faith and orientation. Recently, their home church in Bozeman, St. James Episcopal Church, voted to become a reconciling, affirming community of believers.

> At the age of forty-five, I feel like I am finally doing what I was born to do all along: loving and speaking up for LGBT people. I was raised in a conservative church that taught [that] homosexuality was a choice and a sin. I believed what I was told for most of my life. It has not been easy to come to an affirming stance.
>
> I am grateful for the journey that has led me to now know without a doubt, being gay is not a choice and it is not a sin. I have also let go of other beliefs that I learned, not from God but in a legalistic church. I am more spiritually free than ever before. My relationship with God is open, authentic, and life-giving. I have learned so much from my LGBT friends and family and will always be grateful to them, and to God for putting them in my life!

Caroline Cheek, 28, is married and an artist who lives in Charlotte, North Carolina. She's always enjoyed strong connections to reforming traditions in the Presbyterian Church. She attends Caldwell Presbyterian

Church, where she is an elder and co-chair of Education and Spiritual Formation. Motivated by faith, Caroline participates in her community and advocates for the oppressed and impoverished. She lives out a belief that is core to her worship: "Love your neighbor."

I met Caroline one August in Charlotte, when, for the sake of equality for her little brother, she joined me in the Wall of Love standing between the street preachers and the Charlotte Pride festival-goers.

> When my younger brother came out, I thought my parents and sister would remain stagnant, but that wasn't true. My family was transformed! That opened my eyes to the possibility that people could change their beliefs. My mom told me some painful stories from years earlier when she [had] shared her non-affirming beliefs with another parent of an LGBT child and hurt the woman. The tears came streaming down my mother's face when she realized the pain that she caused that family.

> The process of becoming an advocate for LGBT inclusion in Christian churches has informed my faith in new and beautiful ways. I began to believe that, through dialogue and relationships, people can change. Straight allies and advocates are such important storytellers and bridge builders within the Christian community.

Becoming an ally for equality and inclusion in the Christian church

Perhaps you are now standing on the precipice of decision and wondering how you might fit in and work toward creating fully safe, welcoming, and inclusive Christian churches. If you're ready for more education and want to build personal relationships with lesbian, gay, bisexual, and transgender Christians, here are some practical steps you can consider:

Meet LGBT believers in their faith communities. The website www. gaychurch.org has a listing of most, but not all, churches that are affirming of the LGBT community. LGBT Christians enjoy equal status in the more than 7,500 churches worldwide that are on the list. Additional churches may be found at the organizational websites of the denominations listed at the beginning of this chapter.

Don't just go to church; plan on having a meal with congregants afterward. You may feel nervous or shy, but seek relationships and get to know them. You'll be surprised how many LGBT Christians have attended Christian colleges and seminaries. I suggest calling the pastor beforehand to see if he or she would facilitate your joining members for a meal after church. The friendliness and hospitality I've experienced in the LGBT Christian community is extraordinary.

Read and watch documentaries. The "Resources" tab on my website, www.canyonwalkerconnections.com, lists books and videos for your consideration. Pick the one suitable for your level of investigation. When you're done, pick another one.

Expand your relationships with LGBT Christians. Participate in their lives when invited, and invite them into your social life. This will stimulate conversation in various directions as your circle of friends expands.

As a next level of involvement, you might consider some of the following actions:

Gather a group together for a meal and conversation about a book from the "Resources" list mentioned above, or share some popcorn and watch *Through My Eyes* or *For the Bible Tells Me So*.[25] Then discuss your reactions.

Depending on how ready your home church is, offer to lead such a conversation for other members of your congregation.

---

[25] Daniel G. Karslake, dir., *For the Bible Tells Me So* (First Run Features, 2008).

Facilitate a group discussion about your church's policy and LGBT inclusion. Talk openly about how your policy regarding LGBT Christians aligns with your church's mission statement.

Know that in any of these scenarios, you don't need to have the answers. You do, however, need to have the conversation.

More direct involvement in the issue of sexual orientation and gender identity and the intersection with faith can happen at conferences, such as the following:

The Gay Christian Network[26] hosts an annual conference each January. The most recent one, in 2014, had over seven hundred lesbian, gay, bisexual, and transgender Christians and their families and allies in attendance. More than 10% of attendees were straight Christian allies. Pastors who are navigating their way through this issue are *most* welcome. There's a specific learning and discussion track created for pastors, parachurch leaders, and other ministers. Arrangements can be made to assist you and keep your attendance private so that you might freely seek answers otherwise unavailable to you.

The Reformation Project,[27] led by Matthew Vines, author of *God and the Gay Christian*, hosts several regional conferences each year to educate and help empower Christians who are committed to making their churches affirming, inclusive, and safe places for LGBT Christians. This is an excellent venue for pastors and church leadership to discuss issues they may not be able to raise in their own congregations. Pastors will find as much privacy and safety as they need while they investigate these issues without pressure to come to any final resolution.

---

26 Gay Christian Network, www.gaychristian.net.
27 The Reformation Project, www.reformationproject.org.

Keep going forward until the church aligns with your Christian values

Some of these steps took years for me to progress through. Wherever you are, just keep moving forward until your home church, your denomination, or the church at large aligns with your Christian vision. Maybe your guiding principles include welcoming all, or service to all. Move toward that end.

We are in the midst of change brought on by a growing awareness of the witness of LGBT Christians, the efforts of many to revisit Scripture for more accurate translations and interpretations, the willingness of LGBT Christians to tell their stories and stay in churches, and the strength of straight allies and advocates who will repair the breach by working toward civil and Christian justice.

Allies who personally promote equal rights and treatment can be among the most effective and powerful voices within a movement. As humans, we naturally recognize patterns. When someone from the majority steps out and advocates for the minority, it disrupts the existing pattern, and we notice. People who might not otherwise listen to LGBT Christians begin to do so. This is one reason allies of LGBT Christians are so essential to bringing parity for *all*.

For those of us who do advocate for the LGBT Christian community, it is important that we maintain our respect for tradition, faith, and morality. We need to be credible witnesses so our audience will identify with us.

Above all, conversations need to be motivated, guided, and empowered by our unity in Christ, who has made us all brothers and sisters. Resist any actions and attitudes that work against that bond of unity that has been entrusted to us to preserve.

Tell your own story about why you're an advocate. Build relationships. Proof-texting, or debating isolated verses out of context, is not the best tactic; an exchange of this type can go on and on with little understanding gained. Define your terms and listen to the other person to make sure you understand what his or her main concerns are. Practice self-control. Don't engage in tit-for-tat, name-calling, or one-upmanship. If the conversation starts to go downhill, graciously exit. No "win" is worth mistreating a fellow brother or sister in Christ. Even though you may see the "other" as an enemy, or he or she may treat you as the enemy, the "other" is made in the image of God—just as you are—and deserves to be treated with respect.

In short, strive to live out the words of Ephesians 4:1-6:

> . . . walk worthy of the calling with which you were called, with all lowliness and gentleness, with longsuffering, bearing with one another in love, endeavoring to keep the unity of the Spirit in the bond of peace. There is one body and one Spirit, just as you were called in one hope of your calling; one Lord, one faith, one baptism; one God and Father of all, who is above all, and through all, and in you all. (NKJV)

Repairers of the Breach
Final Thoughts

The roots of my passion

When I was a kid growing up in a predominantly Irish Catholic neighborhood in New York City during the 1950s and 1960s, my mom got a divorce. My father had been unfaithful and left her with three young children. Then, while still legally married to my mom, he married another woman and did the same thing: He got her pregnant and abandoned her with their six-month-old.

After the divorce, my mother was shunned, not only by neighbors but also by our parish priests, for a situation beyond her control—the "sin" of being divorced. She was looked down upon if she dared go to church, and she was *certainly* not welcome to receive communion.

When it came time for me to enter parochial school, my mother was told there was "no room" at the school my brothers were already attending; they did not want any more children of a divorced woman. My mom didn't want me to go to public school, which forced her to enroll me in the Catholic school in the next parish. So as a little seven-year-old, I walked the ten-block distance to and from school each day, by myself because my mother had to work.

I was the only girl in my school from a divorced family. The *only* one. I had no language to express the overwhelming shame the Irish Catholic culture placed on my mother, my family, and me.

My teachers, the nuns, didn't help me; no one from the church helped me. No one acknowledged my family situation—divorce was just too shameful. Even my mother couldn't help me to deal emotionally with the stigma; she was barely surviving the ostracism herself. So I kept my mouth shut about our family situation. I evaded friends' questions. I lied. I pretended I had a father like everyone else just to fit in. I wore a mask constantly.

The cover-up played out in unhealthy ways during my adolescence and throughout college. Though I excelled academically, I was in shambles on the inside. Eventually, in my late twenties, when I became a Christian, I began to get my life on a healthy course toward feeling loved, accepted, and worthwhile.

Recently, I've begun to realize that my passion for justice is rooted in the deep pain those church leaders of my youth inflicted on my family and me. They used a few verses in the Bible as a license to condemn my mother and, in turn, her children. I was an outcast, the victim of religious judgment.

Of course, the Catholic Church no longer holds quite such harsh attitudes toward those who divorce. Eventually, with my encouragement, my mother even returned to her faith at the age of seventy-four, but my brothers have not done so. They walked away from the church and from God altogether. Too much damage had been done to our family, simply because a few Bible passages were thought to be God's final word sentencing divorced people to damnation.

"Can I turn around and walk with you?"

Fifty years later, we've moved on from the stigma of divorce, yet the Christian church is in a similar place in terms of lesbian, gay, bisexual, and transgender Christians. Once again we've used a few Bible passages, out of context and poorly translated, this time to shame gay and transgender people. LGBT people are today's religious outcasts, condemned for conditions they cannot change: their sexual orientation or gender identity.

Throughout this book, you've read numerous stories about LGBT believers and the devastating effects of cultural and religious oppression and rejection on their lives. Before the late 1970s, for the most part Christians stayed out of the societal fray, but in their "unholy union" with conservative politics, conservative Christians not only failed to fight injustice—they actively participated in it.

When I turned around on that hiking path in 2001 and began a relational journey with Netto, I was *sure* my beliefs about gay people were consistent with the Word of God. Though I had never studied the issue on my own, I trusted the teaching of the evangelical culture in which I was cocooned. Gradually, I began to meet other gays and lesbians. My attitudes about equality and civil rights softened and became more inclusive, yet I still hadn't dared to consider that "untouchable" space where faith and sexual orientation meet.

About six years into our friendship, Netto and I were coming back down the trail, chatting away. She was telling me about a predominantly lesbian RV camp-out she was going on the next weekend. "I'm not safe and welcome in places where you are," she said. "This camp-out is the only place I feel completely accepted and safe. Look, Kathy, you don't understand. In this society, I'm the lowest of the low. I am a Native American. I am a woman of color. I have a Hispanic last name. I am a lesbian. Not even God loves me." I can point to the spot on a dirt trail where I *heard* those words from my dear friend. "Not even God loves me." My heart ached; I stopped on the trail, stupefied, and cried.

For the next several days, those words cycled in my head. I asked God earnestly, almost in disbelief, "Is that *true?* God, do You really not love my gay friends just because they are gay? How could You be like that? *I'm* just a person, and *I* love them. But You, You're *God,* and You are supposed to love better than I can."

It was a simple, yet critical, juncture for me. At that point, after several years of close relationships with gays and lesbians, I was finally willing to critically examine my theology concerning faith and orientation. *I was open to being wrong.*

Later that same year, as I shared at the opening of this book, answers came in a most unexpected way as I found myself among several hundred LGBT believers at the Gay Christian Network conference. During worship on the first night, I recognized the clear movement of the Holy Spirit among a beautiful and diverse group of people whom the conservative church had excluded from its fellowship.

Similar scenarios are happening to many of our fellow Christians, even the most conservative among us. There is a disconnect between what we have been taught as biblical truth and what we come to know in our relationships with gay and trans* people. This dissonance has compelled many of us to go back to the Word to investigate for ourselves what the Bible says—and what it does not say.

For me, the impetus was a single friendship that had started one day when I simply asked a stranger, someone outside my comfort zone, "Do you mind if I turn around and walk with you for a while?" From there, I got to know—more, I turned and *walked with*—more people, who also happened to be gay or lesbian or transgender. Though it was often uncomfortable, I decided to lay aside entrenched beliefs and get to know people who were different (though not as much as I first thought) from me.

Eventually, my passion for justice led me to wonder how the gay and transgender community came to be the keen focus of cultural and religious derision. My search for answers took me farther than I ever anticipated. Each layer of information led to more questions. I kept researching until I could see a clear timeline of events in which culture, psychology, history, politics, and religion intertwined. I hoped to dig the beauty of the life-giving sacrifice and love of Jesus Christ out from under the rubble of ruinous actions carried out by some (not all)

Christians. And, to use another metaphor, rather than interpreting the Bible through eyes clouded by cataracts of myth, assumptions, and destructive teachings, I wanted to dislodge the flawed filters in order to gain a clearer view of Scripture. This book is the result of that questioning, searching, digging, and dislodging.

You may have picked up this book for any one of dozens of reasons. Depending on the filters through which you have viewed the LGBT community, some chapters may have resonated with you more than others. Over a lifetime of experiences, relationships, and theological teachings, I had believed that a person's sexual orientation was a choice, whether the conscious or unconscious product of unhealthy family dynamics, and I believed LGBT people could be "fixed." I had a gut-level negative reaction to the question "Can a person be gay or transgender *and* Christian?" Because I believed that homosexuality was a sin, the concept of non-discrimination—much less marriage equality—was foreign to me.

Over the past several years, my theology and ideology about sexual orientation and gender identity have evolved. Knowing the damage done by Christians to the LGBT community, in 2008 I started going to Gay Pride events wearing a hand-painted tee-shirt that read: "Hurt by Church? Get a #str8apology here."

In 2011, I went to Charlotte Pride in North Carolina, where some friends and I had learned that a religious leader planned to bring a group of over two hundred Christians. Indeed, they came, all wearing red tee shirts declaring the "good news" that God wanted to bring "wholeness and transformation" from out of people's transgender identity or homosexual orientation.[1] I attended because I wanted to participate in offering a counter-message of unconditional Christian love.

---

[1] Kathy Baldock, "God Does Have a Better Way: Don't Stand in the Path of It," *Canyonwalker Connections*, August 2011, http://canyonwalkerconnections.com/god-has-a-better-way-about-to-write-need-comments-of-how-this-would-make-you-feel/. See also: http://canyonwalkerconnections.com/god-has-a-better-way-dont-stand-in-the-path-of-it/.

I usually position myself right in front of street preaches who blast hate-filled rants with bullhorns while carrying banners condemning everyone but themselves. Supported by fellow LGBT Christians and allies, we form a "Wall of Love" as a buffer for the festival-goers.[2] We talk to hundreds of people. It's the young adults who rip me to the core. When they come out, many are rejected and shamed, and many who were raised in the Christian faith leave church, never to return. After how they've been treated by church people, they simply cannot imagine that there would be a Christian church to welcome them.

Many young adults know me as "the straight apology lady," having seen me at events or on YouTube.[3] Sam was one such young woman. She had seen me on YouTube and was so delighted to meet me in Charlotte. We chatted. Her story was painfully similar to many I've heard. She came out as a lesbian and got kicked out of her family, her church, and her home. I listened to her pain, offered her love, a hug, and suggestions of more than a dozen churches in the Charlotte area where she would be welcome. She was joyous and gave me an enthusiastic hug in return.

The following year, Sam ran up to me. Her appearance had changed. She was dressing more masculinely and had shaven her hair close to her scalp. "Hey, straight apology lady, do you remember me from last year?" Of course, I did; I recognized her unique voice instantly. We hugged. She was genuinely delighted to be remembered and "known." I caressed her face with my hands, kissed her cheeks and forehead, and looked at her closely. I asked, "Honey, do you realize how *beautiful* you are to God? You are beautiful." Sam teared up, cast her eyes down, and turned her head away. She couldn't even look at me; she had heard too many times that she was an abomination to Christians and to God.

---

[2] Kathy Baldock, "'Wall of Love' at Pride Charlotte: Standing against Hate in Love," *Canyonwalker Connections*, August 2013, http://canyonwalkerconnections.com/wall-of-love-at-pride-charlotte-standing-against-hate-in-love/.

[3] Kathy Baldock, "'Wall of Love' Standing against Hate at Gay Pride" (video), September 8, 2012, https://www.youtube.com/watch?v=ucntaxT39Gs&list=PLFqSvKiowXh6Id-Q4R-xJLMql9lzc_wmyl.Kathy.

Likely, within a decade, we as a culture and as believers will be in a different place in terms of understanding what it means to be gay or transgender. Bolstered by the growing and undeniable witness of LGBT Christians, we'll also have greater insights into the biblical passages about same-sex behavior. In the meantime, what might be your place in the movement toward creating safe, inclusive faith communities for LGBT people?

As I stated at the outset, I wish the book you have just read had been available to me ten years ago; then I could have examined my ideology and beliefs against the historical, cultural, psychoanalytical, political, and scriptural records. But now, chapter by chapter, I have attempted here to unravel the injustices against the LGBT community.

There is no possible way to make up for the damage done, or to redeem lives lost to destruction or suicide. It is highly improbable, if not impossible, to re-engage people who have decided to *never again* look for the good in Christianity. We can, however, begin to take an active part in repairing the breach.

If you have arrived at a new understanding of the historical account of how the LGBT community has been treated, and of how the Bible calls us to treat gay and transgender people, I invite you to join me and growing numbers of Christ-followers in becoming Repairers of the Breach.

> Is this not the fast that I have chosen:
> To loose the bonds of wickedness,
> To undo the heavy burdens,
> To let the oppressed go free,
> And that you break every yoke?
> Is it not to share your bread with the hungry,
> And that you bring to your house the poor who are cast out;
> When you see the naked, that you cover him,
> And not hide yourself from your own flesh?
> Then your light shall break forth like the morning,

Your healing shall spring forth speedily,

And your righteousness shall go before you;

The glory of the Lord shall be your rear guard.

Then you shall call, and the Lord will answer;

You shall cry, and He will say, "Here I am."

If you take away the yoke from your midst,

The pointing of the finger, and speaking wickedness,

If you extend your soul to the hungry

And satisfy the afflicted soul,

Then your light shall dawn in the darkness,

And your darkness shall be as the noonday.

The Lord will guide you continually,

And satisfy your soul in drought,

And strengthen your bones;

You shall be like a watered garden,

And like a spring of water, whose waters do not fail.

Those from among you

Shall build the old waste places;

You shall raise up the foundations of many generations;

And you shall be called the Repairer of the Breach,

The Restorer of Streets to Dwell In.

Isaiah 58:6-12 (NKJV)

About the Author

Kathy Baldock is the founder and Executive Director of Canyonwalker Connections, whose mission is to help repair the breach between the Christian church and the LGBT community through education, encouragement, and engagement.

She is one of the most vocal advocates for inclusion within the conservative church and the founder of the "str8apology" movement, bringing LGBT people and straight Christians together at Gay Pride events to reflect the love of Jesus.

She is the mother of two straight adult children, and is honored to serve as a spiritual mother to hundreds of lesbian, gay, bisexual, and transgender children. Kathy is an ordained minister who lives in Reno, Nevada.

Contact author at: Kathy@canyonwalkerconnections.com

Acknowledgments

Walking the Bridgeless Canyon is the fruit of many kind, generous, gifted, and wise friends, advisors, mentors, confidantes, and encouragers. I came into the gay, lesbian, bisexual, and transgender community as a stranger and have become a family member.

Though it was frightening to step out of the mainstream to follow a passion and a calling, God's provisions through people have made it possible. As I have travelled about over the past years, the generosity in the form of donations, meals, beds, tanks of gas, and airline miles has been overwhelming.

Thank you to those who support Canyonwalker Connections financially. Your gifts have kept the important research on this book and other work moving forward. I appreciate: Gregory Guest, Andrea White, Michael Wong, Devin Buckner, Rayona Sharpnack, Michele Grabbe, Lori Morford, Ryan Kuseski, Michael Watt, Jana Currier, Dee De Herrera, Paul Creekmore, Howard Carver, Mark Metz, Naomi Harvey, Scott W., David Farmer, Desert Oasis Chapel of Palm Springs, David and Steven Medina of Dapstep Ministries, Darren Potter, Wes Snow, Marty Jacobson, Michael Bower, Beau Cannon, Kristen Gil, Jason Stevens, Verlin Byers, Gary Jarnigan, Scott Westrup, Chris Bailey, Sean Caras, Open Door Ministries of Long Beach, Scott Carpenter, Michael Bower, Dean Johnson, Richard Archambault, David Jones, Wendy Wilson, Shirley Sartin, Jonathan Shinn, Henry Dela Peña, Jason

Kamrath, Brent and Janet Conrad, Joy Paul Schwenke, John Paulk, Nick Warner, Sharon Hare, Mark Williams, Doreen Mannion, Mike Castro, David Brown, Melanie Storrusten, Jennifer Zins, Amy Haupman, and Kathyn Sisson.

Thank you to the many people who have hosted me in their homes over the years. Gui Alvarenga and Michael Schlemmer of San Jose, CA who treated me like a princess. Once they ran a plastic red tablecloth from the street to their door to welcome me on a "red carpet." Roby Sapp and Dotti Berry, and furry "Sister," of Blaine, WA, let me luxuriate in their cottage and love—ahhh! Jose Jordan, an architect in Orlando, creates peace and beauty in his surroundings. He barely knew me when he invited me into his home. Rosie Freemyer, of Belgrade, MT, offered mountains and serenity and cushioned me in her love and wisdom. Lisa Salazar, of Vancouver, B.C., is like a sister to me. I wish I could have the peaceful chats and hikes nearby and more often. Carolyn Cheek and Joe Lublinkhof, of Charlotte, NC, opened their doors after just one meeting on the streets of Charlotte. David Jones and Jorge Piza of Greenville, SC, treated me like a treasure and offered a refuge when I next go back. Deb Windham made sure I was well taken care of while in Long Beach, CA, and gave me a stack of her old reparative therapy tapes as original documents! Stephanie Wilson lent me her condo at Kirkwood Ski Resort, where I escaped with my dogs to hike and write for several days. Likewise, Bob and Norma loaned me their timeshare at the onset of this journey. I left my snowboard at home and hunkered down in Squaw Valley, California, to do the first draft of this book.

Thank you to the friends who gave of their endless wisdom and encouragement—I appreciate you. Lisa Darden, of Frederick, Maryland, shared long phone calls filled with insights, encouragements, "hang-in-there's," and sister-love. Lisa *knows* people and how they all connect; she is a gem. Thank you to Stan Maszczak, who has graciously, and often with lightning speed, edited my blog, always making me look smarter than I am. Thank you to "Moms" Darlene Bogle and her partner-for-life, Becky Lake, who have encouraged and loved me and always made sure I go to conferences and gatherings they *knew* I should attend when I was busy dragging my feet. The beautiful quilt they made me covers me in their love nightly. Thank you to Claudia Ness, Tina Wood, Doug Sewell, Connie Barker, and Eric Weiss for the many reference book suggestions. I threatened to "unfriend" them if they sent any more!

Thank you to Mike Castro, who has filled my refrigerator and freezer with countless meals and produce from the Central Valley of California so that I stayed healthy and kept working. One should always have a Filipino chef as a close buddy! I rarely go to or from the Bay Area without spending the night with "the East Bay's Premiere Gay Couple," Mike and husband, David Brown. They create a refuge of love.

Thank you to my hiking buddies, who have endured listening to *endless* stories and research information every time they hiked with me. I tend toward passionate storytelling, and they each tolerated my enthusiasm. All of you listened and gave feedback, which helped me to process the research and connect complex events and concepts. I appreciate you: Netto Montoya, Josh Glanz-Hucks, Ren Curry, Mark Worsnop, Yvette Cantu Schneider, and Iris Shimabukuro.

Thank you to the many who offered personal stories for the book. My prayer is that your words will bless and heal others. May your wisdom be far-reaching: Ted Hayes, Kingston, NY; David and Colin Evans-Carlson, White Rock, B.C.; David Farmer, Springfield, VA; Connie Barker, Santa Rosa, CA; Wendy Wilson and Abby McMillen, Bozeman, MT; Suzanne Lindsey, Baltimore, MD; Lee Walker, Houston, TX; Jerry Reiter, Palm Desert, CA; Michael Watt, Memphis, TN; Darlene Bogle, San Jose, CA; Emily Reese, Reno, NV; Jonathan Shinn, CA; Chad Boone, Jacksonville,

FL; Lynn Golden, Greensboro, NC; Angie Campbell, Auckland, New Zealand; Chet de Rouen, Gilbert, AZ; Wesley T.; Mark and Cheri Worsnop, Reno, NV; Gloria J.; Bruce Strine, Westminster, MD; Mark L., Houston, TX; Rev. Greg Smith, Bozeman, MT; Rev. Gerald Green, San Diego, CA; Kevin Diaz, Longview, CO; Pastor Maria Caruana, San Francisco, CA; Pastor Dan Burchett, Long Beach, CO; Pastor Randy Morgan, Atlanta, GA; Marsha Stevens-Pino, St. Petersburg, FL; Missa and Jena Borah, Charleston, IL; Emilee Friesen, Calgary, Alberta; Eunice Friesen, Grande Prairie, Alberta; Nick Norton, Detroit, MI; Tim Rosenberger, Lakewood, OH; Devin Kennamer, Birmingham, AL; Megan Rhinehart, Atlanta, GA; Matt, Los Angeles, CA; Mateo Williamson, Phoenix, AZ; Jeffrey Hoffman, New York, NY; Anthony Venn-Brown, Sydney, Australia; Pastor Danny Cortez, La Mirada, CA; Pastor Brett Glanzman, Sparks, NV; Kelly and Bryan Lee, Columbia, MO; Ruth Cooper, Royal Palm Beach, FL; Ryan Kuramitsu, Urbana, IL; Betsy Johnson, Ottawa, Ontario; AnaYelsi Sanchez, Washington, D.C.; Lisa Bohn, Jonesboro, AR; Michele Grabbe, Belgrade, MT; and Caroline Cheek, Charlotte, NC.

Thank you to Owen Korsmo, who, with his creative thinking, came up with the title for the book one night long ago when the idea was not even an outline. Good conversation and a bottle of wine became magic.

Immense gratitude to Dr. Ken Lewes, of New York City, author of *Psychoanalysis and Male Homosexuality*. He gave his time and valuable insights, which allowed me to write Chapter 2 in this book. Ken helped me understand the importance of what was happening in psychoanalysis from the early 1900s to the late 1990s.

Thank you to Matthew Vines, author of *God and the Gay Christian* and founder of The Reformation Project. We've shared *many* hours in conversation, not just about theology, but about people, politics, Christian living, equality, and life. It has been an honor getting to know Matthew and to call him friend. The simplicity and accuracy with which I am able to present the scriptural information in Chapters 9 and 10 are partially attributable to conversations with Matthew and to my involvement on the board of, and as a participant in, The Reformation Project.

Thank you to Netto Montoya. Without Netto, my transformation would not have begun. God picked the *exact* person who would click with me to place on my hiking trail. Netto has listened, advised, and loved me over thousands of miles on and off the trails. Many friends have walked away from me over the years; Netto has been loyal, supportive, and irreplaceable.

Thank you to my *awesome* team of editors—actually I call them a "murder of editors," as they were *relentless* with great clarifying questions, fact checking, commas, footnotes, structure, and reorganization. Each gave of their time and talent so generously to ensure that this work was not only completed, but well done. Elaine Bellamore Phillips, of Vancouver, B.C., attacked each document quickly and eliminated— well, *tried* to eliminate—my rampant "that" habit. Jerry Reiter, of Palm Desert, CA, has wide and deep knowledge about so many topics in the book and kindly gave of his wisdom and cleverness. Tim Rymel, of Sacramento, CA, *almost* hit his lifetime limit of suggesting footnotes. Though I groaned with each suggestion, I came to appreciate his diligence and humor. His time and involvement, along with Jerry's, in leading Christian reparative therapy afforded excellent insights. David Farmer, of Springfield, VA, can spot missing and out-of-place punctuation as if he were gifted with a superhuman quality. He did the precise work I am not naturally inclined to do.

Then there is Wendy Prell Danbury, of Orange, CA. My goodness! I had met her *one time* while speaking at a church in Long Beach before she sent me an email early one Sunday morning offering to edit the book. I jumped at the offer! We hardly knew one another, but now, she is an extension of my mind and thinking. She "gets" me and made awesome suggestions, not only to my writing and structure, but to the timelines which are essential to the flow of this book. Wendy shaped me into a better writer, and more importantly, I have a friend for life. And now, I have time to go dancing with her too.

Thank you to Heidi Mann of Final Touch Proofreading & Editing, Hendrum, MN who interviewed me for an article several years ago and, at the time, offered to edit a future book. Heidi took the "final" manuscript, worked magic on what I thought was a good book, and made it flow and shine! Her diligence, professionalism, and excellent talents have blessed me to tears. Heidi is an ordained ELCA minister who poured her spirit and talents into a book that also reflects her passions for the marginalized. As a team, my "murder of editors" fashioned my research into a discovery process easy for the reader to follow and understand.

Thank you to Rodger Peden of Tustin, CA, for the cover design and for moving me beyond the far-too-complicated image floating in my head toward this beautiful cover that expresses my "come along with me on this journey" heart for the readers.

Thank you to Carol Fuss Reed, BlueStem, who painstakingly indexed this book. She made the insights, research, stories, and information findable and accessible. Carol is the Christian parent of a gay child and wanted to use her talents for equality.

Thank you to Buck Sommerkamp and John Yuelkenbeck of Kansas City, MO, who designed the logo for Canyonwalker Press. I met them while they were filming for The Reformation Project's first leadership conference. They lent their talents so willingly. Thank you to Mark Worsnop, of Reno, NV, for the book website design and for hours of video work so that younger people could find me on YouTube. Videos save lives.

Thank you to Pastor Maria Caruana of Freedom in Christ Evangelical Church in San Francisco and to the members of the congregation, who were the first LGBT church to fully embrace me. Member Ed Ness boldly pursued me to become involved with them and invited me to learn "who we are" in the many events where I joined them in the early years.

Thank you, Justin Lee, of the Gay Christian Network, who likewise welcomed me to conferences from the first year of my journey toward understanding. I called him on the phone in 2006 and asked if I could come to the GCN conference, and he so graciously said, "Sure, Kathy, you are welcome to join us." I now serve on the Advisory Board of this excellent organization. Other LGBT organizations that have poured wisdom and welcome into me have been The Evangelical Network, led by Todd Ferrell, and Joshua Ministries, led by Pastor Tony Hoult, of Grace Fellowship in Christ Jesus, Dallas, TX. Both groups have an abundance of gay, lesbian, and transgender pastors who reflect the grace and love of Jesus Christ so richly.

Thank you to my friends, Board members, and publishers, Jan and Bob Bare, of Dallas, TX, who sought me out several years ago *specifically* with the intention of helping me. Bob and Jan have been wise and creative mentors throughout the years. Bob set up Canyonwalker Press in part to help fund the ministry work of Canyonwalker Connections. Canyonwalker Press has become a haven for authors rejected by Christian publishing houses that refuse LGBT-affirming Christian content. The Bares, whose story is in Chapter 7, have ensured that *Walking the Bridgeless Canyon* got out quickly and professionally.

Thank you to my other Board members: Michael Bussee, Lisa Salazar, Naomi Harvey, Richard Archambault, Dean Johnson, and Samantha Baldock. You all keep me in line and balanced.

Thank you to my children, Andrew Baldock, property manager and extraordinary skier, mountain biker, and river guide, of Squaw Valley, California, and Samantha Baldock, public policy MPA with Empire State Development, New York City. People ask me *all the time*, "Are your kids okay with what you do?" Thank you to the "cores-of-my-heart" for being more than okay with me. I am sure a "normal" mom would be less controversial and easier to take to garden parties, yet both encouraged me and allowed me to continue to grow and help the children other parents have rejected. I got my "mom training" with these two wonderful humans.

Finally, this book would not be possible without the generous spirit of my mother, Roberta McCormack, of Surprise, Arizona. My mom is kind, funny, caring, attentive, protective, and giving. For over two years, she had to listen to my stories and research every day on the phone. She listened so patiently as I yammered on about subjects often obscure to her. All that is good in me is a reflection of her and my Father in heaven.

I am grateful, oh so grateful, for everyone who touched my life and made this book possible.

Reference List

Achtemeier, Mark. *The Bible's YES to Same-Sex Marriage*. Louisville: Westminster John Knox Press, 2014.

After Stonewall. Dir. John Scagliotti. Perf. Various. First Run Features, 2005. DVD.

Allen, Jimmy Raymond. *Burden of a Secret: a Story of Truth and Mercy in the Face of AIDS*. Nashville, TN: Moorings, 1995.

Arthur, L. *Sex Texts: Sexuality, Gender, and Relationships in the Bible*. S.l.: Dorrance Pub Co, 2013.

Badinter, Elisabeth. *XY, on Masculine Identity*. New York: Columbia University Press, 1995.

Balmer, Randall Herbert. *Thy Kingdom Come: How the Religious Right Distorts the Faith and Threatens America, an Evangelical's Lament*. New York, NY: Basic Books, 2006.

Balmer, Randall Herbert. *God in the White House: a History: How Faith Shaped the Presidency from John F. Kennedy to George W. Bush*. New York: HarperOne, 2008.

Before Stonewall. Dir. Greta Schiller. Before Stonewall Inc., 2004. DVD.

Bess, Howard. *Pastor I am Gay*. Palmer, Alaska: Palmer Publishing, 1995.

Blumenthal, Max. *Republican Gomorrah: Inside the Movement that Shattered the Party*. New York, NY: Nation Books, 2009.

Bogle, Darlene. *A Christian Lesbian Journey: A Continuation of Long Road to Love*. United States: BookSurge, 2007.

Brown, Peter. *The Body and Society: Men, Women, and Sex Renunciation in Early Christianity*. New York: Columbia University Press, 1988.

Brownson, James. *Bible Gender Sexuality: Reframing the Church's Debate on Same-Sex Relationships*. Grand Rapids, MI: William B. Eerdmans Publishing Company, 2013.

Bryant, Anita. *The Anita Bryant Story*. Old Tappan, NJ: Revell, 1977.

Buxton, Amity. *The Other Side of the Closet: the Coming-Out Crisis for Straight Spouses*. Santa Monica, CA: IBS Press, 1991.

Call Me Troy. Dir. Scott Bloom. Frameline, 2007. DVD.

Carmack, Brad. *Homosexuality: A Straight BYU Student's Perspective*. Provo, UT: B. Carmack, 2010.

Chambers, Alan. *Leaving Homosexuality*. Eugene, OR: Harvest House Publishers, 2009.

Changing our minds. Dir. Richard Schmiechen. Perf. Evelyn Hooker. Frameline, 1991. DVD.

Chauncery, George. *Gay New York: Gender, Urban Culture, and the Making of the Gay Male World 1890-1940*. New York City: Basic Books, 1994.

Coogan, Michael David. *God and Sex: What the Bible Really Says*. New York: Twelve, 2010.

Coontz, Stephanie. *The Way We Never Were: American Families and the Nostalgia Trap*. New York, NY: BasicBooks, 1992.

Coontz, Stephanie. *Marriage, a History: from Obedience to Intimacy or How Love Conquered Marriage*. New York: Viking, 2005.

Cory, Donald Webster. *The Homosexual in America: A Subjective Approach*. [1st ed. New York: Greenberg, 1951.

Countryman, Louis William. *Dirt, Greed, and Sex: Sexual Ethics in the New Testament and Their Implications for Today*. Philadelphia, PA: Fortress Press, 1988.

Dallas, Joe. *A Strong Delusion*. Eugene, OR: Harvest House Publishers, 1996.

Dannemeyer, William. *Shadow in the Land: Homosexuality in America*. San Francisco: Ignatius Press, 1989.

Day, David. *Things They Never Told You in Sunday School: a Primer for the Christian Homosexual*. Austin, TX: Liberty Press, 1987.

Dochuk, Darren. *From Bible Belt to Sun Belt: Plain Folk Religion, Grassroots Politics, and the Rise of Evangelical Conservatism*. New York City: W. W. Norton, 2005.

Falwell, Jerry. *Listen, America!*. Garden City, NY: Doubleday, 1980.

Gary, Sally. *Loves God, Likes Girls: a Memoir*. Abilene, TX: Leafwood Publishers, 2013.

Gritter, Wendy. *Generous Spaciousness: Responding to Gay Christians in the Church*. Grand Rapids, MI: BrazosPress, 2014.

Gulley, Philip. *If the Church Were Christian: Rediscovering the Values of Jesus*. New York, NY: HarperOne, 2010.

Handel, Linda. *Now That You're Out of the Closet: What about the Rest of the House?*. Naperville, IL: Sourcebooks, 2000.

Helminiak, Daniel A. *What the Bible Really Says about Homosexuality*. San Francisco, CA: Alamo Square Press, 1994.

Hill, Wesley. *Washed and Waiting: Reflections on Christian Faithfulness and Homosexuality*. Grand Rapids, MI: Zondervan, 2010.

Himes, Andrew. *The Sword of the Lord: the Roots of Fundamentalism in an American Family*. Seattle, WA: Chiara Press, 2011.

Hodge, Candace. *Bulletproof Faith: a Spiritual Survival Guide for Gay and Lesbian Christians*. San Francisco: Jossey-Bass, 2008.

Horwitz, Robert Britt. *America's Right: Anti-Establishment Conservatism from Goldwater to the Tea Party*. Malden, MA: Polity, 2013.

Hubbard, Peter. *Love into Light: the Gospel, the Homosexual and the Church*. Greenville, SC: Ambassador International, 2013.

John, Smid. *EX'D OUT*. Charleston, SC: Self Published, 2012.

Johnson, David K. *The Lavender Scare: the Cold War Persecution of Gays and Lesbians in the Federal Government*. Chicago: University of Chicago Press, 2004.

Jones, Mike, and Sam Gallegos. *I Had to Say Something: the Art of Ted Haggard's Fall*. New York: Seven Stories Press, 2007.

Katz, Jonathan. *The Invention of Heterosexuality*. New York: Dutton, 1995.

Kaye, Bonnie. *Straight Wives: Shattered Lives: Stories of Women with Gay Husbands.* U.S.: Airleaf Publishing, 2006.

Kaye, Bonnie. *Straight Wives: Shattered Lives: Stories of Women with Gay Husbands | Vol. 2.* British Columbia: CCB Publishing, 201.

Kaye, Bonnie, and Doug Dittmer. *Over the Cliff: Gay Husbands in Straight Marriages.* Terrace], B.C.: CCB, 2011.

Kirk, Marshall, and Hunter Madsen. *After the Ball: How America Will Conquer its Fear and Hatred of Gays in the '90s.* New York, NY: Doubleday, 1989.

Klaich, Dolores. *Woman Plus Woman; Attitudes Toward Lesbianism.* New York: Simon and Schuster, 1974.

LaHaye, Tim F. *The Unhappy Gays: What Everyone Should Know about Homosexuality.* Wheaton IL:Tyndale House, 1978.

Leavitt, David. *The Man Who Knew Too Much: Alan Turing and the Invention of the Computer.* New York: W.W. Norton, 2006.

Lee, Justin. *Torn: Rescuing the Gospel from the Gays-vs-Christians Debate.* New York: Jericho Books, 2012.

Lewes, Kenneth. *Psychoanalysis and male Homosexuality.* Northvale, NJ: J. Aronson, 1995.

Liebman, Marvin. *Coming out Conservative: An Autobiography.* San Francisco: Chronicle Books, 1992.

Lofgren, Mike. *The Party is Over: How Republicans Went Crazy, Democrats Became Useless, and the Middle Class Got Shafted.* New York: Viking, 2012.

Marcus, Eric. *Making History: the Struggle for Gay and Lesbian Equal Rights, 1945-1990: an Oral History.* New York, NY: HarperCollins Publishers, 1992.

Marsden, George M. *The Outrageous Idea of Christian Scholarship.* New York: Oxford University Press, 1997.

Miller, Neil. *Sex-Crime Panic: A Journey to the Paranoid Heart of the 1950s.* Los Angeles: Alyson Books, 2002.

Moegerle, Gil. *James Dobson's War on America*. Amherst, NY. Prometheus Books, 1997.

Myers, David G., and Letha Scanzoni. *What God has Joined Together?: a Christian Case for Gay Marriage*. San Francisco: HarperSanFrancisco, 2005.

Nussbaum, Martha Craven. *From Disgust to Humanity: Sexual Orientation and Constitutional Law*. Oxford: Oxford University Press, 2010.

Paulk, Anne. *Restoring Sexual Identity*. Eugene, OR: Harvest House Publishers, 2003.

Pennington, Sylvia. *But Lord, They're Gay: A Christian Pilgrimage*. Hawthorne, CA: Lambda Christian Fellowship, 1982.

Pennington, Sylvia. *Ex-Gays There Are None*. Hawthorne, CA: Lamda Christian Fellowship, 1989.

Pennington, Sylvia. *Good News for Modern Gays: A Pro-Gay Biblical Approach*. Hawthorne, CA: Lambda Christian Fellowship, 1985.

Pepin, Jacques. *The Origins of AIDS*. Cambridge, UK: Cambridge University Press, 2011.

Rauch, Jonathan. *Gay Marriage: Why it is Good for Gays, Good for Straights, and Good for America*. New York: Times Books/Henry Holt and Co., 2004.

Reuben, David R. *Everything You Always Wanted to Know About Sex, but Were Afraid to Ask*. New York: D. McKay Co., 1969.

Richardson, Sarah S. *Sex Itself: the Search for Male and Female in the Human Genome*. Chicago: University of Chicago Press, 2013.

Rigsbee, Ron, and Dorothy Fanberg Bakker. *The Agony of Deception*. Shreveport, La.: Huntington House, 1983.

Rodgers, William D. *The Gay Invasion: A Christian Look at the Spreading Homosexual Myth*. Denver: Accent Books, 1977.

Ryan, Caitlin, and Donna Futterman. *Lesbian & Gay Youth Care & Counseling*. New York City: Columbia University Press, 1998.

Rymel, Tim. *Going Gay*. Elk Grove, CA: CK Publishing, 2014.

Sachs, Roger. *Not by Might Nor by Power" The Jesus Revolution.* Santa Monica, CA: Freedom Press, 2012.

Salazar, Lisa. *Transparently: Behind the Scenes of a Good Life.* Vancouver: Lisa Salazar, 2011.

Sanford, James C. *Blueprint for Theocracy: The Christian Right's Vision for America.* Providence, RI: Metacomet Books, 2014.

Scanzoni, Letha, and Virginia R. Mollenkott. *Is the Homosexual My Neighbor?: Another Christian View.* San Francisco: Harper & Row, 1978.

Schroth, Laura. *Trans Bodies, Trans Selves: a Resource for the Transgender Community.* New York City: Oxford University Press, 2014.

Seventh-Gay Adventists. Dir. Daneen Akers. Watchfire Films, 2013. DVD.

Sharlet, Jeff. *The Family: the Secret Fundamentalism at the Heart of American Power.* New York, NY: HarperCollins, 2008.

Sharlet, Jeff. *C Street: the Fundamentalist Threat to American Democracy.* New York: Little, Brown & Co., 2010.

Shilts, Randy. *And the Band Played On Politics, People and the AIDS Epidemic..* New York: Souvenir Press, 2011.

Sterling, Anne. *Sex/Gender: Biology in a Social World.* New York: Routledge, 2012.

Strub, Sean O. *Body Counts: A Memoir of Politics, Sex, AIDS, and Survival.* New York City: Scribner, 2014.

Sylvia, Pennington. *Good New for Modern Gays.* Hawthorne, CA: Lambda Life Publications, 1985.

Vines, Matthew. *The Reformation Project Reading Materials.* Wichita, KS: The Reformation Project, 2013.

Vines, Matthew. *God and the Gay Christian: the Biblical Case in Support of Same-Sex Relationships.* New York City: Convergent, 2014.

Weekly, R. D. *Homosexianity: Letting Truth Win the Devastating War between Scripture, Faith, and Sexual Orientation.* Saint Louis, Mo.: Judah First Ministries, 2009.

Weekly, Romell. *The Rebuttal.* St. Louis: Judah First Publishing, 2011.

White, Mel. *Stranger at the Gate: to Be Gay and Christian in America.* New York: Simon & Schuster, 1994.

White, Mel. *Holy Terror: Lies the Christian Right Tells Us to Deny Gay Equality.* New York: Magnus Books, 2012.

Williams, Ritch C. *The New Gay Teenager.* Cambridge, Mass.: Harvard University Press, 2005.

Wilson, Ken. *A Letter to My Congregation: An Evangelical Pastor's Path to Embracing People Who Are Gay, Lesbian and Transgender in the Company of Jesus.* Canton: Read The Spirit Books, 2014.

Winters, Michael Sean. *God's Right Hand: How Jerry Falwell Made God a Republican and Baptized the American Right.* New York: HarperOne, 2012.

Wolfson, Evan. *Why Marriage Matters: America, Equality, and Gay People's Right to Marry.* New York: Simon & Schuster, 2004.

Yarhouse, Mark. *Understanding Sexual Identity: A Resource for Youth Ministry.* Grand Rapids: Zondervan, 2014.

Index

CPSIA information can be obtained
at www.ICGtesting.com
Printed in the USA
BVHW01s2238040218
506819BV00004B/457/P